PLEASURE AND GUILT ON

THE GRAND TOUR

MANCHESTER
UNIVERSITY PRESS

To Vincent Woropay,
and also to Carolyn Hayman,
to whom I promised this dedication
in a childhood pact.

Pleasure and guilt on the Grand Tour

Travel writing
and imaginative geography
1600–1830

✧

CHLOE CHARD

Manchester University Press
Manchester and New York

distributed exclusively in the USA by St. Martin's Press

Published by Manchester University Press
Oxford Road, Manchester M13 9NR, UK
and Room 400, 175 Fifth Avenue, New York, NY 10010, USA
http://www.man.ac.uk/mup

Distributed exclusively in the USA by
St. Martin's Press, Inc., 175 Fifth Avenue, New York,
NY 10010, USA

Distributed exclusively in Canada by
UBC Press, University of British Columbia, 6344 Memorial Road,
Vancouver, BC, Canada V6T 1Z2

British Library Cataloguing-in-Publication Data
A catalogue record for this book is available from the British Library

Library of Congress Calaloging-in-Publication Data applied for

ISBN   0 7190 4804 4   *hardback*
       0 7190 4805 2   *paperback*

First published 1999

06 05 04 03 02 01 00 99   10 9 8 7 6 5 4 3 2 1

Typeset by
D R Bungay Associates, Burghfield, Berks

Printed in Great Britain
by Biddles Ltd, Guildford and King's Lynn

Contents

Illustrations

Preface

I first began to work on travel writing while writing a PhD thesis on 'Horror and Terror in Literature of the Grand Tour, and in the Gothic Novel', in the English Faculty, at Cambridge. The thesis had originally been concerned with the British and French country house novel in the eighteenth century; I was especially interested in the role that the architectural space of houses and castles plays in Gothic fiction, and, after a while, I started to read some of the travel writings from which Gothic novels draw many of the details and general themes of their characteristic *mise-en-scène* of the foreign and the forbidden. During a very happy few months of research in Rome, in 1981, I discovered the travel room at the Biblioteca Hertziana; I swiftly came to see travel writing as a domain of freedom – more precisely, a domain of untrammelled curiosity and cheerful intellectual digressiveness – in contrast to the claustrophobic preoccupation with home and family that I had come to associate with country house novels (even with Gothic novels, in which family life often seems to assume a dramatically aberrant character!). I felt an enormous sense of liberation when I realised, at the beginning of my third year of research, that there was nothing to stop me adopting travel writing and imaginative geography as the primary focus of my work. I finished my thesis at the beginning of 1985; when I began to write this book, some years later, I was delighted at the thought that I was now free to concentrate on the pleasures of travel writing.

For much of the period over which I worked on *Pleasure and Guilt on the Grand Tour*, I lived a life almost completely apart from academic institutions. (My contact with such institutions was derived mainly from the desolate drudgery of part-time lecturing.) When I first began to work on travel writing, travel was of interest to very few scholars, outside a small group of art historians and architectural historians who were concerned with the Grand Tour. Over the last ten years or so, many academics, in a variety of disciplines, have begun to write about travel literature, but their approaches and emphases have, in most cases, been very different from mine. I am therefore especially grateful to those who made me aware that there were others interested in the more baffling, unexpected and extraordinary aspects of imaginative geography: above all, to Helen Langdon, who urged me, against all the odds, not to sink into despair, and to Gill Perry and Wendy Wassyng Roworth, who were both immensely generous in opening up for me new possibilities of intellectual exchange. Nicholas Thomas, Director of the Centre for Cross-Cultural Research, at the Australian National University, in Canberra, invited me to take up a Visiting Fellowship at the Centre in 1997; it was this Fellowship, above all else, that enabled me to finish the book.

Many thanks are due to friends and colleagues who have read parts or all of the book, and offered comments and criticisms: Rosemary Bechler, Michael Hitchcock, Helen Langdon, Donna Merwick, Nicholas Thomas and Vincent Woropay (to whom I owe an overwhelming debt of gratitude for his affectionate support and forbearance throughout the realisation of the project). Jonathan Lamb, who read my typescript for Manchester University Press, made suggestions that were of enormous help in my final revision. I often turned to Simon Pembroke for advice when considering references to Greek and Latin literature, and when worrying about diverse intellectual problems; I feel very sad that he is no longer alive, and that no one will ever again answer my questions with such wit, erudition, and engaging unpredictability. Conversations with friends have often enlivened and invigorated my work on *Pleasure and Guilt*; among those not already mentioned, I should especially like to thank Bice Benvenuto, Deirdre Coleman, Richard Hamblyn, Todd Longstaffe-Gowan, Pasquale Pasquino and Richard Wrigley. During the academic year 1996–7, I used parts of my book in the course of teaching an MA option on 'England and Italy in the Eighteenth Century', at the University of Sussex: the responses of my students, Elisabeth Herles, Jeannie Labno, Roxane Nash, Sheila Saphier and Andrew Whithey, allowed me to gain a clearer sense of how I wished to shape the final text.

For help with picture research, I am much indebted to David Alexander, Alex Coldham, Lisa Heer, Tim Knox, Helen Langdon, Sir Denis Mahon, Wendy Wassyng Roworth, Mary Sheriff and Kim Sloan. Jenny Newell, at the Centre for Cross-Cultural Research, Canberra, provided valuable bibliographic assistance.

I should also like to thank Anita Roy and Matthew Frost, of Manchester University Press, for help and encouragement during – respectively – early and late stages of the book's development.

I am very grateful indeed to the London Library Trust, for generously providing grants to subsidize my membership of the London Library over a number of years, and so allowing me to continue my research, in the face of numerous practical difficulties.

I received several research grants towards the completion of this book from Wimbledon School of Art, at which I lectured (on a part-time basis) from 1986 to 1996. I also wish to acknowledge an Enid Welsford research grant for the project, from Newnham College, Cambridge.

Different versions of sections of some of the chapters of this book have appeared – or are soon to appear – within articles or essays. Parts of Chapter 1 were first published in 'The Intensification of Italy: Food, Wine, and the Foreign', in *Food, Culture and History: Papers of the London Food Seminar: I*, edited by Gerald and Valerie Mars (London: The London Food Seminar, 1993), pp. 95–118. Parts of Chapter 3 are concerned with the same sources and the same themes as sections of: 'Grand and Ghostly Tours: The Topography of Memory', in *Eighteenth-Century Studies*, 31:1 (Fall, 1997), pp. 101–8; 'The Road to Ruin: Memory, Ghosts, Moonlight and Weeds', in *Roman Presences: Receptions of Rome in European Culture, 1789–1945*, edited by Catharine Edwards (Cambridge: Cambridge University Press, 1999), pp. 125–39; 'Comedy, Antiquity, the Feminine and the Foreign: Emma Hamilton and Corinne', in *Aspects of the Grand Tour: Some Writers, Architects and Artists in Italy 1600–1845*, edited by Clare Hornsby (The British School at Rome, forthcoming), and 'Women who Transmute into Tourist Attractions: Spectator and Spectacle in the Warm South', in *Romantic Geographies: Discourses of Travel in the Romantic Period*, edited by Amanda Gilroy (Manchester: Manchester University Press, forthcoming). Parts of Chapter 4 are adapted from the same initial draft as my essay 'Crossing Boundaries and Exceeding Limits: Destabilization, Tourism and the Sublime', in *Transports: Travel, Pleasure and Imaginative Geography, 1600–1830*, edited by myself and Helen Langdon (New Haven and London: Yale University Press, 1996), pp. 117–49.

Introduction

Pleasure and the language of travel writing

Travel writers have often reflected on the pleasures that their commentaries might offer the reader. One of the more unexpected analyses of such pleasures is found in the Marquis de Sade's novel *Juliette* (1797); the eponymous heroine explains, with delicate irony, that she feels that her readers, their imaginations inflamed by the proliferation of 'détails lubriques' within her narratives, may feel a certain relief when she interrupts the tale of her sexual adventures in order to offer an account of her travels in the environs of Naples, thereby providing the opportunity to fall back restfully upon 'des descriptions plus douces.'[1]

Other travellers, in contrast, have defined writing about the foreign as possessing a power of its own to inflame the imagination. Lévi-Strauss, at the beginning of *Tristes Tropiques* (1955), suggests that travel books promise to restore to the reader a sense of otherness – an excitement in encountering cultural difference which has been lost in travel itself, as a result of the distressing seepage of the 'sous-produits maléfiques' of Western civilization into the rest of the world: 'Je comprends alors la passion, la folie, la duperie des récits de voyage. Ils apportent l'illusion de ce qui n'existe plus et qui devrait être encore, pour que nous échappions à l'accablante évidence que 20 000 ans d'histoire sont joués.'[2] Evelyn Waugh, in *Labels: A Mediterranean Journal* (1930), analysing a less subtle genre of travel writing, 'the advertisements of shipping companies', discerns in these advertisements a similar power to displace mundane reality. He considers their attractions for 'the middle-aged widow of comfortable means':

---

1 In Sade, *La Nouvelle Justine*, vol. IX, pp. 338, 339: 'lubricious details'; 'more soft and gentle descriptions'.

2 p. 27: 'harmful by-products'; 'I understand, then, the passion, the madness, the deception of travel books. They bring with them the illusion of that which no longer exists and which should once again be present before us, in order for us to escape the overwhelming evidence that twenty thousand years of history have played themselves out.'

These widows, then, celibate and susceptible, read the advertisements of steamship companies and travel bureaux and find there just that assembly of phrases – half poetic, just perceptibly aphrodisiac – which can produce at will in the unsophisticated a state of mild unreality and glamour. 'Mystery, History, Leisure, Pleasure', one of them begins. There is no *directly* defined sexual appeal...3

Giuseppe Baretti's explanation of the appeal of travel writing, at the beginning of his *Account of the Manners and Customs of Italy* (1768), seems, initially, very different from these visions of alluring exoticism:

Few books are so acceptable to the greatest part of mankind, as those that abound in slander and invective. Hence almost all accounts of travels, published within my memory, have quickly circulated, and were perused, at least for a while, with great eagerness, because they have been strongly marked with these characters.4

At this point, however, Baretti identifies the quality within the foreign that 'slander and invective' so successfully offer up to the reader:

Men are fond of *the marvellous* in manners and customs as well as in events; and a writer of travels, who would make himself fashionable in his own country is generally polite enough to bring from abroad abundant materials for gratifying at once, the malignity and the love of novelty, that must predominate in so many of his readers.5

He voices, in other words, an assumption spelt out more explicitly by Lévi-Strauss and Waugh: the assumption that a traveller engaged in translating the foreign into discourse will set himself or herself the task of producing an effect of pleasure by imposing on the topography of foreignness a demand for some form of dramatic departure from the familiar and the mundane.

Baretti, Lévi-Strauss and Waugh all imply that the travel writer who finds a lack of evidence of otherness within the foreign can always invent such otherness – or, at least, conjure it up through some form of rhetorical 'duperie'. Writings that exclude this possibility often register anxiety or disappointment at an absence of alterity. Rousseau, discussing how to manage travel in *Émile* (1762), laments the difficulty that the traveller encounters in the contemporary world, which he sees, like Lévi-Strauss, as one in which 'les caractères originaux des peuples, s'effaçant de jour en jour, deviennent en même raison plus difficiles à saisir'. For Herodotus,

---

3 pp. 41, 42; emphasis added.

4 Vol. I, p. 1.

5 *Ibid.*; emphasis added.

Ctesias and Pliny, in contrast, grasping the traits of different peoples in their full diversity was relatively easy, since distinctions between them were far more strongly marked.[6]

Without constructing any such grand historical vision of encroaching sameness, a great many writings include complaints about the lack of alterity in individual places: the lament 'It might be London', uttered by the heroine of E.M. Forster's novel *A Room with a View* (1908) on her first evening in a Florentine *pensione*, recurs, in various forms, throughout the history of writing about the foreign.[7] Waugh, in *Labels*, remarks: 'The only place that I can think of at all like the town of Gibraltar, is Shoreham-by-Sea in Sussex' – a comment that only produces its full effect of venom when he explains: 'For those who have at any time had occasion to pass through it, or, worse, to stop there, I will add this modification – that they must think of Gibraltar as a Shoreham deprived of its two churches, and scoured of all the ramshackle, haphazard characteristics which make it relatively tolerable.'[8]

Travellers, then, impose on the foreign a demand that it should in some way proclaim itself as different from the familiar. At the same time, they define their own task as one of grasping that difference. Travel writings regularly note the disadvantages of those travellers who, for whatever reason, are unresponsive to alterity. Giovanni Battista Belzoni, in his *Narrative of the Operations and Recent Discoveries within the Pyramids, Temples, Tombs, and Excavations, in Egypt and Nubia* (1820), describes a type of traveller who, having lived too long among foreigners, 'is so thoroughly initiated into their customs and manners, that those which shock at first sight, lose their effect on him; he... does not reckon any thing he beholds extraordinary or worth attention, though perhaps even of the greatest consequence'.[9] Byron contemptuously describes a woman 'fast asleep in the most anti-narcotic spot in the world' (in Switzerland, between the Château de Chillon and Clarens), and then cites yet another example of dispiriting unresponsiveness: 'I remember at Chamouni – in the very eyes of Mont Blanc – hearing another woman – English also – exclaim to her party – "did you ever see any thing more *rural*" – as if it was Highgate or Hampstead – or Brompton – or Hayes.'[10]

---

[6] pp. 593, 594: 'the original characters of different peoples, growing fainter from day to day, become for that reason more difficult to grasp'.

[7] p. 23.

[8] p. 158.

[9] p. 109.

[10] Byron, *Letters and Journals*, vol. V, p. 97. Byron continues: '– "Rural" quotha! – Rocks – pines – torrents – Glaciers – Clouds – and Summits of eternal snow far above them – and "*Rural!*"'

In acclaiming the foreign as gratifyingly dissimilar from the familiar, travel writing employs a range of concepts of otherness: 'the marvellous', as cited by Baretti, for example, the 'wonder', and concepts of the strange, the singular and the astonishing. Accounts of foreign places also make use of a range of specific tropes and rhetorical strategies, some of which recur in writings of many different periods, in order to affirm that the subject of commentary has managed to grasp the topography in its full alterity, and is offering it up to the reader as an object of pleasurable speculation. The simplest of such strategies is to sprinkle the commentary lavishly with foreign words; conveniently made visible even at a casual glance through the use of italics, terms borrowed from other languages assure the reader that the traveller has indeed managed to collect evidence of a difference from the familiar. Hester Piozzi, in her *Observations and Reflections Made in the Course of a Journey through France, Italy, and Germany* (1789), asks: 'What... can make these Roman ladies fly from *odori* so, that a drop of lavender in one's handkerchief... is to throw them all into convulsions thus? Sure this is the only instance in which they forbear to *fabbricare su l'antico.*'[11]

One particular rhetorical trope plays a major part in representing the foreign as dramatically different. This is the trope of hyperbole: the same rhetorical figure that Byron sees the Englishwoman at Chamonix as so signally failing to achieve, when she reaches for the cosy familiarity of the term *rural*. Specific varieties of hyperbole are considered in detail in the chapters that follow. All these varieties elide alterity with drama; in acclaiming the topography as dramatic, striking and remarkable, they affirm at the same time that it has supplied the evidence of difference expected and required of it. Travel writings often suggest that the perception of a need for hyperbole is one of the features that differentiates the traveller from those without experience of travel. Horace Walpole comments on his own description of the journey over the Alps: 'This sounds too bombast and too romantic to one that has not seen it, too cold for one that has.'[12] Byron remarks in a footnote to a dramatic account of an Italian sunset in Canto IV of *Childe Harold's Pilgrimage* (1818): 'The above description may seem fantastical or exaggerated to those who have never seen an Oriental or an Italian sky, yet it is but a literal and hardly sufficient delineation of an August evening... as contemplated... during many a ride along the banks of the Brenta.'[13]

[11] Vol. I, 417–18.

[12] Walpole, *The Yale Edition*, vol. XIII, p. 182; letter to Richard West; this section of the letter is headed 'Aix in Savoy, Sept. 30th'.

[13] Byron, *Complete Poetical Works*, vol. II, p. 228; note to stanzas 27–9.

A theme that recurs throughout the history of travel writing, and that presents the topography itself as endorsing the impulse to move beyond boundaries inscribed in the structure and etymology of hyperbole (a 'throwing beyond'), is excess. The diversity of utterances produced by this theme include – unsurprisingly – much 'slander and invective' of the kind described by Baretti. The Gothic novels of the 1790s enthusiastically exploit the hyperbolic potential of immoderation in the warm South: Ann Radcliffe's *Sicilian Romance* informs the reader that the lives of the Marquis de Mazzini and Maria de Vellorno 'exhibited a *boundless* indulgence of violent and luxurious passions'.[14]

The proliferation of hyperbole in travel writing is also endorsed through elisions between, on the one hand, the rhetorical impulse beyond constraining limits realized within this trope, and, on the other, the traversals of geographical boundaries entailed in travelling. Chapter 4, 'Destabilized Travel', considers the symbolic traversals of bounds that are presented as accompanying the geographical crossing of limits in late eighteenth-century and early nineteenth-century writings. 'Destabilized Travel' and 'Hyperbole and Observation' both examine elisions between hyperbole, travel and yet another exceeding of bounds: the movement beyond the mundane and familiar entailed in confrontations with the sublime.

Hyperbole, however, is, at various points in the history of travel writing, defined as a trope that involves taking grave rhetorical risks: a trope, in other words, that lays the traveller open to accusations of affectation, pretentiousness, a craven reliance on the conventional formulations of others, a naïve proclivity to be much too easily impressed, or simply a general lack of discrimination.[15] Travellers often parody the hyperbolic language of their precursors: as Paul Fussell has pointed out, Evelyn Waugh mocks a well-established convention of declaring 'I shall never forget...' when he observes: 'I do not think I shall ever forget the sight of Etna at sunset... Nothing I have ever seen in Art or Nature was quite so revolting.'[16]

---

[14] p. 194; emphasis added.

[15] As Nicholas Thomas points out in 'Fear and Loathing in the South Pacific: Colonial and Postcolonial History in Popular Fiction', contemporary travel writing ('much of what appears in *Granta*, for example') often avoids the 'overplayed interests in discovery or adventure' that have provided nineteenth-century and twentieth-century travellers with one means of generating hyperboles, and instead finds satisfaction in those details that allow the reader to adopt a stance of lofty postmodernist detachment: 'the failures of nationalism, the flaking paint, the natives with personal stereos, the fake tribal dances, are dull and sleazy and tell us little about a wider world except that we are the only ones able to detect the ironies' (*In Oceania*, pp. 156–67; p. 167).

[16] Waugh, *Labels*, p. 139. See Fussell, *Abroad*, p. 183.

Such parodies are especially common between (roughly) the 1740s and the 1830s, when travel writing makes great use of a rhetoric of intense emotional responsiveness. John Moore, mocking hyperbolic responses to works of art in *A View of Society and Manners in Italy* (1781), observes that 'if you are violently bent upon being thought a man of very refined taste, there are books in abundance to be had, which will… furnish you with suitable expressions for the whole climax of sensibility'.[17] Unsurprisingly, travel writings of this period often employ a self-protective irony, which acknowledges the temptation to become carried away by linguistic immoderation, and proclaims the traveller's ability to view this temptation from a stance of critical detachment. Patrick Brydone, descending Mount Etna in his *Tour through Sicily and Malta* (1773), indulges in some giddily 'elevated' musings: in such regions, he loftily observes, 'the mind considers the little storms of the human passions as equally below her notice'. Slipping on the ice, however, he suffers a sprain: 'and your poor philosopher was obliged to hop on one leg, with two men supporting him, for several miles over the snow'. This calamity prompts him to detach himself, with some show of embarrassment, from his previous rhetoric of hyperbole: 'our wags here allege, that he left the greatest part of his philosophy behind him, for the use of Empedocles's heirs and successors.'[18] Thomas Gray, in a synopsis of the 'Travels of T.G., Gent.', includes an ironically inflated account of crossing the Alps, which might be seen as defending his other epistolary accounts of this experience from charges of naïve effusiveness: 'visits the Grande Chartreuse:…horrours and terrours on all sides. The author dies of the fright.'[19]

The trope of digression or divagation, which also plays a conspicuous role in travel writing, provides one means of generating such self-protective ironies, and so countering the incipient effusiveness of hyperbole: just as the traveller seems to be working up to a 'climax of sensibility', as John Moore puts it, he or she veers off towards some completely different object of commentary. The structure of hyperbole is transgressive, involving a movement beyond the bounds of mundane or trivial utterances (and, in its more extreme form, a movement beyond the bounds of verisimilitude); digressiveness, therefore, deflates hyperboles by deflecting their transgressive thrust. The first-person narrative of travel – a genre much used to comment on the foreign during the period considered in this book – is inherently divagatory, simply in the sense that it allows the subject of commentary to move

---

17   Vol. I, p. 63.

18   Vol. I, pp. 216, 217, 219, 219.

19   Gray, *The Poems of Thomas Gray*, p. 114; letter dated '*March* 12, *N.S.* 1740'.

easily between one domain of objects and another, to shift back and forth at will between specific objects of commentary, and to pause in the account of a particular place, in order to reflect at length on some idea that springs to mind.[20] De Sade, scornfully rejecting the Abbé Richard's tidy-minded accounts of Italian cities, affirms his own freedom, in describing Naples, to call up individual objects of commenatary at will: 'Je n'ai suivi aucun ordre dans cette tournée parce que j'ai vu que cette manière méthodique et pédantesque ne servait jamais à rien.'[21] Charles Dupaty, at the Palazzo Pitti, in Florence, draws attention to the pleasurable disorderliness of following the train of thought prompted by specific objects – in this case, paintings depicting the death of the rich and the death of the poor – by eliding thematic and geographical digression. The images before him prompt him to reflect sadly on social injustice; by the time he reaches the gardens, the divagatory impulse has somehow led him over the Atlantic: 'mon imagination avoit passé en revue tous les maux de la civilisation; elle entroit dans les forêts du Canada, pour interroger, sur le bonheur, la vie sauvage'.[22]

In many cases, digressions distract the reader by introducing a proliferation of bathetically mundane and trivial details. Gray's ironic synopsis of his travels includes observations which imply that the traveller, attempting to appropriate the foreign in tones of hyperbolic drama, will nonetheless inevitably be drawn to trivia: 'Returns to Lyons; gets a surfeit with eating ortolans and lampreys', 'Locked out of Parma on a cold winter's night… Despises that city', and (at Modena), 'How the duke and dutchess lie over their own stables, and go every night to a vile Italian comedy; despises them and it, and proceeds to Bologna.'[23]

---

20 James Clifford, in *Routes*, p. 66, notes the range of different preoccupations of first-person travel narratives when emphasizing the contrast between the *récit de voyage* and the specialized genres of the nineteenth and twentieth centuries – such as the account of anthropological fieldwork. Digressiveness has often been seen as characteristic of the novel (see, for example, Cascardi, *The Subject of Modernity*, p. 113). My own view of the relation between the two genres is that travel writing can more easily establish a sense of order and closure, simply by reference to the structure of the traveller's itinerary (real or fictionalized), and, authenticated and anchored by the narrative framework of a journey, can indulge in a more untrammelled digressiveness.

21 Sade, *Voyage d'Italie*, p. 385: 'I have not followed any particular order in this tour, because I saw that this methodical, pedantic style was completely pointless.'

22 Dupaty, *Lettres*, vol. I, p. 186: 'my imagination had passed in review all the evils arising from the state of civilization; it was entering the forests of Canada, to reason upon happiness, and a savage life' (*Sentimental Letters*, vol. I, p. 146). For an account of a much more elaborate geographical digression, in William Beckford's account of St Peter's, Rome, in *Dreams, Waking Thoughts and Incidents* (1783), see Shaffer, '"To remind us of China"', pp. 224–35.

23 Gray, *The Poems of Thomas Gray*, p. 114; letter dated '*March* 12, *N.S.* 1740'.

Aldous Huxley, in *Along the Road: Notes and Essays of a Tourist* (1925), defines his own proclivity for digressive fantasy as a major advantage on his travels: 'excessive and promiscuous inquisitiveness, so fatal to a man who desires to mix in society' is, he claims, 'nothing less than a necessity' to the traveller.[24] An equally resolute commitment to divagation is registered in one of the most influential of late eighteenth-century travel narratives: Laurence Sterne's *Sentimental Journey through France and Italy* (1768), in which the traveller-narrator, Yorick, replaces the major sights of the Grand Tour by a series of minutely analysed social encounters (for the most part, flirtatious encounters with women). In Paris, Yorick directly explains the importance of digression to the assimilation of the foreign: 'The man who either disdains or fears to walk up a dark entry may be an excellent good man, and fit for a hundred things; but he will not do to make a good sentimental traveller.' *A Sentimental Journey* ends with a triumphant displacement of hyperbole by the digressive details of social exchange: just as the traveller is embarking on the traversal of the Alps, he is sidetracked into a complex 'Case of Delicacy' with a woman in an inn.[25]

Hyperbole and digression, as this last example suggests, map out two conflicting approaches not only to travel writing but also to travel itself: the traveller can either be swept beyond the bounds of the mundane, or can evince a paradoxical fascination with varieties of mundaneness even when confronting the topography of the foreign. Most travel narratives oscillate between the two approaches, but some register a decided preference for one or the other. W.H. Auden, in the letter 'Hetty to Nancy' in his *Letters from Iceland* (1937), a book compiled in conjunction with Louis McNeice, sets up an ironic opposition between, on the one hand, the sublime natural features such as the cascade of the Gullfoss that he and McNeice visit in the course of a camping trip, and on the other, the incidental events that punctuate their journey. Auden's intermittent hyperboles are, for the most part, rhetorically straightforward, in the manner satirized by Gray: at the Gullfoss, '*I was scared stiff.*' He nonetheless proclaims the attractions of a more digressive approach by establishing – and recklessly exploiting – a self-conscious pretence that he is a female traveller, Hetty, writing archly and loquaciously to a female friend. McNeice, too, becomes a woman, Maisie, who encourages an irreverent attitude towards the sights: 'While the others were taking a morning look at the rainbow spray of the Gullfoss Maisie and I had our first lapse from esprit de corps and sneaked into the little tin house which caters for

---

24   (London: Chatto and Windus, 1925), pp. 26–7.

25   Sterne, *A Sentimental Journey*, pp. 107, 120.

trippers where we had some very good coffee.' Maisie's very opposition to intense encounters with the sublimities of nature – 'the Grand Open Spaces' – is recorded in language of such a stream-of-consciousness kind that it precludes any possibility of hyperbolic intensity:

> Talking of the G.O. Spaces Maisie says they are a closed book. I have been wondering if this would be considered an epigram because I couldn't see that it was very funny and Maisie is supposed to be witty, but then it is different in London, where people have always been drinking sherry before you say anything to them.[26]

Imaginative geography and the Grand Tour

Travel writings, it should be evident from the commentaries quoted so far, are, throughout their history, closely concerned with the traveller-narrator's own rhetorical strategies, and with the rhetoric of other travellers: the task of finding the forms of language to translate the topography into discourse is a recurrent object of discussion. Travel writings usually acknowledge, too, that travel entails the construction of particular myths, visions and fantasies, and the voicing of particular desires, demands and aspirations. Byron, in Venice, writing to his sister Augusta, self-consciously offers her the pleasures of the Gothic novel's imaginative vision of the Roman Catholic South, as a fantasmatic mise-en-scène of the foreign and the forbidden: 'I am going out this evening – in my *cloak* & *Gondola* – there are two nice Mrs. Radcliffe words for you.'[27]

At the same time, travel writings include utterances in which the subject of commentary claims to be concerned primarily with the ordering of knowledge of the world. All the writings discussed in this book provide information about a particular topography of the foreign – whether or not they define the provision of information as their primary aim. Many of them also assume that the reader might visit that topography in person, and might well make practical use of some of the information – whether in finding acceptable inns to stay in, in selecting the principal works of art to view in a specific city, or in avoiding unhappy emotional entanglements with foreigners. Even works that proclaim themselves as fictional offer both information and practical advice. The visit to Capri in de Sade's *Juliette*, which provides the heroine and her two female friends with a chance to speculate about whether they can imitate the debauches of Tiberius, is introduced by a description that would hardly

---

26 Auden, *Letters from Iceland*, pp. 161, 172, 155.

27 Byron, *Letters and Journals*, vol. V, p. 145.

seem out of place in a guide book: 'L'île de Caprée, qui peut avoir environ dix milles de circuit, est partout environnée des plus hauts rochers; on n'y aborde, ainsi que je viens de vous le dire, que par le petit port qui est en face du golfe de Naples...'[28] Ann Radcliffe, embarking on a narrative of horror in her *Mysteries of Udolpho* (the novel implicitly invoked by Byron in the letter just quoted), published in 1794, does not disdain to give the reader a hint about the good sense, when travelling in the Pyrenees, of 'providing against part of the evil to be encountered from a want of convenient inns, by carrying a stock of provisions in the carriage'.[29]

Both these sets of claims on the part of the subject of commentary – the claim to be manipulating language and engaging in a form of imaginative seduction, on the one hand, and, on the other, the claim to be ordering knowledge and, however obliquely, offering practical advice – are constantly combined within travel writings. The intersection of these two claims produces a network of rhetorical and theoretical strategies for understanding and appropriating the foreign that I term an *imaginative topography* or *imaginative geography:* to borrow the formulations used by Christian Jacob in defining the concept of a map, an imaginative geography marks out both a 'space of privileged projection for desires, aspirations, affective memory, the cultural memory of the subject' and, at the same time, a space governed by the demands of a field of knowledge.[30]

This book is concerned with one particular imaginative topography: the topography mapped out by reference to the practice, theoretical rationalization and fantasmatic vision of travel on the Grand Tour. Its primary focus is on the ways in which pleasure of various kinds is registered in

---

28 Sade, *La Nouvelle Justine*, vol. IX, p. 364: 'The island of Capri, which measures around ten miles in circumference, is everywhere surrounded by extremely high rocks; it is only possible to land there at the little port, opposite the Bay of Naples.'

29 p. 28.

30 Jacob, *L'Empire des cartes*, p. 16: 'un espace de projection privilégié pour les désirs, les aspirations, la mémoire affective, la mémoire culturelle du sujet'.

The terms *imaginative geography* and *imaginative topography* are used here to name both particular regions, in their roles as fantasmatic *mises-en-scène* of foreignness, and the activity of mapping out and delimiting them. (The practice of imaginative geography, in other words, produces a range of different imaginative geographies of foreignness.) Edward Said, in *Orientalism*, defines imaginative geography in the latter sense when he notes that 'men have always divided the world up into regions having either real or imagined distinction from each other' (p. 39). Some pages later (p. 71), he offers a more extended definition: 'Imaginative geography... legitimates a vocabulary, a universe of representative discourse... Underlying all the different units of Orientalist discourse... is a set of representative figures, or tropes. These figures are to the actual Orient... as stylized costumes are to characters in a play.'

the language of travel writing: the rhetorical strategies that serve to appropriate this topography as a source of pleasure, the specific concepts of pleasure, enjoyment and gratification that are formed (including the pleasure of
travel itself as well as the delights of this specific category of the foreign) and
the pleasure located in the process of translating the topography into discourse. As a number of the writings quoted so far demonstrate, many of the
strategies that serve to register pleasure are also employed in accounts of
quite different regions of the world, written at quite different periods of history: all imaginative topographies to which the genre of the first-person narrative of travel is allotted authorize the freedom of digressiveness, for
example. I am concerned, obviously enough, both with the features of travel
writing in general that are shared by writing about the Tour and with the
concepts and strategies formed in relation to the specific desires and
demands that the topography of the Tour is seen as inviting.

Like most other scholars in the field, I view the concept of the Tour as
one that determines the way in which travel in Europe is envisaged and
undertaken from the beginning of the seventeenth century up until 1830 or
so.[31] Towards the end of this period, approaches to travel – not only to this
topography, but also to others – split into two opposing attitudes, both of
which still play a crucial part in determining the ways in which encounters
with the foreign can be described or imagined today. One of these
approaches, which is first discernible in travel writing at the very end of the
eighteenth century, is the view that travel is a form of personal adventure,
holding out the promise of a discovery or realization of the self through the
exploration of the other: according to this view – which, for convenience,
may be termed the *Romantic* approach – travel entails crossing symbolic as
well as geographical boundaries, and these transgressions of limits invite
various forms of danger and destabilization.

The second approach appears at about the same time, and presents itself
in more or less explicit opposition to the Romantic view of travel. This is the
approach of the tourist, who recognizes that travel might constitute a form
of personal adventure, and might entail danger and destabilization, but, as a
result of this recognition, attempts to keep the more dangerous and destabilizing aspects of the encounter with the foreign at bay.

Both tourism and the Grand Tour are most frequently defined by
scholars as social practices, to be located within the field of social history.
Bruce Redford, for example, in *Venice and the Grand Tour*, declares:

---

31 Edward Chaney, in *The Evolution of the Grand Tour*, places some emphasis on English trav-
    ellers who visited Italy slightly before this period (see pp. 58–87), but nonetheless asserts
    that the late eighteenth century 'may be regarded as the climax of the Grand Tour' (p. 114).

For purposes of this study... the Grand Tour is not the Grand Tour unless it includes the following: first, a young British male patrician (that is, a member of the aristocracy or the gentry); second, a tutor who accompanies his charge throughout the journey; third, a fixed itinerary that makes Rome its principal destination; fourth, a lengthy period of absence, averaging two or three years.[32]

John Urry, in *The Tourist Gaze,* defines the Grand Tour less narrowly, noting changes in its thematic focus and in the relation between the traveller and the objects of commentary, as well as in the social groups travelling over the period between 1600 and 1800. Once he distinguishes between the Grand Tour and tourism, however, he returns to social history for the terms in which to define the historical discontinuity:

> But before the nineteenth century few people outside the upper classes travelled anywhere to see objects for reasons unconnected with work or business. And it is this which is the central characteristic of mass tourism in modern societies, namely that much of the population in most years will travel somewhere else to gaze upon it [*sic*] and stay there for reasons basically unconnected with work.[33]

My own analyses of the Grand Tour, of Romantic travel and of tourism have a quite different focus. In approaching the Tour by reference to the history of its imaginative geography, rather than its social history, I attempt to chart not changes and discontinuities in travel itself, but changes and discontinuities in the forms of language employed in travel writing. More specifically, I am concerned with a discourse of travel: with the range and limits of what can be said or written about the topography of the Grand Tour over the seventeenth, eighteenth and early nineteenth centuries.[34] This book sets out to analyse various aspects of the rules and regularities of such a discourse: the delimitation of a field of objects, the positions that the speaking subject is able to assume (in relation to these objects, for example, and in relation to various forms of authority), the concepts formed within it, and its themes, arguments, assumptions,

---

[32] p. 14.

[33] p. 5.

[34] The term *discourse* is used here with reference to the account of what constitutes a discourse given by Michel Foucault in *L'Archéologie du savoir*; see, in particular, pp. 44–101; see also the account of how it is possible to intervene in a discourse in Foucault's article 'Réponse à une question', pp. 850–74 (in particular, 852–3). Like Lisa Lowe, in *Critical Terrains*, p. 10, I feel that it is worth emphasizing that I view a discourse not as 'fixed' and 'monolithic', but as 'a multivalent, overlapping, dynamic terrain'.

rhetorical strategies and theoretical options.[35] I also trace some of the ways in which the discourse of European travel maps out its relation to other discourses: writing about the Grand Tour draws, for example, on concepts and theoretical options formed within discourses such as aesthetic theory, art criticism, geology, botany and demography, and within other discourses of travel, such as primitivism, Orientalism, and Romantic Hellenism.[36]

It is worth emphasizing at this point that I am not primarily concerned here with defining the rules of a particular genre of travel writing. Over the course of the seventeenth and eighteenth centuries, various types of discursivity, invested with their own specific literary or non-literary status, are allotted to the domain of the foreign. These types of discursivity include, for example, the practically orientated listing of places to visit and objects to view, first-person narratives of journeys composed for publication or circulation among friends, diaries of private jottings, theoretical exposition and scientific enquiry, poems concerned with particular places, or with some general theme that prompts reference to the foreign, and fictional narratives. Some of these types of discursivity are identified by contemporaries as forms that predominate in a number of individual works, and such bodies of works are classified as genres.[37] Much of the material

---

35 These last two categories are viewed here as two aspects of the same category; all rhetorical strategies embody various theoretical assumptions, and map out some kind of explicit or implicit argument, while all theoretical options assume some kind of rhetorical function.

  Concepts, it should be emphasized, are seen here neither as corresponding to lexical definitions nor as consisting of abstractions, situated in the realm of thought, and invested with an identity exterior to the particular linguistic forms that they may assume; they are viewed, rather, as indissociable from the network of rhetorical and theoretical options that constitute the conditions of their formation. My interest lies not with what was thought or felt about the foreign, but with what it was possible to say and write about it.

36 For an account of the relation between geology and travel writing, over the later part of the period of the Grand Tour, see Hamblyn, 'Private Cabinets and Popular Geology', pp. 179–205.

37 The definition of the term *genre* that is adopted here, then, is that of a notional unity conferred on a body of individual texts over a particular historical period, on the basis of certain features that these texts all share. This definition is one that is put forward, for example, in Tzvetan Todorov's *Les Genres du discours*, p. 49.

  One of the main points of difference between a discourse and a genre, as defined here, lies in the fact that a genre is always identified on the basis of the definition of certain groups of utterances as possessing some overall coherence that allows them to be described as individual 'texts', 'works' or 'books'. The regularities by which a discourse is defined, on the other hand, are found within a field of utterances that may, individually or in groups, be situated within any written or spoken context whatsoever, whether or not they form part of a sequence of utterances that can be defined as a single literary whole.

analysed here is taken from works that situate themselves within the genre of the first-person narrative of travel, but much is also taken from works of other genres, such as novels, aesthetic treatises, and essays on art.[38]

The Grand Tour as narrative

How, then, can the Grand Tour be defined, once the terms of definition have been shifted out of the domain of social history into that of imaginative geography? First, by noting a crucial determinant of the ways in which the traveller is able to claim the topography of the Grand Tour as a source of pleasurable alterity, when translating it into forms of language: the movement from North to South that the Tour entails. William Beckford, for example, presents his own origins in northern Europe as essential to the delight that he feels in travelling through 'a continual bower of vines' near Lucca:

> These arbours afforded us both shade and refreshment; I fell upon the clusters which formed our ceiling, like a native of the north, unused to such luxuriance: one of those Goths, which Gray so poetically describes, who
>
>> Scent the new fragrance of the breathing rose,
>> And quaff the pendant vintage as it grows.[39]

Attempts to define the Grand Tour on the part of social historians often become enmired in debates about whether or not the Tour should be seen as a narrowly British practice, and about the exact extent of the area that it covered: whether or not, for example, it included travels to Greece, and whether northern European countries such as Holland and Germany should be seen as an integral part of it.[40] My own way of handling these questions is simply to adopt the view that a traveller on the Grand Tour, in order to be identifiable as such, should locate the point of origin of his or

---

[38] The first-person narrative of travel is taken as the point of definition of a genre throughout the seventeenth and eighteenth centuries. From about the mid-eighteenth century onwards, however, works appear such as Thomas Nugent's *The Grand Tour*, in which the reader is offered practically orientated, impersonally presented enumeration of sights to visit. Such works are seen as constituting a new, quite different genre of travel writing: that of the guide book. The definition of the narrative of travel then shifts slightly in relation to this new genre; the personal nature of the impressions that first-person narratives offer is more strongly emphasized, and such narratives acquire a more markedly 'literary' status.

[39] Beckford, *Dreams*, p. 152; Beckford quotes Thomas Gray, 'The Alliance of Education and Government: A Fragment', Essay 1, lines 56 and 57.

[40] See, for example, chapter 2 of Black, *The British Abroad*, pp. 14–85.

her journey somewhere in northern Europe, should aim to travel to the southern side of the Alps (whether he or she plans actually to cross these mountains or to arrive in Italy by sea), and should register a desire or intention to visit Rome, whether or not such a visit actually proves possible.[41] For most of the history of the Tour, this practice of travel also entails an assumption that the traveller is likely to return to northern Europe. (Such an assumption is intermittently thrown into question within the approach to travel as transgressive and destabilizing. Byron, in Canto IV of *Childe Harold's Pilgrimage* (1818), leaves some room for doubt as to the answer when he asks himself: 'and should I leave behind / The inviolate island of the sage and free, / And seek me out a home by a remoter sea.')[42]

An analysis of the discourse of European travel, then, could easily include writings in most of the languages of northern Europe. I limit my area of enquiry here, however, for the most part, to writings in French or English, which situate themselves in some way within European culture (as opposed to works in these languages that unequivocally establish the traveller's point of origin somewhere outside Europe), and describe the Alps and Italy. English and French writings exhibit an array of shared discursive regularities, and are so closely interlinked through networks of reference and quotation that any study of English writings would in any case constantly be concerned with references to and adaptations of French commentaries, and vice versa.[43] One particular French account of the works of art to be viewed in Italy – Charles Nicolas Cochin's *Voyage d'Italie* (1758) – is extensively quoted and adapted – often without acknowledgement – by

---

[41] Early seventeenth-century travellers often note the dangers, for Protestants, of visiting Rome, and describe the adjustments to their travel plans which they make as a result. See George Sandys's account of Rome in *A Relation of a Journey*, p. 309, beginning: 'Having staid here foure dayes (as long as I durst)…'. Thomas Coryate, in *Coryats Crudities*, fails to proceed towards Rome from northern Italy, but 'Richardus Cordet' nonetheless obliquely defines Coryat's journey as a movement in the direction of the Eternal City in the poem that he contributes to the verses that precede the traveller's narrative (lines 17–18; unpaginated prefatory section): 'No more shall man with mortar on his head / Set forwards towards Rome'.

[42] Stanza 8, lines 7–9, in Byron, *Complete Poetical Works*, vol. II, p. 127.

[43] To note the close interconnections between French and English writings is not to deny that some distinctions might be drawn between them, within a study that set out to identify such distinctions. John Barrell, in *The Political Theory of Painting*, pp. 39–45, argues that there is a major difference in approaches to pleasure and civic virtue in British and French art criticism – an area of commentary that overlaps to a large extent with accounts of travel in Italy. This book, however, is concerned with charting discursive regularities that can be discerned within writings in both languages, and not with establishing the extent of any variation between travel literature in English and in French.

British travellers.[44] Early nineteenth-century British travellers in Italy constantly refer to Germaine de Staël's novel *Corinne; ou, l'Italie* (1807), in order to define and reflect on their own experiences of travel.[45] Writings in German and other northern European languages are, with a few exceptions, only rarely drawn into this particular network of cross-reference; the one striking instance of a body of work by a German writer that English and French travellers repeatedly invoke is supplied by the writings of Johann Joachim Winckelmann, usually cited by these travellers with reference to French or Italian translations.[46]

The Grand Tour, as just defined, has a clear narrative structure. Richard Colt Hoare, quoting Conyers Middleton's *Letter from Rome* (1729), maps out a version of this narrative:

> I have often been thinking (says Mr. Middleton in his Letter from Rome,) that a voyage to Italy might properly enough be compared to the common stages of journey of life. At our setting out through France, the pleasures that we find, like those of our youth, are of the gay fluttering kind, which grow by degrees, as we advance towards Italy, more solid, manly, and rational, but attain not their full perfection till we reach ROME; from which point we no sooner turn homewards, than they begin again gradually to decline; and though sustained for a while in some degree of vigour, through the other stages and cities of Italy, yet dwindle at last into weariness and fatigue, and a desire to be at home, where the traveller finishes his course, as the old man does his days, with the usual privilege of being tiresome to his friends, and by a perpetual repetition of past adventures.[47]

Other travel writings, too, implicitly proclaim the traveller's assumption that the Grand Tour has its own established sequence by anticipating

---

[44] Compare, for example, the accounts of a *Judith and Holophernes*, attributed to Caravaggio, at the Palazzo Zambeccari in Bologna, in Cochin, *Voyage d'Italie*, vol. II, p. 158, and in Miller, *Letters*, vol. II, pp. 27–8; for direct references to Cochin, see Miller, *Letters*, vol. I, pp. 130, 131, 254, 257, 281, vol. II, pp. 19–20. Compare also the descriptions of Veronese's *Judith and Holophernes* in Cochin, *Voyages d'Italie*, vol. III, p. 157 and Gibbon, *Gibbon's Journey*, p. 74.

[45] See, for example, Anna Jameson, *Diary of an Ennuyée*, pp. 110, 206, 209.

[46] In English and French travel writing, Winckelmann's most famous work, his *Geschichte der Kunst des Altertums* (1764) is usually cited (where travellers acknowledge the reference) in one of the two French translations or in Carlo Fea's Italian edition of 1783. Germaine de Staël's *Corinne* is one of the few works published in French or English over the period of the Grand Tour that frequently alludes to German literature.

[47] Hoare, *A Classical Tour*, pp. 96–7; Hoare quotes, almost word for word, Conyers Middleton, *A Letter from Rome*, p. 8.

specific increases or decreases of strangeness, drama or pleasure as the traveller progresses. Piozzi, visiting a 'conservatory' of 'syrens' in Venice, exclaims: 'Will Naples, the original seat of Ulysses's seducers, shew us any thing stronger than this? I hardly expect or wish it.'[48] Gilbert Burnet charts a sequence of increasing and decreasing fascination through an explanation of his decision to travel back northwards by sea:

> It is true, I lose the sight of *Turin, Genoa,* and some other Courts: but though I am told these deserve well the pains of the Journey, yet when one rises from a great Meal, no Delicacies, how much soever they might tempt him at another time, can provoke his Appetite. So I confess freely that the sight of *Naples* and *Rome* have so set my stomach that way, that the Curiosity of seeing new Places, is now very low with me, and indeed these which I have of late seen, are such, that places which at another time would please me much, would now make but a slight and cold Impression.[49]

One chapter of this book – 'Destabilized Travel' – is especially concerned with elements of the narrative of the Grand Tour. This is because, in examining the Romantic approach to travel, the chapter considers the partial displacement, at the end of the eighteenth century, of the view of travel as a form of detached observation by the view of travel as a form of personal adventure, which entails transgression – the crossing of boundaries – and, as a consequence, also entails risks and dangers. The Grand Tour, as narrative, entails a number of traversals of boundaries: the traveller crosses not only the great natural barrier of the Alps but also, for example, the boundary represented by the Roman Campagna, which supplies a space of anticipation in which to await the momentous encounter with the Eternal City itself, and the boundary of the Pontine Marshes, which separates Rome from Naples and the warm South.[50] Hoare, in designating Rome as the site of 'solid, manly, and rational' pleasures, at their point of greatest perfection, structures the narrative of the Grand Tour so as to exclude any alternative pleasures that might erupt within Italy itself: other late eighteenth-century and early nineteenth-century travellers, however, identify the region beyond Rome – Naples and its environs – as a region of irresponsible, free-floating enjoyment.

---

48 Piozzi, *Observations and Reflections*, vol. I, p. 177.

49 Burnet, *Some Letters*, p. 180.

50 For an analysis of the sense of crossing a threshold experienced by travellers (in particular, by artists), on arriving in Rome, see Wrigley, 'Infectious Enthusiasms', pp. 79–87.

Sights and wonders

The narrative of the Grand Tour is punctuated by 'sights'. Travellers express an eagerness to visit places that others before them have deemed worth seeing. In de Sade's *Juliette*, the heroine classifies St Peter's as noteworthy by making an exception to her usual rules and principles of life in order to visit it: 'Malgré le serment que j'avais fait de n'entrer dans aucune église, je ne pus tenir en arrivant à Rome, au désir de visiter celle de Saint-Pierre.'[51] Travellers often emphasize the importance of sights in ordering their experience of the foreign by complaining if their visits to such places are obstructed or prevented. Piozzi, for example, recounts an especially cruel rebuff in Venice, when she attempts to see a painting defined as one of the principal sights there: Veronese's *Marriage at Cana:*

> When we arrived, the picture was kept in a refectory belonging to friars...,
> and no woman could be admitted. My disappointment was so great that I
> was deprived even of the powers of solicitation by the extreme ill-humour
> it occasioned; and my few intreaties for admission were completely disre-
> garded by the good old monk, who remained outside with me, while the
> gentlemen visited the convent without molestation. At my return to Venice
> I met little comfort, as every body told me it was my own fault, for I might
> put on men's clothes and see it whenever I pleased, as nobody then would
> stop, though perhaps all of them would know me.[52]

Sydney Morgan encounters an equally distressing obstacle when attempting to order mules to visit the cascade at Terni, and discovering 'that the
mules which carried strangers to the waterfall were a monopoly of government', and that her party would have to wait another day until any of these
official mules became available: 'in place of a natural wonder, so often and so
beautifully described, we have here to record one of those petty extortions
of despotism, which press upon the every-day enjoyments of humanity.'[53]

While travellers pay deference to an established itinerary by such declarations, however, they also, from at least the middle of the eighteenth
century onwards, intermittently chafe against the constraints of the
accepted itinerary, and suggest their own revisions of it. In doing so, they

---

[51] Sade, *La Nouvelle Justine*, vol. VIII, p. 100: 'Despite the vow that I had made never
to enter a church, I could not resist the desire to visit St Peter's when I arrived in
Rome.'

[52] Piozzi, *Observations and Reflections*, vol. I, p. 172.

[53] Morgan, *Italy*, vol. II, pp. 164–5.

nonetheless reaffirm the assumption that the Grand Tour is structured as a sequence of noteworthy places and objects. One of the most famous of such proposals for revision is Yorick's declaration, in Sterne's *A Sentimental Journey*, that the main 'thirst' that 'has led me from my own home into France – and from France will lead me through Italy' is a thirst not for 'pictures, statues, and churches', but for knowledge of the female heart.[54] Other travellers, more modestly, simply suggest that particular sights should be removed from the list, or demoted to some inferior position on it. Lady Morgan, inveigled into visiting the Tarpeian Rock by 'a dirty stable-boy' who offers to lead her 'to this great shrine of classic homage', scornfully repudiates both the rock itself and the 'affected raptures' of those who acclaim this scene of ancient brutality (the spot from which prisoners were thrown to their death):

> It were vain, under such unfavourable circumstances, to conjure up one classical association, to affect one of those *thrills* which vibrate in the hearts of all true Corinnas, when the very sound of the *Tarpeian Rock* meets their ear; but even had it been seen under the consecrated authority of those arch-mystagogues of all classic lore, Signori Fea and Nebbi, to the heart of an unlearned woman it could bring no throb of pleasure; nor could its view increase the sum of interest or respect which the Capitoline heroes still awaken in the minds of the most erudite.[55]

In response to the need to affirm the drama of the topography, the itinerary of the Grand Tour is often mapped out as a pared-down sequence of those sights sufficiently remarkable to be accorded the status of wonders. (Lady Morgan, unable to acquire the mules to the *Cascata delle Mormore*, is at pains to point out that the 'petty extortions of despotism' have prevented her from seeing not merely a sight but a wonder.) Most of the wonders of the Tour – the cascade at Terni, St Peter's, the cascade at Tivoli and Mount Vesuvius, for example – are invested with greatest drama and imaginative fascination in the seventeenth century, when Italy is defined as a country remarkable, in particular, for its profusion of objects of extreme singularity. Since Naples and its environs are viewed as especially rich in wonders, the emphasis on such objects allows the city to be present, in these early writings, as the place where the pleasures of the Tour reach

---

54 p. 84.

55 Morgan, *Italy*, vol. II, pp. 179, 179, 180, 179. Lady Morgan's references are to the heroine of Germaine de Staël's novel *Corinne: ou, l'Italie* (1807), and to the various guides to Rome and writings on the city by the archaeologists Carlo Fea and Antonio Nibby.

their climax, in contrast to its later role (discussed in Chapter 4, 'Destabilized Travel') as a place that lures travellers beyond the self-confirmatory pleasures of Rome. John Evelyn, in his *Diary,* designates Naples 'the Non ultra of my Travells', and describes himself: 'sufficiently sated with roling up and downe... since from the report of divers experienc'd and curious persons, I had ben assur'd there was little more to be seene in the rest of the civil World, after Italy, France, Flanders and the Low-Country, but plaine and prodigious Barbarisme'.[56] John Raymond, in his *Itinerary Contayning a Voyage Made through Italy* (1648), comments on Vesuvius: 'This Mountaine was the *Ultima Meta* of our voyage to *Naples,* wherefore having with much content seen these wonderfull things of Antiquity, Nature, and Curiosity; after some few dayes we parted from *Naples* to *Rome*' (Figure 1).[57]

Relative familiarity: ancient history and literary mediation

The imaginative topography of the Grand Tour can also be defined by reference to the confidence with which the traveller expects it to satisfy one of the demands that all travel writings impose on the foreign, alongside the demand for alterity. This is the demand that the topography should not be so radically different from the topography of the familiar that it resists all attempts at understanding and assimilation. Two of the assumptions incorporated in writing about Italy, throughout the period of the Grand Tour, make it especially easy to define the topography of the Tour as one that satisfies this demand. First, the traveller takes it for granted that the topography bears the traces of an ancient past, which has been rendered familiar either by male classical education or by a more general diffusion of knowledge of classical civilization. Seventeenth-century and early eighteenth-century writings present the ancient past as, in one sense, unfalteringly present in the contemporary topography: the 'fame' attached to particular places as a result of their role in myth and history is seen as enduring, however thoroughly the material vestiges of the past have been destroyed. During the late eighteenth and early nineteenth centuries, on the other hand, travel writings frequently present the ancient past as distressingly remote – a strategy that might seem to place in jeopardy the option of using references to antiquity to invest the topography with relative familiarity. At this period, however, antiquity is often presented as accessible to efforts of

---

[56] Vol. II, p. 354.
[57] p. 163.

A. *The entrance of the Grot of Pausilype*   B. *The Castell of Saint Elmo.*   D. *Castello dell ouo.*
towards Naples.   C. *Castello noua.*   E. *The mountaine Vesuuius.*

Figure 1 Engraving of the entrance to the Grotto of Posillipo, and the Bay of Naples, from
George Sandys, *A Relation of a Journey begun An: Dom: 1610* (London, 1615); engraving
(including captions): 11.2 x 12.2 cm.

intuitive understanding, even in the case of ancient sites where classical
scholarship offers little elucidation: travellers regularly demonstrate their
ability to convert historical time into personal time. Part of my third chapter, 'Spectator and Spectacle', is concerned with the attempt to shift
ancient history into a domain of the intuitive and personal, and with the elisions between the antique and versions of the feminine that play a part in it.

The second assumption that permeates writing about Italy, and that
plays a major part in determining the imaginative topography of the
Grand Tour, is the assumption that the traveller's experience of this
topography will be heavily subject to mediation – above all, to literary
mediation (including the mediation of the ancient authors). In almost all
accounts of the journey from Northern Europe across the Alps to Italy –
and even in most guide books concerned with this itinerary – the subject of
commentary indicates to the reader that he or she is already familiar with

the places visited from books, or is reading books on the spot that suggest ways of approaching the places and people in question. Anna Jameson defines Germaine de Staël's *Corinne* as intervening especially vigorously in her experience of Florence when, intending to reread the novel in that city (which the heroine visits at an especially unhappy stage of her life), she throws it down, 'resolved not to open it again', and declares, with reference to the unfortunate love affair that has driven Jameson herself to Italy in the hope of recovery: 'I can suffer enough, feel enough, think enough, without this.'[58]

Pleasure and 'improvements'

Another crucial feature of the imaginative topography of the Grand Tour, as mapped out by travel writing, is the assumption that this topography supplies forms of pleasure that merge easily (if not always seamlessly) with cultural benefit – or 'knowledge and improvements', as Yorick terms the advantages of travel in his 'Preface' to *A Sentimental Journey*. James Howell, recounting his arrival in Naples in *Epistolæ Ho-Elianæ* (1645), defines his travels through Italy as offering both pleasure and 'improvements', and implies by his smooth transition from 'Delight' to 'usefull and solid Knowledge' that the one is continuous with the other:

> And though these frequent removes and tumblings under climes of differ-
> ing temper were not without som danger, yet the delight which accompa-
> nyed them was far greater; and it is impossible for any man to conceive the
> true pleasure of Peregrination, but he who actually enjoyes, and puts it in
> practise: Believe it, Sir, That one yeer well employed abroad by one of
> mature judgment (which you know I want very much) advantageth more in
> point of usefull and solid knowledg then three in any of our *Universities*.[59]

Other writings explicitly discuss what the relation between the pleasures of the Grand Tour and its benefits might be. In *The Compleat Gentleman: or, Directions for the Education of Youth as to their Breeding at Home and Travelling Abroad* (1678), Jean Gailhard, defining 'travelling abroad' primarily with reference to the tour of Italy, muses over this question:

> Now the two ends of Travelling are profit and pleasure; the last subordinate
> to the former, arising from the satisfaction one hath about the first, and from

---

58 Jameson, *Diary*, p. 110 (see Staël, *Corinne; ou, l'Italie*, vol. II, pp. 232–46; book XVIII, chapters 3–6).

59 Sterne, *A Sentimental Journey*, p. 12; Howell, *Epistolæ Ho-Elianæ*, vol. I, p. 77.

the variety of objects: for that which Frenchmen call *divertissement,* or recreation, comes from diversity, which certainly causes a pleasure, almost every day one seeing different things: but benefit is a thing I mind most of all, 'tis a thing gotten by Travels, as confirmed by the practice of all polished and civilized Nations, ancient and modern.[60]

Gailhard's pious assertion that pleasure must clearly be subordinate to 'profit' does not represent a consensus: travel writings vary widely in the views that they put forward as to the specific relation that the traveller should construct between 'improvements' and delight. During the eighteenth and early nineteenth centuries, the need to combine the two is, in fact, usually defined negatively: that is, it is asserted not through the precise formulations of seventeenth-century speculations on travel, but, more nebulously, through dismissals of inadequate travellers. Lady Mary Wortley Montagu, for example, in a letter to her daughter, offers a generalized view of travellers to Italy as failing in the task of appropriation ('They return no more instructed than they might have been at home by the help of a Map'), and then locates this failure in a tendency to allow either one or the other of the aims of the Tour to assume an ascendancy: 'The Boys only remember where they met with the best Wine or the prettyest Women, and the Governors (I speak of the most learned amongst them) have only remark'd Situations and Distances, or at most Status and Edifices.'[61] One of the inadequate travellers who most resolutely refuses to mingle 'improvements' with his attempt to derive gratification and entertainment from travel in Italy is the comte d'Erfeuil in *Corinne*: a Frenchman who, in Rome, comments on the taste for visiting ancient ruins: 'Un plaisir qu'il faut acheter par tant d'études, ne me paroît pas bien vif en lui-même.'[62] Those resistant to pleasure are dismissed with yet greater scorn. The most famous example of such a dismissal is the account of 'the learned SMELFUNGUS' – or Smollett, in his role as traveller-narrator of his *Travels through France and Italy* (1766) – in Sterne's *Sentimental Journey*. 'Smelfungus', Yorick explains, 'set out with the spleen and jaundice, and every object he pass'd by was discoloured or distorted'. Not only does Smelfungus fail to appreciate the great sights of the Grand Tour, such as the Pantheon ('*– 'tis nothing but a huge cock-pit*, said he – I wish you had said nothing worse of the Venus of Medicis, replied I'), but he complains bitterly about his treatment

---

60 Part II, pp. 5–6.

61 Montagu, *Complete Letters*, vol. II, p. 495; letter of 8 December 1751.

62 Staël, *Corinne; ou, l'Italie*, vol. I, p. 139 (book VI, chapter 1): 'A rapture which one must purchase by study cannot be very vivid in itself' (*Corinne; or, Italy*, p. 88).

at the hand of foreigners: 'He had been flea'd alive, and bedevil'd, and used worse than St. Bartholomew, at every stage he had come at –'.[63] Anna Jameson, in her *Diary of an Ennuyée* (1826), also sets up a category of travellers who ignore the need to extract pleasure from the foreign:

> I have met persons who think they display a vast deal of common sense, and very uncommon strength of mind, in rising superior to all prejudices of education and illusions of romance – to whom enthusiasm is only another name for affectation – who, where the cultivated and the contemplative mind finds ample matter to excite feeling and reflection, give themselves airs of fashionable *nonchalance,* or flippant scorn – to whom the crumbling ruin is so much brick and mortar, no more – to whom the tomb of the Horatii and Curatii is a *stack of chimneys,* the Pantheon *an old oven,* and the Fountain of Egeria a *pig stye.*[64]

A failure to appropriate the topography of the Grand Tour as a source of pleasure or benefit – or both – is very often identified with a failure in writing about the topography. Both Yorick's account of Smelfungus's reaction to the Pantheon and Jameson's description of a string of misjudged responses characterize the travellers in question through their chosen words, and specify the precise faults that the words display: Smelfungus, Yorick explains, has written an account of his travels, 'but 'twas nothing but the account of his miserable feelings', while Jameson's purveyors of 'flippant scorn' are guilty of 'an affectation a thousand times more gross and contemptible, that that affectation... which they design to ridicule.'[65]

One of the most ludicrous attempts to translate the topography of the Grand Tour into forms of language is conjured up in Aphra Behn's play *The Feigned Courtesans* (1679), in which Mr Tickletext, a tutor accompanying a young Englishman to Rome, carries with him 'a small volume... into which I transcribe the most memorable and remarkable transactions of the day'. Tickletext's idea of a 'memorable and remarkable' encounter with the foreign is typified by the entry: 'The twenty-second, nine of our twelve chickens getting loose, flew over-board, the other three miraculously escaping, by being eaten by me, that morning for

---

63 Sterne, *A Sentimental Journey*, pp. 28–9. See Smollett, *Travels*, pp. 258, 227; Sterne's summary of Smelfungus's complaints echoes the reference to 'Bartholomew flaed alive' in Smollett's lament that, in Italy, 'the labours of painting should have been so much employed on the shocking subjects of the martyrology' (p. 257).

64 pp. 207–8.

65 Sterne, *A Sentimental Journey*, p. 29; Jameson, *Diary*, p. 208.

breakfast.'[66] A similar lack of understanding of how to use words to make a convincing gesture of appropriation is charted by Byron, in the context of a slightly more distant destination: the poet mockingly quotes some 'Lines in the Travellers' Book of the Macri Family' which, like the journal entry of Mr Tickletext, unwittingly testify to a complete failure in delight and profit:

> Fair Albion, smiling, sees her son depart
> To trace the birth and nursery of art:
> Noble his object, glorious is his aim;
> He comes to Athens, and he writes his name.[67]

Many travel books dismiss other travellers for offering erroneous information, for plagiarism, or for laziness in their enquiries. De Sade, in his notes on Naples, accuses the Abbé Richard of copying from a guide book, and being so careless in his borrowings that he describes a church that has been burnt down nine years before his visit to the city.[68] John Chetwode Eustace, in his *Tour through Italy* (1813), condemns the sloppy research of travellers when assessing the manners and morals of 'females of rank' in Naples. His argument is simple: 'superficial observers' will obviously find it much easier to make the acquaintance of women 'totally lost to all sense of duty and delicacy', since these women are, almost by definition, 'of much easier access': 'they may be seen in every large party and at every public amusement, and are seldom deficient in affability and condescension, particularly to foreigners.' 'Persons of virtue and reputation', on the other hand, 'appear in select societies to which few strangers are admitted, and receive the visits of such only as are introduced by their intimate and habitual friends'.[69]

This preoccupation with ways in which writing about the topography of the foreign is likely to go wrong affirms very strongly the importance of writing itself as an instrument of appropriation, through which the traveller can claim to be extracting pleasure and benefit from the topography. Travellers commenting on Italy implicitly define the task of recording their travels and describing the topography as evidence that they possess the abilites required in order to enjoy the prestige due to full participants

---

[66] p. 46 (Act III, scene 1).

[67] Byron, *Complete Poetical Works*, vol. I, p. 279. Byron comments, unsparingly: 'But yet, whoe'er he be, to say no worse, / His name would bring more credit than his verse' (lines 3–4 of the poet's reply; 1810).

[68] Sade, *Voyage d'Italie*, p. 405.

[69] Vol. II, p. 52.

in the Tour, as a practice of travel determined by the patrician ideal of the cultured, cosmopolitan gentleman.[70]

Curiosity

One of the ways in which travellers affirm that pleasure is readily elided with the quest for 'improvements' is by deploying concepts of curiosity. Seventeenth-century travel writings are full of accounts of curiosities: that is, of objects which, by virtue of their ability to function as bearers of meaning, arouse responses of wonder, eager enquiry and enthralled speculation. Stephen Bann, defining the curiosity with reference to the collection of the seventeenth-century traveller John Bargrave, and distinguishing the rhetoric of curiosity at this period from the rhetoric of late eighteenth-century sensibility, suggests: 'For Bargrave, desire follows the logic not of a greater whole completed by the imagination but, rather, of an intricate structure revealed by intensive study.'[71]

The concept of curiosity, however, is formed not only within accounts of the objects that draw upon themselves such eager enquiry, but also in analyses of the motivating forces that prompt investigation. Hobbes, in *Leviathan* (1651), charts a quest for the pleasure of 'knowing causes' that, in various transmuted forms, plays a part in the emplotments of desire traced out by travel writings throughout the period of the Grand Tour:

> *Desire*, to know why, and how, CURIOSITY; such as is in no living creature but Man; so that Man is distinguished, not onely by his Reason; but also by this singular Passion from other *Animals*; in whom the appetite of food, and other pleasures of Sense, by prædominance, take away the care of knowing causes; which is a Lust of the mind, that by a perseverance of delight in the

---

70 John Barrell's definition of the way in which a concept of prestige functions in the 'civic discourse on the fine arts' in eighteenth-century Britain, in *The Birth of Pandora*, p. 68, provides a useful point of reference in analysing the various forms of prestige claimed by the speaking subject within the discourse of European travel:

> As long as the possibility of appreciating the higher genres of the art was thought of as available only to the aristocracy, it was certainly imagined that an informed concern with painting and sculpture conferred status on the noble or gentle connoisseur; it confirmed his standing as a patrician in the fullest sense of the word, as someone not only born to exercise power, but fit to exercise it. As a result, a form of prestige became attached to the ability to articulate the civic discourse, and that ability could remain to some extent a source of prestige when the discourse came to be spoken by, and addressed to, those with no claim to be regarded as patricians.

71 Bann, *Under the Sign*, p. 103; see also pp. 9–17, for a useful discussion of the concept of the curiosity. See, too, the chapter 'La Culture de la curiosité', in Pomian, *Collectionneurs*, pp. 61–80.

continuall and indefatigable generation of Knowledge, exceedeth the short vehemence of any carnall Pleasure.[72]

Eighteenth-century writings often applaud the power of such a 'Lust of the mind' to create continuities between pleasure and benefit: Lord Kames, in his *Elements of Criticism* (1762), observes:

Men tear themselves from their native country in search of things rare and new; and curiosity converts into a pleasure, the fatigues, and even perils of travelling. To what cause shall we ascribe these singular appearances? The plain account of the matter follows. Curiosity is implanted in human nature, for a purpose extremely beneficial, that of acquiring knowledge. New and strange objects, above all others, excite our curiosity; and its gratification is the emotion... known by the name of wonder.[73]

Edward Gibbon writes in his *Memoirs of my Life and Writings* (1796): 'in a foreign country, curiosity is our business and our pleasure; and the traveller, conscious of his ignorance, and covetous of his time, is diligent in the search and the view of every object that can deserve his attention.'[74] The article on 'Voyage (Education)' in the *Encyclopédie* defines the educational value of the topography of the Grand Tour by specific reference to its ability to excite curiosity: 'Il est en particulier un pays au-delà des Alpes qui mérite la curiosité de tous ceux dont l'éducation a été cultivée par les lettres'.[75] Pierre-Jacques-Onésyme Bergeret de Grancourt claims for Rome a similarly intensified power to prompt efforts of investigation: in this city, 'ceux qui ne sont pas curieux doivent le devenir, car on ne voit que choses rares, même pour les gens du pays'.[76]

At the same time, however, as Nicholas Thomas has noted, 'the nature of curiosity', in the eighteenth century, 'is not fixed but morally slippery': 'the legitimacy of curious inquiry is uncertain'.[77] Concepts of curiosity are formed with reference to two impulses that are defined, in the eighteenth century, as difficult to reconcile with the pursuit of 'improvements': the

---

[72] p. 124.

[73] Vol. I, pp. 319–20.

[74] In Gibbon, *Autobiography*, p. 125.

[75] In D'Alembert and Diderot (editors), *Encyclopédie*, vol. XVII, p. 477: 'There is in particular a country beyond the Alps which merits the curiosity of all those whose education has been cultivated by reading and study.'

[76] Bergeret and Fragonard, *Journal*, p. 163: 'those who are not curious have to become so, for one only sees rarities, which seem exceptional even to the local inhabitants.'

[77] Thomas, 'Licensed Curiosity', p. 122. For another study of tensions and equivocations within accounts of concepts of curiosity, see Benedict, 'The "Curious Attitude"'.

desire for novelty, and restlessness. Edmund Burke, in his *Philosophical Enquiry into the Origin of our Ideas of the Sublime and Beautiful* (1757), declares: 'By curiosity, I mean whatever desire we have for, or whatever pleasure we take in novelty.' He observes:

> But as those things which engage us merely by their novelty, cannot attach us for any length of time, curiosity is the most superficial of all the affections; it changes its object perpetually; it has an appetite which is very sharp, but very easily satisfied; and it has always an appearance of giddiness, restlessness and anxiety. Curiosity from its nature is a very active principle; it quickly runs over the greatest part of its objects, and soon exhausts the variety which is commonly to be met with in nature; the same things make frequent returns, and they return with less and less of any agreeable effect.[78]

Samuel Evers, in his *Journal Kept on a Journey from Bassora to Bagdad* (1784), also identifies curiosity with 'the love of novelty', and presents it as a motive that, however admirable, needs to be defended:

> Man is a creature too imperfect and unsteady to be invariably content: he is ever restless in pursuit, ever wandering with ceaseless avidity from one object to another: This principle it is true is the fruitful cause of many evils, but is is also productive of many advantages; without such an impulse, how dull and insiped [*sic*] would be the state of human life! It would be little better than the contracted existence of a particular species of shell fish, which are stationed as it were on a rock, and never move from the narrow spot assigned them, 'till the moment of their dissolution arrives.[79]

Both these commentaries, in their emphasis on restlessness, align curiosity not only with the pursuit of novelty, but with purposeless movement onwards: in other words, with a form of travel which, where it is mentioned in eighteenth-century writings, is rejected as evidence of complete inadequacy in managing the experience of the foreign. Movement for its own sake provokes severe strictures from Rousseau ('Voyager pour voyager, c'est errer, être vagabond... Je voudrais donner au jeune homme un intérêt sensible à s'instruire') and also from Dr Johnson, whose *Journey to the Western Islands of Scotland* (1775) presents those who engage in 'capricious and casual' migrations (in the manner of the Scottish highlanders) as

---

[78] p. 31.

[79] pp. i–ii.

travellers so inadequate that firm authority is needed to keep them under control:

> When Caesar was in Gaul, he found the Helvetians preparing to go they
> knew not whither, and put a stop to their motions. They settled again in
> their own country, where they were so far from wanting room, that they had
> accumulated three years provision for their march.[80]

A variant on this strategy of equating curiosity with lack of purpose is to define the curiosity that motivates the traveller as 'idle': John MacCulloch, in *On Malaria* (1827), comments darkly on Paestum: 'dearly have many paid for the idle curiosity which prompted them to seek a reputation for taste in exploring its classical ruins.'[81]

As motives for aimless wandering, then, curiosity and the pursuit of novelty can be seen as conflicting with the need to extract benefit from the topography: their maleficent effect, it is implied, stems from their tendency to displace any ordered programme of observation and enquiry. Love of novelty, in addition, is presented as compromising the traveller's ability to engage in a balanced assessment of the relative merits of the foreign and the familiar. (An ability which, I argue at the very beginning of Chapter 1, is defined in the eighteenth century as crucial to the understanding of the relation between different cultures and places.) Joseph Addison, in his *Remarks on Several Parts of Italy* (1705), argues that it is only 'Uncommonness' that makes us 'astonish'd' at Roman ruins, as though the novelty-value of the unfamiliar is a quality that must be discounted if the traveller is to manage the encounter with the foreign in a properly even-handed manner: 'There are indeed many extraordinary Ruins, but I believe a Traveller would not be so much astonish'd at 'em, did he find any Works of the same kind in his own Country.'[82] The same assumption that the foreign and the familiar are in competition for the traveller's attention and admiration, and the same anxiety that the pleasures of novelty might give the foreign an unfair advantage, are inscribed within Lord Kames's account of novelty; despite a relative detachment of tone, a reference to 'foreign luxuries' elides the attractions of the foreign with potentially corrupting pleasures:

---

80 Rousseau, *Émile*, p. 596: 'travelling for its own sake is wandering, being a vagabond…
     I should like to impart to the young man embarking on his travels a lively interest in
     educating himself'; Johnson, 'A Journey', p. 198.

81 p. 376.

82 p. 225.

When two things equally new and singular are presented, the spectator balances betwixt them. But when told that one of them is the product of a distant quarter of the world, he no longer hesitates, but clings to this as the more singular. Hence the preference given to foreign luxuries and to foreign curiosities, which appear rare in proportion to their original distance.[83]

Guilt

'Opposition and Intensification', the first chapter of this book, begins by examining this assumption that the foreign and the familiar are in a relation of opposition to each other, and that attraction towards one must entail a rejection of the other. I argue here that the eighteenth-century commentary of opposition produces an effect that may be termed *guilt*. The feature of eighteenth-century travel writing that first drew my attention to this effect of language was a very obvious one: the proliferation, between around 1720 and the final decades of the century, of expressions of censure. As I grew more accustomed to reading travel writing of this period, I became more aware of the responses of intense pleasure set alongside condemnatory accounts of Italian culture. I found myself, as a result, viewing expressions of censure as strategies for disavowing a pleasure that was defined as forbidden: strategies which, in fact, end up drawing attention to the effects of language that they attempt to erase.

Concepts of curiosity, then, in eighteenth-century writings, become entangled in this tension between pleasure and guilt. The definitions of curiosity that are formulated in travel writing of this period appear yet more equivocal if they are considered not only in the context of assumptions about how the traveller should assess the pleasures of the foreign, but also in the context of assumptions about the traveller's aims and methods in translating the foreign into discourse. A central aim of travel writing is always assumed to be that of offering pleasures of various kinds to the reader: the pleasure of anticipating a future visit to the places described, for example, or the pleasure of imaginative geography itself: of speculating on a topography of dramatic otherness. Both hyperbole and digression are deployed not only as methods of describing this topography, and rendering it accessible to understanding, but also as strategies for seducing the reader into speculating pleasurably on the foreign. While hyperbole is

---

presented as a trope that invites the reader to share in a response of wonder, digression promises opportunities for the indulgence of curiosity.

In twentieth-century travel writings, these pleasures are often proclaimed in a tone of cheerful irresponsibility. Aldous Huxley, for example, when elaborating on the uses of his own 'excessive and promiscuous inquisitiveness', declares happily: 'The most uninteresting human being seen at a little distance by a spectator with a lively fancy and a determination to make the most of life takes on a mysterious charm, becomes odd and exciting.' In pursuing an analogy between travelling and reading, he suggests that those few 'morally admirable' people 'who travel... with purpose and a definite system' may not necessarily produce the best results when writing about their experiences:

> Some of the most self-indulgent and aimless of travellers and readers have known how to profit by their vices. Desultory reading was Dr. Johnson's besetting sin... And yet his achievement was not small. And there are frivolous travellers, like Beckford, who have gone about the world, indulging their wanton curiosity, to almost as good purpose.[84]

Waugh, in *Labels,* is yet more insouciant in proclaiming the uses of digressiveness in translating the topography into language. In Istanbul, he tells the story of 'a procession of pimps demanding a higher percentage to cover the increased cost of living', as a result of the 'unfair amateur competition' that the emancipation of women has set 'against the regular trade'. He then explains the principle on which he has selected such a snippet of information:

> This may or may not be true. It did not seem to me my business to investigate statements of this kind, but simply to scribble them down in my notebook if they seemed to me amusing. But then, I have had three weeks in Fleet Street at one stage in my career. That is what people mean, I expect, when they say that newspaper training is valuable to an author.[85]

Eighteenth-century writings register rather greater anxiety about the possibility that digressiveness might slide into 'self-indulgent and aimless' speculation, directed not at assembling knowledge but at providing an entertaining commentary. Baretti's declaration that 'a writer of travels, who would make himself fashionable in his own country' will seek to gratify his readers' 'love of novelty' at the expense of any fair-minded

---

[84] Huxley. *Along the Road,* pp. 26–7, 32.
[85] p. 117.

pursuit of accurate information has already been quoted.[86] Even such a
determinedly divagatory work as Sterne's *Sentimental Journey* acknowledges the rhetorical dangers of aimlessness, by setting up a category of
inquisitiveness next to which Yorick's own digressive curiosity appears
positively purposeful. Satirizing the demographic commentaries of contemporaries such as Smollett, Yorick launches into reflections on the question of why the French are so small, and imagines an inquisitive traveller
pursuing a series of pedantically pointless enquiries:

> A medical traveller might say,'tis owing to undue bandages – a splenetic
> one, to want of air – and an inquisitive traveller, to fortify the system, may
> measure the height of their houses – the narrowness of their streets, and in
> how few feet square in the sixth and seventh stories such numbers of the
> *Bourgoisie* [*sic*] eat and sleep together.[87]

The argument changes slightly, however, as the passage proceeds. Yorick
produces a further explanation for the tiny stature of the French that is
palpably ludicrous, but which he utters with a triumphant awareness that
it is, in its ebullient absurdity, far more entertaining than any information
that inquisitive travellers, rhetorically trammelled by their fussy preoccupation with precise measurements, might ever hope to reveal:

> But I remember, Mr. Shandy the elder, who accounted for nothing like any
> body else, in speaking one evening of these matters, averred that children,
> like other animals, might be increased almost to any size, provided they
> came right into the world; but the misery was, the citizens of Paris were so
> coop'd up, that they had not actually room enough to get them – I do not
> call it getting any thing, said he – 'tis getting nothing – Nay, continued he,
> rising in his argument, 'tis getting worse than nothing, when all you have
> got, after twenty or five and twenty years of the tenderest care and most
> nutritious aliment bestowed upon it, shall not at last be as high as my leg.
> Now, Mr. Shandy being very short, there could be nothing more said
> about it.[88]

In the eighteenth century, then, as well as the twentieth, the need to offer
the reader an entertaining commentary can serve to endorse 'a lively fancy'
and a taste for enquiry and speculation. In branding curiosity as potentially
blameworthy, travel writing at the same time defines the pleasures of

---

86 Baretti, *An Account*, vol. I, p. 1.

87 Sterne, *A Sentimental Journey*, p. 59.

88 *Ibid*, p. 59

curiosity as essential to the process of describing and commenting on foreign places.

It should be evident by now that this book, in examining the eighteenth-century rhetoric of pleasure and guilt, is concerned more with the forms of language that claim the foreign as a source of pleasurable speculation than with the guilt-laden language of disapproval. It is concerned, too, with the transformations that separate this rhetoric of pleasure and guilt both from the rhetorical strategies of seventeenth-century travel writing, in which expressions of pleasure are allowed to proliferate almost unrestrainedly, and from the rhetoric of pleasure, enjoyment and danger that begins to play a part in travel writing from the 1780s onwards. The two final chapters in this book are concerned with the two variants of this later rhetoric that have already been mentioned: destabilizing travel and tourism.

The use of terms such as *pleasure* and *guilt* will, perhaps, raise an expectation in some readers that this book might offer psychological explanations for the rhetorical and theoretical strategies employed in travel writing. It is therefore worth emphasizing at this point that my concern here is with what it was possible to say or write about the foreign over a particular period, and not with what travellers felt or thought, consciously or unconsciously. In attempting to identify preconditions for the formation of particular concepts and the use of particular theoretical and rhetorical strategies, the domain within which I hope to locate these preconditions is the rhetoric of travel writing itself: that is, neither the domain of psychology nor (as already noted) that of social history.[89]

In my penultimate and final chapters, I am primarily concerned with arguments, assumptions, themes and concepts that mark departures from earlier travel writing, and that are in many ways continuous with present-

---

[89] It seems especially important to make this point because, in the historical narrative of rhetorical transformations that I construct, I end up at a point where a number of the assumptions and arguments about human desire registered within travel writing are continuous with assumptions and arguments still current today – in particular, with emplotments of desire that have been codified in more specialized terms within the discourse of psychoanalytic theory. Some such assumptions operate so forcefully, in guiding late twentieth-century readings of language, that it is difficult to avoid scrutinizing the travel writing of earlier periods for implicit recognition or confirmation of them: reference to psychoanalytic theory produces what Stephen Greenblatt terms 'the curious effect of a discourse that functions as if the psychological categories it invokes were not only simultaneous with but even prior to and themselves causes of the very phenomena of which in actual fact they were the results' ('Psychoanalysis and Renaissance Culture', in *Learning to Curse*, pp. 131–45; p. 142). For an account of travel writing that, in contrast to mine, does in fact examine aspects of the psychology of travel, see Porter, *Haunted Journeys*.

day approaches to travel and pleasure; in other words, I do not set out to chart the discontinuities between early concepts of destabilizing travel and tourism and the corresponding concepts now in use, but concentrate, instead, on disjunctions between, on the one hand, Romantic and touristic approaches to the foreign and, on the other, the approaches that they displace. (References to later writings, which I use throughout the book to emphasize or elucidate particular points, are, as a result, especially frequent in these two chapters.)

The first three chapters, on the other hand, examine ways of describing the foreign, and commenting on the topography of foreignness, that I see as, in large part, discontinuous with the rhetorical options available to the traveller today. At the same time, a number of such options continue to be used even after their importance is diminished by new rhetorical strategies. The eighteenth-century strategy of symmetrical opposition between the foreign and the familiar, for example, never entirely disappears.

Masculinity, femininity, manliness and effeminacy

The five chapters of this book, then, are all concerned with changes in the formation of concepts of pleasure in writings about the Grand Tour, and in the desires and demands imposed upon the topography of the Tour in order to extract pleasure from it. Such changes are, of course, dependent upon an array of other transformations in the discourse of European travel. One series of concepts undergoes some especially dramatic changes: the concepts of gender that become entangled with the idea of travelling to Italy in search of pleasure and benefit. The sources of authority to which the speaking subject is able to lay claim, when appropriating the foreign as a source of pleasure, are determined, in part, throughout the period of the Grand Tour, by the versions of masculinity, femininity, manliness and effeminacy that play a part in the positioning of the speaking subject in relation to the objects of commentary. In most travel narratives, the gender identity of the traveller-narrator is fixed as male or female either on the title page or through clues swiftly offered at the outset of the journey, and the subject of individual utterances within the text is consistently positioned as one writing as a man or writing as a woman. However firmly this identity is established, a range of different concepts of gender will nonetheless play a part in the claims to various kinds of authority and expertise that the subject of commentary establishes. The gender identity of the traveller-narrator, moreover, is not always established immediately and unequivocally: Byron, in a letter to John Murray, retracts a ferocious printed riposte to a traveller who has claimed to have refused to meet him, as he suddenly realizes, with some embarrassment, that the travel book in question is not in fact written by a man:

> I open my letter to say – that on reading more of the 4 volumes on Italy – where the Author says '*declined* an introduction' I perceive (horresco referens) that it is written by a WOMAN!!! In that case you must suppress my note and answer – and all I have said about the book and the writer. – I never dreamed of it till now – in extreme wrath at that precious note – I can only say that I am sorry that a Lady should say anything of the kind. – What I would have said to a person with testicles – you know already.[90]

Before the early to middle decades of the eighteenth century, it is difficult to argue that the subject of commentary in an account of the Grand Tour can be defined as female and yet claim the authority of a participant in the Grand Tour. (Because of the absence of published writings that situate the female traveller as a being able to pronounce authoritatively on the foreign, I adopt a convention of using only male personal pronouns and possessive adjectives when referring to writings of this early period.) From the middle of the eighteenth century, however, a number of travel books are published that name a female author on the title page – and, at intervals throughout the text, refer explicitly or obliquely to the female gender of the traveller-narrator. Books naming the author as female become extremely common in the early nineteenth century. One of the transformations in the discourse of European travel that allows women to be invested with the authority to comment on the foreign is the change from a commentary of scholarly compilation to a commentary of viewing, charted in Chapter 2, 'Hyperbole and Observation': during the early decades of the eighteenth century, the authority of the classical scholar is displaced, to a large extent, by the authority of the eye-witness. Since women are readily admitted as beings able to visit particular places, and to describe them and comment on them as eye-witnesses, female travellers are no longer excluded from the position of authoritative subject within the discourse of European travel. Around the middle of the eighteenth century, the authority of the eye-witness is supplemented by an authority derived from an ability to respond emotionally to the objects of

---

[90] Byron, *Letters and Journals*, vol. VIII, p. 183; according to Leslie A. Marchand, the note was to be printed at the end of *Marino Faliero*, and attacks the author of *Sketches Descriptive of Italy*, of which the author was Jane Waldie (see footnotes, vol. VIII, pp. 173, 183).

commentary. In travel writing of this period, as in many other cultural contexts, emotional responsiveness is marked as a feminized attribute, and the female subject is readily admitted as capable of pronouncing on the foreign in a responsive manner. Responsiveness, in the late eighteenth century, is nonetheless defined as compatible with manly simplicity and restraint: by adeptly combining hyperbole with rejections of too immoderate an effusiveness, both male and female travellers are positioned as feminine yet manly.

The concepts of gender that play a part in definitions of the Grand Tour, moreover, and of travel in general, change dramatically over the period considered here. The Tour is explicitly defined in seventeenth-century writings as a confirmation of masculinity. Richard Lassels, for example, in his *Voyage of Italy* (1670), defines travel as a means of achieving manly self-reliance and avoiding effeminate softness:

> Traveling preserves my yong nobleman from surfeiting of his parents, and weanes him from the dangerous fondness of his mother. It teacheth him wholesome hardship; to lye in beds that are none of his acquaintance; to speak to men he never saw before; to travel in the morning before day, and in the evening after day; to endure any horse and weather, as well as any meat and drink. Whereas my country gentleman that never traveled, can scarce go to *London* without making his *Will*, at least without wetting his *handkercher*. And what generous mother will not say to her son with that ancient? *Malo tibi malè esse, quam molliter: I had rather thou shouldst be sick, then soft.*[91]

During the late eighteenth and early nineteenth centuries, however, various concepts of travel to Italy as feminizing are formed; the rhetoric of emotional responsiveness, with its insistence that some versions of the feminine are compatible with manliness, proves useful in endorsing such concepts. Viewing works of art, for example, and growing accustomed to foreign society and manners, are described as activities that, far from forming part of the 'wholesome hardship' of travel, confer on the traveller a certain feminizing polish and sophistication. Excessive identification with a rough-hewn version of masculinity is mocked, in some writings, as evidence of a failure in acquiring such polish. In Lancelot Temple's *Short*

---

91 Part I, unpaginated preface; the quotation is attributed by Lassels to Seneca. The concept of softness is regularly elided with that of effeminacy, with reference to the Latin *mollitia*, which can refer to either quality. For a discussion of the relation between the Grand Tour and British concepts of masculinity, see Cohen, *Fashioning Masculinity*, chapter 4, 'The Grand Tour of the English Gentleman', pp. 54–64.

Ramble through some Parts of France and Italy (1771), the traveller, exclaiming at the beauty of the *Apollo Belvedere*, in the Vatican, invokes an imaginary group of spectators who, in objecting to such beauty in a male figure, reveal themselves as crudely resistant to any feminizing preoccupation with aesthetic matters: 'I have heard sensible people say that a man has nothing to do with beauty – That a man is handsome enough if he does not frighten his Horse, is a coarse kind of Proverb.'[92]

Late eighteenth-century travel writing, then, both incorporates expressions of responsiveness that are defined as feminized and presents some of the feminizing effects of travel as legitimate and desirable. At the same time, writing of this period is consistently censorious about the effeminacy of the inhabitants of the warm South – an effeminacy that is located either in their languor and indolence or in the fervour of their passions. The traveller, it is assumed, is protected from the contaminatory effects of such effeminacy by the ease with which he or she is able to take up the position of a detached spectator, viewing the foreign as a distanced pictorial spectacle.

Such protection is, however, sometimes thrown into uncertainty: even detached, pictorial viewing allows the topography of effeminacy to compromise the traveller to some extent, by inviting him or her to identify with figures within the topography, or to view them in an enthralled, absorptive manner. By the early nineteenth century, the effeminacy of the warm South is defined both as more dangerous to the traveller and as more attractive. One of the forms of destabilization envisaged as a danger that crossing boundaries might entail is that of succumbing to 'a climate which', as James Johnson puts it in *Change of Air* (1831) 'unmanned not only the conquering Romans but the conquerors of Rome'.[93] At the same time, travellers positively welcome the unmooring, and loss of a sense of bounded selfhood, that such an effemination entails: Anna Jameson, in Naples, charts a diminution of her sufferings as all her faculties 'seemed lost and swallowed up in an indolent delicious reverie, a sort of vague and languid enjoyment'.[94]

The alternative approach to the foreign that travellers begin to adopt around the end of the eighteenth century, moreover, that of the tourist, takes it for granted that travel entails a temporary removal from a domain of duty and responsibility: in other words, from a domain that provides

---

[92] pp. 35–6.

[93] p. 293.

[94] Jameson, *Diary*, p. 262.

crucial confirmation of masculinity and manliness. The touristic identification of travel with an escape from the burden of authoritative but mundane identity survives today, and supplies a central theme of many travel
brochures. ('Jacket and tie or smart dress are decidedly not required in
Kiribati. You only need lightweight casuals and a determination to escape
the rat race.')[95]

Nonetheless, an awareness of the view of travel propounded by Lassels
– travel as confirmation of patrician masculinity – is registered in travel
writings long after it is generally acknowledged that travel to Italy is not the
exclusive preserve either of members of the aristocracy and gentry or of
men. From time to time, eighteenth-century travel writings register
unease about the inclusion of women as participants in the Grand Tour;
women are most often classified as inadequate travellers in utterances
where the discourse of European travel intersects with discourses in which
the authority of the female traveller to describe and comment is less firmly
established. John Moore, in his *View of Society and Manners in Italy*,
defines as risible anomalies those women travellers who, by virtue of their
eye-witness experience of Italy, are able to transmute themselves into participants in the discourse of art criticism: 'Ladies, who have remained
some time at Rome and Florence, particularly those who affect a taste for
virtù, acquire an intrepidity and a cool minuteness, in examining and criticizing naked figures, which is unknown to those who have never passed
the Alps.'[96]

Travellers who proclaim a female identity, moreover, intermittently
define the experience of travel as one that invites an identification with various specifically masculine approaches to determining the relation between
the self and the world. One of the most obvious examples of the curious
effect of writing as a woman identifiying with masculine authority is found
in Mary Wollstonecraft's remark, in Sweden: 'At supper my host told me
bluntly that I was a woman of observation, for I asked him *men's questions*.'[97]
Anna Jameson, identifying with a male experience of feminine allurements, remarks: 'One leaves Naples as a man parts with an enchanting mistress, and Rome as we would bid adieu to an old and dear-loved friend.'[98]

The identification of travel with masculine experience of the world,
however, does not necessarily guarantee that a claim to experience of

95 Anon., *The South Pacific*, p. 11.

96 Vol. II, pp. 424–5.

97 Wollstonecraft, *Letters*, p. 68.

98 Jameson, *Diary*, p. 308.

travelling is defined as a source of authoritative manliness. On the contrary: in eighteenth-century writings, such an identification can affirm all the more strongly that the pleasures of travelling are guilty pleasures. An earlier instance of the metaphor of the traveller and topography as a man and his mistress is found at the end of Piozzi's *Observations and Reflections*, in an account of the effects of travel on different personalities. For Piozzi, however, the man is not enchanted, but all too cavalier:

> Others there are, who, being accustomed to live a considerable time in places where they have not the smallest intention to fix for ever, but on the contrary firmly resolve to leave *sometime*, learn to treat the world as a man treats his mistress, whom he likes well enough, but has no design to marry, and of course never provides for.[99]

---

[99] Vol. II, p. 387

I

Opposition and intensification

The commentary of opposition

Thomas Broderick, in his *Travels* (1754), declares, in riddling manner: 'At Venice one hardly sees the face of a woman that one may not have if one has a mind to it. You are not to suppose, from this, that all the Venetian women are whores, but whores are the only women at Venice who suffer one to see their faces.' Whereas 'there is no making a mistake about these ladies', mistakes are, it seems, much more easily made in the English capital: 'I remember a young fellow of our acquaintance once picked up the dutchess of *** for a common prostitute, at one of the publick places, but here there is no possibility of such an error.'[1] Having drawn attention to an extreme singularity in Venetian manners, in other words, Broderick then emphasizes cultural difference through a binary opposition between the foreign and the familiar: women in the category represented by 'the dutchess of ***' are classified as beings whose behaviour is the exact opposite of that of respectable Venetian women.

For much of the eighteenth century, this device of constructing binary, symmetrical oppositions between the familiar and the foreign constitutes one of the most common strategies for translating foreignness into discourse – both in accounts of the imaginative geography of the Grand Tour and in writings concerned with other domains of alterity. Proclaiming a power of comparison conferred by the experience of travel, the speaking subject adopts his or her own native region as a constant point of reference. Robert Gray, for example, in his *Letters during the Course of a Tour through Germany, Switzerland and Italy* (1794), declares: 'In England, thanks to the existence of religion and a respect for the true happiness of life, the value of fidelity and virtue are still felt; and they who depart from them are compelled to affect their appearance or to retreat from society: – such, alas! is not the case at Naples...'[2]

---

1 Vol. I, p. 330.
2 p. 399.

In setting up symmetrical oppositions between the foreign and the familiar, travel writings often obliquely invoke the oppositions between North and South established in Montesquieu's *De l'esprit des lois* (1741). One extended comparison between the two regions sets up contrasts between industry and idleness and between liberty and slavery:

> Il y a dans l'Europe une espèce de balancement entre les nations du midi et celles du nord. Les premières ont toutes sortes de commodités pour la vie, et peu de besoins; les secondes ont beaucoup de besoins, et peu de commodités pour la vie. Aux unes, la nature a donné beaucoup, et elles ne lui demandent que peu; aux autres, la nature donne peu, et elles lui demandent beaucoup. L'équilibre se maintient par la paresse qu'elle a donnée aux nations du midi, et par l'industrie et l'activité qu'elle a données à celles du nord. Ces dernières sont obligées de travailler beaucoup, sans quoi elles manqueraient de tout, et deviendraient barbares. C'est ce qui a naturalisé la servitude chez les peuples du midi: comme ils peuvent aisément se passer de richesses, ils peuvent encore mieux se passer de liberté. Mais les peuples du nord ont besoin de la liberté, qui leur procure plus de moyens de satisfaire tous les besoins que la nature leur a donnés. Les peuples du nord sont donc dans un état forcé, s'ils ne sont libres ou barbares: presque tous les peuples du midi sont, en quelque façon, dans un état violent, s'ils ne sont esclaves.[3]

A commentary in Hester Piozzi's *Observations and Reflections Made in the Course of a Journey through France, Italy, and Germany* (1789) both invokes Montesquieu's contrast between southern plenty and northern industry and discreetly adjusts it, so that England is invested not only with the merits of industry but also with the benefits of climate which *De l'esprit des lois* denies to northern Europe:

> God has kindly given to Italians a bright sky, a penetrating intellect, a genius for the polite and liberal arts, and a soil which produces literally, as

---

3 Montesquieu, *De l'esprit des lois*, Vol. II, pp. 28–9 (book 21, chapter 3): 'In Europe there is a kind of balance between the southern and northern nations. The first have every convenience of life, and few of its wants: the last have many wants, and few conveniences. To one, nature has given much, and demands but little; to the others, she has given but little, and demands a great deal. The equilibrium is maintained by the laziness of the southern nations, and by the industry and activity which she has given to those in the north. The latter are obliged to undergo excessive labour, without which they would want every thing, and degenerate into barbarians. This has naturalized slavery to the people of the south: as they can easily dispense with riches, they can more easily dispense with liberty. But the people of the north have need of liberty, which alone can procure them the means of satisfying all those wants which they have received from nature. The people of the north, then, are in a forced state, if they are not either free or barbarians. Almost all the people of the south are in a state of violence, if they are not slaves' (*The Spirit of Laws*, vol. II, pp. 22–3).

well as figuratively, almost spontaneous fruits. He has bestowed on
Englishmen a mild and wholesome climate, a spirit of application and
improvement, a judicious manner of thinking to increase, and commerce
to procure, those few comforts their own island fails to produce. The mind
of an Italian is commonly like his country, extensive, warm, and beautiful
from the irregular diversification of its ideas; an ardent character, a glow-
ing landscape. That of an Englishman is cultivated, rich, and regularly
disposed; a steady character, a delicious landscape.[4]

Travellers construct oppositions between the foreign and the familiar even
when commenting on relatively trivial aspects of the topography of foreignness. Joseph Spence, complaining about the 'noise and hubbub' made
by Italian preachers, in a letter of 1732, observes with mock indulgence
that their exertions in the pulpit allow them more 'wholesome' exercise
than their English counterparts, and adds: 'Beside that, they have very
much the advantage of us on frosty mornings, for, let the weather be as cold
as it will, they are sure to bawl till they are all over in a sweat. You see that
I am not prejudiced in my religion, but would give the papists the preference where they really deserve it.'[5]

As noted in the Introduction, eighteenth-century writings quite often
simply take it for granted that the foreign and the familiar are placed in a
relation of rivalry to each other, and that the task of the traveller is to
choose between them: any opinion about the foreign, it is assumed, must
entail some corresponding, symmetrically contrasted opinion about the
familiar, and vice versa. Thomas Gray neatly satirizes this assumption
when he writes, in a letter of 1739 from Genoa to his friend Richard West,
back in England: 'We are fallen in love with the Mediterranean Sea, and
hold your lakes and rivers in vast contempt.'[6] Thomas Watkins, concluding his account of the 'conjugal infidelity' of the Italians, ostentatiously
displays his fair-mindedness through a reference to his own country:
'Shocking as it is, I must observe that the Italians are less culpable in this
respect than the British women, whose consorts are generally the objects of
their own, not of their parents choice.'[7]

---

4   Piozzi, *Observations*, vol. II, p. 140.
5   Spence, *Letters*, p. 93; letter of 29 February 1732.
6   Gray, *Poems of Thomas Gray*, p. 107; letter dated '*Nov.* 21, 1739'. See also James Barry's
    lengthy protest against the tendency of commentators crudely to dismiss the merits either
    of the South or of the North, in *Inquiry*, pp. 79–81.
7   Watkins, *Travels*, vol. II, pp. 371, 372.

The tameness of the familiar
(and the excitement of the foreign)

Comparative commentary, as the remarks just cited suggest, often registers an implicit awareness that the traveller may have difficulty in maintaining a position of lofty detachment. One threat to properly detached comparison noted in eighteenth-century writings has already been mentioned in the Introduction: the demand for novelty, which, according to Lord Kames, explains 'the preference given to foreign luxuries and to foreign curiosities, which appear rare in proportion to their original distance'.[8] More oblique- ly, travel writings identify another agent of imbalance: the hope and expec- tation that the foreign will supply a drama and excitement in which the familiar is lacking. Such an expectation raises the constant possibility that travellers will indeed be prompted to praise the foreign at the expense of the familiar: while Italy is regularly presented as gratifyingly dramatic, the traveller's own country – or the entire North of Europe – is assigned con- trasting attributes, such as tameness, insipidity, or mediocrity. John Moore, considering 'the fine expressive style of the Italian countenance' in his *View of Society and Manners in Italy* (1781), observes: 'Here you have few or none of those fair, fat, glistening, unmeaning faces, so common in the more northern parts of Europe.' He then launches into an anecdote that mocks the 'completely vacant' expression of a British aristocrat.[9] In Henry Swinburne's *Travels in the Two Sicilies* (1783-5), the traveller expresses his disappointment at finding in Taranto the tame and insipid scenery that he associates with England: 'the banks that inclose the bay are so gently sloped off as to create no very striking effect; there is a tameness in the prospect not unlike the insipidity of the artificial lakes and elegant swells in our fashion- able gardens in England, totally different from the bold beauties of Italian landscape'.[10]

When they express pleasure in the drama of the foreign, most eigh- teenth-century travellers nonetheless employ strategies of caution, limiting

---

8 Kames, *Elements of Criticism*, vol. I, p. 331.

9 Vol. II, pp. 65–6. Moore's contrast between expressive and 'unmeaning' countenances invokes Winckelmann's well-known denigration of the English (see Winkelmann, *Histoire de l'art*, vol. I, p. 64); such contrasts are one of the instances of injustice towards England that James Barry cites in *Inquiry*, p. 80.

10 Vol. I, p. 227. See, too, Lady Morgan's complaint, in a much later work, that her dramatic expectations of Lake Avernus are defeated: 'sites that awed the spirits of Hercules and Ulysses, now looked invitingly gay; and the terrible Avernus of antiquity resembled the carp and tench lake of an English park'; *Italy*, vol. II, p. 337 (footnote).

and qualifying their expressions of delight. In doing so, they register an unease at the possibility that the dramatic qualities of Italy might outweigh the merits and attractions of their own country. One of the comparative commentaries in Piozzi's *Observations and Reflections* begins with an unequivocal expression of delight in the 'striking' character both of Venice and of Italy as a whole. The traveller then, however, hastily reaffirms that her own country possesses pleasures of its own, as though these pleasures must ineluctably be called into question by the initial acclamation of foreign drama:

> I do believe that Venice, like other Italian beauties, will be observed to possess features so striking, so prominent, and so discriminated, that her portrait, like theirs, will not be found difficult to take, nor the impression she has once made easy to erase. British charms captivate less powerfully, less certainly, less suddenly: but being of a softer sort, increase upon acquaintance; and after the connexion has continued for some years, will be relinquished with pain, perhaps even in exchange for warmer colouring and stronger expression.[11]

A similarly hasty reaffirmation of the pleasures of the familiar is found in a passage in the Gothic novel *Montalbert,* by Charlotte Smith (1795), which describes the journey of the heroine, Rosalie, from England to Italy. During Rosalie's travels, the narrator notes, with apparent sympathy and approval, that 'her mind was exalted by scenes so much superior to any she had ever formed an idea of either from the efforts of the pen or the pencil, she seemed transported to a world of higher rank in the universe than that she had inhabited while she was in England.' Then, however, there is a sharp reversal; the sentence continues: 'and she was of an age and disposition to forget, or at least be indifferent to those circumstances which can hardly fail to remind English travellers, that, though other countries may have more bold and attractive scenery, their own is that where life is enjoyed with the greatest comfort'.[12] The narrator, in other words, firmly establishes that she herself speaks as a more adequate traveller-spectator than her inexperienced young heroine, and is able to compare Italy and England without allowing herself to be carried away by the more striking attractions of the former.

The plot of an awareness of foreign attractions followed by a recollection of more basic and essential advantages reproduces, in a more elaborate, sharply polarised form, that of a repeated declaration of loyalty to the familiar by Spence, in a letter of 1732, from Florence. The sense of rivalry

---

11   Vol. I, pp. 150–1.
12   Vol. II, p. 144.

between the two domains is softened in this latter commentary by the effect of ironic bathos, as the traveller adopts a disarmingly down-to-earth and unpretentious stance in making claims for his own country, but Spence nonetheless suggests, just as Smith does, that travellers must make some sort of choice between immediate charms and solid comforts:

> And indeed, though Italy be the country for the sights, England is the country to live in, for my money. I have come here from seeing Julius Caesar and the Capitol, when I have wished in vain, after it, to sit down to a good piece of mutton; and though the statues here in the Great Duke's gallery are something better than what we meet with at Hyde Park Corner, the Florentine beef is not half so good as our English.[13]

Guilt and censure

Commentaries such as these, then, in taking such elaborate care not to disparage the familiar in the course of praising the foreign, establish that pleasure in foreign attractions poses a potential challenge to the familiar, and that such a challenge must be countered. In some commentaries, the traveller explicitly disavows any inclination to value the foreign more highly than his or her own region of origin: William Beckford, in one of the letters in *Dreams, Waking Thoughts and Incidents* (1783), declares: 'I have only to add, that whatever judgment you may form of the strictures this letter contains, you will not infer from them, that I ran abroad, only to admire other countries, at the expence of my own.'[14]

Some eighteenth-century travellers, moreover, launch into sudden attacks on the very activity that they themselves claim to be describing; travelling, such writings suggest, is especially reprehensible because of the disloyalty towards the familiar that it induces, or that prompts it in the first place. Piozzi's account of the traveller's propensity 'to treat the world as a man treats his mistress' has been noted in the Introduction; another of the objections to travel that she marshals at the end of *Observations and Reflections* is that many of those who spend several years away from Britain 'bring back with them an alienated mind'.[15] At the conclusion to Moore's

---

13 Spence, *Letters*, p. 125; 11 October 1732. The allusion to 'Hyde Park Corner' presumably refers to John Cheere's statuary yard there; the sculptures on show in this yard included casts and copies of the famous classical sculptures, such as those in the Grand Duke's collection in the 'Gallery', now known as the *Uffizi,* in Florence.

14 p. 261.

15 Vol. II, pp. 386–7.

View of Society and Manners in Italy, the traveller describes 'the neigh-bouring nations' beholding with astonishment 'such numbers of British subjects, of both sexes, and of all ages, roaming discontented through the lands of despotism, in search of that happiness, which, if satiety and the wanton restlessness of wealth would permit, they have a much better prospect of enjoying in their own country'.[16]

Sterne, in his *Sentimental Journey,* satirically reproduces the paradox by which eighteenth-century travel writing, devoted to the extraction of pleasure from the foreign, is nonetheless constrained to limit this extrac-tion of pleasure, and pay tribute to the delights of the familiar. At Calais, Yorick retires to 'an old Desobligeant', or one-person carriage, to write his preface. In considering the chances of obtaining 'useful knowledge and real improvements' from travel, he pronounces:

> I am of opinion, That a man would act as wisely, if he could prevail upon himself to live contented without foreign knowledge or foreign improve-ments, especially if he lives in a country that has no absolute want of either – and indeed, much grief of heart has it oft and many a time cost me, when I have observed how many a foul step the inquisitive Traveller has meas-ured to see sights and look into discoveries; all which, as Sancho Pança said to Don Quixote, they might have seen dry-shod at home.[17]

The ironic overstatement of the case, emphasized by the redundancy of 'oft and many a time', is taken yet further, as the argument that knowl-edge is available 'at home', as well as in other places, is abruptly trans-muted into a claim that not only knowledge but all sorts of other benefits are most particularly in evidence in the country which the traveller has left behind:

> It is an age so full of light, that there is scarce a country or corner of Europe whose beams are not crossed and interchanged with others – Knowledge in most of its branches, and in most affairs, is like music in an Italian street, whereof those may partake, who pay nothing – But there is no nation under heaven – and God is my record (before whose tribunal I must one day come and give an account of this work) – that I do not speak it vauntingly – But there is no nation under heaven abounding with more variety of learning – where the sciences may be more fitly wooed, or more surely won than here – where art is encouraged, and will soon rise high – where Nature (take her altogether) has so little to answer for – and, to close all, where there is more

---

16   Vol. II, p. 502.
17   In Sterne, *A Sentimental Journey,* pp. 8, 12.

wit and variety of character to feed the mind with – Where then, my dear
countrymen, are you going –[18]

This final question is revealed in the following paragraph as one addressed
to two Englishmen who have approached the carriage to find out why it
had been thrown into motion (an effect produced by Yorick's 'agitation' as
he composes his preface). Placed at the culmination of Yorick's remarks on
travel, however, it reads as though the traveller is upbraiding the whole
British nation for their inclination towards foreign pleasures.

The commentary of opposition, then, is, as Yorick suggests here,
always in the grip of a conflict between the need to extract pleasure from
the foreign and the need to contain or negate that pleasure in some way, so
as to avoid any confirmation of the suspicion – which is constantly aroused
– that the subject may be registering a desire to abandon the familiar for the
delights of drama and alterity. In many commentaries, this conflict is
implicitly mapped out in gendered terms, as a choice between the solid
advantages of manly liberty and the superficial charms of effeminate luxury. Piozzi, describing the delights of the Borromean islands, is suddenly
prompted to reflect 'that liberty, security, and opulence alone give the true
relish to productions either of art or nature', and to assure herself 'that
freedom can make the currants of Holland and golden pippins of Great
Britain sweeter than all the grapes of Italy'. She continues:

... while to every manly understanding some share of the government in a
well-regulated state, with the every-day comforts of common life made
durable and certain by the laws of a prosperous country, are at last far preferable to splendid luxuries precariously enjoyed under the consciousness of
their possible privation when least expected by the hand of despotic power.[19]

The strategies of caution already mentioned are not the only rhetorical
devices through which travellers attempt to deny a culpable attraction
towards the foreign: a ploy more commonly adopted is that of ensuring that
expressions of pleasure are always counterbalanced by expressions of censure. In eighteenth-century travel literature, praise and delight constantly
alternate with criticism and condemnation. Censure often follows pleasure in
a plot of hasty reversal of the same kind that serves to introduce revaluations
of the familiar: Piozzi, just after she has described 'the most excellent, the
most incomparable fish I ever eat', in Naples, observes: 'almond and even

---

[18] *Ibid.*, pp. 11–12.
[19] Piozzi, *Observations*, vol. II, p. 224.

apple trees in blossom, to delight those who can be paid for coarse manners and confined notions by the beauties of a brilliant climate.'[20] Charles Dupaty, looking out from the Certosa di S. Martino, in the same city, remarks:

> C'est dans ce couvent que fut dit un mot bien profond. Un voyageur, à l'aspect de cette vue magnifique, s'écria, devant un chartreux: *le bonheur est ici! oui*, repartit le solitaire, *pour ceux qui passent.*[21]

The commentary of intensification: hyperbolic pleasure

The strategy of investing the foreign with difference by setting it in direct, symmetrical opposition to the familiar is not confined to eighteenth-century writings; as suggested in the Introduction, this strategy has survived the various transformations in travel writing that have taken place in the nineteenth and twentieth centuries, and has become naturalized as part of the array of methods for ordering knowledge of travel and foreignness that any late twentieth-century writer might use. A recent Italian travel book, Sergio Benvenuto's *Capire l'America: Un europeo negli States di oggi* (1995), briskly establishes a series of oppositions between America and Europe. These include – to cite a few at random – oppositions between the respective symbolic resonances of *downtown* and *centro storico*, between American children who show off their computer skills and their Italian counterparts who recite lists of dates and battles, and between the American proclivity for heating houses in winter and cooling them in summer, and the relative continuity between indoor and outdoor temperatures in Europe.[22]

---

20 *Ibid.*, vol. II, p. 58. Within oppositions between foreign extremity and familiar mediocrity, this balancing of pleasure and censure is often achieved through the establishment of an equivalence, in the topography of the warm South, between excess in the good and excess in the bad. Piozzi declares: 'In all hot countries... flowers and weeds shoot up to enormous growths: in colder climes, where poisons can scarce be feared, perfumes can seldom be boasted' (vol. I, p. 128.) In Martin Sherlock's *Nouvelles Lettres d'un voyageur anglois* (1780), the account of Naples – and of Italy in general – offers an extended series of analogies between praiseworthy and regrettable excesses, beginning with the declaration: 'La médiocrité ne se trouve guère ici, tout est extrême' (p. 36): 'Mediocrity is rare here; every thing is in extremes' (*New Letters*, p. 45).

21 Dupaty, *Lettres sur l'Italie*, vol. II, p. 285;
   It was in this convent that an answer was given, containing deep reflection, and profound thought.
     A traveller, struck with the glorious and magnificent prospect of the country, exclaimed before one of the monks – *here happiness must dwell* – yes, replies the pensive recluse, *for the strangers who visit us*.
   (*Sentimental Letters*, vol. II, p. 203).

22 Benvenuto, *Capire l'America*, pp. 18, 24, 20–1.

The enduring usefulness of the device of symmetrical opposition to travellers describing foreign places makes it difficult to imagine any way of mapping out the difference between the foreign and the familiar that would elude such a device. In seventeenth-century commentary, however, the foreign is only very rarely placed in a relation of direct opposition to the familiar; in defining Italy as different from northern Europe, travel writing much more often deploys a strategy of intensification. Travellers, in other words, regularly claim that, while the warm South incorporates many features that are also found in England or France, it displays these features in an intensified form. As in eighteenth-century travel writing, the subject of commentary registers a strong desire to discover a dramatic difference from the familiar within the topography of the foreign: this difference, however, is a difference of degree rather than of kind.

The element of drama, therefore, is never, in this earlier form of commentary, placed in direct opposition to any contrasting quality within the familiar; instead, it is greeted as an effect produced by an unusual intensity, concentration, or extremity within objects and attributes which are in themselves perfectly familiar – such as the 'huge Citrons' observed by John Evelyn in Genoa in 1644, which strain credulity not because of their exoticism but simply because of their size: they are described as fruits 'that one would have believed incredible should have been supported by so weake branches'.[23] The drama that the foreign supplies is very precisely identified with intensification rather than with unfamiliarity in the description of the Campania Felix in Fynes Moryson's *Itinerary* (1611): 'Here the beautie of all the World is gathered as it were into a bundle.'[24]

The absence of any structure of opposition, in seventeenth-century travel writing, allows the subject of commentary to express delight in the foreign without at the same time implying any denigration of the familiar. Expressions of pleasure, therefore, require no disavowal, of the kind constantly voiced in eighteenth-century travel writing through expressions of censure, but are allowed to proliferate without qualification or restraint. The primary strategy employed to invest the topography of the Grand Tour with intensity is the adoption of a rhetoric of hyperbolic delight.

Travel writings register delight and approbation of a wide range of different domains of objects – including, for example, works of art, architectural monuments and natural wonders. The sites of intensity that are most

---

[23] Evelyn, *Diary*, vol. II, p. 176; diary entry for 17 October 1644.
[24] Part III, p. 106.

frequently designated as objects of overwhelming pleasure, however, are fertile tracts of countryside: travel writings are full of enraptured descriptions of the fruitfulness of the Italian terrain. This fruitfulness is further affirmed, in a more oblique manner, through unrestrained approbation of Italian food and wine; gastronomic products are constantly adopted as metonyms for the land from which they are produced.

The selection of natural fertility as the primary source of pleasure makes it possible, in fact, for the wines and foodstuffs of Italy to be defined as objects at least as worthy of attention as art and architecture. The brief assessment of Vicenza in Jean Huguetan's *Voyage d'Italie Curieux et Nouveau* (1681), for example, includes wine among the main features to be noted in that town: 'Les Palais y sont beaux; le vin y est excellent, et la campagne tres fertile.'[25]

The status of wine as a worthy object of commentary is sometimes affirmed directly – though always with a self-protective gesture of irony. John Raymond's *Itinerary Contayning a Voyage Made through Italy* (1648) describes Albano as a town which 'deserves seeing, if not for the Antiquity, yet for the good Wine; one of the best sorts in *Italy'*. The same travel book comments on the villa of Caprarola: 'In the Garden the Cataracts of water, are very admirable; But that for which this place is most spoken of, is the Sellar.'[26] In Richard Lassels's *Voyage of Italy* (1670), the traveller also pauses to consider the two rival attractions of Caprarola, and concludes by making a similar choice: 'Having walked this garden about, youl deserve after so much water, a little wine, which will not be wanting to you from the rare *cellar* lyeing under the great *Terrasse* before the house: and perchance youl think the *wineworks* here as fine as the *waterworks*.'[27]

In including food and drink among the objects of commentary particularly worthy of note, the subject is able to proclaim an especially formidable power of extracting pleasure from the terrain: the power to enjoy Italy through more than one of the senses. Descriptions of a multiplication of sensory delights are regularly deployed, in seventeenth-century travel writing, in order to render the rhetoric of pleasure yet more hyperbolic. A claim to multi-sensory appropriation of the topography is elaborated at some length, for example, at the beginning of Jean Gailhard's *Present State of the Princes and Republicks of Italy* (1650):

---

[25] pp. 245–6: 'The *palazzi* there are beautiful; the wine is excellent, and the country very fertile.'

[26] pp. 267, 65.

[27] Part I, p. 249.

That must needs be a Rare Country which is pleasant and plentifull, watered with many Rivers; at the season adorned with Corn in the fields, and Grass in the Meadows, with delightful Land-skips, that in most parts hath a wholesome Air, that abounds in strong and stately Cities, where the eye is delighted with most sumptuous buildings, recreated with variety of Pictures and Statues, the ear pleased with as great a variety of harmonious Musick as can be upon earth; where the Palate is satisfied with the best fruits, and other delicacies, and the rarest wines in *Europe;* where in a certain Season, the nose enjoys the smell of *Orange* and *Jasmin* flowers, which lay over head or under feet; and at the same time, and in the same place to behold fine perspectives, and hear the murmur of several fountain waters: In a word, that Country which produces plenty and variety to please all the Senses, and which hath the Alpes of one side for walls, and the Sea on the other for bounds, must needs be an excellent Country; such is *Italy*.[28]

John Clenche's *Tour in France and Italy* (1676) supports the description of Italy as 'most of it fertile, beyond expression', by a declaration that 'its Wines are incomparable, and of infinite variety and delicacy, pleasing at once both scent and tast'.[29] The account of Posillipo in George Sandys's *Relation of a Journey begun An: Dom: 1610* (1615) elaborates the theme of profusion through a multiplication of sensory pleasures, in noting 'those orchards both great and many, replenished with all sorts of almost to be named fruite trees: especially with oranges and lymons, which at once do delight three senses'.[30] Fruit and fruit trees are regularly presented as a source of delights supplementary to those of the palate: Richard Fleckno describes the gardens of Genoa as 'planted with all sorts of delicious fruit, Oranges and Limmons amongst the rest, in so great abundance, as their flowers perfume the sea all the way you passe along', while Raymond declares: 'The Hesperian Apple, or Orange Tree is of a most ravishing beauty perpetually Verdant, bearing an Hortyard of Blossoms, greene and ripe Fruite altogether.'[31]

Comparison and incomparability

Within the commentary of intensification – in sharp contrast to that of opposition – there is no need for the traveller to refer to the familiar at all;

---

28 pp. 1–2.

29 p. 122.

30 p. 262.

31 Fleckno, *A Relation*, p. 22 (see also Evelyn, *Diary*, vol. II, p. 171; 15 October 1644); Raymond, *An Itinerary*, unpaginated introduction.

where the traveller's own region of origin is mentioned, it is usually introduced merely as a point of reference that allows the traveller to indicate the
scale of foreign intensity – as in Clenche's comment on food in Italy: 'The
Provisions of all sorts excellent, exceeding *England* in some things, and
France in all', and in Gilbert Burnet's assessment of Naples: 'if it is not
above half as big as Paris or London, yet it hath much more beauty then
either of them' (Figure 1).[32]

In one of the rare instances of a commentary that sets the foreign and
the familiar in a relation of rivalry to each other – the description of
Mantua in *Coryats Crudities* (1611), by Thomas Coryate – it is made clear
that the two domains are not in fact being subjected to a symmetrically
structured comparison, taking account of their relative delights and benefits, but are being assessed according to quite different criteria; the familiar
has claims on the traveller that have nothing to do with any ability to match
the overwhelming pleasures of the foreign:

> Truely the view of this most sweet Paradise, this *domicilium Venerum et
> Charitum* did even so ravish my senses, and tickle my spirits with such
> inward delight that I said unto my selfe, this is the Citie which of all other
> places in the world, I would wish to make my habitation in, and spend the
> remainder of my dayes in some divine Meditations amongst the sacred
> Muses, were it not for their grosse idolatry and superstitious ceremonies
> which I detest, and the love of Odcombe in Somersetshire, which is so
> deare unto me that I preferre the very smoke thereof before the fire of all
> other places under the Sunne.[33]

Another of the rare seventeenth-century accounts of the foreign and the
familiar as rival sources of attraction does in fact make an attempt to apply
similiar criteria to each domain (as Coryate does, briefly, in considering the
disadvantages of Italian 'idolatry'), but is deflected from constructing a
symmetrical opposition between the two by the demands of the commentary of intensification. As the traveller in Sandys's *Relation of a Journey*
turns back towards his native land after a voyage to Egypt and the Levant,
he declares his affection for England. When he begins to compare that
country with others, however, he can only define it as representing a degree
zero against which to measure the intensificatory 'additions' offered by the
foreign: after the hyperbolic opening to this declaration, the application of
hyperbole to the familiar is revealed as unsustainable, as the 'beloved soile'

32 Clenche, *A Tour*, p. 122; Burnet, *Some Letters*, p. 200.
33 p. 120.

is revealed to be a cautiously 'provident' parent, who supplies his devoted son merely with 'whatsoever is usefull':

> Now shape we our course for England. Beloved soile: as in site
> — *Wholly from all the world disjoynd:*
> so in thy felicities. The Sommer burnes thee not, nor the Winter benums thee: defended by the Sea from wastfull incursions, and by the valour of thy sonnes from hostile invasions. All other Countries are in some things defective, when thou a provident parent, doest minister unto thine whatsoever is usefull: forrein additions but onely tending to vanity, and luxury.[34]

The strategy of symmetrical opposition is entirely precluded, moreover, by one of the main themes through which the superior intensity of the foreign is affirmed: the theme of incomparability, which explicitly defines the object of commentary as destabilizing any attempt to find some rival or equivalent object with which to compare it. A general survey of Italy in Moryson's *Itinerary,* for example, culminates in an assurance that points of comparison for the country cannot be found, at least within the same continent:

> *Italy* worthily called the Queene of Nations, can never be sufficiently praised, being most happy in the sweete Ayre, the most fruitfull and pleasant fields, warme sunny hils, hurtlesse thickets shadowing groves, Havens of the Sea, watering brookes, baths, wine, and oyle for delight, and most safe forts or defences as well of the Sea as of the Alpes. Neither is any part of Europe more inhabited, more adorned with Cities and Castles, or to be compared thereunto for tillage and husbandry.[35]

A declaration of incomparability does, of course, presuppose an initial attempt at comparison. There is no need at all, however, for the objects of comparison to be taken from the traveller's own region of origin: a stronger affirmation of intensity is produced by designating as the area of scrutiny Italy itself – the land within which rival points of incomparability may be expected: Evelyn comments on the Mole of Genoa: 'doubtlesse of all the

---

[34] p. 218; a marginal note gives the original Latin version of the quotation, with a reference to '*Virg. Ecl.* I': '– penitus toto divisos orbe Britannos'.

[35] Part III, p. 105. Like the themes of profusion and excess, and many other characteristic features of the rhetoric of intensification – the allegory of Paradise, for example – this theme of incomparability is not limited to writings on Italy and southern Europe, but is employed in descriptions of a wide range of different regions, both during the seventeenth century and for some centuries before it. Mary B. Campbell, in *The Witness and the Other World*, identifies in Columbus's journals, and in other Renaissance writings concerned with the New World, a number of the same intensificatory effects of language that later appear in writings on Italy.

wonders of Italy, for the art, & nature of the designe nothing dos parallel this'.[36] Jean-Jacques Bouchard, describing the fountains of Naples, observes: 'pour ce qui est de la beauté et bonté naturelle elles surpassent de beaucoup Rome, et peut estre toutes celles de l'Europe'.[37]

Yet more hyperbolically, other commentaries locate their points of comparison within some conspicuously vast sweep of terrain, such as the whole world, or the whole range of geographical locations within the traveller's experience or imagination. (The last of these categories is often indicated obliquely, through a generalized designation of a particular feature as incomparable.) Evelyn comments on the 'Streetes & buildings' of Genoa: 'by reason of their incomparable materials, beauty & structure: never was any artificial sceane more beautifull to the eye of the beholder; nor is any place certainly in the World, so full for the bignesse of well designed & stately Palaces.'[38] *Coryats Crudities* asserts that Venice 'is indeed of that admirable and incomparable beauty, that I thinke no place whatsoever, eyther in Christendome or Paganisme may compare with it'.[39] Sandys presents the southern harbour of Syracuse as 'the most goodly and most famous that ever Nature or Art had a hand in', while Bouchard comments on Posillipo: 'je ne croi pas qu'il y ait aujourd'hui lieu plus delicieus et où se facent plus de galenteries que cette coste de Pausilype'.[40]

One point of incomparability is not defined as incompatible with another, even when the two might appear to rival each other in the same form of excellence; objects that surpass all others of their kind are unworriedly described in swift succession, as in Evelyn's account of rooms in the Villa Medici 'full of incomparable Statues & Antiquities': 'above all, & happly preferable to any in the World are the two Wrestlers, for the inextricable mixture with each others armes & leggs plainely stupendious; In the great Chamber is the naked *Gladiator* whetting a knife; but the *Venus* is without parallel... certainly nothing in Sculpture ever aproched this miracle of art.'[41]

[36] Evelyn, *Diary*, vol. II, p. 177 (18 October 1644).

[37] Bouchard, *Journal*, vol. II, p. 243: 'in their beauty and their natural wholesomeness they far surpass those of Rome, and perhaps those of all Europe'.

[38] Evelyn, *Diary*, vol. II, pp. 172–3 (17 October 1644); see also, for example, vol. II, p. 338 (8 February 1645).

[39] pp. 171–2.

[40] Sandys, *A Relation*, p. 241; Bouchard, *Journal*, vol. II, p. 425: 'I don't believe that there is at present any place more full of delight and amorous dalliance than this coast of Posillipo.'

[41] Evelyn, *Diary*, vol. II, p. 286 (29 November 1645).

The crucial precondition for this designation of first one object and then another as incomparable is a strategy that might be termed *itemizing*: concentrating on one object at a time, and considering each in its own uniqueness.[42] This strategy also supplies a precondition for the formation of three concepts that play a large part in seventeenth-century commentary on the topography of the Grand Tour: the rarity, the curiosity and the wonder. These three concepts often merge, since all are defined with reference to the same attribute: that of an extreme singularity, which invests an object with incomparability by removing it, partially or entirely, from any category of objects with which it might be compared. François Misson, in his *Nouveau Voyage d'Italie* (1691), obliquely notes this difficulty of comparison when he describes the Roman Amphitheatre at Verona as 'une chose qui surprend d'autant plus, que les yeux ne sont past accoutumez à en voir de semblables'.[43]

Stephen Greenblatt, in his essay 'Resonance and Wonder', emphasizes the status of the wonder as a localized exception when he notes its power 'to stop the viewer in his tracks, to convey an arresting sense of uniqueness, to evoke an exalted attention'.[44] This 'arresting sense of uniqueness' is, for example, identified by Evelyn in 'the Campanile or Settezonio' of Pisa; having described this structure as 'built exceedingly declining by a rare adresse of the imortal Architect', the traveller adds: 'and realy I take it to be one of the most singular pieces of workmanship in the World.'[45] Coryate emphasizes the power of singularity to supply foreign visitors with drama: 'Such is the rarenesse of the situation of Venice, that it doth even amaze and drive into admiration all strangers that upon their first arrival behold the same.'[46] Raymond explicitly defines the uniqueness of the wonder as an occasion for hyperbole: 'truly if a traveller Hyperbolise in any part of his voyage of *Italy,* the most fit Theame he can take, are the Wonders a little distant from *Naples*; and first the *Tractus Puteolanus scatens hominum ac naturæ miraculis.*'[47]

42 The term *itemizing*, used in this sense, is put forward to describe the way in which a curiosity is defined as such by the traveller John Bargrave, in Bann, *Under the Sign*, p. 102.

43 Vol. I, p. 112: 'a thing so much the more surprising, because we do not frequently meet with such Monuments of antiquity' (*A New Voyage*, vol. I, p. 116).

44 In *Learning to Curse*, p. 170.

45 Evelyn, *Diary*, vol. II, p. 180; 20 October 1644.

46 Coryate, *Coryats Crudities*, p. 160.

47 Raymond, *An Itinerary*, p. 142.

Profusion and excess

The second theme that serves to establish the superior intensity of the foreign is that of profusion – as deployed in Moryson's description of Capua as 'a place abounding with all dainties', or his remarks on Spoleto: 'the soile of this Dukedome is most fruitfull, of corne, wine, almond, and olive trees, and of most sweet fruits'.[48] This theme is often combined with the theme of incomparability, in order to increase the effect of intensification. Bouchard's journal describes at Posillipo a profusion of the incomparable: 'dans ce petit espace là se peut dire qu'est compris et renfermé tout ce que l'Europe a de plus miraculeus et de plus magnifique, tant pour les choses naturelles que pour les artificieles.'[49] A passage in Evelyn's diary presents the incomparable 'amœnitie' of Baiæ as the product of an incomparable abundance of individual points of incomparability:

> And thus we leave the Baiæ so renowned for the sweete retirements of the most opulent, & Voluptuous Romans, and certainly they were places of incomparable amœnitie, as their yet lasting & tempting site, and other circumstances of natural curiosities easily invite me to believe; since there is not certainly in the whole World so many stupendious rarities to be met with, as there are in the circle of a few miles which inviron these blissful aboades.[50]

The theme of profusion, like that of incomparability, plays a major part in ordering commentary on art and antiquities, as well as commentary on the terrain. In assessing particular cities, palaces and villas, travellers regularly specify how abundantly these cities or buildings are supplied with paintings and scultures. Misson notes: 'On assure qu'il n'y a pas moins de belles peintures à Venise qu'à Rome, et nous en avons deja veû quantité.'[51] The Marquis de Seignelay's account of his travels in 1671 begins the commentary on the Villa Borghese, in Rome, with the assertion: 'Ce qu'il y a de plus remarquable dans cette vigne est *la quantité* des statues anciennes et celles du Bernin.'[52] The description of Rome in Jacob Spon's *Voyage d'Italie, de*

---

48 Moryson, *An Itinerary*, part I, pp. 108, 101.

49 Vol. II, p. 311: 'in that little space it can be said that all that Europe has that is most miraculous and magnificent, both natural and artificial, is brought together and enclosed.'

50 Vol. II, pp. 352–3 (8 February 1645).

51 Misson, *Nouveau Voyage*, vol. I, p. 164: 'They give out, that there are as many fine Paintings at *Venice*, as at *Rome*, and we have already seen good store of them' (*A New Voyage*, vol. I, p. 171).

52 Seignelay, *L'Italie en 1671*, p. 157: 'What is most remarkable in this *vigne* is the *quantity* of ancient statues and of sculptures by Bernini' (emphasis added).

Dalmatie, de Grèce, et du Levant (1678) enumerates in detail the profusion of incomparable material suitable for satisfying a series of artistic and anti-quarian interests. The traveller initially praises the sculptures in that city for their incomparability ('La Sculpture vous plaît-elle?... Pour celle des anciens Grecs et Romains, elle passe jusqu'au prodige'); he then, however, describes them as even more remarkable for their extreme abundance:

> J'ajoute seulement que rien ne m'a tant surpris que de voir que Rome, apres avoir été si souvent saccagée, puisse avoir conservé tant de belles choses. Le Palais Palestrine a plus de 60 Statuës, qui pour la plus grande partie ont été trouvées dans le terrain de la maison. Celuy de Justiniani en a environ 150, dans une seule Sale, de sorte qu'on pourroit encore dire de Rome ce qu'on disoit autrefois d'Athenes, que le peuple n'y étoit pas en si grand nombre que les statuës.[53]

In accounts of the natural fertility of Italy, the theme of profusion is regu-larly transmuted into a yet more intensificatory theme: that of excess. Bouchard's description of Fondi mentions a natural fruitfulness that goes beyond expected boundaries, and that produces a dramatic excess of sup-ply over demand: 'il y a aussi quantité de beaus jardins tous plantez d'or-angers et citroniers qui rompent, tant ils sont chargez de fruit, qui se perd à faute de gens qui le recueillent.'[54]

Other travel writings affirm that Italian profusion far exceeds demand by observing that in Italy it is possible to obtain food and wine without pay-ing for it. Evelyn notes: 'At Fundi... we had Oranges & Citrons for noth-ing, the trees growing in every corner infinitely charged with fruite, in all the poore people's Orchyards.'[55] Coryate relates that on the road between Brescia and Bergamo, 'I did oftentimes borrow a point of the law in going into their vineyardes without leave, to refresh my selfe with some of their grapes. Which the Italians like very good fellowes did winke at, shewing

---

53 Spon, *Voyage d'Italie*, vol. I, pp. 41–2: 'Do you care for sculpture?... As far as the sculp-ture of the ancient Greeks and Romans goes, its beauty is prodigious'; 'I only wish to add that nothing surprised me so much as seeing that Rome, after being sacked so often, can have kept such beautiful things. The Palazzo Palestrina has more than sixty statues, which for the most part have been found on the land belonging to the house. The Palazzo Giustiniani has about a hundred and fifty, in one room, so that it is still possible to say of Rome what was said of Athens in the past, that the people were not so numerous as the statues.'

54 Bouchard, *Journal*, vol. II, p. 171: 'there are, too, numerous gardens all planted with orange and lemon trees, so heavily laden with fruit – which is left to go to waste, for want of anyone to collect it – that they break under the strain.'

55 Evelyn, *Diary*, vol. II, p. 322 (29 January 1645).

themselves more kind unto me then the Germans did afterward in Germany'.[56] The ease with which both food and wine are obtained for nothing is emphasized particularly strongly, as a feature of his native country affectionately remembered by an Italian in exile, in Giacomo Castelvetro's *Brieve racconto di tutte le radici di tutte l'erbe di tutti i frutti che crudi o cotti in Italia si mangiano* (1614).[57]

In seeking out points of the greatest possible intensity, the subject of commentary, in seventeenth-century travel writing, not only scrutinizes the topography of the Grand Tour for instances of immoderate profusion of the kind just cited, but also registers a strong impulse to extend the scope assigned to the theme of excess, by moving from profusion and unrestraint in natural productiveness to unrestraint in consumption of the fruits of that productiveness. Travel writings regularly comment on the opportunities for excessive consumption that Italy offers. Bouchard's journal states that 'les Capuans sont encore aujourdhui fort delicieus en toutes choses, et surtout en manger', and notes that the traveller himself, in Capua, was treated 'fort friamment et splendidement, avec quantité de pasticeries, confitures et pastes, et autres galanteries de sucre'.[58] Evelyn's diary describes the traveller arriving 'at the 3 Kings, a Place of treatement of excesse, as we found by our very plentifull fare all the tyme we were in Naples, where provisions are miraculously cheape, & we seldome sat downe to fewer than 18 or 20 dishes of the most exquisite meate & fruites'.[59]

Accounts of excess in consumption of food and wine, however, seldom attribute extreme bibulousness or gourmandise to the Italians themselves; where they do so, such unrestraint is always limited to the inhabitants of a particular area, as in Bouchard's commentary on Capua, just quoted, or to the period of carnival, described by Moryson as one of 'unspeakable luxury in meate, wantonnesse, and all pleasures'.[60] In attempting to maintain and extend the theme of excess, seventeenth-century travel writings energetically wrestle with the problem that the Italians are very firmly classified as 'sparing' in eating and drinking. Castelvetro, in a paragraph of his treatise entitled 'perché gl'Italiani mangino più erbaggi e frutti che carne', begins by presenting the consumption of vegetables as a reaction to a failure in

---

[56] Coryate, *Coryats Crudities*, p. 341.

[57] pp. 39, 48.

[58] Vol. II, p. 449: 'the Capuans today are very fond of pleasure in everything, especially in eating'; 'very indulgently and splendidly, with lots of little cakes, sweetmeats and pastries, and other sugary confections'.

[59] Vol. II, p. 325 (31 January 1645).

[60] Moryson, *An Itinerary*, part III, p. 50.

natural profusion – a relative scarcity of meat – but then argues that vegetables are in fact eaten out of preference, as a response to extremes of heat.[61] Moryson, noting a similar moderation in the consumption of meat by the Italians, attempts not only to restore the theme of profusion but also to insist that the traveller has observed positive gluttony: 'howsoever they are not so great flesh-eaters as the Northerne men, yet if the bread bee weighed, which one of them eates at a meale, with a great Charger full of hearbes, and a little oyle mixed therein, beleeve mee they have no cause to accuse Northerne men for great eaters.'[62]

The strategy most commonly employed to ensure that Italy is invested with a high degree of intensificatory excessiveness in eating and drinking, however, is the simple device of transferring attention away from the behaviour of the Italians towards that of foreigners travelling in Italy. One of the past travellers whose adventures provide a proleptic narrative of temptation to excess, anticipating future departures from moderation, is the character described in de Rogissart's *Les Délices de l'Italie* (1706) as 'Gentilhomme *Allemand,* grand amateur du Jus *Bachique'*, who, in Montefiascone, 'mourut pour en avoir trop bû'.[63] (It is from this story, travel writings maintain, that the wine of this town acquired its name, *Est Est Est:* the German sent his servant on ahead to write *Est* on the doors of inns supplying good wines – or, according to another version, on vessels containing these wines – and on reaching one particular inn, or bottle, the servant was so enraptured that he repeated this affirmation two or three times.)[64]

With reference to a further proleptic figure, 'the Emperour *Fredericke* the Third', *Coryats Crudities* emphasizes the gastronomic incomparability and profusion of Venice by noting an instance of temptation to excess in eating. Having described, at some length, 'the marveilous affluence and exuberancy of all things tending to the sustentation of mans life' in that city, Coryate focuses, in particular, on a 'speciall commodity... which is one of the most delectable dishes of a Sommer fruite of all Christendome, namely muske Melons'. A hyperbolic account of the abundance of these melons is followed by a direct warning about the dangers posed by their excellence:

---

61 Castelvetro, *Bnieve raccouto*, p. 37: 'why it is that the Italians should eat more fruit and vegetables than meat'.

62 Moryson, *An Itinerary*, part III, p. 113.

63 Vol. I, pp. 198–9: 'a German gentleman, a great lover of the Bacchic juice'; 'died from drinking too much of it'.

64 See, for versions of this part of the story, Evelyn, *Diary*, vol. II, p. 210 (4 November 1644), Huguetan, *Voyage*, p. 45, and Bromley, *Remarks*, p. 320.

But I advise thee (gentle Reader) if thou meanest to see Venice, and shalt happen to be there in the sommer time when they are ripe, to abstaine from the immoderate eating of them. For the sweetnesse of them is such as hath allured many men to eat so immoderately of them, that they have therewith hastened their untimely death: the fruite being indeed γλυκύ πικρου, that is, sweete-sowre. Sweete in the palate, but sowre in the stomacke, if it be not soberly eaten. For it doth often breede the *Dysenteria,* that is, the bloudy fluxe: of which disease the Emperour *Fredericke* the Third died by the intemperate eating of them...[65]

In accounts of the indulgence of other passions, the Italians are not classified as so 'sparing'. Even in accounts of sexual excesses, however, which are presented as among the most striking features of manners in Italy, travel writings often focus primarily on the danger that such excesses pose to travellers, rather than on the behaviour of the Italians themselves. Evelyn's diary mentions, in Naples, the 'Courtisans' who 'by a thousand studied devices seeke to inveagle foolish young persons', and remarks that 'some of our Company did purchase their repentance at a deare rate, after their returne'.[66] Lassels's *Voyage of Italy* comments sternly on young travellers who 'desire to go into *Italy,* onely because they heare there are fine *Curtisanes* in *Venice*' and will 'travel a whole month together, to *Venice,* for a nights lodgeing with an impudent woman': 'And thus by a false ayming at breeding abroad, they returne with those diseases which hinder them from breeding at home.'[67] James Howell's *Instructions and Directions for Forren Travell* sets an account of the character of the Italians within a passage of advice to the young traveller:

> And being now in *Italy, that great limbique of working braines,* he must be very circumspect in his cariage, for she is able to turne a *Saint* into a *Devill* and deprave the best natures, if one will abandon himselfe to pleasure, and become a prey to dissolut courses and wantonnes, the *Italian,* being the *greatest embracer of pleasures,* and the *greatest Courtier of Ladies* of any other. Here he shall find vertue and vice, Love and hatred, Atheisme and Religion in their extremes; being a witty contemplative people; and *Corruptio optimi est pessima. Of the best wines you make the tartest vinegar.*[68]

The subject of commentary quite often emphasizes – as Howell does here – that the temptations of the Grand Tour constitute a source of delight as

---

65   Coryate, *Coryats Crudities,* pp. 257–8.

66   Vol. II, p. 332; 6 February 1645.

67   Unpaginated preface.

68   p. 55.

well as of danger; excess in social conduct is regularly invested with implicit attraction by elisions with gratifying excess in the domain of nature. In both Moryson's *Itinerary* and Lassels's *Voyage of Italy*, the proleptic narrative of the maleficent effects of Capuan luxury and debauchery on Hannibal's army, anticipating the perilous allurements to be encountered by the contemporary traveller in Italy, is offered as confirmation of the extremity of pleasure offered by the Campania Felix:

> The Capuan delights, corrupting the Army of *Hanniball*, are knowne to all the World. This Province is an earthly Paradise, where *Bacchus* and *Ceres* strive for principalitie.[69]

> It was this country which with its delights, broke *Hannibals* army; which neither *snow could coole, nor Alpes stop, nor Romans Vanquish*, sayth Seneca.[70]

Howell implicitly endorses Italian immoderation by invoking a figure of Nature who actively encourages such unrestraint: 'They are generally indulgent of themselves, and great embracers of pleasure, which may proceed from the luscious rich Wines, and luxurious Food, Fruits, and Roots, wherwith the Countrey abounds, Insomuch, that in som places, Nature may be said to be *Lena sui, A Baud to her self*.'[71]

Both the deflection to the behaviour of travellers and the naturalization of Italian excess help to ensure that censure only very occasionally predominates over pleasure – at least until the final decades of the century. Instances of depravity among the Italians are not often seen as demanding any particular effort of explanation or assessment, of a kind that might produce the elaborate accounts of foreign failings and iniquities found in eighteenth-century commentaries; rather, travellers assume that the vices of Italy are so well known that they can simply be taken for granted – as they are, for example, when Evelyn, listing exhibits in the Uffizi, casually mentions 'an Italian lock for their wanton Wives or jealous Husbands'.[72]

The tropes of intensification

Accounts of incomparability, profusion and excess are supported by a series of highly intensificatory rhetorical tropes. All these tropes constitute versions of the figure of hyperbole, or are merged with this figure.

---

69 Moryson, *An Itinerary*, part III, p. 106.

70 Lassels, *Voyage*, part II, p. 268.

71 Howell, *Epistolæ Ho-Elianæ*, part I, p. 85.

72 Evelyn, *Diary*, vol. II, p. 192 (24 October 1644).

As noted in the Introduction, hyperbole constantly thematizes its own etymological origins in 'excess', or 'throwing beyond', by constructing visions of excess within the topography. One of the tropes most commonly employed is a hyperbole of enumeration, in which the traveller testifies to Italian abundance by providing an extensive list of natural products, natural or artificial 'wonders', works of art, or other noteworthy objects – not necessarily all from a single category. Sandys's *Relation of a Journey*, for example, provides a hyperbolically enumerative survey of Sicily: 'Vines, sugar-canes, hony, saffron, and fruites of all kindes it produceth: mulberry trees to nourish their silke-wormes, whereof they make a great income: quarries of porphyre, and serpentine. Hot bathes, rivers, and lakes replenished with fish...'[73] Edmund Warcupp's account of 'the Territory of Verona', in *Italy, in its Original Glory, Ruine and Revival* (1660), incorporates a description of the incomparability of the local apples within a hyperbolic enumeration:

> Towards *South* and by *East,* thirty Mils to the *Ferrarian* or *Mantovan* confines, of most fertile Countreys, being no less pleasant than fruitfull of whatever can be desired. It hath Mountains, Hills, Woods, diverse navigable Rivers, clear fountains, oyl, good Corn, good Wine, Hemp, and great plenty of Fruit, and Trees bearing Apples, more sweet, fresh, and of longer keeping than any other Country: It hath Fowl, and Flesh of all sorts, divers sorts of Stone, and Chalk, Villages with fair Fabricks, and foundations of antient Towers.[74]

Coryate's description of the Veneto deploys enumeration as the preface to an expression of unrestrained delight: 'It is wholly plaine, and beautified with such abundance of goodly rivers, pleasant meadowes, fruitfull vineyards, fat pastures, delectable gardens, orchards, woodes, and what not, that the first view thereof did even refocillate my spirits, and tickle my senses with inward joy.'[75]

A second form of hyperbole regularly adopted in seventeenth-century travel writings is a hyperbole of accumulation. Burnet, for example, progresses through several examples of mere gastronomic excellence, at Chavennes, in northern Italy, before introducing a climactic instance of incomparability: 'Both here and in the Grisons the meat is very juicy, the Fowl is excellent, their Roots and Herbs very tastful, but the Fish of their

---

[73] p. 235.

[74] pp. 53–4.

[75] Coryate, *Coryats Crudities*, p. 93.

Lakes is beyond any thing I ever saw.'[76] The same trope is employed in Misson's description of the delicacies of Pesaro: 'Les Olives en sont admirables, mais les figues surpassent tous les autres fruits, en bonté et en réputation.'[77] Howell's account of Naples includes the remark: 'The Clime is hot, and the constitutions of the Inhabitants more hot.'[78]

The intensity of Italy is affirmed, too, through a hyperbole of substitution: a relatively modest object within the foreign is said to resemble some more intensified object within the familiar. (This hyperbole, therefore, follows the strategy, already noted, of introducing the familiar simply as a point of reference to enable the traveller to affirm the scale of foreign intensity all the more emphatically.) The source of intensity, within this substitution, is often size. Burnet comments on Chavennes: 'I never saw bigger Grapes then grow there, there is one sort bigger then the biggest Damascene Plums that we have in England.'[79] Moryson's *Itinerary* remarks on Italy in general: 'All the fields are full of fig trees, not small as with us, but as big in the body as some Appel-trees, and they have broad leaves.'[80] William Bromley's *Remarks in the Grande Tour of France and Italy* (1692) notes, in Naples, that 'whereas I rarely saw in the Pope's Dominions Orange-Trees, unless in Pots, and preserved with Care and Art; here they appeared as Apple-Trees in our *English* Orchards, so frequent and so large'.[81]

A very common hyperbole of substitution is the observation that winter in the South resembles the more intensified season of summer, as it is experienced in northern Europe. At Fondi, Moryson declares: 'The Orange trees at one time have ripe and greene fruites and buds, and are greene in winter, giving at that dead time a pleasant remembrance of Summer.'[82] Evelyn comments on Naples: 'The very winter here is a summer, ever fruitefull, & continualy pregnant, so as in midst of February we had Melons, Cheries, Abricots and many other sorts of fruite.'[83]

---

[76] Burnet, *Some Letters*, p. 94.

[77] Misson, *Nouveau Voyage*, vol. I, p. 216: 'The Olives are admirable; but the Figs in goodness and esteem surpass all other Fruits' (*A New Voyage*, vol. I, p. 223). See also, for example, Warcupp, *Italy*, p. 4, describing the cherries of Marostica, and Huguetan, *Voyage*, pp. 164–5, describing two different sorts of mustard.

[78] Howell, *Epistolæ Ho-Elianæ*, part I, p. 75.

[79] Burnet, *Some Letters*, p. 93.

[80] Part III, p. 110.

[81] pp. 282–3. Bouchard's commentary on Sorrento devises a variation on this substitution of large for small, in which figs and grapes resemble pears and plums not in size but in firmness (*Journal*, vol. II, pp. 427–8).

[82] Moryson, *An Itinerary*, part I, p. 105.

[83] Evelyn, *Diary*, vol. II, p. 353 (8 February 1645).

The rhetoric of self-conscious extravagance

So far, in all the seventeenth-century commentaries cited, the subject uttering the account of the foreign has claimed to be transcribing either visual
observations of the topography or some other kind of first-hand experience
of it – such as an experience of smelling or tasting. In travel writing of this
period, however, the commentary is also regularly presented as the product
not of any kind of empirical engagement with the objects described but,
rather, of rhetorical artifice and ingenuity: the speaking subject is positioned, in many cases, as a self-conscious stylist, devising forms of language
which, through their hyperbolic extravagance, will provide a verbal equivalent to the extravagance and intensity of the topography. A passage from
Coryats Crudities, for example, incorporates a hyperbole of substitution in
which all pretence at direct observation of the topography is abandoned,
and the traveller devotes himself entirely to the exercise of rhetorical ingenuity, openly treating the natural world as a store of signs to be selected and
combined at will; the definition of his task as one requiring literary contrivance rather than eye-witness experience is emphasized especially
strongly by the declaration that the hyperbole employed is in fact borrowed
from a friend: 'To conclude this introduction to Lombardy, it is so fertile a
territory, that (as my learned and eloquent friend *M. Richard Martin* of the
middle Temple once wrote to me in a most elegant letter) the butter thereof
is oyle, the dew hony, and the milke nectar.'[84]

Another substitutive hyperbole proclaims the subject's commitment to
ingenuity and extravagance all the more strongly by reaching out beyond
the natural world in search of a substitution fit to convey the pleasures of
Italian intensity: Raymond describes Frascati as 'a place of such ravishing
delights, as fitter's for the Gods to inhabit then men', and Coryate uses the
same formula to affirm the incomparability of Lombardy: 'For it is the
fairest plaine... that ever I saw, or ever shall if I should travell over the whole
habitable world: insomuch that I said to my selfe that this country was fitter
to be an habitation for the immortall Gods then for mortall men.[85]

The affinity that is forged between hyperbolic language and the intensified topography, within such descriptions, is a form of metonymy founded
on a conceit: it is recognized that language and the topography are quite
unlike each other, but the gap between them is seen as providing the subject
of commentary with a perfect opportunity for displaying his rhetorical

---

[84] p. 93.

[85] Raymond, *An Itinerary*, p. 117; Coryate, *Coryats Crudities*, p. 99.

legerdemain, by upholding the pretence that they exhibit striking points of resemblance. The conceit of establishing an equivalence between the terrain described and the language that describes it is quite often employed in seventeenth-century travel writings in a form that explicitly emphasizes the whimsical character of such a ploy. Sir Robert Dallington's *Survey of the Great Dukes State of Tuscany* (1605) comments on the more mountainous part of the Tuscan countryside: 'no marvaile... though the discourse be like the hilles themselves, barraine.'[86] The preface to Lassels's *Voyage of Italy* includes in a list of anticipated criticisms the suggestion: 'Others will say, I change stile often, and sometimes runn smoothly, sometimes joltingly: True: I traveled not allwayes upon smooth ground, and paceing horses...'[87] A letter by John Dennis, describing the Alps (1693), draws attention to the traveller's ability to equal the 'extravagancies' of Nature:

> I am afraid you will think that I have said too much. Yet if you had but seen what I have done, you would surely think that I have said too little. However Hyperboles might easily here be forgiven. The *Alpes* appear to be Nature's extravagancies, and who should blush to be guilty of Extravagancies, in words that make mention of her's.[88]

In striving to match the intensity of Italy through rhetorical ingenuity, the subject of commentary necessarily places himself in complicity with the topography of intensification, setting himself up in emulation of it as a purveyor of extravagance.[89] The more dazzling his display of resourcefulness and wit, the greater the complicity. Where the ebullience of the rhetoric places the subject unmistakably on the side of intensification, the censure that might otherwise be attached to observations of excesses in Italian forms of behaviour is partially or wholly displaced. In Bouchard's journal, the subject claims the misdemeanours of the inhabitants of the environs of Naples as, above all else, a gratifying occasion for a show of wit:

> A la verité, à voir tous ces feus, ces fumées, ces bruits sousterrains, ces eaus bouillantes et ces puanteurs de soufre, il est bien difficile de s'empescher de croire que les Enfers ne soint en ce païs là; mais la raison qui me le

---

[86] p. 27.

[87] Unpaginated preface.

[88] Dennis, *Miscellanies*, p. 140 (letter dated 15 October 1688).

[89] To repeat a point made in the Introduction: since the speaking subject is almost invariably presented as male in seventeenth-century travel writing, male personal pronouns and possessive adjectives will be used here in referring to seventeenth-century subjects of commentary.

persuaderoit plus qu'aucune autre, c'est que les habitans de toute cette contrée là de la Campagne sont de vrais diables.[90]

In Misson's *Nouveau Voyage d'Italie*, censure of the Neapolitans is displaced
by a gratified awareness that the traveller has found a satisfactory aphorism
to encapsulate a combination of natural and behavioural excess: 'On n'a pas
mal rencontré, quand on a dit que Naples estoit un Paradis habité par des
Diables.'[91] A pun on the word *Lemmon*, which serves to introduce the topic
of the city's 'thirty thousand Courtesans Registred, that paid taxes for their
pleasure', accomplishes a similar displacement of censure in Raymond's
Itinerary: '*Naples* is extremely populous, and consequently vitious, he that
desires to live a retired, or indeed chaste life must not set up there; as the gardens are fild with Oranges, so the houses want not for Lemmon.'[92]

Hyperbole and allegory

The kind of rhetorical excess that hyperbole embodies has often been associated with a movement beyond the limits of verisimilitude. In the first group
of tropes of intensification examined above, the hyperbole never in fact
reaches this point; a claim to verisimilitude is maintained by a plausible positioning of the speaking subject as an observer. Where there is an acknowledgement of literary contrivance, however – in the second group of tropes of
intensification – the commentary does begin to reach out beyond any pretence at accuracy and, in doing so, becomes more strongly hyperbolic.

This freedom from the need to maintain verisimilitude stems from a
partial liberation of the rhetoric of intensificatory ingenuity from the need
to refer to an exterior world at all. One of the tropes employed in order to
achieve this partial liberation is that of irony. In commentaries that recognize their own status as artificial constructions, audaciously claiming an
equivalence to the world rather than stemming from experience of it, the
hyperbole is always at least incipiently ironic: the subject is divided between
an ingenious stylist who composes the commentary and a detached ironist
who reflects on this commentary. The first, naïve subject indulges a pro-

---

[90] Vol. II, p. 316: 'In truth, to see all these fires, these smokes, these subterranean noises,
these boiling waters and these sulphurous stenches, it is extremely difficult not to believe
that Hell was here in this country; but what persuades me of this more than anything else
is the fact that the inhabitants of all this country of Campania are real devils.'

[91] Vol. I, p. 292: 'They did not hit amiss, who said, That *Naples* is a Paradise inhabited with
Devils' (*A New Voyage*, vol. I, p. 308).

[92] pp. 141–2.

clivity for wordplay and self-congratulatory wit. The subject of the ironic metacommentary, on the other hand, recognizes the self-indulgent irresponsibility of the naïve subject, and redeems this irresponsibility by the perspicacity and frankness implicit in such an acknowledgement: by the addition of irony, hyperbole is deprived of the blameworthy tendency towards outright mendacity that might otherwise be attributed to it.

This redemptive function, however, does not entail any return to the commentary of observation; on the contrary, the presence of an element of irony introduces a subject who has no responsibility to refer to an exterior world at all: his task is to comment on the language of the naïve subject. By embarking on this metacommentary, he places himself in a position of superior wisdom, and acquires much greater authority than the subject on whose utterances he comments; the abandonment of observation, therefore, is strongly authenticated by its association not only with self-congratulatory wit, but also with sophisticated self-awareness.

A self-protective irony, for example, is introduced into Raymond's description of 'the Wonders a little distant from *Naples*' as 'the most fit Theame' for hyperbole, and in Dennis's declaration, in the Alps, that 'Hyperboles might easily here be forgiven': the justification of hyperbole incorporates a playful, disarming recognition not only that the correspondence between topography and language is merely a conceit, but also that the main purpose of this conceit is to authorize the traveller's display of self-aggrandizing ingenuity. In the three hyperbolic descriptions cited above, by Bouchard, Misson and Raymond, in which hyperbole displaces censure, the very naïveté of the subject's triumph in his exercise of wit marks out within the commentary a place for a second subject who recognizes this self-congratulatory stance and claims indulgence for it.

This impulse towards ever greater heights of hyperbolic language, freed from the requirement that a pretence at observation should be maintained, is protected not only by irony but also by allegory – a trope that has been described as disrupting and disqualifying 'all claims to referential and temporal presence', and as tracing out explicitly the movement of all literary language towards 'an upsurge of freedom, an irruption of nothingness in the determined massiveness of the world'.[93]

Allegory, it has often been pointed out, has a disjunctive structure: as Pierre Fontanier notes, 'l'allégorie est un discours... qui paroît toute autre chose que ce qu'on a besoin de faire entendre'.[94] This structure, Paul de

---

[93] Melville, *Philosophy Beside Itself*, p. 125 (summarizing the view of allegory propounded by Paul de Man in 'The Rhetoric of Temporality'; see below, p. 67–8).

Man argues, 'necessarily contains a constitutive temporal element': 'it
remains necessary, if there is to be allegory, that the allegorical sign refer to
another sign that precedes it'. It is this reference back which allows a preoccupation with language itself to displace any commitment to making sense
of an exterior reality, since the relationship between signs is one 'in which
the reference to their respective meanings has become of secondary importance': 'The meaning constituted by the allegorical sign can then consist
only in the *repetition*... of a previous sign with which it can never coincide,
since it is of the essence of this previous sign to be pure anteriority.'[95]

As a trope sanctioned by literary tradition, therefore, allegory provides an
endorsement of the subject's eagerness to proclaim his own linguistic ingenuity at the expense of any more measured assessment of the foreign. Several
of the passages quoted above are, in fact, allegorical as well as ironic: Dennis
introduces a female personification of Nature, who behaves extravagantly in
creating the Alps, while Bouchard elaborates an allegory of Hell and Misson
allegorically invokes traditional visions both of Hell and of Paradise.

In seeking out forms of language to supply the place of direct reference
to the topography, seventeenth-century travel writings (like most writings
within which allegory is deployed) draw on an inherited literary and
mythological typology. Literary tradition is defined, within such allegories, as a domain of exceptionally hyperbolic language, to which the subject resourcefully turns in order to seek out linguistic formulations
possessed of the required degree of intensificatory force. A description of
the view from the tower of Milan Cathedral in *Coryats Crudities*, for example, first describes the 'variety' of objects that present themselves to the
gaze as 'unspeakable', but then discovers within 'the verses of Poets' a
series of allegories through which to speak of the unspeakable:

> The territory of Lombardy, which I contemplated round about from this
> Tower, was so pleasant an object to mine eyes, being replenished with such
> unspeakable variety of all things, both for profite and pleasure, that it
> seemeth to me to be the very Elysian fieldes, so much decantated and cele-
> brated by the verses of Poets, or the Tempe or Paradise of the world.[96]

---

94 Fontanier, *Les Tropes*, vol. I, p. 178; 'allegory is a discourse... which appears to be some-
    thing quite different from that which we need to understand.'

95 de Man, *'The Rhetoric of Temporality'*, p. 207. In travel writing, the anterior sign that is
    'repeated' in the allegory is almost always a descriptive reference to the topography of for-
    eignness: allegorizing provides a displaced means of saying something about the other,
    and thematizes its own structure and etymology, as a trope 'speaking an other' (that is,
    repeating the previous sign), through this displaced concern with otherness.

96 p. 99.

Another feature of allegory, which contributes towards its power to replace or absorb direct references to the topography, in the interests of unrestrained hyperbole, is its expansiveness: an allegory has often been defined as a figure that elaborates and continues a metaphor, either through narrative or through some other device, such as personification.[97] Not only is each allegory by definition already extended, moreover, so as to constitute an assemblage of parts, but, within all the allegories employed in seventeenth-century travel writing, there is nothing to prevent the addition of extra parts at will, producing an effect of extravagant hyperbole and ingenuity: each new extension offers a further opportunity to construct or maintain a conceit of correspondence between allegorical invention and the topography. The general survey at the beginning of Lassels's *Voyage of Italy* proclaims especially dramatically the lack of any principle of limitation governing the proliferation of allegorical language; the effect of hyperbolic insouciance and irresponsibility is further increased by the capricious disregard for consistency with which different allegories are combined. The initial allegory of an indulgent Mother Nature is pursued through a series of permutations that allow two subsidiary allegories to be fitted in: the fight between Bacchus and Ceres, and Italy as a human body, or sequence of human bodies, which can sweat, appear shaven, seem barren, and become pregnant:

> For the Country it self, it seemed to me to be *Natures Darling*, and the *Eldest Sister* of all other countryes; carrying away from them, all the greatest blessings and favours; and receiving such gracious lookes from the *Sun* and *Heaven*, that if there be any fault in *Italy*, it is that Mother Nature hath cockered her too much, even to make her become Wanton. Witnesse luxuriant *Lombardy*, and *Campania* antonomastically *Fœlix*, which *Florus*, *Trogus* and *Livy* think to be the best parts of the world, where *Ceres* and *Bacchus* are at a perpetual strife, whether of them shall court man the most, she by filling his barnes with corne; he by making his cellars swimme with wine: Whiles the other parts of *Italy* are sweating out whole *Forests* of *Olive-trees*, whole woods of *Lemmons*, and *Oranges*, whole fields of *Rice*, *Turky wheat*, and *Muskmillons*, and where those Bare Hills, which seem to be shaven by the Sun and cursed by Nature for their barrennes, are oftentimes great with child of pretious *Marbles*, the ornaments of Churches and Palaces, and the Revenews of *Princes*: witnesse the *Prince* of *Massa*: whose best Revenues are his Marble Quarries: *Nature* here thinking it a farre more noble thing to feed Princes, Then to feed sheep.[98]

---

97 See, for example, Fontanier, *Les Tropes*, vol. I, p. 178: 'l'allégorie n'est même qu'une métaphore continuée'.

98 Part I, pp. 1–2.

A commitment to linguistic extravagance is registered, here, through the absorption of any direct visual reference to the topography into the network of allegorical narratives: even the 'Bare Hills', which initially seem to throw the allegory of indulgent Nature into disarray, are soon triumphantly marshalled as further evidence of indulgence. The allusion to the figure of antonomasia, as the determinant of the name *Campania Felix*, presents the terrain as one that positively invites an effort of ingenious wordplay – a view of the region reaffirmed by the reference back to the precursors in ingenuity who provide a point of origin for the allegorical narrative of Bacchus and Ceres: '*Florus, Trogus* and *Livy*'.[99] Later in *The Voyage of Italy*, when commenting once again on this same region, Lassels claims a precursor for the allegory of 'Natures Darling' as well: 'I call this country *Natures Favourite*, in imitation of *Pliny*, who calls it, *Opus gaudentis naturæ*, that is, *a country made by nature when she was in a good humour*.'[100] Ellis Veryard, in *An Account of Divers Choice Remarks, as well Geographical as Historical, Political, Mathematical, Physical and Moral, taken in a Journey through the Low-Countries, France, Italy, and Part of Spain* (1701), presents Italy as actively propelling literary precursors – Pliny and 'the Poets' – into these same allegorical fictions:

> The temperateness of the Air, and great abundance of all things necessary for the preservation of Life, made *Pliny* imagin Nature to have been in a merry Mood when she made it, and induc'd the Poets to feign Bacchus and Ceres at variance, and emulously contending which shall most contribute to the delight and benefit of the Inhabitants.[101]

In both these two surveys of Italy, then, the forms of language that are put forward as fit to be matched up against the intensity of the country are invested with extravagance by virtue of the inventiveness and expansiveness of allegory itself. They are also, more conspicuously, invested with extravagance through the narratives of exceeding limits traced out within the allegorical fictions that travellers invoke. Lassels's survey locates a strong element of immoderation both in Mother Nature's favouritism and indulgence ('Mother Nature hath cockered her *too much*') and in the wantonness that this indulgence produces in her favoured

---

[99] *Antonomasia* is usually defined as the figure of substituting a proper name for a common noun (as in 'He's a bit of a Lothario'), or replacing a proper name with a recognizable characterization of the person, place, or other possessor of the name (as in Lassels's example of 'Campania Felix'). See Marchese, *Dizionario*, p. 23.

[100] Part II, p. 268.

[101] p. 262. See also Warcupp, *Italy*, pp. 255–6.

child. The competition between Bacchus and Ceres is extravagant in itself, since it attests to a will to 'exceed' on the part of each of the combatants and, in addition, is a source of a spectacularly immoderate overproduction of food and wine. Unrestrained physicality, moreover, is suggested in the allegory of Italy sweating out her various natural products. In Veryard's survey, Nature is happily preoccupied with indulging her own caprice, rather than with following the dictates of sober responsibility, while Bacchus and Ceres are again presented as spectacularly unrestrained in their self-aggrandizing competitiveness.

Other versions of the allegory of indulgent Nature also generate narratives of immoderation: in one of the letters in Howell's *Epistolæ Ho-Elianæ*, Nature indulges in a fit of unbridled vanity: 'At *Puzzoli* not far off amongst the *Grotts*, ther are so many strange stupendous things, that nature her self seem'd to have studied of purpose how to make her self there admir'd'. In another letter, issuing a warning to a less experienced traveller, a maternal generosity in nourishment is displaced from Nature to Italy herself, who, in this role of mother, combines unrestrained indulgence with a lack of discrimination that produces extremes of behaviour in the Italians:

> You are now under the chiefest clime of wisdom, fair *Italy*, the darling of Nature, the Nurse of Policy, the Theater of Vertue; But though *Italy* give milk to *Vertue* with one dug, she often suffers *Vice* to suck at the other, therefore you must take heed you mistake not the dug; for there is an ill favord saying, that *Inglese Italionato, è Diavolo incarnato;* An *Englishman Italianat,* is a Devill incarnat.[102]

The allegory of Bacchus and Ceres, too, is employed in other writings of the period as a narrative of immoderation that affirms untrammelled excess within the topography: Warcupp invokes this allegory, in an adapted form, in his account of the countryside around Gaeta:

> You may with delight here have the prospect of *Capua*, the Countreys *Falerna, Stellata,* and *Leborina,* the most beautiful parts of *Italy,* whose hills are plentifully fraught with good wines, whence who delight to drink well and to be intoxicated, fetch from far these wines for the celebration of that *gusto;* and here the antients were wont to say, an important combate was fought between the Father *Liberio* the Finder of wine, and *Ceres* the Goddesse...[103]

---

102 Vol. I, p. 76; vol. III, p. 51.
103 Warcupp, *Italy*, pp. 255–6.

Another allegory of competition, this time between Art and Nature, maps out a wider range of reference for itself, and therefore produces yet more audacious hyperboles: every element within the topography can be marshalled as evidence of the unrestrained competitiveness of one or the other of the combatants. Sandys describes Pozzuoli and 'the places adjoyning' as an area 'where the wonderfull secrets of Nature are epitomized, and Art had congested together her incredible performances'.[104] Spon refers to Tivoli as 'un lieu, où il semble que l'art et la nature disputent à qui fera parêtre plus de merveilles', while Evelyn deploys this same allegory to affirm the intensity of one of the sights of Bologna:

> The rest of the After noone was taken up in *St. Michall in bosco,* built on a steepe hill, on the Edge of the Citty: & is for its fabric, Celars, pleasant shade, & groves, Cellars, dormitory & prospect one of the most delicious retirements that in my whole life I ever saw: Art & nature contending whither shall exceede, so as 'till now I never envied the life of a Frier, who here live so sweetly as nothing can be more desird.[105]

Paradise and Hell

Allegories of Paradise and Hell incorporate no narratives of extravagance or competition, but depend for their hyperbolic effect on the gesture by which the traveller reaches out beyond the mundane, observable world for a point of incomparability with which a particular place can be identified. In Moryson's commentary on Naples, the invocation of Paradise supplies a culminatory affirmation of pleasure, for which an allusion to the Garden of the Hesperides merely prepares the way:

> On all sides the eye is as it were bewitched with the sight of delicate gardens, as well within the City, as neere the same. The gardens without the wals are so rarely delightfull, as I should thinke the Hesperides were not to be compared with them; and they are adorned with statuæs, laberinthes, fountaines, vines, myrtle, palme, cetron, lemon, orange, and cedar trees, with lawrels, mulberies, roses, rosemary, and all kinds of fruits and flowers, so as they seeme an earthly Paradice.[106]

---

104 Sandys, *A Relation*, pp. 261–2.

105 Spon, *Voyage*, vol. I, pp. 47–8: 'a place, where it seems that art and nature are quarrelling over who can produce more wonders.' Evelyn, *Diary*, vol. II, p. 423 (May, 1645); de Rogissart, *Les Délices*, vol. I, pp. 132–3, uses the same allegory to describe the same spot, but transmutes it into a narrative of co-operation between nature and art.

106 Moryson, *An Itinerary*, part I, p. 112.

At the same time, his description invokes the concept of Paradise that is necessarily summoned up by an awareness of its etymological derivation from the Greek term παραδεισος, or 'garden'. A vision of the impossible incomparability of the 'earthly Paradice', inconceivable within the limits of the real, observable world, is authenticated, here, by the traveller's eagerness to elide such a vision with the observable qualities of garden-like Italy. Spon deploys a similar elision when he comments almost casually on 'les beaux Jardins et les Maisons de plaisance de Rome': 'ce sont de vrays Paradis terrestres et commes des lieux enchantez.'[107] Coryate's description of the countryside around Venice invokes Italy's garden-like qualities in support of the allegory of Paradise at the very point at which the affirmation of the area's incomparability becomes most inventively elaborate:

> Surely such is the fertility of this country, that I think no Region or Province under the Sunne may compare with it. For it is passing plentifully furnished with all things, tending both to pleasure and profit, being the very Paradise and Canaan of Christendome. For as Italy is the garden of the world, so is Lombardy the garden of Italy, and Venice the garden of Lombardy.[108]

The ease with which the traveller can move between this-worldly observations and other-worldly visions, through self-conscious manipulation of language, is vaunted by Raymond, with ironic extravagance, when he remarks, in his description of Vesuvius: 'Upon this Hill, or (changing a Letter) Hell...'[109] More often, travellers who identify a particular place as Hell hasten to endorse their use of such an audaciously intensificatory allegory by invoking the authority of the ancients. Sandys introduces the allegory of hell, at Lake Avernus, entirely through references to ancient sources: 'This was supposed the entrance into hell by ignorant Antiquity: where they offered infernall sacrifice to *Pluto,* and the *Manes,* here said to give answers. For which purpose *Homer* brought hither his *Ulysses,* and *Virgil* his *Æneas.*'[110] Nicolas Bénard comments on this same natural feature: 'son eau est fort noire et espoisse, toutesfois chaude et sulphurée...

---

107 Spon, *Voyage,* vol. I, p. 45: 'the beautiful gardens and *maisons de plaisance* of Rome'; 'they are true earthly paradises and places that seem to be enchanted.'

108 Coryate, *Coryats Crudities,* pp. 92–3.

109 Raymond, *An Itinerary,* p. 161.

110 Sandys, *A Relation,* p. 279. See also Moryson, *An Itinerary,* part I, p. 117, Evelyn, *Diary,* vol. II, p. 346 (8 February 1645), describing the same lake, and Lassels's description of the crater of Vesuvius (*Voyage,* part II, pp. 287–8).

c'est pourquoi Virgile dit que Eneas conduict par la Sibille descendit aux enfers par ceste abysme sulphurée'.[111]

Travel and the sedentary scholar: intensification through fame

Such references to secondary sources, morover, do not only provide authentication for hyperbolic allegory, but themselves supply a means of intensifying the topography, by affirming its 'fame'. It has already been noted that reference back to secondary sources is a recurrent feature of allegory in general: not only allegories of the underworld, but all the other major allegories of seventeenth-century travel writing draw on literary and mythological models. In commentaries of other kinds, too, the subject of commentary, at this period, is often positioned as a scholar, seeking out the forms of language supplied by texts. As with the position of self-conscious stylist, the adoption of this position of scholarly compiler banishes any pretence that the subject is attempting to offer as immediate as possible a transcription of first-hand, eye-witness experience of the topography. Even when Moryson explicitly declares, in his account of ruins near Naples, that he is consulting his own notes, made on the spot, he places these notes at much the same distance from himself, the scholar compiling the travel book back in England, as the other sources which he considers. At the same time, he emphasizes that he is just as embroiled with his text as he is with the topography, through a conceit of correspondence between the 'Laberinth' of scholarly problems in which he is caught up and the 'intricate caves' within the terrain:

> Upon the Sea shore lies the bath, commonly called of *Cicero*... and this Bath lieth neere the ruines of the Village of *Cicero*, called his Academy. I know not whether this Village (or rather Pallace) had the name of Academy or no; for I finde in my notes a Village of *Cicero* in the way from *Naples* to *Pozzoli*, and likewise the mention of this bath of *Cicero*, and his Academy, neere the Lake of *Avernus*. And *Leander* mentions a village of his in both places: but *Villamont* speaks of a Village neere *Pozzoli*, and of a Pallace in this place called *Accademy*; and these differ not much from my notes: but others confound the Village and the Bath, putting both together, so as writing of these intricate caves under the earth, my selfe am fallen into a Laberinth, wherein I had much rather die, then goe backe to *Naples* for searching the truth.[112]

---

[111] Bénard, *Voyage*, p. 394: 'Its water is very black and thick, yet hot and sulphurous... This is why Virgil says that Aeneas, conducted by the Sibyl, descended to hell by this sulphurous abyss.'

[112] Moryson, *An Itinerary*, part I, p. 118.

One precondition for the major role that scholarly reference plays in determining the ways in which knowledge of the foreign is ordered in the seventeenth century is the assumption that the objects of commentary acquire their identity to a large degree from their 'fame' – their reputation, and the accretion of mythological, literary, historical and anecdotal detail which has attached itself to them – and from the 'esteem' in which they are held. One of the subject's main tasks, therefore, is that of assessing the fame of particular objects – a task which necessarily entails reference back to the descriptive and narrative language of the past. Accounts of particular locations usually refer to the writings that have made them 'famous', or to the events for which they are 'famous', as transmitted by such writings. An entry in Evelyn's diary, for example, begins: 'Pisa, for the famous mention thereof in History, whiles it contended with Rome, Florence, Sardinia, Sicily, & even Carthage herselfe, is as much worthy the seeing as any city in Italy.'[113] The trope of fame is, like that of allegory, incipiently hyperbolic, in that it allows reference to other forms of language to assume a primacy over reference to the exterior world, and so removes one of the guarantees of sober verisimilitude. Quite often, eyewitness observation is wholly or largely excluded by allusions to the reputation and history of a place or object of commentary; such a displacement occurs even in accounts of works of art – objects that might be expected to prompt the traveller to pay specific attention to their visual qualities. In Lassels's commentary on Rome, the traveller observes that he has viewed a well-known painting, but entirely excludes any reference to its appearance, and remarks only on its fame (to which he alludes twice in one sentence): 'From hence I went to *Cardinal Mazzarinis* Pallace, and there saw in the garden, the famous picture of the *Aurora* made by *Guido Rheni* famous over all *Rome.*'[114]

While the source invoked in order to affirm the fame of an object is situated in the past (whether distant or recent), the fame itself is always assumed to endure within the present. The renown that objects acquire, by virtue of the utterances that establish them as a presence in language, is viewed as independent of any noteworthy qualities that they may exhibit as objects of observation; fame, in other words, is uncompromised by the mutability of the material world. In Sandys's account of Bauli, for example, a narrative of ancient excesses on this spot is elaborated at some length, as something that remains part of the place's fame; the observation that all visual traces of these

---

113 Vol. II, p. 179 (19 October 1644).
114 Lassels, *Voyage*, part II, p. 150.

excesses have been erased is consigned to a parenthesis, as an incidental
remark which can hardly be expected to halt the flow of hyperbolic language:

> Here *Hortensius* the Orator had his Villa (the ruines whereof are now buried
> in earth, and covered with water) who greatly delighted in his fish-stues,
> and was nick-named *Triton* by *Tullie;* for the fishes herein would come to
> his hand when so called: who wept for the death of a Lamprey: and to a
> friend that begged two Barbels of him (called *Mulli* in Latin) replied, that
> he had rather give him two mules for his litter.[115]

De Rogissart presents the intensity inscribed within the fame of the city of
Capua as utterly uncompromised by the erasure of such intensity within the
topography observed by the traveller. The initial sentence of his description
is interrupted by a sequence of relative clauses which, in elaborating the
ancient profusion and excess for which the city is famous, consign to a position of relative insignificance the brief, long-delayed observation that it no
longer exists: 'Capoue, qui étoit autrefois la ville Capitale de la *Campanie*, si
fameuse pour sa fertilité et pour son abondance en toute sorte de choses, et
pour ses délices célébres, qui ont été la cause de sa ruine et de sa destruction,
aussi bien que de celle de l'Armée d'*Annibal*, n'est plus.'[116]

The concept of fame, therefore, like the concept of 'memory', as
defined by Derrida, 'preserves an essential and necessary relation with the
possibility of the name, and of what in the name assures preservation'.
Fame continues the process of establishing an object of commentary as
something present in language which the name begins, and so assumes the
same power as the name to allow the object to survive independently,
untouched by the mutability of the world outside language: 'In calling or
naming someone while he is alive, we know that his name can survive him
and already survives him; the name begins during his life to get along without him...'[117]

Seventeenth-century travel writings themselves, in fact, implicitly recognize the name as the starting-point of fame, and the initial guarantee of
immortality, by regularly presenting the task of investigating the name of a
place as the first stage in the exposition of its fame. (Naming is almost always
discussed through a double reference back: the subject of commentary
implicitly refers back to classical or other textual sources which themselves

---

115 Sandys, *A Relation*, p. 294.
116 Rogissart, *Les Délices*, vol. II, p. 435: 'Capua, which was in the past the capital city of
     Campania, so famous for its fertility and for its abundance in all varieties of things, and for
     its celebrated delights, which were the cause of its ruin and destruction, and that of
     Hannibal's army as well, is now no more.'
117 Derrida, *Memoires*, p. 49.

refer back to the name and the process of its formation.) Moryson's commentary on Pozzuoli, for example, includes an extended discussion of the naming of the town: 'I say it hath the present name of the Italian word *Pozzo*, signifying a well, though some will have it named presently of *Puzzo*, which signifies a stink...'[118]

The name, like all other utterances in which the fame of the topography is inscribed, serves as a bearer of intensity, in affirming that an object of commentary has exhibited qualities sufficiently remarkable for it to be judged worthy of translation into language at some point in the past. Sandys's *Relation of a Journey* and Bouchard's journal offer accounts of the etymology of *Posillipo* which are completely different from each other, but which both emphasize gastronomic intensity: profusion of wine in the one instance, and incomparability of eels in the other:

> Hard without the City the way is crossed with *Pausilype*: the name doth signifie a releaser from cares, for that the wine (wherewith this mountaine is richly furnished) is an approved remedy for those consuming infirmities.

> Il s'appelle Pausilype à cause de cette fameuse Villa Vedii Pollionis, où il nourissoit de si belles anguilles à qui il jettoit de ses serfs pour mangeaille, et encore aujourd'hui prend on les plus belles anguilles de tous ces quartiers là à la pointe de Pausilype.[119]

The citing of names as bearers of intensity is not limited to such enquiries into ancient etymologies: Raymond's account of Verona embarks on an unashamedly retrospective attempt to find an etymological motivation for the title of that city which might proclaim its advantages with a sufficient degree of hyperbole:

> Tis the vulgar Criticisme on this Name, that if it bee syllabizd, it comprehends the first letters of the three head Cities of *Italy Ve – Venetia. Ro – Roma. Na – Napoli.* Others leave the verbal derivation, and more strictly interpret it, that whatsoever is containd in those three Cities may bee found in *Verona.*

> Her wealth may be compar'd to that of *Venice;* Her Monuments of Antiquity equall even those of *Rome*, neither is the delightfull situation inferiour to that of *Naples.*[120]

---

118 Moryson, *An Itinerary*, part I, p. 115; the derivation from *Puzzo* has been suggested, Moryson informs the reader, 'because of the smell of brimstone in these parts'.

119 Sandys, *A Relation*, p. 262; Bouchard, *Journal*, vol. II, pp. 309–10: 'It is called Posillipo because of the famous Villa Vedii Pollionis, where Pollio nurtured such beautiful eels, to whom he threw his slaves for food, and today the most beautiful eels of any region are still found there, at the promontory of Posillipo.'

120 Raymond, *An Itinerary*, p. 226.

Affirming fame:
travellers invoke hyperbole, esteem and drama

Accounts of fame follow three main strategies, all of which overlap. The first strategy is to cite the intensified forms of language which have at some point in the past been used to describe an object of commentary within the topography. This strategy is employed in all the topographically specific allegories discussed above; the designation of the past as a source of intensified language has already been noted as a feature of the allegories employed in seventeenth-century travel literature. The second option, which is also adopted in many of the allegories cited so far, is to note the 'esteem' in which the object of commentary is or has been held. The third strategy – employed in Bouchard's account of Pollio's extreme devotion to his eels – is to describe or narrate the dramatically intensified passions and actions which have been attached to a particular spot, either by credible histories or by literary and mythological tradition.[121]

The hyperbolic language of the past is regularly summoned up not only in allegories, but also in other allusions to 'the Poets', and to ancient myths and fables. Evelyn remarks: 'Returning towards the Baiæ we againe passe the Elysian Fields so celebrated by the Poets, nor unworthily for their situation & verdure, being full of Myrtils & sweete shrubs, and having a most incomparable prospect towards the tyrrhen sea.'[122] Bouchard's description of the Bay of Naples (Figure 1) invokes the allegory of incomparable seductiveness supplied by the Greeks:

> Si vous prenez le costé de la mer, il ne se peut rien voir de si delicieus, de plus superbe et de plus beau que ce golphe de Naples, rond comme une coupe, dont les Grecs luy donerent le nom de κρατηρ et où ils logerent les

---

121 See, for example, Sandys's account of the incomparable excesses of the ancients at Baia (*A Relation*, p. 291), in which the traveller asserts that '*Ægyptian Canopus...* was a schoole of vertue compared to the voluptuous liberty of this City'. Seventeenth-century travel literature incorporates as a firmly established assumption the view that the ancient Romans were inclined to immoderation in the indulgence of their sexual, gastronomic, and architectural proclivities, and also to extremes of cruelty. Architectural excess is noted, for example, in Bénard's account of the Grotta di Posillipo: 'c'est un travail extréme et de despence excessive faicte du temps des Romains' (*Voyage*, p. 388: 'it is a work of an extreme kind, and of excessive expense, carried out in the time of the Romans'); extremity of cruelty is emphasized by narratives of Nero's murder of his mother Agrippina – for example, in Moryson, *An Itinerary*, vol. I, p. 118, and Sandys, *A Relation*, p. 294.

122 Evelyn, *Diary*, vol. II, p. 351 (8 February 1645).

Sirenes, come dans le golphe le plus voluptueus non seulement de l'Europe, mais encore de l'Asie et de l'Afrique.[123]

The strategy of invoking intensified language often overlaps with that of invoking 'esteem' – as in the case of the two commentaries just cited, or in Coryate's account of the wines of Venice:

> Some of these wines are singular good, as their *Liatico*, which is a very cordiall and generose Liquor: their *Romania*, their *Muscadine*, and their *Lagryme di Christo*; which is so toothsome and delectable to the taste, that a certaine stranger being newly come to the citie, and tasting of this pleasant wine, was so affected therewith, that I heard he uttered this speech out of a passionate humour: *O Domine Domine, cur non lachrimasti in regionibus nostris?* that is, O Lord, O Lord, why hast thou not distilled these kinde of teares into our countries?[124]

Other references to esteem, however, draw not on intensified forms of language but on accounts of the intensified actions and passions excited by the objects of commentary. Evelyn, describing the crater of Vesuvius, observes: 'This horrid Barathrum engaged our contemplation for some whole houres both for the strangnesse of the spectacle, and for the mention which the old histories make of it, as one of the most stupendious curiosities in nature, & which made the learned & inquisitive Pliny adventure his life, to detect the causes, & to loose it in too desperat an approch.'[125] Narratives of the downfalls of Hannibal at Capua and of the foreign bishop at Montefiascone, already mentioned as prolepses of the temptation to excess facing the contemporary traveller, also proclaim the intensity of the topography of the Grand Tour by emphasising noteworthy reactions to this topography.[126]

---

123 Bouchard, *Journal*, vol. II, p. 307: 'If you take the coastal side of the city, there is nothing more delightful, more splendid and more beautiful than this Bay of Naples, round as a drinking cup, which was the reason why the Greeks gave it the name of κρατηρ, and it was where they gave the Sirens their dwelling place, as though to situate them in the most voluptuous bay not only of Europe, but of Asia and Africa too.'

124 Coryate, *Coryats Crudities*, p. 288.

125 Evelyn, *Diary*, vol. II, p. 335 (*c.* 7 February 1645). Evelyn relates, at some length, two of the other events which have contributed towards the fame of the 'Vorago': 'It is likewise famous for the Stratagemm of the rebell Spartacus... But, especialy, notorious it is, for the last conflagration, when in Ann: 1630 it burst out beyond what it had ever don since the memory of any history' (vol. II, pp. 335–6).

126 See, for example, Sandys's account of Hannibal and his army 'by vices vanquished' (*A Relation*, p. 291) and Huguetan's narrative of the bishop's enthusiastic over-consumption (*Voyage*, p. 45). (This latter story, of course, also provides another demonstration of esteem, on the part of the servant who writes *est* three times on the door or the vessel where the best wine is to be found.)

Accounts of actions and passions that testify to esteem sometimes play a part in asserting the incomparability of works of art. *Coryats Crudities* comments on a sculpture on the inner side of the doorway into the Palazzo Ducale in Venice: 'That statue of *Eve* is done with that singularity of cunning, that it is reported the Duke of Mantua hath offered to give the weight of it in gold for the Image, yet he cannot have it.'[127] Lassels's account of 'an *old picture* made in the time of the *Pagans* representing a *mariage* after the old *Romans* fashion' earnestly informs the reader: 'the rarity of it is so great, that *Cavalier Pozzo* (a brave Gentleman and a great *Virtuoso*,) got leave to copie it out.'[128] Other commentaries simply note the high regard in which specific works are held, without invoking any particular authenticating narrative. Evelyn describes a painting by Raphael, probably the *Transfiguration*, as a piece which is 'esteemed one of the rarest in the world', while Bromley comments on the Cathedral at Parma: 'The *Cupola* is painted by *Corregio*, and esteemed one of the greatest Works in the World.'[129] Misson remarks, in Venice, that 'le S. Pierre martyr de Titien est regardé comme un des plus excellens tableaux qui ayent jamais esté'.[130]

The traveller uttering the commentary occasionally provides a personal endorsement of the incomparability attributed to a painting or sculpture – as in Evelyn's account of the *Laocoon*: 'Plynie says this statue is to be esteem'd before all pictures & statues in the World, and I am altogether of his opinion, for in my life I never beheld anything of Art approch it.'[131] More often, however, travellers cite the respect for a particular work evinced by those possessed of a specialized expertise. The expertise invoked is often that of the 'connoisseur' or 'virtuoso': Misson, commenting on Titian's *St Peter Martyr*, observes that 'les meilleurs connoisseurs sont enchantez de cette piéce'.[132] The account of Raphael's *St Cecilia* in William Lodge's *Painter's Voyage of Italy* (1679) informs the reader that

---

127 p. 193. See also Evelyn's account of 'the Adonis of Parrian Marble which once my L: of Arundel would have purchas'd, if a greate price would have been taken for it' (*Diary*, vol. II, p. 217; 6 November 1645). Esteem is also linked to financial valuation through simple allusions to the price paid for a work, and through more vaguely hyperbolic assertions; see Bromley, *Remarks*, p. 253 ('a Basin and Ure, Painted by *R. Urbin*, that cost 100 Pistols') and p. 274, describing a *Trinity* by Guido Reni as a work 'of an inestimable value'.

128 Lassels, *Voyage*, part II, pp. 149–50.

129 Evelyn, *Diary*, vol. II, p. 313 (25 January 1645); Bromley, *Remarks*, p. 102.

130 Misson, *Nouveau Voyage*, vol. II, p. 8: 'The *St. Peter Martyr* of Titian is reputed to be one of the finest Pictures that ever was made' (*A New Voyage*, vol. II, p. 9).

131 Evelyn, *Diary*, vol. II, p. 304 (18 January 1645).

132 Misson, *Nouveau Voyage*, vol. II, p. 8: 'The best Judges are charm'd with this Piece' (*A New Voyage*, vol. II, p. 9).

'all the *Virtuosi* which travel by the way of *Bolognia* cannot depart this City without a sight of such a marvellous Piece'.[133] At other points, travel writings invoke the expertise of an artist: Bromley's catalogue of works in Parma notes 'above the rest, *Venus* and *Cupid*, by *Titian*, esteemed by Painters one of the greatest Pieces of Art in the world'.[134] Lassels refers to both sources of authority in an account of one of Michelangelo's sculptures in Florence: 'That which represents *Night*, is a rare statue, and hugely cryed up by all *Sculptors* and *Virtuosi*.'[135]

Outside the context of commentary on art, no source of authority is explicitly invested with a privileged authority of this kind. A diverse array of different subjects of judgement are summoned up, and are all assigned an equivalence, as subjects who, at some previous date, whether recent or long past, have translated one of the objects of commentary into language. Italian proverbs are often cited in authentication of the intensity of specific towns. Raymond comments on Padua: 'It stands in a most delicious and fertile Plaine, which produceth so great abundance of things necessary to humane life, that the vulgar Proverb goes *Bolonia la grassa ma Padova la passa*.'[136] Coryate's account of Padua moves without any sense of disjunction from classical references, affirming the degree of esteem in which the plane tree was formerly held (and, in a reference to 'the Poets', the intensified, allegorical language which was formerly employed to describe it), to an allusion to the equally superlative esteem with which the contemporary Italians now regard the pistachio nut:

> The Poets doe faine that *Jupiter* dallied with *Europa* under this kinde of tree. And it was in former times so highly esteemed amongst the Romans by reason of the shadow, that they were wont sometimes to nourish the roote of it with wine poured about it. Also I saw a very prety fruit which is esteemed farre more excellent then Apricocks, or any other dainty fruit whatsoever growing in Italy. They call it *Pistachi*, a fruit much used in their daily banquets.[137]

Unsurprisingly, however, the store of references on which seventeenth-century travel literature draws most frequently, in accounts of esteem as well as in invocations of hyperbole, is classical literature. Moryson vaunts the incomparability of the wine of Spoleto through a quotation from

---

[133] p. 33.

[134] Bromley, *Remarks*, p. 106.

[135] Lassels, *Voyage*, part I, p. 160.

[136] Raymond, *An Itinerary*, p. 208; see also, for example, Huguetan's account of Milan (*Voyage*, p. 265) and Lassels's account of Genoa (*Voyage*, part I, 82–3).

[137] Coryate, *Coryats Crudities*, p. 149.

Martial, translated as 'If with *Spoleto* bottels once you meet, / Say that *Falerno* must is not so sweet.'[138] In Warcupp's account of incomparability in Padua, the straightforward declaration that 'the bread they make here is the whitest of *Italy*' is immediately followed by a scholarly allusion to a classical source: 'And the wine is by *Plinie* accounted amongst the most noble and excellent.'[139] Descriptions of Baia by Moryson, Sandys and Evelyn all cite versions of the words of Horace, in order to supply both intensified forms of language and a hyperbolic declaration of esteem:

> Hence we passed to *Baie*, an ancient Citie, and for the sweetnesse preferred to *Rome* by *Horace:*
>
> > *Nullus in urbe locus Baijus prælucet amœnis.*
> > No place of *Rome* sweete *Baie* doth excell.
>
> A place so endued by Nature, and so adorned by art, that the *Lyric* Poet doth celebrate it as of pleasure incomparable:
>
> > No place on earth surpasseth pleasant *Baiæ.*
>
> And now we enter'd the haven of the Baiæ where once stood that famous Towne so call'd from the Companion of Ulysses here buried; certainly not without greate reason celebrated for one of the most delicious places that the Sunn shines on in the World, according to that of *Hor:*
>
> > Nullus in Orbe locus Baijs prælucet amœnis[140]

The familiarity of the ancient past

One of the features of travel writing that invests classical texts with greater attractions than all other such points of reference, in confirming the fame of Italy, is the desire to find relative familiarity amid the strangeness of the foreign. Coryate welcomes a plane tree in 'the goodly garden of the City' in Padua as an object which, though unprecedented in his empirical experience of the world, is nonetheless already familiar from classical texts: 'Amongst the rest I saw a certaine rare tree whereof I have often read both in *Virgil* and other Authours, but never saw it till then.'[141] Raymond, noting

---

138 Moryson, *An Itinerary*, part I, p. 101; the lines translated are given as '*De Spoletanis quæ sunt curiosa lagenis | Malveris, quam si musta Falerna hibas*'.

139 Warcupp, *Italy*, p. 19.

140 Moryson, *An Itinerary*, part I, pp. 118–19; Sandys, *A Relation*, p. 290 (the Latin is given in the margin as 'Nullus in orbe locus Baijs prælucet amœnis'); Evelyn, *Diary*, vol. II, pp. 348–9 (8 February 1645).

141 Coryate, *Coryats Crudities*, pp. 148–9.

the 'superior endowments' conferred on Italy in more recent times, nonetheless declares: 'Yet most certainly had *Romulus* his Successours aspird no farther then the Mud wall hee left them; had those Legions of Worthies never beene borne there, wee should never have had such an esteeme of this *Cisalpine* clod.'[142]

The intensity conferred on Italy by its classical past, travel writings suggest, is derived not only from the intensified character of that past and its writings, but also from the pleasure that the traveller derives from reminders of texts with which he is already familiar. Bouchard's journal situates the delights of the Villa Hortensii, near Naples, in the resurgence of a past to which the traveller has already become attached:

> Nous disnasmes sous l'une de ces arches, couchez par terre sur les tapis de Turquie de nostre felouque, et les poissons furent cuits par les mariniers en belle pleine campagne... entre autres nous eusmes deus *mullos*, qui ne cedoint je pense gueres à ces deus qu'Hortensius tenoit en ce mesme lieu... J'eus tous les plaisirs du monde en mangeant en ce lieu, m'imaginois de voir ce bon Hortensius mettre des pendans d'oreilles à ses murenes et leur doner à manger dans sa main, puis le voir pleurer et prendre le deuil pour la mort d'un de ces poissons là.[143]

It has already been suggested that the desire that the foreign should not prove too bafflingly unfamiliar is registered in travel writing of all periods, alongside the opposing desire to find, within the foreign, a dramatic difference from the topography to which the traveller is accustomed. In seventeenth-century accounts of fame, these two conflicting desires are regularly reconciled through a paradox: the foreign is defined as more intensified than the familiar – and, therefore, as gratifyingly different – partly because it supplies stronger and more numerous reminders of a domain of familiarity, for which the traveller feels an affection sufficient to invest a visit to an ancient site with 'tous les plaisirs du monde'.

---

142 Raymond, *An Itinerary*, unpaginated introduction.
143 Vol. II, pp. 341–2: 'We dined under one of these arches, lying on the ground, on the Turkish carpets of our felucca, and the fish were cooked by the sailors in the open air... among others, we had two mullets, which, I think, were scarcely inferior to those which Hortensius kept in this same place... I had all the pleasures in the world in eating in this place; I imagined seeing the good Hortensius putting earrings on his morays and feeding them out of his hand, then seeing him weeping and putting on mourning for the death of one of the fish.'

2

Hyperbole and observation

Hyperboles of the unrepresentable

In many of the varieties of hyperbole discussed in the last chapter, there is, as already emphasized, little or no pretence at visual scrutiny of the topography of the Grand Tour; the subject of commentary concentrates instead on seeking out forms of language sufficiently intensified to match the drama of the topography. In contrast to this confident recourse to the language of intensification, one of the most common forms of hyperbole adopted in late eighteenth-century and early nineteenth-century commentary is the declaration that no linguistic formulation can hope to convey to the reader the dramatic intensity of a particular object of commentary, as experienced visually by the traveller. Patrick Brydone, on the summit of Mount Etna, remarks: '*But here description must ever fall short*; for no imagination has dared to form an idea of so glorious and so magnificent a scene.'[1] Charles Dupaty concludes his description of the Bay of Naples by proclaiming: 'tout cela forme un tableau, une situation, un enchantement, *qu'il est impossible de rendre*.'[2] Eruptions of Vesuvius elicit from Sir William Hamilton the observation that '*It is impossible to describe* the beautiful appearance of these girandoles of red hot stones, far surpassing the most astonishing artificial fire-work', and from Hester Piozzi an account of 'a thick cloud', which, 'charged heavily with electric matter, passing over, met the fiery explosion by mere chance, and went off *in such a manner as effectually baffles all verbal description*'.[3] Such hyperboles of indescribability are

---

1   Brydone, *A Tour*, vol. I, p. 202; emphasis added.
2   Dupaty, *Lettres sur l'Italie*, vol. II, p. 164; emphasis added: 'All these form a scenery, a situation, and an enchantment, impossible to be described' (*Sentimental Letters*, vol. II, p. 117; further translations in footnotes are all taken from this edition).
3   Hamilton, *Observations*, p. 8. Piozzi, *Observations*, vol. II, p. 5; emphasis added in both quotations. For an early example of the hyperbole of indescribability, see Thomas Gray's description of Mount Cenis, in a letter of 1739, in *The Poems of Mr. Gray*, p. 64; letter dated 7 November, N.S.

often reinforced by the claim that a particular scene defeats all attempts at *visual* representation. Henry Swinburne, on the island of Capri, declares: 'The magnificence of this scene would baffle the skill of the greatest painter; how feeble then must be the idea my description can convey of the prospect enjoyed from the chapel of Santa Maria.'[4]

Having noted that the topography resists all efforts at description, travellers, in many cases, happily proceed to describe it. Marie Anne Fiquet du Boccage, in the Alps, declares: 'Les points de vue terribles et charmants qu'on y rencontre, sont faits pour nourrir l'imagination des Poëtes; mais leurs tableaux n'en peuvent rendre la réalité, et me dégoûtent de vous la crayonner.' On the very next page, she offers her own verses on Alpine scenes.[5] Dupaty acknowledges no incompatibility between his long, rapturous description of the *Venus de' Medici* and his declared conviction that 'elle échappera toujours au pinceau, au cizeau et à la parole: il n'existe aucune langue au monde, qui puisse modéler tant de charmes'.[6]

The eye-witness and the commentary of visual observation

One rhetorical task that travellers accomplish, when they utter hyperboles of indescribability, is that of affirming their own status as eye-witnesses, who have encountered the objects of commentary in person, and undergone an experience beyond the imaginative grasp of those who know these objects only through the mediation of literature and art. It is the eye-witness alone, such hyperboles suggest, who is capable of experiencing the sense of uniqueness that supplies the precondition for wonder. Lord Kames, defining wonder as the emotion experienced when curiosity is gratified, presents this gratification as the reward for undergoing 'the fatigues and even perils of travelling' – fatigues and perils that the spirit of enquiry renders positively pleasurable. Hyperboles of indescribability endorse his suggestion that wonder represents the culminatory point of a narrative of first-hand investigation, in which the traveller is propelled by curiosity towards 'new and singular objects'.[7]

---

4 Swinburne, *Travels*, vol. II, p. 3. See also, for example, Jameson, *Diary*, p. 267.

5 Boccage, *Recueil*, vol. III, pp. 135, 136: 'The dreary prospects which are there to be seen might furnish matter to the imagination of poets, but is is impossible for any picture to come up to the reality; and for that reason I am afraid to give you a sketch of them' (*Letters*, vol. I, p. 121).

6 Dupaty, *Lettres*, vol. I, p. 146: 'She will always baffle the pencil, the chissel, and the pen: there exists no language in the world that can model so many charms' (vol. I, p. 115).

7 Kames, *Elements of Criticism*, vol. I, pp. 320, 323.

The claim to unmediated, eye-witness experience provides travellers, from early in the eighteenth century onwards, with a new strategy for endorsing their own authority to describe and comment. Du Boccage begins her declaration that poets can never adequately describe the Alps by asserting the importance of viewing them as she has, at first hand: 'On ne peut se faire une juste idée des hautes montagnes qu'on ne les ait parcourues.'[8] The 'rights' of the eye-witness to translate the foreign into discourse are crisply identified at the very beginning of Sterne's *Sentimental Journey*, in Yorick's explanation of the motives for his travels:

> – They order, said I, this matter better in France –
> – You have been in France? said my gentleman, turning quick upon me with the most civil triumph in the world. – Strange! quoth I, debating the matter with myself, That one and twenty miles sailing, for 'tis absolutely no further from Dover to Calais, should give a man these rights – I'll look into them.[9]

Such 'rights' are eagerly inscribed within the titles of some travel books: Sacheverell Stevens's *Miscellaneous Remarks Made on the Spot, in a Late Seven Years Tour through France, Italy, Germany and Holland* (1756), for example, and Adam Walker's *Ideas, Suggested on the Spot in a Late Excursion through Flanders, Germany, France and Italy* (1790). In their emphasis on on-the-spot immediacy, such travellers pointedly dismiss the work of compilation to which Coryate refers in the extended title of *Coryats Crudities* (1611): the 'crudities', though 'hastily gobled up in five Moneths travells', have been 'newly digested in the hungry aire of ODCOMBE in the County of Somerset'. Anne, Lady Miller, in her *Letters from Italy* (1776), registers a sharp awareness that her authority to comment depends upon a claim to immediate observation rather than sedentary cogitation: describing the works of art in the palaces in Bologna, she explains that 'for fear of errors, I take my notes *upon the spot*, which I assure you is often very troublesome, as I am frequently obliged to write in my pocket-book standing, and at times placing it on the pedestal of a statue, or the moulding of a surbase'.[10]

The status of the speaking subject as eye-witness is affirmed by disparaging references to the two strategies that are viewed as compromising this status most alarmingly: self-conscious literary extravagance and

---

8   Boccage, *Recueil*, vol. III, p. 135: 'You cannot form a just idea of these lofty mountains without having passed over them' (*Letters*, vol. I, p. 121).

9   p. 3.

10 Vol. II, p. 18; emphasis added; see also, for example, Piozzi's account of Raphael's *Transfiguration*, which relates a conversation with the friar showing the painting (*Observations*, vol. II, pp. 109–10).

scholarly reference to classical sources. Patrick Brydone, in his *Tour through Sicily and Malta* (1773), echoes a passage from Pope's 'Peri Bathous' (1727) in noting ironically that Virgil and the Sicilian poet Raitano have both 'been greatly outdone by the wonderful imagination of our great countryman Sir Richard Blackmore; who accounts at once for the whole phænomena of Ætna, by the simple idea of giving the mountain a fit of the colic'.[11] Allegories are not entirely excluded from eighteenth-century travel writing, but are often introduced briefly and unassertively, and embedded in visual observations.[12] Martin Sherlock, in his *Nouvelles lettres d'un voyageur anglois* (1780), registers a strong sense of unease when he deploys one of the allegorical affirmations of intensity most often incorporated into earlier travel commentaries: he attempts to assimilate the allegory of indulgent Nature into an account of the visual delights of Italy by changing Nature from a mother into an artist, striving to produce pleasing aesthetic effects.)[13]

In rejecting scholarly annotation, travellers frequently disparage Joseph Addison's *Remarks on Several Parts of Italy* (1705), despite Addison's own eagerness to establish his commitment to observation as well as to scholarship: he has, he says, read passages from classical authors 'as it were, upon the Spot', comparing them with 'the Natural Face of the Country'.[14] Sterne, in *Tristram Shandy* (1759-67), nonetheless describes 'the great Addison' as writing 'with his satchel of school-books hanging at his a—'.[15] Henry Fielding, in the preface to his *Journal of a Voyage to Lisbon* (1755), suggests, more temperately, that Addison is 'to be considered... as a commentator on

---

[11] Vol. I, pp. 268–9; see also vol. I, pp. 37–8. See Pope, 'Peri Bathous' pp. 142–3. For further discussion of disparaging references to Blackmore's allegory, see Chard, 'Rising and Sinking' pp. 66–7.

[12] Joseph Spence, in an account of the environs of Naples (*Letters*, p. 105; letter of 1732), and Thomas Watkins, concluding an account of a visit to Vesuvius (*Travels*, vol. II, p. 83), both introduce allegories of Hell and Paradise, but do so only after naming the specific visual qualities in the landscape that prompt them.

[13] pp. 11–12. Sherlock's attempts to combine observation with self-conscious manipulation of language, in this passage and in others, are criticized by the *Monthly Review;* see vol. 62 (1780), p. 597.

[14] Unpaginated preface. Addison, in this preface, explicitly proclaims his intention of quoting only 'such Verses as have given us some Image of the Place, or that have something else besides the bare Name of it to recommend 'em' – in other words, those that might provide material for comparison with on-the-spot observations, rather than those that merely serve to establish 'fame'.

[15] p. 462. Sterne continues: 'there is not a galloper of us all who might not have gone on ambling quietly in his own ground... and have wrote all he had to write, dryshod, as well as not.'

the classics, rather than as a writer of travels'.[16] In later eighteenth-century writings, the traveller frequently attempts to keep at bay any such accusations of sedentary scholarship by implying that classical allusions spontaneously spring to mind in the presence of striking repositories of cultural memory. Piozzi assures the reader: '*I have examined* the place where Sylla massacred 8000 fellow-citizens at once.'[17] Henry Swinburne, at the site of the Battle of Cannae, remarks: '*My eyes now ranged at large* over the vast expanse of unvariegated plains... My thoughts naturally assumed the tint of the dreary prospect, as I reflected on the fate of Rome and Carthage.'[18]

Tedious repetition and diminished hyperbole

Empirical observation has often been presented as a strategy for gathering and ordering knowledge that allows a range of eighteenth-century discourses to transform themselves in ways that open up new and enlivening rhetorical and theoretical possibilities.[19] The claim to be speaking as an eye-witness, however, whatever its transformatory force (and whatever excited awareness of that force is registered in representations of foreign places), nonetheless, in its early stages, produces two rhetorical problems within the discourses of travel, which are only overcome as a result of a further set of changes in the options open to the traveller-narrator. One such problem, registered in many early eighteenth-century writings, consists of a fear that the traveller-narrator is in constant danger of repeating the words of previous travellers. The commentary in which particular objects are described will, it is assumed, as a transparent transcription of visual observation, necessarily repeat the accounts offered by those who have viewed the same objects on a previous occasion. Far from registering dramatic difference, therefore, the commentary may, the traveller

16 Fielding, *Jonathan Wild and The Journal of a Voyage to Lisbon*, p. 185. See Walpole, *Yale Edition*, vol. XIII, pp. 85–90 (letter of *c.*15 October 1735), for Walpole's parody of Addison's profusion of Latin quotations and vol. XIII, p. 231 (letter to Richard West, headed 'Florence, Oct. 2, 1740', N.S.) and vol. XVI, p. 52 (letter to the Rev. Henry Zouch, dated 'March 20, 1762'), for disparaging references to Addison's proclivity for citing Latin poets rather than observing the topography of Italy. See also, for example, Miller, *Letters*, vol. II, pp. 155–7.

17 Piozzi, *Observations*, vol. I, p. 381; emphasis added.

18 Swinburne, *Travels*, vol. I, p. 169; emphasis added.

19 See, for example, Stafford, *Voyage into Substance*, pp. xxi, 29, 287, 421–3. For an account of new possibilities opening up in visual orderings of knowledge, as a result of 'the mode of perception and expression which artists... tended to acquire as a result of the conditions imposed upon them on scientific voyages', see Smith, in *European Vision*, p. 3.

anxiously suggests, seem tediously familiar to the reader. Edward Wright, in *Some Observations* (1730), remarks, when considering paintings in the Palazzo Pitti: 'I forbear entering into the Particulars, this having been done by others; and particularly of late by Mr. *Richardson.*' At the *Stanze di Raffaele* in the Vatican, he declares: 'I shall not pretend to give any particular Description of these admirable Performances; 'twould be but *actum agere;* they have been so largely and fully describ'd by *Bellori* and others formerly, and by Mr. *Richardson* of late.'[20] Walpole greets Herculaneum with relief, as an object too newly discovered for his account of it to have become hackneyed: 'One hates writing descriptions that are to be found in every book of travels; but we have seen something to-day that I am sure you never read of, and perhaps never heard of.'[21]

One way of reading these expressions of anxiety about repetition is to view them in terms similar to those that Anthony Cascardi adopts, in *The Subject of Modernity*, when considering equivocations within the novel, from Cervantes' *Don Quixote* (1605-15) onwards. Novels, Cascardi suggests, confront a world 'that has been disenchanted, secularized, rendered prose', and attempt to re-enchant this world by invoking the alluring fictions of romance. At the same time, they strive to reconcile these fictions with the demands of verisimilitude, grounding them in a world that seems objective, rational and real. Early eighteenth-century travel writings, defined in these terms, can be seen as so committed to the verisimilitude necessary to endorse the authority of the traveller as eye-witness that they deny that the topography can entrap the subject of commentary into any of the flights of fancy – rhetorical or imaginative – that might produce points of divergence between one travel book and the next. They nonetheless voice a fear that a world that so easily eludes such flights of fancy might prove tedious when translated into forms of language.[22]

---

20 Vol. II, p. 421; vol. I, p. 262; see also, for example, vol. II, p. 436. Wright refers to *An Account of some of the Statues, Bas-Reliefs, Drawings and Pictures in Italy, &c with Remarks* (1722), by the Jonathan Richardsons, Senior and Junior.

21 Walpole, *Yale Edition*, vol. XIII, p. 222; letter to Richard West, headed 'Naples. June 14, 1740 N.S.'; see also vol. XIII, pp. 206–7, 209 (letter to West, written jointly by Walpole and Thomas Gray, and headed 'Rome, April 16, 1740, N.S.'), for further allusions to the danger of repetition. William Bromley, describing his visit to Rome at the end of the seventeenth century, already envisages the possibility that readers might fear repetition, but dismisses this fear, noting that 'Travellers Observations do as much differ as their Genius's, and what one slights as trivial, escapes not the other's Notice' (*Remarks*, pp. 154–5).

22 Cascardi, *The Subject of Modernity*, p. 120; see Cascardi's chapter on 'The Theory of the Novel and the Autonomy of Art', pp. 72–124.

Travellers also obliquely register an anxiety that the topography mapped out by the eye-witness – a subject of commentary deprived of opportunities for rhetorical extravagance, and stolidly resistant to the illusions and distortions of the imagination – might fail to generate hyperboles. Lady Miller, in Genoa, demonstrates the expendability of hyperbole to the traveller intent upon claiming the authority of on-the-spot observation when she observes: 'Upon the whole, I own the idea I had acquired in England, of the wretched situation of a galley-slave, was exaggerated, perhaps by my own imagination's forming a picture much too strong from what I had read or heard.'[23] While often disowning any susceptibility to 'exaggerated' fictionalizing, eighteenth-century traveller-narrators nonetheless continue to assume that hyperbole is one of the tropes most urgently necessary to them. Fielding, in the 'Author's Preface' to *The Journal of a Voyage to Lisbon*, outlines the problems of the traveller who is expected to establish a claim to first-hand observation, but finds the commentary of sober veracity discomfitingly tame, and hankers quixotically after 'the wonderful'. The novelist, assuming this rhetorical dilemma to be more or less universal and unchanging, comments ironically, but forgivingly, on those travel writers who achieve hyperbole at the expense of trustworthiness, and invent for themselves more exciting and dramatic objects than their topographies of foreignness supply:

> What motive a man can have to sit down, and to draw forth a list of stupid, senseless, incredible lies upon paper, would be difficult to determine, did not Vanity present herself so immediately as the adequate cause. The vanity of knowing more than other men is, perhaps, besides hunger, the only inducement to writing, at least to publishing, at all. Why then should not the voyage-writer be inflamed with the glory of having seen what no man ever did or will see but himself? This is the true source of the wonderful in the discourse and writings, and sometimes, I believe, in the actions of men.[24]

Fielding pointedly fails to extend the same indulgent understanding towards travellers who fail to show a proper commitment to hyperbole, but 'waste their time and paper with recording things and facts of so common a kind, that they challenge no other right of being remembered than as they had the honour of having happened to the author, to whom nothing seems trivial that in any manner happens to himself'. He cites the 'ignorant

23 Miller, *Letters*, vol. I, p. 131; for an early example of this trope, see Misson's rejection of the hyperbolic style that, he argues, other travellers learn from the Italians, in the (unpaginated) 'Avertissement' at the beginning of his *Nouveau voyage d'Italie*.

24 Fielding, *Jonathan Wild and The Journal of a Voyage to Lisbon*, p. 187.

pedant', Mr Tickletext, in Aphra Behn's *The Feigned Courtesans* (1679), as an example of a traveller who, 'before his departure from a town, calls for his journal to record the goodness of the wine and tabacco, with other articles of the same importance, which are to furnish the materials of a voyage at his return home'.[25]

Censure: excess and transgression

A transmutation of one of the major themes of travel writing does, however, provide a means of rescuing the topography of the Grand Tour from the prosaic, while at the same time maintaining a commitment to verisimilitude: from around the 1720s onwards, travellers begin to construct elaborate visions of Italy as a *mise-en-scène* of the forbidden, by transforming the theme of excess into the theme of double excess, or transgression. An act of transgression is presented, within the context of Italian society and manners, as an excess of licence produced by an excess of restraint. In other words, it now becomes possible to define Italian immoderation as an aspect of society and manners that invites curious enquiry, rather than simply exhibiting itself as yet another aspect of the natural excessiveness of the country. As a result, travel writings embark on more lengthy analyses of such immoderation – and so produce an effect of more dramatic censoriousness.

Two specific instances of improper restraint, within the topography of the Grand Tour, are seen as producing a proliferation of improper licence: the forms of restraint located within the customs of monasticism and cicisbeism. In analyses of these customs, women are assigned the role of transgressors much more frequently than men; since females are assumed to be everywhere subject to greater restriction and limitation than males, their transgressions can be invested with greater drama, as instances of the more powerful impulse required in order to infringe prohibitions enforced with greater rigour. When commenting on monasticism, for example, travellers focus on nuns far more often than on monks: eighteenth-century travel writings attack very strongly the parental and priestly tyranny which consigns young girls to a life of celibacy, imposing on them a prohibition so unnatural and severe that it positively invites infringement. Wright tells the story of an acquaintance who, when visiting a convent, encounters a nun, 'detain'd there contrary to her Inclinations': the unhappy woman 'came, in a perfectly frantick manner, into the *Parlatorio*, tearing her Hair, and making hideous Complaints, and crying, *Pregate Dio per mi' son' desperata*. "Pray to God for

25 *Ibid.*, pp. 187–8; see above, pp. 24–5.

me, I am in Despair.'" Having established that monasticism entails
misplaced and cruel restrictions, the traveller speculates on the reaction
which such restrictions may provoke: "tis certainly a most grievous
Hardship upon these poor Creatures (whether menaced or decoy'd into
Profession, at an Age they cannot judge what they are doing) to keep them
there afterwards contrary to their Inclination, and perhaps the violent
Impulses of a Constitution, which may become more rebellious through the
Notion of a perpetual Restraint.'[26]

The other major example of an improper freedom produced by an
improper restraint that is cited in eighteenth-century travel writings is the
custom of cicisbeism, by which a married woman is expected to find a man
other than her husband to escort her to social occasions, and spend much
of his time with her. (Unsurprisingly, the precise role of the cicisbeo was
the object of an enormous amount of speculation by English and French
travellers.) The excess of restraint that prompts the excess of licence is
most frequently located, in eighteenth-century writings, within the
restrictions placed upon young girls: their education in convents, secluded
from the pleasures of society, and the arranged marriages that are imposed
upon them: 'their being led to the altar as victims, for sacrifice to any disagreeable wretch their parents think proper to bestow them upon', as Lady
Miller puts it.[27] Watkins's *Travels* constructs a direct contrast between
extreme harshness and extreme 'liberty':

> Before marriage their women are nuns, and after it libertines. At twelve
> years they are immured in a convent, from which there is no return, but
> upon the hard condition of receiving from their parents a husband whom
> they have never seen. If dissatisfied with him (as it generally happens) they
> are at liberty (from universal custom) to chuse their *Cavalieri Serventi*, or
> *Cecisbèi*, who attend them to all public places, for the husbands dare not,
> assist at their toilette, and, in a word, do every thing they are ordered; for
> which the ladies sacrifice their own virtue, and their husband's honour.[28]

A second plot of restraint and licence that is also employed to explain cicisbeism, sometimes alongside the first, classifies the licentious excesses of
the Italians as the product of an absence of political freedom, which prevents men from entering public life, and confines them to a feminized

---

26 Wright, *Some Observations*, vol. I, p. 229. See, too, Brooke, *Observations*, pp. 112–13. For
    speculations on the reactions of nuns to the 'restraint' placed upon them, within the
    'seducing climate' of Campania, see Moore, *View of Society*, vol. II, pp. 313–15.

27 Miller, *Letters*, vol. II, p. 61.

28 Vol. II, pp. 371–2.

domain of frivolity and flirtation. Moore explains that, in 'despotic states... where it is dangerous to speak or write on general politics... love becomes a first, instead of being a secondary object... and on this account women are the objects of greater attention and respect in despotic than in free countries'. 'Most Englishmen', Moore observes, 'will be astonished how men can pass so much of their time with women.' He explains this phenomenon:

> This, however, will appear less surprising, when they recollect that the Italian nobility dare not intermeddle in politics; can find no employment in the army or navy; and that there are no such amusements in the country as hunting or drinking... Even an Englishman, in those desperate circumstances, might be driven to the company and conversation of women, to lighten the burden of time.[29]

The use of the theme of excess to invest the topography with drama is extended in another way in eighteenth-century travel writing: immoderation is now located not only in society and manners, and in the natural world, but also in works of art, which are previously defined as instances of incomparability or profusion, rather than unrestraint. Travel writings, around the middle of the century, begin to focus on scenes of violence – especially on martyrdoms, which can be defined, explicitly or implicitly, as part of a meretricious theatrical spectacle stage-managed by the Roman Catholic church.[30] Earlier descriptions of such paintings register little interest in the narrative content of the scenes depicted: the Marquis de Seignelay's account of the paintings in St Peter's, as viewed in 1671, lists a representation of violence with breezy unconcern, as a work equivalent in its beauty to others with quite different narrative preoccupations: 'Sur tous les autels de l'église, il y a de fort beaux tableaux: les principaux sont un du Guerchin, qui est une Vierge qu'on enterre; *un de Poussin, qui est Saint Érasme à qui on arrache les boyaux;* un du cavalier Bernin, qui est une Vierge qu'on présente au juge...' (Figure 2).[31]

---

29 Moore, *View of Society*, vol. II, pp. 398–9, 416. Within this second plot of constraint and excess, it is often suggested that male attentiveness towards women is not only the product of political servitude but itself entails an improper degree of servility. See *ibid.*, vol. II, pp. 409–10, Watkins, *Travels*, vol. II, p. 372, and Montesquieu, *Voyages*, vol. II, p. 293.

30 See, for example, Smollett, *Travels*, p. 257.

31 Seignelay, *L'Italie en 1671*, p. 145; emphasis added: 'On all the altars of the church, there are extremely beautiful paintings: the main works are one by Guercino, which depicts the burial of the Virgin; one by Poussin, which depicts St Erasmus, with executioners tearing out his entrails; one by the Cavaliere Bernini, which is the Virgin being presented to the judge...'

Figure 2 Nicolas Poussin, *The Martyrdom of St Erasmus*, engraved by Guglielmo Mitelli; 41.9 x 27 cm.

Late eighteenth-century commentaries, on the other hand, strongly emphasize the narratives of blood and suffering that such works represent. In doing so, they classify these paintings (or, occasionally, sculptures) as excessive in two ways. First, they define the inner body, in the painting, as indecorously exceeding its proper boundary – the skin of the outer body – and placing itself on display. Secondly, they imply that such indecorum produces an excess of effect – that it impinges too uncomfortably on the imagination of the beholder. Thomas Gray, in his notes on Poussin's *Martyrdom of St Erasmus*, one of the paintings described by Seignelay, deplores, at some length, the impropriety of representing such a scene of blood:

> I do not apprehend why a scene, that on account of its horror (even suppos-
> ing it capable of being ever so lively represented,) would be utterly improp-
> er to introduce in a drama... should be thought a fit subject to be set before
> the eyes in a picture; in the present case, the saint is extended on his back in
> all the paleness and agonies of so terrible a death; a hardened ruffian is tear-
> ing out his entrails, which are wound round a wooden roller by another; the
> expression of men inured to blood, and cruel by habit, as strongly painted in
> their faces and attitudes as possible; a priest of Hercules in white drapery (a
> noble figure) is pointing to a statue of that god, and trying to instil his faith
> into the poor sufferer: several other figures, larger than life.[32]

Impulsive spontaneity

In this account of excess of effect, the traveller's reference to the immediate impact of the scene of horror, as it is 'set before the eyes', explains and
endorses his hyperboles. After 1750 or so, travel writings frequently define
such immediacy as both demanding and authenticating hyperbolic forms
of language. Moving beyond the mere claim that he or she has viewed the
objects of commentary on the spot, the traveller often claims to be com-
posing this commentary in the presence of these objects. In Sterne's
Sentimental Journey, the excitement of a commentary composed in the
heat of the moment is hyperbolically affirmed when some curious
Englishmen observe that the carriage in which Yorick is sitting has actually
been thrown into motion – a motion that he attributes to 'the agitation...
of writing a preface'.[33] Dupaty, in his account of the *Venus de' Medici*,

---

[32] *Works*, IV, 251; Gray's notes were compiled during or after his travels in 1739 and 1740.
[33] p. 13.

declares: 'Je suis assis devant elle, la plume à la main.'[34] Piozzi, listing antiquities around Naples, literally deploys on-the-spot immediacy to exclude any suspicion of the prosaic: demanding 'who can write prose however in such places!', she exclaims: '- let the impossibility of expressing my thoughts any other way excuse the following VERSES.'[35]

The claim to on-the-spot composition is established, in many commentaries, through an exclamatory, loosely structured syntax that mimics the informality of speech, and so produces the effect of a reaction voiced in the actual presence of the objects of commentary – particularly when combined with words such as *here* and *now*, which establish a common space in which both the subject and the objects are located. 'But here's Guercino's sweet returning Prodigal, and here is a *Madonna disperata* bursting as from a cavern to embrace the body of her dead son and saviour', cries Piozzi, in the Palazzo Colonna, in Rome (Figure 3); when describing antiquities around Naples, she manages to employ the word *here* eight times in two sentences.[36] At Tivoli, Dupaty observes excitedly: 'Tout-à-coup le temple de Vesta et celui de la Sybille se montrent. Que l'œil tourne avec plaisir autour de ces belles colonnes!' Similarly exclamatory formulations mark his encounters with an *Assumption* by Guido Reni in Genoa: 'C'est là une Vierge! Ce sont-là des anges! C'est-là monter vers le ciel!', with the beauty of the women of Rome ('Quel teint!... Quel incarnat!'), and with the Coliseum ('Que l'ennui romain était féroce! On ne pouvait l'amuser qu'avec du sang').[37]

---

34 Dupaty, *Lettres*, vol. I, p. 146; Povoleri's translation, however, abandons this immediacy: 'I sat down before her with a pen in my hand' (vol. I, p. 115).

35 Piozzi, *Observations*, vol. II, pp. 8–9 ('VERSES' is printed on a new line, as the title to the poem that follows).

36 *Ibid.*, vol. I, p. 425 (Piozzi describes the first of these paintings at greater length when discussing Leandro Bassano's treatment of the same subject: vol. II, p. 188); vol. II, p. 8. For an early example of a syntax of this kind, in the relatively informal genre of the letter, see Walpole, describing the mountains of Savoy: 'Precipices, mountains, torrents, wolves, rumblings, Salvator Rosa —— the pomp of our park, and the meekness of our palace!' (Walpole, *Yale Edition*, vol. XIII, p. 181; letter to Richard West, dated 'Sept. 28, 1739, N.S.').

37 Dupaty, *Lettres*, vol. I, p. 250: 'Behold! on a sudden the temple of Vesta and that of the Sybil appear! With what transports does the eye wander around these beautiful columns! With what extasy does it gaze!' (vol. I, pp. 193–4); vol. I, pp. 28–9: 'What a Madonna! What angels! – they are real ones; and that is certainly the way to mount to heaven!' (vol. I, p. 25); vol. I, p. 285; 'What a complexion!... What a vermilion!' (vol. I, p. 221); vol. II, p. 62: 'Heavens! How sullen and savage must the Roman *ennui* have been! Nothing but effusion of blood could dissipate or amuse it' (vol. II, p. 43).

Figure 3 Guercino, *Madonna Disperata*, engraved by Luigi Cunego; 43.2 x 26.4 cm.

This rhetoric of the here and now sometimes follows a narrative of accumulation of pleasure, as the traveller progresses from sight to sight. Piozzi, at various points in her *Observations and Reflections*, invests the rhetoric of on-the-spot observation with added drama by appending the term *too* to each exclamation, as though yet further gratification might prove too overwhelming to endure. 'A St. John too, by dear Guercino, transcendent!', she cries, in the Palazzo Barberini, in Rome. 'Such a sky too!', she exclaims, in the description of Guercino's '*Madonna disperata* '(Figure 3); admiring 'a resurrection of Lazarus, by Leandro Bassano', at Capo di Monte, in Naples, she adds: 'the restored Lazarus too – an apparent corpse, re-awakened suddenly to a thousand sensations at once, wonder, gratitude, and affectionate delight!' The same sense of frenzied accumulation is imprinted on her final summary of the sights of that city ('Vesuvius too'), and on her survey of the ancient ruins in its environs ('The end of Caligula's bridge too, but that they say is not his bridge, but a mole built by some succeeding emperor – a madder or a wickeder it could not be...).[38]

This exclamatory syntax – in Piozzi's narrative and in others – invests the topography with the drama required as an endorsement for hyperbolic language simply by classifying the objects of commentary as gratifyingly 'striking': each exclamation mark affirms that the traveller-spectator has been 'struck'. The exclamation operates as a powerful hyperbolic device even in the context of a mere catalogue of objects: an entry in Thomas Martyn's *Gentleman's Guide in his Tour through Italy* (1787) registers a discreet excitement in 'the assumption... with thirteen figures as large as life' when it concludes the listing: 'by Salvator Rosa!'.[39] Where exclamation marks are deployed as quantifications of enthusiasm – as they are, most notably, in Mariana Starke's *Letters from Italy* (1800) – their very arithmetical conciseness produces the impression that the traveller is referring in code to a pleasure too intense to express directly, and so adds yet greater hyperbolic force to the commentary. Starke's account of 'the Palace of Marcellino Durazzo', in Genoa, includes the cumulatively exclamatory sequence: 'a very fine collection of pictures, the most striking of which are, Seneca dying! – Clorinda delivering Olinda and Sophronia!! – and Phineas thrown down by Medusa's head, all three by L. Giordano – and the Magdalene at our Saviour's feet, by Rubens!!!'[40]

---

38 Vol. I, pp. 419, 425; vol. II, pp. 79–80, 86, 8.

39 p. 77.

40 Vol. I, p. 188. See also Morgan, *Italy*, vol. II, pp. 177 (describing the Capitoline Museum, in Rome): 'Of this collection it is sufficient to say, that it contains the FAUN! – the GLADIATOR! and the ANTINOUS!!!'

Intense responsiveness: blushing, weeping, trembling

The rhetoric of spontaneity proclaims not only the immediacy of the response but also its intensity; it positions the subject of commentary as one who is not simply viewing but also responding. The hyperbole of inexpressibility, with which this chapter began, establishes a similar position for the speaking subject; an exclamatory syntax, in fact, is often used to suggest emotions that elude expression, as in Piozzi's comment on the famous Aurora in the casino of the Villa Ludovisi, in Rome: 'But Guercino is *such* a painter!'.[41] (Anna Jameson, viewing Mount Vesuvius, combines on-the-spot spontaneity with a variant on inexpressibility when she declares: 'I can hardly write, my mind is so overflowing with astonishment, admiration, and sublime pleasure.')[42] Such displays of responsiveness, in the late eighteenth and early nineteenth centuries, are, of course, not confined to accounts of the foreign.[43] Intense emotional responses, however, fulfil at least three rhetorical functions that make them especially useful in travel writing. First, they supply a way of avoiding repetition – or, at least, of appearing to do so: by defining the commentary as the product of his or her own personal feelings, the traveller is able to differentiate it from the commentaries of previous travel writers. Sydney Morgan, in *Italy* (1821), voices the assumption that responsiveness invests the commentary with a redeeming individuality when, designating Naples as 'an exhausted subject', she observes: 'to the traveller of the present day nothing is left, but cautiously and briefly to obtrude upon the reader some object of overwhelming importance, whose impression is deep-seated, and whose description, if not new, may at least not be languid.'[44]

Secondly, intense responses endorse the traveller's status as an eye-witness; expressions of 'private sentiments' emphasize very strongly that the traveller has actually gone in person to observe the object described. John Moore explicitly links feeling to on-the-spot viewing when, after noting the grace, elegance, 'mild persuasive devotion' and 'inviting loveliness' of figures in Guido Reni's paintings, he declares: 'It requires no knowledge in the art of painting, no connoisseurship, to discover those beauties in the works of Guido; all who have eyes, and a heart, must see and feel them.'[45] Byron's

---

41 Piozzi, *Observations*, vol. I, pp. 413–14.

42 Jameson, *Diary*, p. 226.

43 For an account of the late eighteenth-century 'fixation upon tears, sighs, and meanings beyond words', within a wider context, see Mullan, *Sentiment and Sociability* (p. 16).

44 Vol. II, pp. 337, 338.

45 Moore, *View of Society*, vol. I, p. 311.

commentary on the *Venus de' Medici* in Canto IV of *Childe Harold's Pilgrimage* also invokes emotion as an adjunct to vision: rejecting 'the paltry jargon of the marble mart', the traveller-narrator proclaims: 'we have eyes: / Blood – pulse – and breast, confirm the Dardan Shepherd's prize.'[46]

Thirdly, such a display of emotional and sensory susceptibility produces a new proliferation of hyperbole; it affirms that the topography can always be rescued from the glumly prosaic effects of eye-witness verisimilitude by the transformatory powers of the emotions and imagination. An especially dramatic hyperbole of responsiveness is produced by the claim that an object of commentary has excited a reaction so strong that it manifests itself physically – as in Byron's reference to his 'blood' and 'pulse'. Dupaty, in the Uffizi, proclaims archly: 'N'entrez jamais dans le cabinet de l'hermaphrodite, si vous ne voulez pas rougir de plaisir et de honte tout-à-la fois.'[47] Vestiges of the ancient past are routinely presented as provoking fits of lachrymosity, as the traveller reflects on the gap between past and present. 'I am almost in tears, when I sit down to write to you of Vespasian's amphitheatre,' says Thomas Broderick, at the Coliseum.[48] 'Mais c'est ici, madame la comtesse, c'est ici où le cœur se fend, ou les larmes coulent malgré soi, lorsqu'on voit ce fameux temple... aujourd'hui changé en une malheureuse église nue et dépouillée,' declares de Sade, at the Pantheon.[49]

Works of art that depict scenes of violence, cruelty or suffering – those works to which the theme of excess is now extended – are regularly singled out as producing physical reactions of disgust and horror. At times, travellers claim to have experienced responses of trembling and shuddering – as in Anne Miller's dramatic account of Caravaggio's *Judith and Holofernes*:

> A Judith in the act of cutting off Holofernes's head. This picture is too well done; it struck me directly, that it must have been taken from the life. The idea threw me into a trembling, and made me very sick; producing the same effects upon me, that perhaps I might have experienced from the presence of a real execution: the separation of the neck, the force she uses, the spouting of the blood from the divided arteries, and her countenance, whilst she turns

46 Canto IV, stanza 50, line 7, lines 8–9; in Byron, *Complete Poetical Works*, vol. II, p. 141.

47 Dupaty, *Lettres*, vol. I, p. 154; 'Never enter the cabinet of the *hermaphrodite*, if you do not wish to blush for pleasure and shame at the same instant' (vol. I, p. 121).

48 Broderick, *Travels*, vol. II, p. 69.

49 Sade, *Voyage d'Italie*, p. 225: 'But it is here, madame la comtesse, it is here that the heart breaks and the tears flow, despite my efforts to stop them, when I see this famous temple... now changed into a miserable, naked, despoiled church.'

away her face from the dreadful work she is about, and which nevertheless
expresses a fierceness and a sort of courage little befitting a woman, joined
with the writhing convulsions of the body of Holofernes, make it a picture
quite improper for the inspection of those who have any degree of feeling.[50]

The physical reaction to such scenes most commonly noted, however, consists merely of an involuntary aversion of the gaze: Miller comments on
Luca Giordano's painting of 'Jezebel devoured by dogs': 'The history it
represents is so horrible, that although I am perfectly convinced one might,
by considering it, have discovered great merit, yet, after a cursory view, I
could not bring myself to dwell upon the representation of a catastrophe
attended with so many disgusting circumstances.'[51] Piozzi describes 'an
Egyptian Mary by Spagnolet, too terrifying to look long at'.[52] The need to
look away is, in some commentaries, elaborated in a way that allows the traveller to claim the work in question as a source of pleasure at the same time
that he or she expresses horror: Arthur Young, in Bologna, remarks: 'A
slaughter of the Innocents, by Guido, which will command attention, how
little inclined soever you may be to give it' (Figure 4).[53] Sydney Morgan,
describing this same painting, charts a variant on the same equivocation:
'There is in this sublime composition so much to melt and to horrify, that it
is often left and often returned to.'[54] Anna Jameson, at the Chapel of San
Severo, in Naples, cites the power of a sculpture to drive the spectator away
as proof of a similarly striking combination of pain and pleasure: after luke-
warm praise of two of the famous works in the Chapel, she observes: 'The
Dead Christ covered with a veil, by Corradini, has merit of a higher class: it
is most painful to look upon; and affected me so strongly, that I was obliged
to leave the church, and go into the air.'[55]

As these commentaries suggest, the very excess that eighteenth-century and early nineteenth-century travel writings locate in such scenes, and
describe censoriously, is also overtly recognized as supplying a pleasurable
drama. Travellers often trace out a similar equivocation between censure

---

[50] Miller, *Letters*, vol. II, pp. 27–8.

[51] *Ibid.*, vol. I, pp. 256–7.

[52] Piozzi, *Observations*, vol. II, p. 83. Piozzi views this painting in Dresden, but in identifying it as the work of Jusepe Ribera, known as 'Spagnolet', or 'Lo Spagnoletto', who
worked in Naples, she implicitly classifies it as representative of Italian art in its immoderate terror.

[53] Young, *Travels*, vol. I, p. 249.

[54] Morgan, *Italy*, vol. I, p. 297.

[55] Jameson, *Diary*, p. 254. The *Veiled Christ* is usually attributed to Giuseppe Sanmartino,
working from an *abbozzo* by Antonio Corradini.

Au Guide Eglise de S.ᵗ Dominique a Bologne.

Fragonard . del.

Saint Non Sc 1772

Figure 4 Guido Reni, *The Massacre of the Innocents*, aquatint by Jean Claude Richard de Saint–Non, from a drawing by Jean-Baptiste Fragonard, in Saint-Non, *Fragments Choisis dans les peintures et les tableaux les plus intéressans des palais et des églises de l'Italie* ([Paris?,] 1772–5); 18.5 x 12cm.

and pleasure by describing themselves as simultaneously repelled by narratives of violence, cruelty and suffering and attracted by the formal qualities (such as force of expression, or strong contrasts of light and shade),
that are seen as characteristic of works that depict scenes of this kind.[56]

Feminized responsiveness and manly restraint

In late eighteenth-century and early nineteenth-century European literature, as in many other cultural contexts, responsiveness is marked as a feminized quality. Yorick, at Calais, proclaiming his susceptibility to feeling in
a reference to his later visit to the grave of Father Lorenzo (a monk whom
he treats first rudely and then apologetically), declares that various features of the scene 'all struck together so forcibly upon my affections, that I
burst into a flood of tears', and adds: '- *but I am as weak as a woman;* and I
beg the world not to smile, but pity me'.[57] Sydney Morgan, embarking on
her account of Milan, claims a heightened susceptibility to 'the influence
of sentiment', and specifically defines this 'bias of affections' as gendered:

> The very name of this city, as I write it, awakens feelings which the impar-
> tiality of veracious narrative should distrust. From pages like the present,
> the bias of affections and the influence of sentiment should be excluded. I
> trust, however, that in a woman's work, sex may plead its privilege; and that
> if the heart will occasionally make itself a party in the *concern,* its intrusions
> may be pardoned, as long as the facts detailed are backed, beyond the pos-
> sibility of dispute, by the authority of contemporary testimonies.[58]

---

[56] See Smollett, *Travels*, p. 278, for an account of 'a picture, by Carlo Maratti, representing
a saint calling down lightning from heaven to destroy blasphemers', in which the traveller
describes the surroundings of the saint as 'tame enough', and comments: 'I imagine
Salvator Rosa would have made a different disposition on the same subject: that amidst
the darkness of a tempest, he would have illuminated the blasphemer with the flash of
lightning by which he was destroyed: this would have thrown a dismal gleam upon his
countenance, distorted by the horror of his situation as well as by the effects of the fire;
and rendered the whole scene dreadfully picturesque.' For an analysis of the rhetoric of
horror, terror, disgust and pleasure in eighteenth-century commentary on art in Italy, see
Chard, 'Horror on the Grand Tour', pp. 3–16.
    The ease with which works repudiated as indecorously immoderate can also be
acclaimed as enthralling is demonstrated by commentaries that manage, unselfcon-
sciously, to transmute the censure of earlier commentaries into expressions of pleasure
and praise. Compare, for example the accounts of Salvator Rosa's *Job* in Weston,
Viaggiana, p. 75 and Piozzi, *Observations*, vol. II, p. 141, and the descriptions of
Veronese's *Judith and Holofernes* in Cochin, *Voyage d'Italie*, vol. III, p. 157 and Gibbon,
Gibbon's Journey, p. 74.

[57] Sterne, *A Sentimental Journey*, p. 21; emphasis added.

[58] Morgan, *Italy*, vol. I, p. 71.

At the same time, the display of a feminized responsiveness is assumed to be readily compatible with manly restraint – an attribute located, in part, in the sincerity and simplicity which guarantee that responsiveness will not spill over into effusiveness. Travellers often carefully place their own heightened responsiveness in opposition to the effeminate tendency towards excessive indulgence of the passions that is attributed to the inhabitants of the warm South. Dupaty explicitly defines the Neapolitans as failing utterly in sincerity and depth of feeling, however readily they express emotion: in Naples, he claims, 'la sensibilité est machinale. A l'aspect de l'homme assassiné et de l'assassin, c'est par le premier que la pitié commence; mais elle passe, bientôt, au second.'[59] Gothic novels, in dramatizing the horrors of southern, Roman Catholic Europe, constantly establish oppositions between the restrained and discriminating exercise of the sentiments, typifying the traveller who approaches the warm South from a position of cautious detachment, and the immoderate indulgence of the passions that characterizes the Italians themselves. Ann Radcliffe's *Mysteries of Udolpho* (1794) establishes an especially crisp distinction between the 'fierce and terrible passions' that 'so often agitated the inhabitants' of the Castle of Udolpho, and, on the other hand, the heroine's 'silent anguish, weeping, yet enduring; not the wild energy of passion, inflaming imagination, bearing down the barriers of reason and living in a world of its own.'[60] As Anne Vincent-Buffault argues, in her *History of Tears*, 'the exaltation which led to the shedding of tears, and the moderation which withheld them, were both curiously part of the same movement, of the same economy of the imagination'.[61]

One of the instances of mingled susceptibility and restraint that Vincent-Buffault cites is, tellingly, that of a Northern European traveller on the Grand Tour, making a strong impression on an Italian woman precisely by virtue of his distinctness from her fellow-countrymen: towards the beginning of Germaine de Staël's novel *Corinne; ou, l'Italie* (1807), the narrator describes the effect of the Scotsman Oswald, Lord Nelvil, upon the eponymous heroine:

> Elle étoit accoutumée aux hommages vifs et flatteurs des Italiens; mais la dignité des manières d'Oswald, son apparente froideur, et sa sensibilité, qui se trahissoit malgré lui, exerçoient sur l'imagination une bien plus grande

59 Dupaty, *Lettres*, vol. II, p. 222: 'Sensibility is but mechanical. At the sight of a murdered man, and the murderer, pity will shew itself for the former, but soon declare for the latter' (vol. II, p. 160).
60 p. 329.
61 p. 110.

puissance. Jamais il ne racontoit une action généreuse, jamais il ne parloit d'un malheur, sans que ses yeux se remplissent de larmes, et toujours il chercoit à cacher son émotion.[62]

'Silly affectations'

In order to claim the manly quality of sincerity, the subject of responsiveness has to allay the suspicion that he or she might be exhibiting a fault to which travellers are seen as especially vulnerable: affectation. Hester Piozzi, in a letter to her daughter, acknowledges the danger of affectation that the Grand Tour brings in its wake, but pointedly mentions her own 'real, & true, & unaffected Delight' at the works of Guido Reni, and argues robustly that the example of the Italians themselves demonstrates that it is in fact possible to approach Italian art directly and sincerely:

> Affectation after all (tho' many People may bring it home with 'em) is certainly no Plant of this Country's Growth: the Folks here live and die quite their own way, & not having any Taste of ridiculing others, or any fear of being ridiculed, behave naturally, & never pretend to be sorry when sad, or insensible when really diverted.[63]

As this commentary suggests, affectation is defined as a particular danger to any traveller venturing to express responses towards works of art. John Moore, mocking travellers who evince hyperbolic horror at scenes of violence, stoutly affirms his own unpretentious common sense:

> I only say for myself, that, on contemplating a painted tragedy, I can never help recollecting that it is acted upon canvas. This never fails to dart such a ray of comfort into my heart, as cheers it up, in spite of all the blood and carnage I see before my eyes. With a mind so vulgarly fabricated, you will not be surprised when I acknowledge, that I have felt more compassion at the sight of a single highwayman going to Tyburn, than at the massacre of two thousand innocents, though executed by Nicholas Poussin himself. This convinces me that I am not endued with the organs of a connoisseur.[64]

---

62 Vol. I, p. 83 (book IV, chapter 1): 'She was accustomed to the lively and flattering tributes of the Italians; but the lordly deportment and apparent coldness of Oswald, through which his tenderness of heart so often broke, in spite of himself, exercised a far greater power o'er her imagination. He never related a generous deed or a tale of misfortune, but his eyes filled, though he strove to hide this weakness' (*Corinne; or, Italy*, p. 25.)

63 Piozzi, *The Piozzi Letters*, vol. I, p. 188. See also, Piozzi, *Observations*, vol. I, p. 250.

64 Moore, *View of Society*, vol I, pp. 62–3. Moore draws on Edmund Burke's comparison of a theatrical production of a tragedy with an execution: see Burke, *Philosophical Enquiry*, p. 47.

The rhetoric of mingled pain and pleasure supplies Moore with further instances of absurdity; he parodies the words of 'a gentleman who affected an enthusiastic passion for the fine arts':

> The Virgin, you'll observe, gentlemen, is only fainting, but the Christ is quite dead. Look at the arm, did you ever see any thing so dead?... – Pray, gentlemen, observe this St. Sebastian, how delightfully he expires: Don't you all feel the arrow in your hearts? I'm sure I feel it in mine. Do let us move on; I should die with agony if I looked any longer.[65]

Whereas the subject of sincere responsiveness is defined as feminized yet manly, then, the subject of affected effusiveness is defined as feminized in a way that renders him or her incapable of manliness. The distinction between the two positions is explicitly established in an attack on 'silly affectations' in responses to art, in James Barry's *Inquiry into the Real and Imaginary Obstructions to the Acquisition of the Arts in England* (1775). Barry, like Moore, links effusiveness to a facile deployment of hyperbole in response to scenes of suffering:

> There is another piece of ridiculous nicety, observable in our age and nation, which better times have been strangers to; we affect such nice feelings and so much sensibility, as not to be able to bear the sight of pictures where the action turns upon any circumstance of distress; we have such extreme good-nature as to turn off with disgust from the whole class of affecting subjects that agitate and call forth our feeling for the distresses of our species, and which the wisest nations have ever regarded, as the noblest, most useful, and most interesting subjects, both for painting and poetry: we mistake grossly in this matter; the best natured people are the furthest from being disgusted with such subjects; and this is so known and so decided a truth, that many excellent writers, from Aristotle down to our own times, have endeavoured to explain and account for the satisfaction and melancholly pleasure the mind receives in such tragical representations.[66]

The painter emphasizes, at this point, that it is not responsiveness itself that compromises the spectator's authority: on the contrary, those devoid of affectation will evince intense responses of their own.

> Who that has ever seen the expiring Laocoon and his children, the plague of Poussin, the death of Ananias by Rafaelle, the possessed boy by Domenichino, the Conversion of S. Bruno by Le Sueur, or even the

---

65 Moore, *View of Society*, vol. I, pp. 64, 65.

66 pp. 156–7.

S. Cecilia by Maderna; what person, of fine feelings, has ever beheld these, and many other similar pictures, without an extreme pleasure?[67]

Barry then concludes his attack by establishing an elision between affectation and an insipid, trivializing version of the feminine – the version to which Mary Wollstonecraft refers when she discusses the influences that turn women into 'creatures of sensation', and encourage them to develop an 'overstretched sensibility', which 'naturally relaxes the other powers of the mind, and prevents intellect from attaining that sovereignty which it ought to attain'.[68] The painter declares: 'I am ashamed to be obliged to combat such silly affectations, they are beneath men who have either head or heart; they are unworthy of women, who have either education or simplicity of manners; they would disgrace even waiting-maids and sentimental milliners.'[69] On the one hand, then, he carefully specifies that both male and female spectators are capable of manly sincerity: women 'who have either education or simplicity of manners' may, like 'men who have either head or heart', rise above affectation. On the other hand, the feminized character of affected emotion is reaffirmed by the assumption that the spectators most susceptible to mawkishness are female: women, when unredeemed by education, are cited as beings from whom little simplicity or sincerity can be expected.

Affectation, however, is located in other qualities as well as effusiveness. The Marquis of Normanby, in one of the sketches in *The English in Italy* (1825), once again presents woman as especially prone to 'affected and ridiculous' language and behaviour, but at the same time indicates a range of different ways in which travellers may diverge from manly restraint and judgement:

Travel... is the hot-bed of affectation; if there be a seed, a germ of it in the disposition, travel will force it to the light, and it is for this reason that womankind are so rarely improved by seeing foreign countries, and return in general so much more affected and ridiculous. Mankind still is far from proof; and he really is one of exemplary sagacity, who doth not return from abroad to his friends at home, with some strange whim or affectation, that but for his voyaging would have remained totally undeveloped. Some go forth ignorant, and return pedantic and over-learned; some go forth regular and moral, and return gallants and libertines; some leave England as saints,

---

67 *Ibid.*, p. 157.
68 Wollstonecraft, *A Vindication*, p. 152.
69 Barry, *Inquiry*, pp. 157–8.

and return to it infidels: others set out thorough John Bulls, contemning and denouncing every object they meet abroad, and return utter Jack Sprats to do the same by every thing they meet in England; the very opposite of their case, *vice versâ*, is no uncommon consequence of tourification.[70]

Such diversity of perils allows travellers to fend off any suspicion of feminized effusiveness, and affirm that responsiveness is in fact perfectly compatible with manly sincerity, by citing some form of affectation, to which the commentary of response can be shown to be sharply opposed. Accounts of works of art very often designate connoisseurs, or other categories of spectators who claim specialized expertise, as affected not because they are effusive but because they are coldly pedantic, pretending not to emotion but to knowledge and critical skills. This strategy is deployed in several of the commentaries quoted above: Moore's declaration that 'it requires no knowledge in the art of painting, no connoisseurship, to discover those beauties in the works of Guido', for example, and Byron's impassioned rejection of 'the paltry jargon of the marble mart'.[71] Piozzi, too, in her account of Bassano's *Raising of Lazarus*, cited above as an example of the commentary of impulsive spontaneity, perceives the usefulness of invoking the frigid formulations of those who claim specialized critical expertise, in order to invest intense responsiveness with simplicity and sincerity. She concludes contemptuously: '– How can one coldly sit to hear the connoisseurs *admire the folds of the drapery?* '[72]

Landscape: sublimity displaces gastronomy

In accounts of the natural scenery encountered by travellers on the Grand Tour, the commentary of eye-witness observation produces two main changes: a questioning of the hyperboles previously lavished on the Italian countryside and Italian gastronomic products, and, as in other areas of commentary, a rhetoric of hyperbolic responsiveness. Travellers reassess the established vision of Italy as a land of incomparable fertility from the late seventeenth century onwards: proclaiming their own authority as

---

70 Normanby, *The English in Italy*, vol. II, pp. 72–3.

71 Moore, *View of Society*, vol. I, p. 311; Byron, *Childe Harold's Pilgrimage*, Canto IV, stanza 50, line 7, in *Complete Poetical Works*, vol. II, p. 141; in stanza 53, this rejection is extended into a yet more scornful dismissal (vol. II, pp. 141–2).

72 Piozzi, *Observations*, vol. II, p. 80. Such dismissals of 'the connoisseurs' are, obviously, in the sharpest possible contrast to the way in which specialized expertise is invoked in seventeenth-century writings, as a means of generating hyperboles by endorsing incomparability.

eye-witnesses, soberly observing what lies before them, they frequently
claim that Italy is a country where natural fruitfulness has been wasted
through human inefficiency.[73] This argument is occasionally developed to
a point where the fertility of the country is denied altogether: Samuel
Sharp, asserting that the country no longer deserves its traditional title of
'the Garden of the World', declares: 'however bold and uncommon the
assertion may appear, I think *England* a better resemblance of a garden
than *Italy*.'[74]

The theme of waste is carried over into accounts of Italian gastronomy.
Commentary on food now focuses less on natural produce – which is still, in
most cases, described as delightful – than on meals encountered at country
inns; when, as often happens, travellers describe these meals as utterly
appalling, they classify them as bearing witness to failings on the part not of
nature but of human culture. Henry Swinburne spells out this argument
explicitly in his account of 'the wine of the district south of the Osanto':
'The grapes have a fine flavour, and might produce excellent liquor, but from
inveterate and rooted ignorance the proprietor brews with them a muddy
unpotable mixture.' More often, accounts of disgusting food and drink simply incorporate an unstated assumption that natural resources have been
mismanaged: Swinburne describes an occasion at an inn on the road from
Naples to Taranto where he is forced to drink 'the water of a cistern full of
tadpoles', mixed with wine 'that resembled treacle much more than the juice
of the grape': 'While I held the pitcher to my lips, I formed a dam with a
knife, to prevent the little frogs from slipping down my throat.'[75] Lady
Miller provides a horrified account of an evening 'at a village called
Maschieri':

> In the dirtiest of all possible inns, and the most miserable bed, 'we courted
> sleep in vain,' after having supped upon, what think you? a pork soup with
> the *bouilliée* in it, namely a hog's head, with the eye-lashes, eyes, and nose

---

73 See, for example, Burnet's suggestion, in Naples, that 'the sloath and laziness of this people renders them incapable of making those advantages of so rich a Soil, that a more indus-
trious sort of People would find out' (*Some Letters*, pp. 191–2); see also Brydone's
extended comparison between Sicily and Switzerland (*A Tour*, vol. II, pp. 62–3). This latter account of waste defines Sicily as a country that 'starves in the midst of plenty' – a
theme also taken up, for example, in Burnet, *Some Letters*, p. 191, Joseph Addison's 'A
Letter from Italy, to the Right Honourable Charles Lord Halifax, in the Year 1701' (lines
113–18), in *Works*, vol. I, p. 35, and Swinburne, *Travels*, vol. II, p. 299.

74 Sharp, *Letters*, p. 64. See also the repudiation of the belief that Italy has a 'delicious
climate' in Young, *Travels*, vol. I, p. 242.

75 Swinburne, *Travels*, vol. I, pp. 182, 208.

on; the very food the wretched animal had last eat of before he made his *exit*
remained sticking about the teeth.[76]

The rhetoric of responsiveness that serves to restore hyperbole to commentary on the terrain, amid such plunges into bathos, is mainly produced
by appeals to the discourse of aesthetic theory. By the second half of the
eighteenth century, reference to the sublime supplies one of the primary
strategies adopted by travellers in order to describe the terrain of Italy.[77] In
theoretical treatises on the sublime, moreover, the subject of commentary
is repeatedly positioned as a traveller as well as a theorist, citing examples
of sublimity from topographies of the foreign, and putting forward principles which, it is assumed, can best be tested out by those enjoying some
degree of geographical mobility.

Travellers, when they voice admiration of sublime natural scenery, and
scrutinize the countryside for scenes of sublimity, transfer their attention
away from those aspects of the Italian terrain that are most strongly
emphasized in seventeenth-century travel writings: the luxuriant fertility
of the land, producing an abundance of food and wine, and the mild, delicious climate. The effect of sublime grandeur, and the qualities that are
defined as contributing to this effect, such as vastness and irregularity, are
located in wild, barren, savage and 'frowning' landscapes, rather than cultivated, fertile, gentle and smiling ones. One result of the proliferation of
enraptured description of natural sublimity, in the late eighteenth century,
is that travel writing manages to suggest that much of Italy is barren and
uncultivated – in other words, to accomplish, covertly, the same rhetorical
task of reversing earlier visions of fruitfulness as that attempted by the
theme of waste – without acknowledging that this suggestion might in any
way seem contentious.

The language in which the sublime is acclaimed, however, unlike
the language that serves to classify Italy as a land of wasted fertility, is a

---

[76] Miller, *Letters*, vol. II, p. 89. See also, for example, Sharp's account of 'the horrors of an
Italian journey' (*Letters*, p. 46) which are above all of a culinary nature, and include 'a soop
like wash, with pieces of liver swimming in it' (p. 45). Piozzi, in Siena, declares: 'I have
eaten too many of these delicious grapes', and explains: 'No wonder, I know few who
would resist a like temptation, especially as the inn afforded but a sorry dinner, whilst
every hedge provided so noble a dessert' (*Observations*, vol. I, p. 372).

[77] Concepts of sublimity are, however, employed in travel writing long before the 1750s. For
an early description of natural sublimity, see, for example, Dennis, *Miscellanies*, pp.
137–40. For a brief discussion of the chronology of the sublime, see Ashfield and de Bolla,
The Sublime, p. 59.

language of hyperbole.[78] Most of the hyperboles of indescribability quoted at the beginning of this chapter describe sublime landscapes, which proclaim their own hyperbolic potential and their sublimity simultaneously. The sublime incorporates a plot of exceeding limits that thematizes, as the theme of excess does, the impulse to move beyond boundaries which is inscribed in the structure and etymology of hyperbole; it also, moreover, strongly endorses this impulse, by situating it in the subject as well as the objects of observation, and linking it to a spirit of aspiration. By adopting the on-the-spot experience of the terrain as an object of curious enquiry in its own right, travellers provide themselves with a language in which eye-witness observation, far from being linked simply to a glum rejection of rhetorical flights of fancy (as it is in accounts of wasted fertility), itself generates new plots of traversing limits.

In *Peri Hypsous,* the founding text of theories of the sublime, Longinus, shifting momentarily from sublimity in rhetoric and poetry to the sublime in nature, explicitly equates the desire for sublimity with an impatience of limits and limitations. The passage is quoted here in William Smith's translation of 1739 – one of many eighteenth-century translations of the text:

> Nature never designed man to be a grov'ling and ungenerous animal, but brought him into life, and placed him in the world, as in a crouded theatre, not to be an idle spectator, but spurr'd on by an eager thirst of excelling, ardently to contend in the pursuit of glory. For this purpose, she implanted in his soul an invincible love of grandeur, and a constant emulation of whatever seems to approach nearer to divinity than himself. Hence it is, that the whole universe is not sufficient, for the extensive reach and piercing speculation of the human understanding. It passes the bounds of the material world, and launches forth at pleasure into endless space. Let any one take an exact survey of a life, which, in its every scene, is conspicuous on account of excellence, grandeur, and beauty, and he will soon discern for what noble ends we are born.[79]

Longinus then argues that this spirit of aspiration leads us to admire natural features that themselves display a proclivity to go beyond bounds: features that not only draw our imagination beyond the limits of the domestic

---

78   Hyperbole is, of course, only one of the range of rhetorical tropes and strategies that characterize the language of sublimity; for some subtle and illuminating comments on language and the sublime, see the chapter 'A Reading of Longinus', in Hertz, *The End of the Line,* pp. 1–20.

79   Longinus, *Dionysius,* pp. 145–6 (section 35).

and familiar, and exceed more mundane objects in size, but, in addition, actively transgress their own boundaries. He cites, for example, the Nile, a river famous for annually overflowing, and Etna, a mountain which, as he emphasizes, is renowned for its eruptions:

> Thus the impulse of nature inclines us to admire, not a little clear trans-parent rivulet that ministers to our necessities, but the *Nile*, the *Ister*, the *Rhine*, or still much more, the Ocean. We are never surprised at the sight of a small fire that burns clear, and blazes out on our own private hearth, but view with amaze the celestial fires, tho' they are often obscured by vapours and eclipses. Nor do we reckon any thing in nature more wonderful than the boiling furnaces of *Ætna*, which cast up stones, and sometimes whole rocks, from their labouring abyss, and pour out whole rivers of liquid and unmingled flame. And from hence we may infer, that whatever is useful and necessary to man, lies level to his abilities, and is easily acquired; but what-ever exceeds the common size, is always great, and always amazing.[80]

Unsurprisingly, given the crucial role of movement beyond boundaries within Longinus's founding text, travel writings implicitly define hyper-bole as the trope proper to description and analysis of the natural grandeur offered to view by the topography of the Grand Tour. Travellers who fail to rise to the hyperbolic heights required by mountain scenery, and remain, rhetorically, within the bounds of the mundane, are often dismissed as inadequate. Byron's account of the two Englishwomen who respond to the Alps by, respectively, falling asleep and exclaiming 'did you ever see any thing more *rural*' has already been quoted in the Introduction.[81] Elisabeth Vigée-Lebrun, in Italy in 1790, is troubled on her journey from Rome to Naples by the presence of a companion who refuses to join her in her cries of admiration, seeing only a threat of rain when he views 'la ligne des Apennins entourée de nuages superbes que le soleil couchant éclairait'; she eventually informs the reader that 'j'étais décidée à ne point me laisser refroidir par ce glaçon'.[82]

The variety of unfamiliarity represented by the sublime, moreover, assumes an especially useful strategic function within the hyperbolic lan-guage required to translate the topography of the Grand Tour into

---

80   *Ibid.*, pp. 146–7.

81   Byron, *Letters and Journals*, vol. V, p. 97.

82   Vigée-Lebrun, *Souvenirs*, vol. I, p. 189: 'the line of the Apennines, surrounded by superb clouds, which were lighted by the setting sun'; vol. I, p. 190: 'I was determined not to let myself be chilled by this iceberg.'

discourse: it invests the topography with a strangeness that is not dependent on novelty. This topography of the not-so-distant foreign is, in some ways, at a disadvantage, when compared with more exotic regions as a domain of drama and difference: not only is it less geographically remote, but it is also, as emphasized in the Introduction, defined as a topography that has already been rendered familiar by the writings of previous travellers. By invoking the sublime, the traveller is able to insist that the Alps and Italy offer an effect of strangeness that is undiminished by familiarity. Piozzi, in the Alps, remarks that even for 'the chairmen who carry one through', to whom 'nothing can be new', 'it is observable that the glories of these objects have never faded'; she cites a native inhabitant of the region who 'told us, that having lived in a gentleman's service twenty years between London and Dublin, he at length begged his discharge, chusing to retire and finish his days a peasant upon these mountains, where he first opened his eyes upon scenes that made all other views of nature insipid to his taste'.[83]

The astonishment excited by the sublime, moreover – a state in which, in the words of Edmund Burke, 'the mind is so entirely filled with its object, that it cannot entertain any other' – is readily elided with the response demanded by another category of natural scenery, possessed of a drama that goes beyond mere unfamiliarity: the 'wonder'.[84] Eighteenth-century descriptions of landscape establish an effortless rhetorical continuity between the difference and drama located in transcendence of limits and the unique, unparalleled and incomparable qualities which, as in earlier writings, are attributed to wonders. Piozzi's account of Vesuvius merges the two varieties of alterity in the simple declaration: 'One need not stir out for wonders sure, while this amazing mountain continues to exhibit such various scenes of sublimity and beauty.'[85]

---

[83] Piozzi, *Observations*, vol. I, p. 42.

[84] Burke, *Philosophical Enquiry*, p. 57. For a brief account of some of the differences between the early seventeenth-century aesthetics of wonder and awe and the eighteenth-century aesthetics of the sublime – modes of discourse that eighteenth-century travel writing often seeks to present as continuous with each other – see Cascardi, *The Subject of Modernity*, p. 54.

[85] Piozzi, *Observations*, vol. II, p. 4. The strategy of selecting wonders as examples of the sublime is endorsed by the founding text of the sublime. Longinus, in his account of natural grandeur, names, alongside the more generalized 'ocean', four features that he designates as wonders simply by singling them out as the objects in the world that most indisputably excite our admiration and amazement: 'the *Nile*, the *Ister*, the *Rhine*' and 'the boiling furnaces of *Ætna* '(*Dionysius*, pp. 146, 167; section 35).

Responsiveness, desire, power and authority

In describing both sublime wonders and other scenes of sublimity, travel writings make use of hyperboles that, as in other areas of commentary, proclaim the traveller's ability to respond emotionally to the topography. This emotional responsiveness, however, is less easily relegated to the domain of the feminine than the responsiveness directed towards other domains of objects. Commentary on landscape, much more clearly than commentary on other objects presented to view by the topography of the Grand Tour, exemplifies the equivocations over categories of gender that Julie Ellison, in *Delicate Subjects: Romanticism, Gender, and the Ethics of Understanding,* traces within romantic writing. She points out that 'the key terms of romantic poetics – the sublime, the haunted, the grotesque, the sentimental, the ironic, memory, desire, imagination – are accompanied by the desire to be understood intuitively'. Ellison then outlines a contradiction central to such a poetics:

> Intuition is marked as a feminine quality, just as most objects of romantic longing are, including childhood, nature, and the demonic. The invention of the romantic subject as the hero of desire is therefore wholly bound up with the feminine. At the same time, romantic writers suspect that desire may be a form of power, understanding a form of science, and women a form of sabotage. Objects of desire are lost or violated in ambivalent allegories of the domestic and the maternal.[86]

In seeking out examples of the sublime, the traveller describing the landscapes of the Grand Tour ostensibly finds a means of voicing this suspicion 'that desire may be a form of power'. A great many contemporary theorists of the sublime have emphasized the opportunity for self-confirmation that sublimity offers. Such theorists usually invoke the narrative of identification mapped out by Longinus in Section VII of *Peri Hypsous*:

> The mind is naturally elevated by the true *Sublime,* and so sensibly affected with its lively strokes, that it swells in transport and an inward pride, as if what was only heard had been the product of its own invention.[87]

Burke, explaining the sublime 'delight' that we experience 'when we have an idea of pain and danger, without being actually in such circumstances', cites this passage:

---

[86] p. 11.

[87] Longinus, *Dionysius*, p. 21.

Now whatever either on good or upon bad grounds tends to raise a man in his own opinion, produces a sort of swelling and triumph that is extremely grateful to the human mind; and this swelling is never more perceived, nor operates with more force, than when without danger we are conversant with terrible objects, the mind always claiming to itself some part of the dignity and importance of the things which it contemplates. Hence proceeds what Longinus has observed of that glorying and sense of inward greatness, that always fills the reader of such passages in poets and orators as are sublime; it is what every man must have felt in himself upon such occasions.[88]

The plot that these commentaries map out is one in which the 'sort of swelling and triumph' is prompted by some threat (the superior grandeur of sublime orators and poets, in Longinus, and the overwhelming and frightening qualities of 'terrible objects', in Burke). It has become commonplace to view this plot as entailing a culminatory moment of self-affirmation; the gratification of this 'sense of inward greatness' in the face of a threatening authority or power is wittily summarised, much later in the history of musings on the sublime, in an early twentieth-century short story, Edith Wharton's 'False Dawn' (1923), when Lewis Raycie gazes 'with a sense of easy equality' at the 'awful pinnacles' of the highest Alpine mountain, and reflects upon the 'thunders' of his overbearing father: 'Had Mr Raycie ever really frightened Lewis? Why, now he was not even frightened by Mont Blanc!'[89] In many descriptions of sublime landscape, however, the subject of commentary, rather that exploiting the dramatic potential of such a moment, locates greater drama and excitement in the threat to stability and mastery, and registers a greater fascination with the more equivocal sense of self that

---

[88] Burke, *Philosophical Enquiry*, pp. 50–1; this is the only point in the *Enquiry* where Burke refers to *Peri Hypsous* directly.

[89] Wharton, *Old New York*, p. 67. See Thomas Weiskel's account of the sublime as entailing an oedipal identification with the power of the father, in *The Romantic Sublime*, pp. 10–11, 91–4, 203. The relations between subject and object in Burke's theory of sublimity are helpfully mapped out by Ashfield and de Bolla in *The Sublime*, p. 128:

> The sublime can be understood as a *pulsation* . . . in which first the conscious mind relinquishes its power over the world it perceives and in which it has experiential encounters in order to open itself to the object, to become suffused with the world. Then, in a secondary pulsation, this experience of opening up or of being overcome leads to an intensification of self-presence and a corresponding re-assertion of the power of the subject over the object.

the experience of this threat produces.[90] Brydone's account of Mount Etna, for example, presents the traveller's loss of control as more note-worthy than the position of mastery that he subsequently attains: 'The senses, unaccustomed to the sublimity of such a scene, are bewildered and confounded; and it is not till after some time, that they are capable of separating and judging of the objects that compose it.'[91] A description of the Alps in a later work, Sydney Morgan's *Italy*, positively denies that the experience of 'the unmastered savagery of remote scenes' entails any culminatory moment when the mind regains a sense of control; in such regions of otherness, where 'man' finds that 'nothing is in conformity with him, all is at variance with his end and being', the mind, Morgan argues, 'is not raised. It is stricken back upon its own insignificance.'[92]

Burke's principle that the sublime is produced by distanced terror, moreover, is often invoked in a manner that registers a sharper awareness of terror than of distancing. Frances Reynolds's account of the sublime, in her *Enquiry concerning the Principles of Taste, and the Origin of our Ideas of Beauty* (London, 1785), throws into uncertainty the question of whether the subject of the sublime can maintain control, having once undergone an experience of danger: 'It is a pinnacle of beatitude, bordering upon horror, deformity, madness! an eminence from whence the mind, that dares to look farther, is lost! It seems to stand, *or rather to waver*, between certainty and uncertainty, between security and destruction.'[93] More mundanely, many travellers express fright when encountering sublime landscapes, but do lit-tle to draw attention to the distanced character of the terror that confronts them. 'My head got giddy and I thought I should have fainted with fright', says Catherine Wilmot, when ascending Vesuvius and 'obliged to totter round the edge of the gulph'.[94]

---

90   Neil Hertz, tracing the movement, in eighteenth-century accounts of the sublime, from 'the notion of difficulty or recalcitrance' (in assimilating the great works of nature, for example) to 'the notion of absolute blockage', points out that the experience of difficulty or blockage, in which the subject is baffled, checked or astonished by the sublime object, is not one of utter destabilization or annihilation: 'although the moment of blockage might have been rendered as one of utter self-loss, it was, even before its recuperation as sublime exaltation, a confirmation of the unitary status of the self' ('The Notion of Blockage in the Literature of the Sublime', in *The End of the Line*, pp. 40–60; p. 53).

91   Brydone, *A Tour*, vol. II, p. 204.

92   Vol. I, p. 22.

93   p. 18; emphasis added. See Burke, *Philosophical Enquiry*, pp. 35–7.

94   Wilmot, *An Irish Peer*, pp. 151, 150; journal entry dated 6 March 1803.

The beautiful: mastery and effemination

Burke's *Enquiry,* however, in forming a concept of the beautiful, in symmetrical opposition to the sublime, provides theorists and travel writers with a powerful rhetorical aid, which makes it much easier for them to preclude any loss of authority that rapturous accounts of wavering 'between security and destruction' might entail. References to the the sublime and the beautiful very often emphasize that each is to be defined by opposition to the other. Swinburne, overlooking the Bay of Naples, declares tersely: 'the sea-view is sublime; the land one most beautiful'.[95] Piozzi, at Livorno, comments: 'The Appenine mountains degenerate into hills as they run round the bay, but gain in beauty what in sublimity they lose.'[96] The alternating qualities of sublimity and beauty are not always named directly, but are regularly invoked by reference to the symmetrically opposed terms of other binary pairs, to which they are closely allied: the wild and the cultivated, the barren and the fertile, the savage and the gentle, the terrible and the agreeable, the frowning landscape and the *paysage riant,* Salvator Rosa and Claude Lorrain. Thomas Watkins, for example, observes: 'The vale of Altdorf would have satisfied the rich fancy of Claude Lorrain, and the descent of Urseven the romantic genius of Salvator Rosa.'[97] Within this structure of binary opposition, writers on the sublime intermittently align the sublime with the masculine and the beautiful with the feminine; Frances Reynolds strongly emphasizes the power of concepts of gender to generate a sharply binary structure, by pursuing the oppositions imposed by such concepts through a sequence of highly diverse examples:

> It is, I imagine, to the principles of the masculine and the feminine character, that we owe the perception of beauty or taste, in any object whatever, throughout all nature and all art that imitates nature; and, in objects which differ from the human form, the principles must be in the extreme, because the object is then merely symbolical. Thus, the meekness of the lamb, and the high-spirited prancing steed; the gentle dove, and the impetuous eagle; the placid lake, and the swelling ocean; the lowly valley, and the aspiring

95 Swinburne, *Travels,* vol. II, p. 58.

96 Piozzi, *Observations,* vol. I, p. 354.

97 Watkins, *Travels,* vol. I, p. 50. One precondition for the ease with which the seventeenth-century allegories of Hell and Paradise are assimilated within the rhetoric of eye-witness observation (see p. 87 n. 12) is, perhaps, the fact that they are endowed with a new rhetorical function as a result of the formation of this sequence of binary pairs.

mountain. It is the feminine character that is the sweetest, the most interesting, image of beauty; the masculine partakes of the sublime.[98]

The introduction of a category in such sharp contrast to the sublime provides, first, a means of assuring the reader of the subject's ability to experience not only intense responsiveness (as demonstrated by his or her
accounts of sublimity), but also untroubled pleasure: the beautiful, when
equated with feminine 'meekness', is defined as a quality that allows the
subject to evince a sense of easy mastery, as opposed to the more complex
sense of self-affirmation in the face of the destabilizing power of nature
that is obtained through the sublime. This concept of the beautiful is outlined by Burke when, establishing a contrast between sublimity and
beauty, he declares: 'we submit to what we admire, but we love what
submits to us; in one case we are forced, in the other we are flattered into
compliance.'[99]

When Burke declares, however, that 'we love what submits to us' as a
result of its power to flatter us 'into compliance', the words 'flattered into
compliance' might lead the reader to suspect that his concept of beauty is
not an entirely straightforward one.[100] At other points in his *Enquiry*, he
does in fact present beauty in terms that invoke not an unthreatening femininity, but dangerously alluring forces of effemination. The concept of
beauty as an effect that depends on an effeminating passivity is formed
within those sections of the *Enquiry* that usually attract the least attention:
the sections concerned with the physiological mechanisms that produce an
experience of beauty or sublimity. Section 19, for example, entitled 'The
physical cause of LOVE', begins as follows:

> When we have before us such objects as excite love and complacency, the
> body is affected, so far as I could observe, much in the following manner.
> The head reclines something on one side; the eyelids are more closed than
> usual, and the eyes roll gently with an inclination to the object, the mouth
> is a little opened, and the breath drawn slowly, with now and then a low
> sigh: the whole body is composed, and the hands fall idly to the sides. All
> this is accompanied with an inward sense of melting and languor.[101]

---

[98] Reynolds, *An Enquiry*, p. 29.

[99] Burke, *Philosophical Enquiry*, p. 113.

[100] *Ibid*. See also, as an instance of Burke's equation between beauty and an unthreatening
version of the feminine, p. 116: 'The beauty of women is considerably owing to their
weakness, or delicacy, and is even enhanced by their timidity.'

[101] *Ibid.*, p. 149.

Burke then embarks on an explanation of such a marked physical effect:

> From this description it is almost impossible not to conclude, that beauty
> acts by relaxing the solids of the whole system. There are all the appear-
> ances of such a relaxation; and a relaxation somewhat below the natural
> tone seems to me to be the cause of all positive pleasure. Who is a stranger
> to that manner of expression so common in all times and in all countries,
> of being softened, relaxed, enervated, dissolved, melted away by
> pleasure?[102]

The *Enquiry* does not itself draw any explicit parallel between this effect of
relaxation and the relaxing effects of a warm climate. In his account of
being 'melted away by pleasure', however, Burke obliquely invokes one of
the most renowned eighteenth-century accounts of bodily relaxation:
Montesquieu's explanation, in *De l'esprit des lois* (1748), of 'combien les
hommes sont différents dans les divers climats'. This section of the work
begins with a contrast between North and South:

> L'air froid resserre les extrémités des fibres extérieures de notre corps; cela
> augmente leur ressort, et favorise le retour du sang des extrémités vers le
> cœur. Il diminue la longueur de ces mêmes fibres; il augmente donc encore
> par là leur force. L'air chaud, au contraire, relâche les extrémités des fibres,
> et les allonge; il diminue donc leur force et leur ressort.
> On a donc plus de vigueur dans les climats froids.[103]

The ways in which the relaxing, enervating effects of a warm climate might
relate to pleasure are explored later in this same chapter of *De l'esprit des
lois*, after Montesquieu's famous account of his experiment of freezing one
half of a sheep's tongue, and discovering that the little pyramids upon it,
which appear to be 'le principal organe du goût', contract and disappear as a
result of this process, and begin to reappear as the tongue thaws:

> Cette observation confirme ce que j'ai dit, que, dans les pays froids, les
> houpes nerveuses sont moins épanouies: elles s'enfoncent dans leurs

---

[102] *Ibid.*, pp. 149–50.

[103] Vol. I, p. 373 (book XIV, chapter 2); 'Of the Difference of Men in different Climates':
A cold air constringes the extremities of the external fibres of the body; this
increases their elasticity, and favors the return of the blood from the extremities to the heart. It contracts those very fibres; consequently it increases also
their force. On the contrary a warm air relaxes and lengthens the extremes of
the fibres; of course it diminishes their force and elasticity.
People are therefore more vigorous in cold climates. (*The Spirit of Laws*,
vol. I, p. 316; further translations in footnotes are all taken from this edition.)

gaines, où elles sont à couvert de l'action des objets extérieurs. Les sensations sont donc moins vives.

Dans les pays froids, on aura peu de sensibilité pour les plaisirs; elle sera
plus grande dans les pays tempérés; dans les pays chauds, elle sera
extrême.[104]

Initially, in Montesquieu's account, such sensibility to pleasure designates
the warm South as the region of effeminate passion rather than effeminate
languor: he explains that 'avec cette délicatesse d'organes que l'on a dans
les pays chauds, l'âme est souverainement émue par tout ce qui a du rap-
port à l'union des deux sexes; tout conduit à cet objet'. Passivity, in his
account of spiritual geography, turns out to lurk in regions yet warmer
than those of passion:

> La chaleur du climat peut être si excessive, que le corps y sera absolument
> sans force. Pour lors, l'abattement passera à l'esprit même; aucune
> curiosité, aucune noble entreprise, aucun sentiment généreux; les inclina-
> tions y seront toutes passives; la paresse y sera le bonheur.[105]

Dupaty, describing the environs of Naples at the very end of his *Lettres sur
l'Italie*, registers an awareness of the continuity between Montesquieu's
concept of the relaxation of the fibres in the warm South and Burke's concept of the relaxation induced by beauty. He begins by eliding effeminacy
of passion with effeminacy of passivity: the ancients' indulgence of
amorous passions, in his account, leads naturally to an abandonment of
active bellicosity (one of the effects of relaxation of the fibres specifically
mentioned in *De l'esprit des lois*):

---

104 *Ibid.*, vol. I, p. 375 (book XIV, chapter 2); 'the principal organ of taste' (vol. I, p. 318):
     This observation confirms what I have been saying, that in cold countries, the
     nervous glands are less spread; they sink deeper into their sheaths, or they are
     sheltered from the action of external objects. Consequently they have not such
     lively sensations.
        In cold countries, they have very little sensibility for pleasures; in temper-
     ate countries they have more; in warm countries their sensibility is exquisite.
     (vol. I, p. 319)
105 *Ibid.*, vol. I, pp. 375–6 (book XIV, chapter 2): 'From this delicacy of organs peculiar to
     warm climates, it follows, that the soul is most sensibly moved by whatever has a relation
     to the union of the two sexes: here every thing leads to this object' (vol. I, p. 319); vol. I,
     p. 376 (book XIV, chapter 2): 'The heat of the climate may be so excessive as to deprive
     the body of all vigor and strength. Then the faintness is communicated to the mind; there
     is no curiosity, no noble enterprize, no generous sentiment; the inclinations are all passive;
     indolence constitutes the utmost happiness' (vol. I, p. 320).

Je suis allé visiter. . . sur-tout ces charmans rivages, si funestes à la pudeur et
si favorables à l'amour, où les zéphirs, où la mer, où l'air, où tout détachoit
les esprits et les cœurs du joug des pensées austères; où parmi les chants
voluptueux de voix et d'instrumens efféminés, mêlés au souffle des zéphirs
et aux accens des oiseaux, venoient se perdre les accens des trompettes
guerrieres.[106]

Dupaty then imagines 'ces lieux de délices' at the hour of the day when he
himself contemplates them: 'à cette heure la plus corrompue de toutes les
heures de la soirée, lorsque tout s'abandonnait ici à la volupté, comme à
une convenance même du soir et du lieu'. Playfully noting his impression
that 'cet air a retenu quelque chose de son ancienne corruption', he
embarks on an account of effeminatory languor that pointedly includes
two of the sources of beauty listed in Burke's *Enquiry:* 'gradual variation',
and sounds that can be seen as parallel to 'the softness, the winding surface,
the unbroken continuance, the easy gradation of the beautiful in other
things':

Je sens mes pensées s'amollir à ces aspects, à cette situation, à cette ombre
vague, légère, qui, successivement, éteint dans le ciel, sur la mer, sur
toutes les montagnes, sur tous les sommets des arbres, les dernieres
lueurs du jour; mes pensées s'amollissent sur-tout à ce silence qui se
répand, du moment en moment, sur ces rivages, et du sein duquel s'élève
par degrés le touchant concert du soir, composé du bruit mélancolique
des rames qui sillonnent les flots éloignés, des bêlements des troupeaux
répandus dans les montagnes, des ondes qui expirent en murmurant sur
les rochers, du frémissement des feuilles des arbres, où les zéphirs ne se
reposent jamais, enfin, de tous ces sons insensibles, épars au loin dans les
cieux, sur les flots, sur la terre, qui forment en ce moment, comme une
voix incertaine, comme une respiration mélodieuse de la nature
endormie![107]

---

106 Vol. II, p. 306: 'I went to see. . . above all, those delightful shores, so fatal to modesty, and
so favourable to love, where the zephyrs, the sea, the air – all contributed to relax the
mind, and the heart, from the severe yoke of thought; where, amidst the voluptuous
accents of voices and effeminate instruments, intermixed with the murmurs of gentle
zephyrs, and the sweet notes of the feathered songsters, were dying away the sounds of
warlike trumpets' (vol. II, pp. 208–9). See Montesquieu, *De l'esprit des lois,* I, 374.

107 *Ibid.,* vol. II, p. 307: 'those delightful shores' (vol. II, p. 209); vol. II, pp. 307–8: 'at that
hour, which is the most inviting of all the evening hours, to soft endearments, and to dalliance; for all then here abandoned themselves to voluptuousness and pleasure, agreeable

The definition of beauty as effeminating invests the beautiful with a strong
element of danger, as Frances Ferguson has pointed out, in a summary of
the role of beauty in Burke's *Enquiry:* 'Although we love (and pity) that
which we see as weaker than we are, the danger in beauty is that its appearance of weakness does not prevent its having an effect, which is always that
of robbing us of our vigilance and recreating us in its own image.'[108] In
Burke's account of 'gradual variation', this danger is located in a giddiness
that aligns it with the 'giddy' loss of mastery described by travellers such
as Catherine Wilmot when confronting sublime landscapes:

> Observe that part of a beautiful woman where she is perhaps the most
> beautiful, about the neck and breasts; the smoothness; the softness; the
> easy and insensible swell; the variety of the surface, which is never for the
> smallest space the same; the deceitful maze, through which the unsteady
> eye slides giddily, without knowing where to fix, or whither it is
> carried.[109]

The device of transferring loss of control from the sublime to the beautiful is extremely useful rhetorically, in rescuing the traveller temporarily
unsettled by the sublime from the suspicion of a feminized loss of restraint
and control: if the beautiful is set up as the site of perilously effeminating
forces, the sublime is, simply by the persuasive power of binary opposition,
defined as an effect that induces a sense of manliness.

Burke reinforces such a definition, moreover, by invoking
Montesquieu's analysis of the effects of climate not only when assuring the

to the charms of the evening and the place' (vol. II, p. 210); vol. II, p. 308: 'the air has
retained something of its ancient corruption' (vol. II, p. 211); Burke, *Philosophical
Enquiry*, pp. 115, 122; Dupaty, *Lettres*, vol. II, p. 309: 'In this aspect, and in this situation,
the thoughts are incessantly rendered more flexible by that vague and light shade, spreading a sable veil over the last glimpses of day, in the heavens, on the sea, and on the summits of the hills and the trees; but above all by the silence, which every moment diffuses
itself on this coast, and from the bosom of which rises by degrees the affecting concert of
the evning, composed of the melancholy sound of oars dashing the foaming waves, of the
distant bleating of flocks, scattered over the mountains; of the hollow murmurs of the sea,
expiring on the rocks; of the rustling of the leaves, where the zephyrs never rest; of all
those insensible sounds, in short, which, extended far off in the heavens, on the water, and
on the earth, form at this instant an uncertain whisper, a kind of melodious breathing of
reposing nature!' (vol. II, pp. 211–21).

108 Ferguson, *Solitude*, pp. 51–2.

109 Burke, *Philosophical Enquiry*, p. 115. Dupaty silently quotes this passage of Burke's
Enquiry, in a context that emphasizes the erotic character of 'gradual variation': a description of the *Venus de' Medici* (*Lettres*, vol. I, pp. 147–8).

reader that 'beauty acts by relaxing the solids of the whole system', but also when explaining the physiological effects of the sublime. Montesquieu, as already noted, emphasizes the vigour that nature has assigned to the inhabitants of the North, in contrast to the indolence of natives of the South; at a later point in *De l'esprit des lois,* he equates this vigour with industry and activity.[110] Burke, in his analysis of the sublime as an effect produced by terror operating in a distanced, indirect manner, defines invigoration as an essential part of such an effect. The topographical implications of this analysis are complicated by an implicit reference to another chapter of *De l'esprit des lois,* which focuses on a specific variety of lassitude that Montesquieu attributes to the English, and which supplies an explanation for the propensity of this people to kill themselves.[111] Such an exception to the overall classification of the North as bracing and the South of relaxing, however, does not prevent an elision between northern industry and sublime invigoration. In a 'languid inactive state', Burke observes, 'the nerves are more liable to the most horrid convulsions, than when they are sufficiently braced and strengthened'. The best remedy for the 'melancholy, dejection, despair, and... self-murder' that result from such 'horrid convulsions' is 'exercise or *labour*'; labour, Burke declares, 'is a surmounting of difficulties, an exertion of the contracting power of the muscles; and as such resembles pain, which consists in tension or contraction, in every thing but degree'. He then moves on from the effect of pain on 'the coarser organs' to 'those finer parts', which must also 'be shaken and worked to a proper degree':

> As common labour, which is a mode of pain, is the exercise of the grosser, a mode of terror is the exercise of the finer parts of the system; and if a certain mode of pain be of such a nature as to act upon the eye or the ear, as they are the most delicate organs, the affection approaches more nearly to that which has a mental cause. In all these cases, if the pain and terror are so modified as not to be actually noxious; if the pain is not carried to violence, and the terror is not conversant about the present destruction of the person, as these emotions clear the parts, whether fine, or gross, of a dangerous and troublesome incumbrance, they are capable of producing delight; not

---

110 See vol. II, p. 28 (book 21, chapter 3).

111 See *ibid.,* vol. I, p. 385 (book XIV, chapter 12): in the suicidal inhabitant of England, Montesquieu argues, 'la machine, dont les forces motrices se trouvent à tout moment sans action, est lasse d'elle-même; l'âme ne sent point de douleur, mais une certaine difficulté de l'existence'; 'the machine whose motive faculties are every moment without action, is weary of itself; the soul feels no pain, but a certain uneasiness in existing' (vol. I, p. 331).

pleasure, but a sort of delightful horror, a sort of tranquillity tinged with terror.[112]

Burke's *Enquiry*, then, supplies travellers with a rhetorical strategy which, whatever their degree of feminized effusiveness, allows them to present themselves as enjoying the manly pleasures of a bracing 'exercise of the finer parts of the system', and eschewing languorous effemination, simply by voicing an attraction towards the sublime.

This claim to be enjoyably invigorated is reinforced by a northerly bias in the geographical affiliations that eighteenth-century writings establish for the sublime. Once travel writings begin to invoke the theory of the sublime, they locate the phase of most dramatic sublimity, within the itinerary of the Grand Tour, just before the crucial transition from North to South takes place, while the traveller is still in a region that, as far as society and manners are concerned, exemplifies the liberty and industry of northern Europe: the phase when the traveller crosses the Alps. During the late eighteenth and early nineteenth centuries, travellers very often observe that the Alps are more strikingly grand, sublime and astonishing than the Apennines. Piozzi comments on 'the mountains after Terni':

> No one who wishes to see the Appenines in perfection must miss this road,
> yet are they not comparable to the Alps at best, which being more lofty,
> more craggy, and almost universally terminating in points of granite devoid
> of horizontal strata, give one a more majestic idea of their original and
> duration.[113]

On the one hand, therefore, enraptured accounts of sublime natural scenery throughout the Italian peninsula allow the traveller to affirm that he or she has experienced dramatic difference. On the other hand, the traveller can choose to locate sublimity just before the beginning of the region that can most easily be classified as dramatically different. The two options are, unsurprisingly, often used in conjunction with each other, without any

---

112 Burke, *Philosophical Enquiry*, pp. 135, 136. In his account of pain as a remedy for melancholy, Burke adapts Montesquieu's account of the propensity of the English to kill themselves (*De l'esprit des lois*, vol. I, pp. 384–5; book 14, chapter 12.)

113 Piozzi, *Observations*, vol. II, pp. 154–5. The new status of the Alps as a major focal point for speculation on natural grandeur is affirmed, too, by the admission of these mountains into the series of localized wonders listed by Longinus: 'the *Nile*, the *Ister*, the *Rhine*' and 'the boiling furnaces of *Ætna*'. Both John Baillie's *Essay on the Sublime* (pp. 5–6) and Alexander Gerard's *Essay on Taste* (pp. 13–14) add the Alps to their adjusted versions of Longinus's list. Lord Kames, in his *Elements of Criticism*, mentions 'the Alps and the pike of Teneriff' as instances of combined 'greatness and elevation' just after citing Longinus's list of sublime natural objects in a footnote vol. I, pp. 265, 264).

acknowledgement of a potential contradiction between acclamations of sublime landscape in the South and an implicit insistence that it is the Alps that are most truly sublime. In citing Burke's *Enquiry*, travel writings very often invoke the aesthetic topography that this treatise maps out: a topography that firmly assigns the effeminating qualities of the warm South to the beautiful, and relocates the sublime in northern regions of manly invigoration. At the same time, these travel writings also include rapturous accounts of sublime wonders in the warm south, and metaphorically elide the drama of these wonders – of Vesuvius, in particular – with southern indulgence of the passions and effeminating southern air. Catherine Wilmot, in her journal of 1803, begins her account of Naples by declaring: 'I will give you first a sketch of the Neapolitans we were acquainted with, almost all of whom partook in the animation of their manners of their Volcanic mountain, of which they are the epitomies.'[114] By the early nineteenth century, travellers begin to examine more closely the relation between the Alpine sublime and the sublime wonders and effeminating climate of the South. Some of the changes that can be discerned within their speculations are considered in Chapter 4.

---

[114] Wilmot, *An Irish Peer*, p. 141. See also, for example, Moore, *View of Society*, vol. II, pp. 212, 315

3

Spectator and spectacle

I: THE FEMININE AND THE ANTIQUE

Women in 'different disguises'

One of Yorick's expositions of his approach to travel in Sterne's *Sentimental Journey* is addressed to a French count, whom the traveller-narrator is visiting at Versailles. Differentiating himself from more morose and censorious travellers, Yorick assures the count that he has 'not come to spy the nakedness of the land'. After a while, the Frenchman returns to the theme of nakedness: '*Hèh bien! Monsieur l'Anglois,* said the Count, gaily – You are not come to spy the nakedness of the land – I believe you – *ni encore*, I dare say, *that* of our women – But permit me to conjecture – if, *par hazard*, they fell in your way – that the prospect would not affect you.' Yorick defends himself against this accusation that he might not object to the sight of naked Frenchwomen:

> Excuse me, Monsieur Le Count, said I – as for the nakedness of your land, if I saw it, I should cast my eyes over it with tears in them – and for that of your women (blushing at the idea he had excited in me) I am so evangelical in this, and have such a fellow-feeling for what ever is *weak* about them, that I would cover it with a garment, if I knew how to throw it on – But I could wish, continued I, to spy the *nakedness* of their hearts, and through the different disguises of customs, climates, and religion, find out what is good in them, to fashion my own by – and therefore am I come.[1]

In the next paragraph, Yorick defines the pleasures of enquiring into the female heart as equivalent to those of viewing works of art; women, he suggests, are easily substituted for the more orthodox sights of the Grand Tour:

---

[1] p. 84.

It is for this reason, Monsieur le Compte, continued I, that I have not seen the Palais royal – nor the Luxembourg – nor the Façade of the Louvre – or have attempted to swell the catalogues we have of pictures, statues, and churches – I conceive every fair being as a temple, and would rather enter in, and see the original drawings and loose sketches hung up in it, than the transfiguration of Raphael itself.[2]

Yorick's insistence on his own unorthodoxy in focusing his powers of investigation on the female heart is, in fact, belied by the regularity with which travel writings include speculations about female desires and female behaviour in their accounts of the topography of the Grand Tour. Commentaries on monasticism, as already noted, almost invariably concentrate on nuns rather than monks. In late eighteenth-century and early-nineteenth-century accounts of ruins and landscape, moreover, female figures often appear – sometimes for no apparent reason. Charles Dupaty, in his *Lettres sur l'Italie* (1788), describes himself in the Coliseum, meditating on the work of time, when suddenly, 'à travers ces dernières lueurs du jour, et ces premières ombres du soir, mêlées ensemble', he sees a young woman. 'Elle étoit belle!', he exclaims, 'elle étoit vêtue avec grace! Ses cheveux et ses vêtements étoient mollement agités par un vent frais.'[3]

In charting the role that women assume in travel writing, one precondition for their rhetorical usefulness immediately suggests itself, in addition to the precondition noted in the last chapter (the assumption that women, being subject to greater restraint than men, will react more dramatically against that restraint). Travellers on the Grand Tour register particular interest in those objects of commentary that resist enquiry especially strongly, and can therefore be deployed as metaphors for difference, unfamiliarity and mysterious otherness – the very qualities that, in all travel writings, are expected and demanded of foreign places. Yorick, in the section of Sterne's *Sentimental Journey* just quoted, emphasizes – however ironically – that his wish is not to encounter Frenchwomen who are literally unclothed, but, metaphorically, to unclothe them himself, and overcome the obstacles to investigation that they present: 'to spy the *nakedness* of their hearts, and through the different disguises of customs,

---

[2] *Ibid.*

[3] Vol. II, p. 64: 'through the last glimpses of the day, and the first shades of the evening, intermixed'; 'How beautiful her countenance, and how graceful her dress! Her hair and her garments were lightly flowing before the evening breeze' (*Sentimental Letters*, vol. II, p. 45; further translations in footnotes are all taken from this edition). See also, for example, Lady Morgan's description of Terracina, where 'a lovely creature. . . with the smile of a young Sibyl' springs out to offer her services as a *cicerone* (*Italy*, vol. II, p. 326).

climates, and religion, find out what is good in them'.[4] Women are easily
defined as beings who present 'disguises' and obstacles. The restraint
placed upon them is often presented as manifesting itself metonymically,
in visual features that, at the same time, also serve as metonyms for a resistance to appropriation. Accounts of monasticism, for example, place some
emphasis on such aspects of the *mise-en-scène* as the nun's habit, the
imprisoning walls, and the bars of the parlatory grate. Such features invest
nuns with an intriguing inaccessibility at the same time that they dramatize
prohibition and restriction: the emphasis on improper restraint is elided
with an implication that the traveller's gaze is itself intruding transgres-
sively into a restricted or prohibited area. Patrick Brydone, in his *Tour
through Sicily and Malta* (1773), notes that several nuns in a Sicilian convent that he visits are 'extremely handsome', and comments: 'but, indeed,
I think they always appear so; and I am very certain, from frequent experience, that there is no artificial ornament, or studied embellishment whatever, that can produce half so strong an effect, as the modest and simple
attire of a pretty young nun, *placed behind a double iron grate*'.[5]

Accounts of cicisbeism have no obvious metonymic objects to invoke,
eliding restraint with inaccessibility in the manner of the parlatory grate.
(Joseph Jérôme le Français de Lalande, in his *Voyage d'un françois en Italie*,
published in 1769, ingeniously turns cicisbei themselves into figures who
obstruct flirtation with Italian women.'[6]) The less tangible obstacles in the
way of understanding the custom are nonetheless emphasized very
strongly; travellers repeatedly promise elucidation and then fail to provide
it. The Earl of Cork and Orrery's summary of cicisbeism in his *Letters from
Italy* (1773) is triumphantly periphrastic: 'Upon the whole, we may pronounce equitably this sentence, that if the *Lady* is chaste, she has great
virtue; if the *Chichisbee* is chaste, he has greater.'[7] Dupaty's account of
cicisbeism in Genoa is phrased almost entirely in the form of questions.[8]

---

4   p. 84.
5   Vol. I, p. 62; emphasis added. See also John Moore's declaration that 'the interest you take
     in a beautiful woman is heightened on seeing her in the dress of a nun' (*View of Society*,
     vol. II, p. 313). The harem, in Orientalist writings, provides an obvious example of a sim-
     ilar site of fascination, in which the obstacles confronting the traveller's gaze – the veil, the
     walls of the seraglio, the eunuchs guarding the seraglio – serve to emphasize both inac-
     cessibility and extremity of restraint. See, for example, Savary, *Lettres*, vol. I, pp. 164–5;
     for an account of the harem as a fantasmatic *mise-en-scène* of this kind, see Grosrichard,
     Structure du sérail, pp. 153–6.
6   Vol. V, p. 142. See also Sade, *Voyage d'Italie*, p. 147.
7   p. 116.
8   Dupaty, *Lettres*, vol. I, pp. 82–3.

Women's resistance to understanding is implicitly defined as a characteristic that must positively invite investigation, and excite an eager curiosity on the part of the reader. Female traveller-narrators, when commenting
on the behaviour and desires of foreign women, are able to claim an addi-
tional authority by reference to their gender: the authority of someone
who, having firmly established that foreign women are not easily understood, can nevertheless claim to enjoy privileged opportunities to enquire
into female manners. Hester Piozzi promises privileged access to female
secrets when she reminds the reader that she is a woman, who will in the
course of everyday events often find herself in situations where other
women will feel free to confide in her:

> The women are not behind-hand in openness of confidence and comical
> sincerity. We have all heard much of Italian cicisbeism; I had a mind to
> know how matters really stood; and took the nearest way to information by
> asking a mighty beautiful and apparently artless young creature, *not noble,*
> how that affair was managed, for there is no harm done *I am sure,* said I.[9]

This pointed observation provokes a reply that repeatedly stops just short
of full elucidation: Piozzi manages to emphasise that she is the privileged
recipient of ingenuous confidences while at the same time ensuring that
the custom retains the fascinations of mystery:

> 'Why no,' replied she, 'no great *harm* to be sure: except wearisome atten-
> tions from a man one cares little about: for my own part,' continued she, 'I
> detest the custom, as I happen to love my husband excessively, and desire
> nobody's company in the world but his. We are not *people of fashion* though
> you know, nor at all rich; so how should we set fashions for our betters?
> They would only say, see how jealous he is! if *Mr. Such-a-one* sat much with
> me at home, or went with me to the Corso; and I *must* go with some gentle-
> man you know: and the men are such ungenerous creatures, and have such
> ways with them: I want money often, and this *cavaliere servente* pays the
> bills, and so the connection draws closer – *that's all.*'[10]

Piozzi then reminds the reader that the fascination of the custom is
derived from distance, by emphasizing that cicisbeism interests her much
more strongly than it interests the Italians:

---

[9] Piozzi, *Observations,* vol. I, p. 100; Piozzi also refers to the potential advantages of 'my
     demi-naturalization' (that is, her marriage to an Italian; vol. I, p. 67), in allowing her priv-
     ileged access to the foreign.

[10] *Ibid.,* vol. I, pp. 100–1.

And your husband! said I – 'Oh, why he likes to see me well dressed; he is very good natured, and very charming; I love him to my heart.' And your confessor! cried I. – 'Oh, why he is *used to it*' – in the Milanese dialect – *è assuefaà.*[11]

Women and antiquities provide 'moderate difficulty'

In all these commentaries on cicisbeism, including Piozzi's, the traveller's failure to define precisely what is going on produces a strong effect of ironic knowingness: such commentaries imply that the resort to obliquity is neces-sary because the truth proclaims itself all too clearly and indelicately. An effect of this kind – in other words, a suggestion that women might not in fact be so difficult to understand – is common in accounts of female behav-iour, and provides a clue to another precondition for the rhetorical useful-ness of women in travel writing: at the same time that versions of the feminine supply metaphors for the intriguing inaccessibility of the foreign, they also promise to satisfy the traveller's demand that the topography of the foreign, however mysterious, should not in the end prove entirely resistant to assimilation and appropriation. At Calais, Yorick describes a woman who, by virtue of his fleeting visual impression of her, eludes and excites his curiosity, while at the same time inducing a cheerful confidence in the pleas-ure if not the accuracy of his own effort of imaginative speculation:

> I had not yet seen her face – 'twas not material; for the drawing was instantly set about, and long before we had got to the door of the Remise, *Fancy* had finished the whole head, and pleased herself as much with its fit-ting her goddess, as if she had dived into the TIBER for it.[12]

The gratification that an antiquary might derive from reconstructing an antique statue serves, here, as a metaphor for a combination of the two attractions that women are seen as supplying: on the one hand, a resistance to understanding and, on the other, a promise that this resistance will not be too overwhelmingly daunting. Yorick, in other words, elides women with the second category of objects that travel writing of the period

---

[11]   *Ibid.*, vol. I, p. 101.

[12]   Sterne, *A Sentimental Journey*, p. 17. To cite a travel book concerned with more distant regions: Frédéric Cailliaud's *Voyage à Méroé* (3 vols (Paris, 1826), vol. 1, 77, 97) con-structs an amusingly precise parallel between the viewing of antiquities and the viewing of women: the two categories of objects are both presented, in successive stages of Cailliaud's travels, as domains to which direct access is forbidden, and which the traveller is forced to view from a distance.

regularly classifies as resistant to appropriation: vestiges of the ancient past. Ruins and antiquities are assumed to be mysterious and inaccessible by virtue of their origins in a remote past. (In Thomas Love Peacock's *Nightmare Abbey*, published in 1818, Scythrop – a figure based on Shelley – dismisses the much-vaunted pleasure of visiting Italy, in order to wander 'among a few mouldy ruins, that are only imperfect indexes to lost volumes of glory', precisely by a metaphor that transmutes the antique into the feminine: 'It is, indeed, much the same as if a lover should dig up the buried form of his mistress, and gaze upon relics which are any thing but herself.')[13] The material remains of this past are nonetheless also defined as objects that are not entirely beyond the reach of the traveller's efforts to understand and assimilate them. Alexander Gerard, in his *Essay on Taste* (1759), emphasizes the gratification to be derived from this paradoxical mixture of mystery and accessibility when he uses antiquities to illustrate the principle that 'the exercise of thought, which moderate difficulty produces, is a principal source of the pleasure we take in study and investigation of every kind':

> Witness the delight, with which antiquaries bestow indefatigable pains on recovering or illustrating ancient fragments, recommended only by their age, and obscurity, and scarce apprehended to be, on any other account, of great importance.[14]

Gerard's antiquary, investigating his 'ancient fragments', is involved in a relatively sober process of enquiry. Yorick, however, addressing 'Fancy', as he considers his own fascination with the woman's face, notes the ease with which objects that resist understanding can stimulate imaginative efforts of a wilder kind:

> But thou art a seduced, and a seducing slut; and albeit thou cheatest us seven times a day with thy pictures and images, yet with so many charms dost thou do it, and thou deckest out thy pictures in the shapes of so many angels of light, 'tis a shame to break with thee.[15]

When Archibald Alison produces his own account of the pleasures of the antiquary, in his *Essays on the Nature and Principles of Taste* (1790), he emphasizes this same 'seducing' power of obscurity to propel the fancy into producing visions of its own:

---

[13] p. 98.

[14] pp. 4–5.

[15] Sterne, *A Sentimental Journey*, p. 17.

The antiquarian, in his cabinet, surrounded by the relics of former ages, seems to himself to be removed to periods that are long since past, and indulges in the imagination of living in a world, which, by a very natural kind of prejudice, we are always willing to believe was both wiser and better than the present. All that is venerable or laudable in the history of those times present themselves to his memory. The gallantry, the heroism, the patriotism of antiquity rise again before his view, softened by the obscurity in which they are involved, and rendered more seducing to the imagination by that obscurity itself, which, while it mingles a sentiment of regret amid his pursuits, serves at the same time to stimulate his fancy to fill up, by its own creation, those long intervals of time of which history has preserved no record.[16]

Like Piozzi in her account of cicisbeism, moreover, Alison introduces figures to whom the objects of enquiry are tediously familiar – who, in the words of Piozzi's informant, are 'used to it' – in order to emphasize, by contrast, the fascinations of viewing the ancient world from the standpoint of someone who is not 'used to it' at all. Asserting that 'there is no man... acquainted with the history or the literature of antiquity, who has not felt his imagination inflamed by the most trifling circumstances connected with such periods', he notes the 'established grandeur' which 'the names of the Ilyssus, the Tiber, the Forum, the Capitol, &c.' assume for us:

No man, however, is weak enough to believe, that to the citizen of Athens, or of Rome, such names were productive of similar emotions. To him they undoubtedly conveyed no other ideas, than those of the particular divisions of the city in which he dwelt, and were heard of consequence, with the same indifference that the citizen of London now hears of the Strand, or the Tower.[17]

Such principles are constantly invoked in travel writings of the late eighteenth and early nineteenth centuries. Joseph Forsyth, commenting on Tivoli in his *Remarks on Antiquities, Arts, and Letters during an Excursion in Italy* (1813), reaffirms the power of obscurity to stimulate a pleasurable effort of the imagination:

In landscape we love ruined temples, a Gothic castle, a moss-grown cell, more than the most elegant villa; because ancient Romans, a feudal baron, and a hermit, being remote from our own times or manners, are more poetical beings than a private gentleman or a modern prince. We know what the

---

16   Vol. I, pp. 39–40.
17   *Ibid.*, vol. I, pp. 106–7.

villa and its inhabitants are; one glance gives us all, and exhausts the subject. But we must fancy what a ruin has been; we trace and we lose its design, we rebuild and re-people it, we call in history, we compose, we animate, we create; and man ever delights in his own creation.[18]

Women of antique appearance and feminized ruins

By selecting objects of commentary that bear the imprint both of the antique and of a version of the feminine, then, the traveller is able to affirm with double insistence that the topography does in fact offer the allurements of mysterious otherness, and, at the same time, is able to suggest – again, with double emphasis – that this topography positively invites an effort of appropriation. One category of sights that merge the antique with a version of the feminine is that of ancient ruins that bear the imprint of a female presence (Figure 5). Accounts of such ruins often emphasize the remote, vanished nature of the past, and the difficulties experienced by the classical scholar in investigating this past, while at the same time suggesting that antique femininity may prove surprisingly accessible to a more artlessly intuitive approach. In Canto IV of Byron's *Childe Harold's Pilgrimage* (1818), the narrator, contemplating the Tomb of Cecilia Metella, explains at enormous length how little we know about the woman whom it commemorates: 'Was she as those who love their lords, or they / Who love the lords of others?', he asks – was she 'Profuse of joy – or 'gainst it did she war, / Inveterate in virtue?' He eventually decides, however, that he has forged a close relationship both with Cecilia Metella and with the ancient past:

> I know not why – but standing thus by thee
> It seems as if I had thine inmate known,
> Thou tomb! and other days come back on me
> With recollected music...[19]

In proclaiming this understanding with the tomb's 'inmate', the speaker uses the conjunction between the antique and the feminine to allow him to convert historical time into personal time – a task that travel writing of this period constantly sets itself, and defines as crucial to the efficient appropriation of the foreign. By defining an ancient monument, fragment or ruin as the site of a ghostly female presence, the traveller, implicitly invoking an

---

[18]   pp. 279–80.

[19]   Stanza 104, lines 1–4; in Byron, *Complete Poetical Works*, vol. II, p. 159.

Sepulcrum Ceciliæ Metellæ, nunc
dictum = Capo di Bove =

*Ecclesia s. Urbani vulgo dicta = alla
Cafarella = Fons Nymphæ Egeriæ,
et Camenarum a Numa frequentatus.*

Figure 5 Engravings of the Tomb of Cecilia Metella and the Fountain of Egeria, from
Marien Vasi [Mariano Vasi], *Itinéraire Instructif de Rome* 2 vols (Rome, 1797), a translation
of Vasi's *Itinerario istruttivo di Roma*, 2 vols (Rome, 1791); 12.7 x 7.15 cm overall.

established elision between the feminine and the personal, makes the vestige of antiquity more easily transportable into a private domain of emotional intimacy. Living women who appear in ancient sites also serve to accomplish this same shift from ancient history into personal emotion. In one of the fictional biographies in William Beckford's *Biographical Memoirs of Extraordinary Painters* (1780), the painter Og of Basan travels down to Italy from northern Europe, and lingers in the 'enchanted region' of Tivoli, embroiled in amorous dalliance with a 'young native'. This 'beloved nymph' not only resembles an antiquity herself ('Her form was perfectly Grecian, and the contour of her face exceeded those of the antique Julia'): she also assumes an active role in Og's experience of moving antiquity into personal time, in indulging, with him, their shared taste for 'the ruins that lay scattered over her country':

> She would often lead him to meadows of greenswerd, where she had observed some sculptured marble overgrown with flowers; when the sun had cast his setting gleams on the Sybil's temple, she would hasten to her love and conduct him to a grove of cypresses, and sing under their shades till the moon dimly discovered the waterfalls to her view.[20]

A similar *mise-en-scène* of gentle pastoral eroticism, deploying a woman as a means of shifting ancient history into an intimate, private world, is set up by Dupaty, when the traveller and his companions are served their dinner in the Temple of the Sibyl at Tivoli, and relish the combination of 'de l'appetit, des mets sains, le sentiment toujours présent du lieu où nous étions'. Among 'tous ces plaisirs réunis', Dupaty lists 'l'arrivée imprévue d'une charmante Tivolienne'. The woman is first identified with the accessible, readily consumable delights that she provides for the travellers: 'du lait blanc et pur, comme ses belles dents, et des fraises, aussi vermeilles que ses jeunes lêvres'. At the same time, the travellers equate her with the ruin – the site of antique femininity – by their eagerness actively to make their mark on each: they first cause the woman to blush, through their smiles and glances, and then proceed to carve their names on the masonry. Dupaty describes this 'dîner champêtre' as supplying 'un des moments les plus doux de ma vie'.[21]

---

[20] p. 44.

[21] Dupaty, *Lettres*, vol. I, pp. 255–6: 'A good appetite, wholesome dishes, the mind present to the place we were in' (vol. I, p. 198); vol. I, p. 257: 'these united pleasures; (vol. I, p. 199); vol. I, p. 256: 'a charming girl of Tivoli brought us milk, pure and white as her own fine teeth, together with strawberries, that vied in colour with the natural vermilion of her lips' (vol. I, p. 199); vol. I, p. 257: 'this rural dinner', 'one of the most delicious hours of my life' (vol. I, p. 199).

Another category of sights that merges the feminine and the antique is that of women who resemble antiquities. (As the classical appearance of Og's 'beloved nymph' suggests, this category often overlaps with that of women who appear in ancient places.) In Germaine de Staël's novel *Corinne; ou, l'Italie* (1807), the heroine is described as 'grande, mais un peu forte, à la manière des statues grecques'. As she makes her initial appearance on the Capitol, in Rome, where she is to be crowned with laurel in recognition of her talents as an *improvvisatrice,* Corinne is dressed in the costume of Domenichino's *Sibyl.* Her identification with the Sibyls of antiquity is reinforced when she reveals that she has chosen for her 'maison de campagne', in Tivoli, a spot where her garden faces the Temple of the Sibyl. (It is in front of this temple, high on its rocky precipice, that Elisabeth Vigée-Lebrun situates the heroine in her allegorized portrait, *Madame de Staël as Corinne,* painted in1807–8; Figure 6.) The narrator exclaims: 'Quel lieu pouvoit mieux convenir à l'habitation de Corinne, en Italie, que le séjour consacré à la Sibylle, à la mémoire d'une femme animée par une inspiration divine!' The scene on the Capitol is witnessed by Oswald, Lord Nelvil, a Scotsman on the Grand Tour, who is struck by Corinne's paradoxical combination of accessibility and mystery – the two qualities with which women and antiquities are so often invested. He feels, in fact, that this combination marks her out as one of the wonders of Italy: 'Ce mystère et cette publicité tout à la fois, cette femme dont tout le monde parloit, et dont on ne connoissoit pas le véritable nom, parurent à lord Nelvil l'une des merveilles du singulier pays qu'il venoit voir.'[22]

Corinne, like the ruins that bear the trace of ancient female presences and the women who appear in ancient sites, accomplishes shifts between ancient history and personal emotion. When she appears on the Capitol, the narrator specifically notes her power to mediate not only between past and present, but also between the public domain, occupied by Sibyls, as priest-esses of Apollo, and the domain of everyday life: 'elle donnoit à la fois l'idée d'une prêtresse d'Apollon, qui s'avançoit vers le temple du Soleil, et d'une femme parfaitement simple dans les rapports habituels de la vie.' At Tivoli, the comment that identifies her talent with the Sibyl's divine

---

22 Vol. I, p. 46 (book. II, chapter 1): 'tall, and, as we frequently see among the Grecian stat-ues, rather robust' (*Corinne; or, Italy*, p. 21; further translations in footnotes are taken from this same edition); vol. I, pp. 45 (book II, chapter 1), p. 216 (book VIII, chapter 4): 'What place could more appropriately have been selected as the home of Corinne than that consecrated to the Sibyl, a woman divinely inspired?' (p. 144); vol. I, p. 44 (book II, chapter 1): 'Such mystery and publicity, united in the fate of a female of whom every one spoke, yet whose real name no one knew, appeared to Nevil [*sic*] as among the wonders of the land he came to see' (p. 19).

Figure 6 Elisabeth Vigée-Lebrun, *Madame de Staël as Corinne* (1807-8); oil on canvas, 140 x 118 cm.

inspiration is followed by a reference to the heroine's ability to elide past and present in a more domestic context: 'La maison de Corinne étoit ravissante; elle étoit ornée avec l'élégance du goût moderne, et cependant le charme d'une imagination qui se plaît dans les beautés antiques s'y faisoit sentir.'[23]

The shift into the sphere of personal emotion is so dramatic, during the visit to Tivoli, that it places Corinne's identification with the Sibyl

---

[23] *Ibid.*, vol. I, p. 46 (book II, chapter 1): 'She gave you at the same instant the idea of a priestess of Apollo advancing towards his temple, and of a woman born to fulfil the usual duties of life with perfect simplicity' (p. 20); vol. I, p. 216 (book VIII, chapter 3): 'The house was charming; decked in all the elegance of modern taste, yet evidently by a classic hand' (p. 144).

under threat, and aligns her with another figure from the ancient past (in this case, from myth and literature). She visits her 'maison de campagne' with Lord Nelvil, whom she has been conducting round the sights of Rome. He is moved by the delights of the spot to suggest to her that 'tu peux, sans crainte, t'unir à mon sort, il n'aura plus rien de fatal'. Corinne, in response, refuses to speculate about fate ('Ne touchons pas à la destinée...'), and so distances herself from the Sibyl, whose role is precisely to make pronouncements about the future. She later shows her lover around her collection of paintings, which include a series of 'tableaux dramatiques tirés de quatre grands poètes'. The first of these depicts the shade of Dido turning away from Aeneas, as he tries to approach her in the underworld. In describing the work, the heroine particularly emphasizes the visual contrast that the painter establishes between Dido, as a ghost, and the Sibyl who guides Aeneas around the lower regions: 'La couleur vapoureuse des ombres, et la pâle nature qui les environne, font contraste avec l'air de vie d'Énée et de la Sibylle qui le conduit.' The scene anticipates Corinne's final improvisation, when, losing her Sibylline power to utter inspired verses to her audience, she is unable to recite her own words in person, and is reduced to a mere ghost of her former self; for Lord Nelvil, she is now 'cette ombre qui lui sembloit une apparition cruelle'. She is, at this point, explicitly described as identifying with Dido; as she sees Oswald, she at first reaches out towards him, but then turns aside, 'comme Didon lorsqu'elle rencontre Énée dans un monde où les passions humaines ne doivent plus pénétrer'.[24]

In her later improvisation at Miseno, in contrast, Corinne's sense of impending sorrow in her personal life, far from compromising her identification with the sibyls of antiquity, allows her to identify with a sibyl all

[24] *Ibid.*, vol. I, pp. 217, 219 (book VIII, chapter 4): 'Fearlessly, then, unite thy fate with mine: there is no danger now!'; 'Well,... let us not disturb this peace by naming Fate'; 'And now come my dramatic *chefs d'œuvre* drawn from the works of four great poets'; 'The vapourous colour of the phantoms, and the pale scenes around them, contast the air of life in Æneas, and the Sibyl who conducts him' (pp. 144, 146); vol. II, p. 297, (book XX, chapter 5): 'she was to him as an apparition that haunts a night of fever'; 'like Dido when she met Æneas in a world which human passions should not penetrate' (pp. 385, 384).

Mary Sheriff, discussing the heroine's identification with the sibyl of Tivoli in the novel, and the selection of Tivoli as the setting for the figure in Vigée-Lebrun's portrait of de Staël as Corinne, emphasizes the provocative stance taken by both novelist and painter in adopting a sibyl – a woman who assumes a public role – as a literary model, within the context of Napoleonic France (*The Exceptional Woman*, p. 241). My own point here is not that de Staël abandons her view that a woman of talent requires public recognition, but that she presents the shift from the historical to the personal as a movement that fatally undermines Corinne's ability to claim such recognition.

the more strongly (Figure 7). Towards the end of her improvisation on '*les souvenirs que ces lieux retraçoient*', she once again muses on fate: 'La fatalité ne poursuit-elle pas les âmes exaltées, les poètes dont l'imagination tient à la puissance d'aimer et de souffrir.' Distinguishing between the sufferings of such exalted souls and the happy indifference of the vulgar, she explicitly mentions one of the ancient sibyls (presumably the Sibyl of Cuma, to whose Grotto she has alluded in her improvisation) as a woman whose genius brings pain and sorrow in its wake:

> Que vouloient dire les anciens, quand ils parloient de la destinée avec tant de terreur? Que peut-elle, cette destinée, sur les êtres vulgaires et paisibles? Ils suivent les saisons, ils parcourent docilement le cours habituel de la vie. Mais la prêtresse qui rendoit les oracles se sentoit agitée par une puissance cruelle.[25]

As though to emphasize that she too is 'agitée par une puissance cruelle', Corinne concludes her performance by fainting. In this act of identification with the Sibyl, she affirms that public brilliance is accompanied by sufferings which, she implies, may well include sufferings in love; just before she collapses into the arms of Lord Nelvil, she reminds her audience that 'les passions exercent en nous une tyrannie tumultueuse, qui ne nous laisse ni liberté, ni repos'.[26] Antique femininity, then, in this chapter, is simultaneously elided with a public display of talent and with personal anguish: Corinne's power to shift antiquity into personal time is presented

---

25 Staël, *Corinne; ou, l'Italie*, vol. II, p. 72 (book XIII, chapter 4): 'the memories that scene recalled' (p. 223); the reference to the Sibyl's cave is also here; vol. II, p. 76, (book XIII, chapter 4); the improvisation from which these two passages are taken is translated, in Isabel Hill's edition (p. 228), by 'L.E.L' (Letitia Landon):

For Destiny compels exalted minds: -
The poet, whose imagination draws
Its power from loving and from suffering.

Why spoke the ancients with such awe of Fate?
What had this terrible Fate to do with them,
The common and the quiet, who pursue
The seasons, and still follow timidly
The beaten track of ordinary life?
But she, the priestess of the oracle,
Shook with the presence of the cruel power.

26 *Ibid.*, vol. II, p. 77 (book XIII, chapter 4). Landon, in Isabel Hill's edition (p. 229), translates these words as:

Tumultuous tyranny
Our passions exercise, and neither leave
Repose nor liberty.

Figure 7 Aubry-Lecomte, lithograph of *Corinne Improvising at Miseno* (1827); 37.6 x42.65 cm; after the painting by François Gérard (1822), which the lithograph reverses.

as all the greater for her proclivity to suffuse her public evocations of antique inspiration with the intensity of intimate emotions.

The past as 'one enormous abeyance'

When Corinne faints at Miseno, she testifies to the power of memory to intervene actively – and in unsettling ways – in the events of contemporary life. From around the middle of the eighteenth century onwards, travel writings frequently map out the relation between the ancient past and the present as one in which the past is always poised to resurge disquietingly within the contemporary topography, and use various repositories of memory, such as ruins, antique fragments, and ghosts, as sites or vehicles for such a resurgence. A conversation in an early twentieth-century novel, Elizabeth Bowen's *The Hotel* (1927), neatly illustrates the mixture of danger and excitement with which such a resurgence is invested. A young girl, Sydney, and a clergyman, Mr Milton, both guests in the hotel of the title, are walking together near the coastline somewhere in the South of France. Looking down on 'the village with its toppling campanili', Mr

Milton asks Sydney if she can tell him why it is walled, and she replies: 'Against the Saracens. They used to land along this coast and ravage the valleys, so they built the villages as high as possible and fortified them.' Mr Milton's bland observation that 'it would be interesting to get in touch with local records' is swept aside to make way for some wilder fantasies:

> 'I don't know whether there are any. Do you remember the *Decameron* lady who fished in the sea near here and was carried off by a pirate whom she liked from the first moment better than her husband?'
> 'Husbands' shares were not good in those days,' he said tolerantly.[27]

This narrative of abduction suggests a way in which the past might resurge, and invest the banalities of the present with an enlivening element of 'dust, panic and ecstasy':

> 'Wouldn't it be nice, she said, suddenly smiling, if the Saracens were to appear on the skyline, land, and ravage the Hotel? They all take for granted – down there – that there aren't any more Saracens, but for all we know they may only be in abeyance. The whole Past, for a matter of fact, may be one enormous abeyance.'[28]

The possibility that the historical past might intervene in the personal dramas of the present is repeatedly raised in late eighteenth-century and early nineteenth-century accounts of ruins that bear the imprint of ancient female presences. Og, in Beckford's *Biographical Memoirs,* places himself at the mercy of a disturbing alliance between historical and personal repositories of memory after abandoning his 'perfectly Grecian' lover: 'At length Og recollected, he was born not to spend all his days at Tivoli, and whilst his beloved nymph was sleeping by his side, he arose, and without venturing to cast one look behind, fled like a criminal towards Rome.' Og enjoys huge professional success in the Eternal City, but is reminded of the woman whom he has abandoned when he contemplates, by moonlight, 'the magnificence of the ancient Romans reduced to heaps of mouldering ruins, objects continually before his eyes'. 'The recollection of Tivoli', we are told, 'now stole insensibly into his mind'; after some disturbing dreams – some which represent the young woman 'on the distant shore of rapid torrents, beckoning him to console her in vain', and some from which he 'would wake in horror, crying, "I drown! I drown!"'– he goes back there and learns from her brother that the nymph has in fact killed herself, by

---

27 pp. 34, 35.
28 *Ibid.,* p. 35.

throwing herself into the river. 'Cowardice,' Beckford blandly remarks, 'generally accompanies guilt':

> Og, terrified at the resolute aspect of the young man, and appalled by the lively sense of his wrongs, retired without making any reply, and remounting his horse, which he had led when he ascended the steeps of Tivoli, galloped away with astonishing swiftness, without determining where to direct his route.[29]

The painter at last stops near the Tomb of Cecilia Metella (Figure 5), by the Via Appia; he seeks shelter within the tomb, but 'noxious birds' drive him out, and although he finds 'some branches loaded with fruit', which 'offered themselves opportunely to allay his hunger', these fruits appear within a 'desolate scene', as though metaphorically reminding him of the fruits of faithless passion. Having spent 'half the night' in 'vain lamentations', he falls asleep only in 'the grey twilight' of dawn, and sees his 'beloved nymph' as an apparition in a dream:

> A fictitious city was stretched out before him, enlightened by a fictitious moon. The shade of her he loved skimmed along a colonnade, which cast its shadows on the plain, and then stood leaning on the lonely pillar, uttered a feeble groan and glided by his side. Her wet garments clinging round her delicate shape, her swollen eyes and drooping hands, announced a melancholy fate. She seemed to say, 'Why do my affections still linger on thee beyond the tomb! – Why doth my pale bosom still cherish its wonted fires! – How comes it that I do not appear riding on a sulphureous cloud, shaking a torch in my hand and screaming out Perjury! – No! my gentle nature forbids me to injure thee. But mark! Quit yonder fatal city; seek the islands of the south, and may'st thou expiate thy crime!' The form next shed some visionary tears, and seemed to mingle with the mists of the morning.[30]

At the Tomb of Cecilia Metella, then, in this narrative, antique femininity acquires a more dangerously dynamic character than at Tivoli: the ancient female presence, far from entering into the kind of affectionate understanding with the traveller that she seems to establish in *Childe Harold*, leaves him to the mercies of another, more alarming bearer of memory. This spectral female describes herself as 'gentle', but it is evident from her effect on Og, propelling him into frenzied motion, that the term belies her destructive power:

---

[29] pp. 45, 50, 51, 52, 53, 54.

[30] *Ibid.*, pp. 55, 56, 56–7, 57–8.

Og, awakened by the sun-beams, recollected his dream, and without even taking leave of the Cardinal Grossocavallo, in whose care he had deposited a coffer containing the rewards of his pencil, heedlessly took the road to Naples, resolving to pass into Sicily, and end his days in that island.[31]

De Staël, in *Corinne*, invests the Tomb of Cecilia Metella with a similar power to disrupt the lives of those who visit it – or, at least, to reinforce processes of disruption that are already at work. When Corinne takes Lord Nelvil to visit the monument, she is reminded of Propertius's elegy on Cornelia, in which the dead woman addresses her husband from beyond the grave. This elegy, in turn, prompts her to see a sad distinction between her own past and Cornelia's unsullied conjugal devotion: 'qu'il est digne d'envie,' she muses tearfully, 'le sort de la femme qui peut avoir ainsi conservé la plus parfaite unité dans sa destinée, et n'emporte au tombeau qu'un souvenir'.[32]

In answer to Oswald's questions, Corinne then explains that, that before she met him, 'mon imagination a pu me tromper sur l'intérêt qu'on m'inspiroit!' Oswald feels his heart seized by 'un sentiment cruel, un soupçon pénible' at this inadvertent confession that Corinne's life will not be marked by the memory of one man alone. The suggestion of a danger threatening the relationship between the lovers, as Corinne is forced to defend her previous sentimental entanglements, is anticipated by the narrator's description of the plants that the two of them observe in the Campagna, as they proceed from the Fountain of Egeria to the Tomb – plants whose resistance to human control foreshadows the unruly passions that are to cause endless trouble in the narrative that follows:

> Ces plantes parasites se glissent dans les tombeaux, décorent les ruines, et semblent là seulement pour honorer les morts. *On diroit que l'orgueilleuse nature a repoussé tous les travaux de l'homme.*[33]

The proleptic role of nature, in indicating the dangers that await Corinne and Oswald, is affirmed, two short chapters later, when Lord Nelvil comments on the *aria cattiva* that blights the entire region, including the

---

31 *Ibid.*, pp. 54, 55, 58.

32 Vol. I, p. 123 (book V, chapter 1): 'How enviable the woman who preserves this perfect unity in her fate, and carries but one remembrance to the grave!' (p. 78).

33 *Ibid.*: 'Must I confess, that, ere I knew you, I might have deceived myself as to the interest with which others inspired me?' 'A cruel suspicion seized the heart of Oswald'; vol. I, p. 121 (emphasis added): 'The parasitic tribes creep round the tombs, and decorate the ruins, as if in honour of their dead. Proud nature... there repulses the care of man' (p. 77). All these references are to book V, chapter 1.

gardens within the city limits, which offer the traveller scenes of beauty
and fertility: '– J'aime, disoit Oswald à Corinne, ce danger mystérieux,
invisible, ce danger sous la forme des impressions les plus douces.'[34]

In other accounts of sites of antique femininity, too, vegetation reinforces the promise or threat that the past might resurge, and display its
enduring vitality – that the passions, in their intrinsic turbulence, might
provide points of continuity between antiquity and the contemporary
world. Byron's description of the Fountain of Egeria (Figure 5) in *Childe
Harold's Pilgrimage* – the spot where Numa, King of Rome, supposedly
met the nymph Egeria for midnight trysts – establishes a series of
metaphorical slippages between the 'fantastically tangled' plant life around
the spring and the perilous, frenzied character of passion. As the traveller-
narrator asks whether the 'transports' of Egeria and Numa were blighted
by satiety – 'the deadly weed which cloys', his musings become yet more
complicatedly enmeshed in vegetable metaphors, and he reflects upon the
'weeds of dark luxuriance, tares of haste' that arise from our passions:

> Flowers whose wild odours breathe but agonies,
> And trees whose gums are poison; such the plants
> Which spring beneath her steps as Passion flies
> O'er the world's wilderness, and vainly pants
> For some celestial fruit forbidden to our wants.[35]

Women who revive the past

When a version of the feminine draws antiquity into the domain of the personal, however, a third variety of narrative is sometimes generated: neither
a straightforward story of simple duplication and reinforcement of gratification, as in Dupaty's 'dîner champêtre' in the Temple of the Sibyl, nor a
tale of disruption and danger. Women who appear in ancient sites often
supply metaphors not for the destabilizing powers of memory but for a
resurgence of life, alongside a recognition of the remoteness of the ancient
world. A well-known resurgence of this kind is charted in a much later text:
Freud's essay 'Delusions and Dreams in Jensen's *Gradiva*' (1907), which
summarizes and analyses Wilhelm Jensen's *Gradiva: ein pompejanisches
Phantasiestück* (1903). In Jensen's novella, a young archaeologist, Norbert

---

34 *Ibid.*, vol. I, pp. 132–3 (book V, chapter 3): "'I love such invisible danger," said Oswald,
    "veiled as it is in delight"' (p. 86).

35 Canto IV, stanza 117, line 1; stanza 119, line 9; stanza120, line 3, lines 5-9; in Byron,
    Complete Poetical Works, vol. II, pp. 163,164.

Hanold, 'has surrendered his interest in life in exchange for an interest in the remains of classical antiquity'. He displays no interest in living women, but is attracted to a bas-relief, which he has discovered, in the past, in a museum of antiquities in Rome, and which represents a young girl, lifting her flowing dress a little to reveal her sandalled feet, and stepping forward in a manner that he finds especially charming; he calls her 'Gradiva': 'the girl who steps along'. A plaster cast of this work hangs in his study in a German university town. Hanold sees Gradiva in a dream, buried in ashes in Pompeii on the day of the eruption of Vesuvius in 79 AD, and is convinced that this has in fact been her fate. His researches soon offer him a pretext for a journey to Italy, and he travels restlessly southwards to Pompeii. At 'the "hot and holy" mid-day hour, which the ancients regarded as the hour of ghosts', he sees the Gradiva of the relief; in the events that follow, this figure is finally revealed to be not a ghost, as Hanold at first thinks, but a living woman, Zoe Bertgang, whom he has known well in the days before 'archaeology took hold of him and left him with an interest only in women of marble and bronze'.[36]

The ancient bas-relief, then, plays a crucial part in reviving the memory of this living woman. Zoe herself, however, assumes an active role in reviving not only the personal past but also antiquity; her fitness for this role of revival is proclaimed in her name, since her first name means 'life' and her surname, Hanold decides, 'means the same as "Gradiva" and describes someone "who steps along brilliantly."' Once an understanding has finally been reached between them, and their mutual attraction avowed, he asks her to stage a visual tableau in which she seems to transform the woman of marble into a living physical presence. It is, as Mary Jacobus comments, 'a moment which Freud takes evident pleasure in rehearsing':

> The delusion had now been conquered by a beautiful reality; but before the two lovers left Pompeii it was still to be honoured once again. When they reached the Herculanean Gate, where, at the entrance to the Via Consolare, the street is crossed by some ancient stepping-stones, Norbert Hanold paused and asked the girl to go ahead of him. She understood him 'and, pulling up her dress a little with her left hand, Zoe Bertgang, Gradiva rediviva, walked past, held in his eyes, which seemed to gaze as though in a dream; so, with her quietly tripping gait, she stepped through the sunlight over the stepping-stones to the other side of the street.'[37]

---

36 See Freud, 'Delusions and Dreams', pp. 36, 37, 59. Some points of comparison between 'Delusions and Dreams' and earlier narratives of encounters with the antique and the feminine are explored in Chard, 'The Road to Ruin'.

37 Freud, 'Delusions and Dreams', pp. 62, 64–5; Jacobus, *Reading Woman*, p. 95.

This narrative of revival, in Jensen's novella and in Freud's essay, draws on a plot that is deployed in a number of late eighteenth-century and early nineteenth-century writings. Lamartine, in a long 'note additionnelle' to his 'Dernier Chant du pèlerinage d'Harold', relates the story of a visit to Pompeii, during which he walks up a street newly cleared of ashes, preceded by three young girls: 'Elles ressemblaient à trois beaux songes de vie égarés dans les régions de la mort. Une seule âme comme la leur repeuplerait un grand sépulchre.' The traveller is invited by the director of a band of archaeological diggers to take a pick and uncover some remains, but hands the pick to the young girls instead; at a few feeble blows, the sand runs away like water. Lamartine observes that 'quand elles relevaient leurs fronts en secouant leurs tresses, on croyait voir dans cette exhumation charmante un jeu ou une allégorie vivante, semblable à ces allégories ingénieuses inventées ou déifiées par l'antiquité'. He resolutely declares, however, that this spectacle is 'ni une allégorie ni un jeu':

> La cendre en s'ébranlant découvrit successivement à nos regards une porte, une cour, un bassin orné de mosaïque, des statuettes admirablement bien conservées dans leur moule de poussière, des instruments de musique, et des peintures sur les murs aussi vives de couleurs que si le pinceau n'était point encore séché. C'était l'art sous toutes les formes, ressuscité par la beauté, et retrouvant à la fois son soleil dans le ciel, et son culte dans les jeux de trois jeunes femmes.[38]

Corinne, dancing the Tarantella at a ball in Rome, is invested with similar powers of revival. She is described taking her inspiration from a distant past, but reanimating that past so as to produce new works of art:

> Corinne connaissoit si bien toutes les attitudes que représentent les peintres et les sculpteurs antiques, que, par un léger mouvement de ses bras, en plaçant son tambour de basque tantôt au-dessus de sa tête, tantôt en avant avec une de ses mains, tandis que l'autre parcouroit les grelots avec une incroyable dextérité, elle rappeloit les danseuses d'Herculaneum, et faisoit

---

38 Lamartine, *Dernier Chant*, p. 298: 'when they lifted their foreheads to shake their hair off, it was as though one saw in this charming exhumation a game or a living allegory, similar to those ingenious allegories invented or deified by antiquity'; 'neither an allegory nor a game'; 'As the ashes were shaken away, they revealed to our eyes in turn a door, a courtyard, a basin ornamented with mosaic work, little statues admirably preserved in their mould of dust, musical instruments, and paintings on walls with their colours as fresh as if the paintbrush were not yet dry. It was art in all its forms, revived by beauty, and finding at one and the same time its sun in the sky, and its cult in the games of the three young women.'

naître successivement une foule d'idées nouvelles, pour le dessin et la peinture.[39]

The suggestion of a reanimation is reinforced by a hyperbolic account of Corinne's dramatic effect on her audience: 'je ne sais quelle joie passionnée, et quelle sensibilité d'imagination électrisoit à la fois tous les témoins de cette danse magique, et les transportoit dans une existence idéale, où l'on rêve un bonheur qui n'est pas de ce monde'[40]

Another woman who is invested with the power to revive the ancient past – in this case, a non-fictional woman, but one whose life assumes all the fascinations of fiction for contemporaries – is Emma Hamilton, who, as the mistress and then the wife of Sir William Hamilton, the British Envoy at Naples, becomes one of the sights of that city in the 1780s and 1790s. In Elisabeth Vigée-Lebrun's account of her visit to Naples in 1790, Emma is first introduced through a contrast between her animated style of beauty (Figure 8) and the more languorous attractions of the comtesse Skawronska, wife of the Russian Ambassador:

> Je peignis madame Harte en bacchante couchée au bord de la mer, et tenant une coupe à la main. Sa belle figure était fort animée et contrastait complétement avec celle de la comtesse; elle avait une quantité énorme de beaux cheveux châtains qui pouvaient la couvrir entièrement, et ainsi en bacchante, ses cheveux épars, elle était admirable.[41]

In accounts of Emma's famous attitudes – which she performed in Naples, and continued to perform after her return to England in 1802 – her vivacity and animation are elided with an ability to animate the past. (This ability is accentuated by an implicit, ribald analogy with her power to animate her elderly husband.) Vigée-Lebrun describes 'ce talent d'un nouveau genre':

---

39 Staël, *Corinne; ou, l'Italie*, vol. I, p. 141 (book V, chapter 1): 'Corinne was so well acquainted with ancient painting and sculpture, that her positions were so many studies for the votaries of art. Now she held her tambourine above her head; sometimes advanced it with one hand, while the other ran over its little bells with a dexterous rapidity that brought to mind the girls of Herculaneum' (p. 89).

40 *Ibid.*: 'every witness of this magic was electrified by impassioned joy, transported into an ideal world, there to dream of bliss unknown below'.

41 Vigée-Lebrun, *Souvenirs*, vol. I, p. 193: 'I painted madame Hart as a bacchante, lying beside the sea, a cup in her hand. Her beautiful face was extremely animated and formed a complete contrast to that of the comtesse; she had an enormous quantity of beautiful chestnut hair, sufficient to cover her entirely, and in this guise of a bacchante, her hair strewn about her, she was admirable.' Vigée-Lebrun emphasizes Emma's equivalence to the heroines of fiction by noting: 'La vie de lady Hamilton est un roman' (vol. I, p. 194; 'The life of Lady Hamilton is a romance').

Figure 8 Elisabeth Vigée-Lebrun, *Emma Hamilton as a Bacchante* (1790); oil on canvas, 134.6 x 157.5 cm.

> Rien n'était plus curieux en effet que la faculté qu'avait acquise lady Hamilton de donner subitement à tous ses traits l'expression de la douleur ou de la joie, et de se poser merveilleusement pour représenter des person-nages divers. L'œil animé, les cheveux épars, elle vous montrait une bac-chante délicieuse, puis tout à coup son visage exprimait la douleur, et l'on voyait une Madeleine repentante admirable.[42]

The comtesse de Boigne, citing the transition from Medea to Niobe in the course of her explanation of the attitudes (she herself, she says, was the young girl who played the part of the victim in both), emphasizes that it is above all the classical past that Emma seeks to revive: 'C'est ainsi qu'elle s'inspirait des statues antiques, et que, sans les copier servilement, elle les

---

[42]   *Ibid.*, vol. I, pp. 194, 195–6: 'this new variety of talent'; 'Nothing was more curious than the faculty that Lady Hamilton had acquired of suddenly imparting to all her features the expression of sorrow or joy, and of posing in a wonderful manner in order to represent dif-ferent characters. Her eye alight with animation, her hair strewn about her, she displayed to you a delicious bacchante, then all at once her face expressed sadness, and you saw an admirable penitent Magdalene.'

rappelait aux imaginations poétiques des Italiens par une espèce d'improvisation en action.'[43]

Women proclaim themselves as different from antiquities

The power of women to revive the ancient past, as portrayed in writings
such as those just quoted, is dependent not only on the ease with which
femininity is elided with antiquity, but also on a recognition that there is a
distinction between the two: a recognition, in other words, that women are
different from ruins and antiquities because they are full of life and antiquities are not.[44] De Staël's account of Corinne dancing the Tarantella
implies that the heroine's ability to inspire artists with new ideas might go
beyond that of the paintings at Herculaneum, despite her resemblance to
them. The desire that women should display an irrepressible liveliness, in
order to guarantee their power to reanimate ancient art, is inscribed,
tellingly, in an account of a much later woman who revives the antique:
Emma Hamilton's Australian successor Pansy Montague, known as 'La
Milo', or 'The Modern Milo', arouses disappointment, when performing
her own representations of ancient statues in London in 1906, by failing to
supply the animation – the power to imbue the art of the past with resur-
gent life – that her audiences had expected. Anita Callaway's summary of
her career quotes an English newspaper as complaining, on behalf of her
audience: 'What did they see? A series of statues, cold, white statues, for all
the world like the statues that they neglect every day of their lives when
they pass the National Gallery.'[45]

In some eighteenth-century and early nineteenth-century descriptions of women who resemble or imitate antiquities, however, the animation necessary to the process of revival is defined as a quality that may
become so irrepressible that, far from affirming continuity and fusion, it
prompts a sharp awareness of the difference between the woman and the
works of art that she evokes. In commentaries on Emma Hamilton, a
recognition of the difference between the feminine and the antique is

---

43 Boigne, *Mémoires*, vol. I, p. 115: 'In this way she took her inspiration from antique statues,
     and without copying them in a servile manner, she summoned them up before the poetic
     imagination of the Italians by a kind of improvisation in action.'
44 In the context of portraiture, the diversity of roles that antique allegorical disguises
     assume in the representation of living women, at this period, has been explored by Gill
     Perry, in '"The British Sappho"', and by Marcia Pointon, in 'Portraiture, Excess, and
     Mythology'.
45 In Kerr, *Heritage*, p. 219.

registered especially strongly. One precondition for this awareness of a split between the two categories is that Emma – unlike Corinne, and unlike the three women in Lamartine's narrative of revival – does in fact present her reanimations of the classical past as allegories and games. De Boigne describes an audience enraptured by the game that Emma sets up for them:

> Un jour elle m'avait placée à genoux devant une urne, les mains jointes dans l'attitude de la prière. Penchée sur moi, elle semblait abîmée dans sa douleur, toutes deux nous étions échevelées. Tout à coup, se redressant et s'éloignant un peu, elle me saisit par les cheveux d'un mouvement si brusque, que je me retournai avec surprise et même un peu d'effroi, ce qui me fit entrer dans l'esprit de mon rôle, car elle brandissait un poignard. Les applaudissements passionnées des spectateurs artistes se firent entendre avec les exclamations de: *Bravo la Médéa!* Puis m'attirant à elle, me serrant sur son sein en ayant l'air de me disputer à la colère du ciel, elle arracha aux mêmes voix le cri de: *Viva la Niobé!* [46]

Such descriptions, in noting the delight of the audience at solving the puzzle, by matching up the physical and facial expression of Emma Hart herself with the mythical or historical figure whom she represents, indicate the importance of the gap between the expressive body and the figure represented – however easily this gap is then overcome. Emma, in other words, resists, at least partially, the fusions and continuities associated with Romantic concepts of the symbol, and instead defines herself as an allegorist, drawing on an established store of signs, and directing the audience towards that store of signs in order to solve the puzzles with which she presents them. Corinne, in dressing as a sibyl on the Capitol, and fainting, at Miseno, when she talks of the suffering of the Sibyl, claims a continuity with this figure of ancient myth; Emma's attitudes, on the other hand, discourage any such sense of passionate identification with the figures represented, through the ease with which she is able to exchange one expression for the next: as Vigée-Lebrun puts it, 'Elle passait de la douleur

---

[46] Boigne, *Mémoires*, vol. I, p. 115: 'One day she placed me on my knees in front of an urn, my hands placed together in the attitude of prayer. Leaning on me, she seemed deep in sorrow, and we both had a wild, dishevelled air. Suddenly, drawing herself up and moving back a little, she seized me by the hair with a movement so abrupt that I drew back in surprise and even a little in fear, which made me enter into the spirit of my part, since she was brandishing a dagger. The passionate applause of the artists in the audience was accompanied by cries of *Bravo la Médéa!* Then pulling me towards her, pressing me against her breast as though she wished to fight with the anger of the gods for me, she drew from the same spectators the cry of *Viva la Niobé!* '

à la joie, de la joie à l'effroi, si bien et avec une telle rapidité que nous en fûmes tous ravis.'[47]

Corinne, discussing her own performances, explicitly defines improvisation as lacking in contrivance and artifice. She presents the art of improvisation as an aspect of 'la libéralité de la nature' in Italy; when Sicilian boatmen improvise verses, 'on diroit que le souffle pur du ciel et de la mer agit sur l'imagination des hommes, comme le vent sur les harpes éoliennes, et que la poésie, comme les accords, est l'écho de la nature'. She then suggests that 'la bonhomie du Midi, ou plutôt des pays où l'on aime à s'amuser sans trouver du plaisir à critiquer ce qui amuse', is necessary to this art: in other countries, the audience's proclivity to mockery – their instinctive adoption of a critical distance – would deprive the performer of the presence of mind required in order to sustain the performance.[48]

The comtesse de Boigne, describing Emma Hamilton's attitudes, also notes the importance of keeping mockery at bay: 'D'autres ont cherché à imiter le talent de lady Hamilton, je ne crois pas qu'on y ait réussi. C'est une de ces choses où il n'y qu'un pas du sublime au ridicule.' Travellers who witness Emma's performances suspend their sense of the ridiculous when watching the attitudes themselves, but perceive an absurdity in the astonishing discontinuity between Emma's talent and her everyday social behaviour. De Boigne remarks: 'Hors cet instinct pour les arts, rien n'était plus vulgaire et plus commun que lady Hamilton. Lorsqu'elle quittait la tunique antique pour porter le costume ordinaire, elle perdait toute distinction.'[49] The Earl of Minto, having noted that 'with men her language

---

47 Vigée-Lebrun, *Souvenirs*, vol. I, p. 199: 'She passed from sorrow to joy, from joy to fright, so well and with such rapidity that we were all enraptured.' See, too, Boigne, *Mémoires*, vol. I, p. 114.

48 Staël, *Corinne; ou, l'Italie*, vol. I, pp. 76, 76-7 (book III, chapter 3): 'this bounty of heaven'; 'one might dream that the pure sea breeze acted on man as on an Eolian harp; and that the one, like the other, echoed but the voice of nature'; 'all the good humour of a country in which men love to amuse themselves, without criticizing what amuses them' (p. 44). For an earlier analysis of improvision as dependent on the absence of any proclivity to mockery among the Italians, see Piozzi, *Observations*, vol. I, pp. 237, 240.

49 Boigne, *Mémoires*, vol. I, p. 113: 'Others have sought to imitate Lady Hamilton's talent; I don't believe that they have succeeded. It's the kind of thing where there's only one step from the sublime to the ridiculous'; vol. I, p. 115: 'Apart from this instinct for the arts, nothing was more vulgar and commonplace than Lady Hamilton. When she took off her antique tunic and put on her ordinary clothes, she lost all distinction.' See, too, Vigée-Lebrun, *Souvenirs*, vol. I, p. 198. The paradoxical character ascribed to Emma is derived, in part, from an awareness that she is a moving statue, who equivocates uneasily between the domain of the animate and that of the inanimate; for a useful account of the fantasy of a sculpture that comes to life, see Gross, *The Dream*. I consider the perception of Emma as a comic figure at greater length in Chard 'Comedy, Antiquity'.

and conversation are exaggerations of anything I ever heard anywhere', is nonetheless impressed by the attitudes: he remarks that 'nothing about her, neither her conversation, her manners, nor figure announce the very refined taste which she discovers in this performance, besides the extraordinary talent that is necessary for the execution'. As though uneasy at voicing such delight in the performances of this 'extraordinary compound', however, Lord Minto swiftly introduces a note of bathos: 'and besides all this, says Sir *Willum*, "she makes my apple-pies"'.[50]

Emma Hamilton is not the only woman to supply effects of unexpected comedy for the traveller on the Grand Tour. Another human sight who aligns herself with the elevated and removed domain of the antique, and converts herself into an inanimate object in her husband's collection, while at the same time displaying an alarming appetite for life in her social behaviour, is Paolina Borghese, Napoleon's sister, renowned – among other things – for the fact that she posed for Canova's neo-classical sculpture of *Venus*. Anna Jameson, viewing Paolina walking in the Borghese Gardens, in Rome, 'sometimes alone but oftener surrounded by a cortege of beaux', moves swiftly from the emulation of the antique ('She is no longer the "Venere Vincitrice" of Canova; but... she still preserves the "andar celeste"') to the amused, bathetic observation: 'Of the stories told of her, I suppose, one half *may* be true – and that half is quite enough.'[51] Charlotte Eaton, too, commenting on 'the Principessa Borghese' in *Rome in the Nineteenth Century* (1820), begins her account of Paolina by aligning her with the work of art: 'Some years ago, Canova sculptured a Statue of this Lady, as Venus, and it is esteemed by himself one of the very best of his works.' She then discreetly notes the incongruity between the Prince's careful control of access to this 'esteemed' statue and his complete failure – or disinclination – to establish any such control over his wife (or indeed, the reader might reflect, over his famous collection of antiquities, most of which he had sold to the French in 1807):

> No one else can have an opportunity of judging of it, for the Prince, who certainly is not jealous of his wife's person, is so jealous of her statue, that he keeps it locked up in a room of the Borghese Palace at Rome, of which he keeps the key, and not a human being, not even Canova himself, can get access to it.[52]

---

50   Minto, *Life and Letters*, vol. II, pp. 364–5, 365–6, 366. An editor's note by the Countess of Minto explains: 'Lady Hamilton's manner of pronouncing her husband's christian name.'

51   Jameson, *Diary*, p. 273.

52   Vol. III, p. 47.

James Galiffe, in *Italy and its Inhabitants* (1820), defines the statue itself as
the site of a split between the ideal and the bathetic, and between antiquity
and the conventions of everyday life, through a narrative (repeated by
Thomas Love Peacock in *Crotchet Castle*) which suggests that, in the traveller's view, different rules might apply to goddesses and to women: 'One
of Canova's best statues is said to be that of Buonaparte's youngest sister,
Princess Borghese, who sat naked for it; and who replied to an English lady
who asked how she could bear to do so, that "there was a very good fire in
the room!"'[53]

Femininity, antiquity and the sights of the Grand Tour

A similar, though much gentler awareness of the comic incongruity
between women and antiquity is produced in Dupaty's account of the
woman who appears in the Coliseum. Instead of fusing with the pleasures
of the antique, like the woman who appears in the Temple of the Sibyl at
Tivoli in the same travel book, this young woman blots out antiquity altogether: 'Le Colisée disparut', Dupaty tells us, and it is only when he judges
himself 'remis de ce léger trouble' that he is once more able to turn his
attention to the scene around him.[54] More surprisingly, the possibility that
the antique and the feminine might split apart, however readily they seem
to merge with each other, is also raised – much more obliquely and tenta-
tively – within commentaries in which the elision between the two seems
to have been established securely and seamlessly. When Yorick deploys the
activity of fitting antique fragments together as a metaphor for speculating
about the facial beauty of a woman, he not only emphasizes that women
and antiquities have something in common, but also proclaims, less insistently and directly than in his interview with the Count at Versailles, the
allurements of his own revision of the orthodox itinerary of sights, so as to
displace the monuments and works of art designated as sights by discourses such as classical scholarship and art criticism by a sequence of
women, poised to yield up to the enquiring traveller the secrets of their
hearts.

What, precisely, is the difference between women and antiquities
in Yorick's definition of the two as alternative categories of sights? This
difference would seem to be located in the very aspect of the feminine

---

53 Vol. I, pp. 254–5. See Peacock, *Nightmare Abbey*, *Crotchet Castle*, p. 189.
54 Dupaty, *Lettres*, vol. II, p. 64: 'The Colisæum disappeared' (vol. II, p. 46); vol. II, p. 65:
    'Recovered from this gentle emotion' (vol. II, p. 46).

Figure 9 Joseph Wright, *Maria, from Sterne* (1777); oil on canvas, 100.3 x 125.7 cm.

emphasized at the beginning of this chapter: the ability of feminine or feminized sights to draw the traveller into a domain of private, intimate emotion. Where women are elided with antiquities and ruins, they can, of course, as already argued, draw these into the same domain. Yorick recognizes this when, at Moulines, on his way to Italy, he visits a 'disorder'd maid', Maria, who has already appeared in Sterne's *Tristram Shandy* (1757–65), and who is elided with the antique in an unexpected way. Yorick finds her 'sitting under a poplar', in an attitude that echoes that of the *Weeping Dacia*, in the classical bas-relief, in Rome: '– she was sitting with her elbow in her lap, and her head leaning on one side within her hand.' One of Joseph Wright's paintings of her emphasizes the resemblance to the *Dacia* especially strongly (Figures 9, 10). The allusion to this classical fragment is reinforced by Yorick's elaborate account of Maria's own proclivity for weeping: he describes how 'the tears trickled down her cheeks', and enlarges on his 'undescribable emotions' when she allows him to wipe these tears away.[55]

---

55   Sterne, *A Sentimental Journey*, pp. 113, 114; see Sterne, *Tristram Shandy*, pp. 600–2 (volume XI, chapter 24). I am grateful to Malcolm Baker for pointing out the resemblance between Maria's attitude, both in Sterne's description and in Joseph Wright's painting of the episode (private collection; 1777), and the posture of the female figure in the antique bas-relief.

In her antique dimension, then, Maria anticipates Yorick's arrival at
Rome – as the woman at Calais does, in eliciting from him the simile of a
statue in the Tiber. By linking women encountered en route to the Eternal

Figure 10 Pompeo Batoni, *Peter Beckford of Stapleton* (1766); oil on canvas, 239 x 162.8
cm. The bas-relief of the *Weeping Dacia* is depicted by Batoni on the plinth that Beckford
leans on.

City in this way, and minutely calibrating his own feelings about them, Yorick ironically draws attention to his own rhetorical audacity, as a traveller who is not afraid to bring trivial, feminized flirtation into affiliation with the weighty and serious discourse of classical scholarship, in which the authority to describe and comment is specifically gendered as masculine. The reader is delicately encouraged to reflect that there might be not only a continuity but also a discrepancy between the tears of the antique woman and those of the living one: while the *Dacia* weeps for her province, conquered by the Romans, Maria has been driven to despair by the faithlessness of her lover, and afflicted not only by the death of her father but also by the desertion of her pet goat. Such a discrepancy provides Sterne with a way of satirizing – however gently – the high seriousness of the discourses that authenticate the conventional sights of the Grand Tour.

II: PICTORIAL VIEWING

The spectacle stares back

When Yorick talks with the Count at Versailles, and expresses his interest in 'the original drawings and loose sketches' to be discerned within 'every fair being', he does not simply express a desire to substitute women for more orthodox sights; he also suggests that women can in fact be viewed in a manner analogous to the viewing of works of art. He reaffirms this suggestion by explaining that 'the thirst of this ... *as impatient as that which inflames the breast of the connoisseur,* has led me from my own home into France – and from France will lead me through Italy'.[56]

Other travel writings of the period make the same assumption that the viewing of a work of art supplies the model-metaphor for the activity of observation – whatever other objects the traveller may choose to substitute for pictures and statues. Pictorial metaphors abound in late eighteenth-century travel writing. Piozzi, for example, breezily incorporates analogies with art within the rhetoric of spontaneity: after admiring Salvator Rosa's *Job,* in 'the Santa Croce palace', in Rome, she moves to a quite different domain of objects, as though impulsively allowing herself to follow up stray associations: 'There are too many living objects here in Job's condition, not to render walking in the streets extremely disagreeable.' Having viewed Guercino's *Aurora*, she remarks: 'We were driving

---

56   Sterne, *A Sentimental Journey*, p. 84; emphasis added.

last night to look at the Coliseo by moon-light... I thought how like a sky of Guercino's it was.'[57]

Travellers of the late eighteenth and early nineteenth centuries register uncertainties, however, about the degree of separation imposed by the boundary that separates the spectator from the spectacle. Two refinements of the strategy of pictorial viewing, in particular, explore the possibilities and dangers of crossing this boundary. One of these two options has a founding text, concerned with a domain of foreignness more exotic than the topography of the Grand Tour: a letter by Lady Mary Wortley Montagu, written on her way to Turkey in 1717, and published in a collected edition of her writings several decades later. The letter seems, initially, to be affirming as strongly as possible the authority of the detached spectator, while reinforcing that authority yet more strongly by invoking the privilege of 'behind the scenes' observation and enquiry available to the female traveller. At Sophia – then part of the Ottoman Empire, and therefore a place where women could be assumed to be veiled and heavily secluded – Montagu visits the women's baths, and observes the women who frequent this establishment 'in the state of nature, that is, in plain English, stark naked, without any beauty or defect concealed'. The traveller pointedly draws attention to the exclusion of men from such scenes, by conjuring up a male spectator who, in her imagination, transgresses the prohibition on viewing these women: 'To tell you the truth, I had wickedness enough to wish secretly that Mr. Jervas could have been there invisible. I fancy it would have very much improved his art, to see so many fine women naked...'[58]

Mary Wortley Montagu herself, however, slides, temporarily, from the position of spectator to that of spectacle. Just before her account of naked beauty at the baths, she expresses her conviction that the naked foreign women must be looking at her with a curiosity that, like hers, is sharpened by a strong sense of cultural difference:

> I was in my travelling habit, which is a riding dress, and certainly appeared very extraordinary to them. Yet there was not one of them that showed the least surprise or impertinent curiosity, but received me with all the obliging civility possible. I know no European court where the ladies would have behaved themselves in so polite a manner to such a stranger. I believe,

---

57 Piozzi, *Observations*, vol. II, p. 141, vol. I, p. 414.

58 Montagu, *Works* (first published, in a collection of Montagu's letters, in 1763), vol. I, pp. 174, 175; letter dated 'April 1 *O.S.* 1717'. The variety of ways in which Montagu makes use of the conventions of travel writing, when describing women, in this letter and in others, is considered by Lisa Lowe, in *Critical Terrains*, pp. 35–52.

upon the whole, there were two hundred women, and yet none of those disdainful smiles and satirical whispers, that never fail in our assemblies when any body appears that is not dressed exactly in the fashion. They repeated over and over to me, 'Guzel, pec guzel,' which is nothing but *Charming, very charming.*[59]

As spectators, these women, however polite, turn out to demand more of their spectacle than Montagu has anticipated: once she has described them in their state of nakedness, she notes that they seem eager to erase the very distinctions of dress that they compliment so agreeably:

The lady that seemed the most considerable among them entreated me to sit by her, and would fain have undressed me for the bath. I excused myself with some difficulty. They being, however, all so earnest in persuading me, I was at last forced to open my shirt, and show them my stays; which satisfied them very well; for, I saw, they believed I was locked up in that machine, and that it was not in my own power to open it; which contrivance they attributed to my husband.[60]

In allowing herself to transmute into spectacle, in this narrative, Lady Mary Wortley Montagu might seem to be taking a major rhetorical risk – to be laying herself open to charges of vulnerability and inadequacy. Travel writings regularly define travellers who slide from the position of spectator to that of spectacle as either, on the one hand, falling prey to a danger that threatens all travellers, but that most would rather not acknowledge, or, on the other hand, revealing themselves as simply not equal to the task of extracting pleasure and benefit from the topography of foreignness.[61]

The first of these two dangers is charted by Sterne. Long before Yorick confidently declares to the count that he has come to spy out his own preferred variety of nakedness, he explains, in a rambling epic simile that concludes by invoking the story of the drunken Noah, that the traveller may indeed find that it is he and not the land that has, metaphorically speaking, become a spectacle of nakedness:

---

59 Montagu, *Works*, vol. I, p. 174.

60 *Ibid.*, vol. I, pp. 175–6.

61 Fear of becoming a spectacle is not confined to travel writing: David Marshall, in *The Figure of Theater*, is concerned, throughout, with the dangers associated with a 'theatrical' exposure before the eyes of the world, in a range of eighteenth-century and nineteenth-century writings. Marshall's analysis of Adam Smith's concept of sympathy (pp. 167–92), as set forth in his *Theory of Moral Sentiments* (1759), is of particular relevance to the relations between spectator and spectacle considered in this chapter.

The man who first transplanted the grape of Burgundy to the Cape of Good Hope (observe he was a Dutch man) never dreamt of drinking the same wine at the Cape, that the same grape produced upon the French mountains – he was too phlegmatic for that – but undoubtedly he expected to drink some sort of vinous liquor; but whether good, bad, or indifferent he knew enough of this world to know, that it did not depend upon his choice, but that what is generally called *chance* was to decide his success: however, he hoped for the best; and in these hopes, by an intemperate confidence in the fortitude of his head, and the depth of his discretion, *Mynheer* might possibly overset both in his new vineyard; and by discovering his nakedness, become a laughing-stock to his people.

Even so it fares with the poor Traveller, sailing and posting through the politer kingdoms of the globe in pursuit of knowledge and improvments.[62]

Piozzi, too, presents the slide into spectacle as a manifestation of vulnerability: observing the signs of everyday life interrupted by sudden death in Herculaneum and Pompeii, she envisages herself and her travelling companions ignominiously reduced first to 'spectacles' and then to mere souvenirs:

How dreadful are the thoughts which such a sight suggests! how *very* horrible the certainty, that such a scene may be all acted over again to-morrow; and that we, who to-day are spectators, may become spectacles to travellers of a succeeding century, who mistaking our bones for those of the Neapolitans, may carry some of them to their native country back again perhaps; as it came into my head that a French gentleman was doing, when I saw him put a human bone into his pocket this morning, and told him I hoped he had got the jaw of a Gaulish officer, instead of a Roman soldier, for future reflections to energize upon.[63]

Transformation into an object to be scrutinized by others is repeatedly cited as a mark not simply of vulnerability but rather of culpable inadequacy in complaints about dissipated young English travellers who make spectacles of themselves on the Grand Tour – on the model of 'the young Æneas' in the fourth Book of Pope's *Dunciad* (1743), whose transformation is introduced through an effect of sudden bathos: 'Intrepid then, o'er seas and lands he flew: | Europe he saw, and Europe saw him too.'[64]

The role of the inadequate traveller who forgoes the advantages of the spectator is defined with reference to a range of concepts of gender. The

---

62 Sterne, *A Sentimental Journey*, pp. 11–12.

63 Piozzi, *Observations*, vol. II, pp. 35–6

64 Lines 293–4.

impulse to make a spectacle of oneself is identified as a manifestation of an attraction towards the effeminate luxury of the warm South, as opposed to the manly liberty of the cold North. Clermont Lynmere, in Fanny Burney's *Camilla* (1796), a traveller returned from the Grand Tour, is described as a man who personifies 'effeminacy in its lowest degradation', and has gained from his experience of the Grand Tour an 'acquired luxuriance' to add to his 'natural presumption'. Men regard him as 'an unmanly fop', while women display a yet sharper awareness of his predilection for acting the part of the spectacle rather than the spectator: they consider him 'too conceited to admire any thing but himself'.[65]

Anna Jameson's *Diary of an Ennuyée* (1826) describes an acquaintance of the traveller-narrator who is similarly drawn towards unmanly luxury and self-display:

> Frattino is a young Englishman who, if he were in England, would probably be pursuing his studies at Eton or Oxford, for he is scarce past the age of boyhood; but having been abroad since he was twelve years old, and early plunged into active and dissipated life, he is an accomplished man of fashion, and of the world, with as many airs and caprices as a spoiled child.[66]

Frattino's lack of English manliness is further emphasized first by noting his resemblance to the *Belvedere Antinous,* a classical sculpture almost invariably cited as an instance of smooth-limbed effeminacy, and, secondly, by explicitly defining him as a traveller who has crossed over from the side of the spectator to the side of the spectacle:

> He is by far the most beautiful creature of his sex, I ever saw; so like the *Antinous,* that at Rome he went by that name. The exquisite regularity of his features, the graceful air of his head, his *antique* curls, the faultless proportions of his elegant figure, make him a *thing* to be gazed on, as one looks at a statue.[67]

---

65 pp. 583, 569.

66 p. 240.

67 *Ibid.,* pp. 240–1. The implications of homosexuality established by referring to the sculpture identified as Antinous, the 'favourite' of the Emperor Hadrian, are absorbed into a more general model of 'effeminate' sensuality by an allusion to Frattino's womanising: 'he possesses high honour and generosity, *where women are not concerned*' (p. 241; emphasis added). Percy Bysshe Shelley's 'The Coliseum: A Fragment' is one of the many writings to classify the *Antinous* as effeminate: Shelley describes a traveller in Rome as resembling the sculpture in 'eager and impassioned tenderness', but lacking 'the effeminate sullenness of the eye, and the narrow smoothness of the forehead' (Shelley, *Essays,* vol. I, p. 169).

Mary Wollstonecraft, in *A Vindication of the Rights of Woman* (1792), emphasizes the place of self-display within a conventional version of the feminine which, in its affectation and narcissism, closely resembles the 'airs and caprices' of Lynmere and Frattino – and which, like these affectations, is defined by opposition to manly powers of observation. Wollstonecraft rejects the system of female education based on the assumption that unmanly devotion to trivial gratification is to be expected and even positively required of women: 'the. . . love of pleasure, fostered by the whole tendency of their education, gives a trifling turn to the conduct of women in most circumstances.' Illustrating her point by citing male and female approaches to travel, she argues that this insipidly 'feminine' version of the love of pleasure is displayed, most strikingly, in an eagerness to assume the position of spectacle:

> A man, when he undertakes a journey, has, in general, the end in view; a woman thinks more of the incidental occurrences, the strange things that may possibly occur on the road; the impression that she may make on her fellow-travellers; and, above all, she is anxiously intent on the care of the finery that she carries with her, which is more than ever a part of herself, when going to figure on a new scene; when, to use an apt French turn of expression, she is going to produce a sensation. Can dignity of mind exist with such trivial cares?[68]

Retaining authority

Far from disparaging Mary Wortley Montagu's role in the scene in the Turkish baths, however, as all these commentaries might lead us to expect, other travel writings eagerly reproduce the plot of crossing over to the side of the spectacle. Mungo Park, in his *Travels in the Interior Districts of Africa* (1799), describes his 'surprise' when, as a prisoner in a remote village, he is visited in his hut by a party of women who wish 'to ascertain, by actual inspection, whether the rite of circumcision extended to the Nazarenes (Christians,) as well as to the followers of Mahomet'.[69] In 'Mrs. Belzoni's trifling account of the women of Egypt, Nubia, and Syria', appended to the first edition of Giovanni Battista Belzoni's *Narrative of the Operations and Recent Discoveries within the Pyramids, Temples, Tombs, and Excavations, in*

---

[68] p. 151.

[69] p. 132. I am grateful to Nicholas Thomas for drawing my attention to this variant on Mary Wortley Montagu's narrative of the spectator in danger of becoming a naked spectacle.

Egypt and Nubia (1820), the narrator offers 'behind the scenes' accounts of foreign women who, returning her curiosity, examine and unfasten her clothing, and inspect her corsets with interest.[70]

Wollstonecraft herself, in her *Letters Written during a Short Residence in Sweden, Norway, and Denmark* (1796), constructs a less dramatic version of this same plot – less dramatic because, unlike the travellers just cited, and unlike Noah in Sterne's simile, she is never at risk of being revealed in a state of vulnerable nakedness:

> My clothes, in their turn, attracted the attention of the females, and I could not help thinking of the foolish vanity which makes many women so proud of the observations of strangers as to take wonder very gratuitously for admiration. This error they are very apt to fall into; when arrived in a foreign country, the populace stare at them as they pass; yet the make of a cap, or the singularity of a gown, is often the cause of the flattering attention, which afterwards supports a fantastic superstructure of self-conceit.[71]

In differentiating herself, here, from other travellers who notice that they are attracting attention, Wollstonecraft spells out the main rhetorical strategies by which Montagu, Park and Mrs Belzoni retain their authority. First, she links her awareness of the spectacle staring back to a recognition of cultural difference, and so affirms her own power to claim from the foreign the primary quality expected and demanded of it: a divergence from tame familiarity. In other words, she makes a gesture of authoritative appropriation that compensates for the threat to her authority that is produced by her slide into spectacle. (At the same time, she also reaffirms the separation between spectator and spectacle: cultural difference guarantees that each side will regard the other across a chasm of 'wonder'.) Secondly, Wollstonecraft carefully distinguishes the adequate traveller from the inadequate one by emphasizing that she manages to remain a spectator at the same time as she transmutes into spectacle; while the inadequate traveller congratulates herself on being the object of observation, the adequate traveller is not content simply to fall into this role, but continues to scrutinize foreigners as they scrutinize her. Mary Wortley Montagu, after her first declaration of an awareness that the women in the baths are observing her, swiftly introduces an analogy with painting, and so re-establishes herself as a detached, pictorial spectator: 'There were', she says, describing the naked women, 'many amongst them as exactly proportioned as ever

70   p. 446.
71   p. 97.

any goddess was drawn by the pencil of a Guido or Titian.'[72] Mungo Park, following this same strategy, outwits his female visitors by pointedly reclaiming his role as subject of vision: informing them 'that it was not customary in my country to give ocular demonstration in such cases, before so many beautiful women', he selects 'the youngest and handsomest' of the group as the sole observer whom he will allow to 'satisfy her curiosity'. Park notes that 'the ladies enjoyed the jest; and went away laughing heartily'.[73]

The traveller, in all these commentaries, registers a desire to enjoy the pleasures and advantages of both the two positions mapped out by pictorial viewing. The transmutation into spectacle is classified as an experience that is enviable and at the same time dangerous: the perils located within it must, travellers suggest, be kept at bay by ensuring that the position of spectator is always maintained.

Piozzi repeatedly adopts this device of gazing at the spectacle as it gazes back. In Milan, she shows how even a notion so essential to the self-satisfaction of the northern European traveller as that of liberty can undergo dramatic and startling adjustments when appropriated by southerners. The words of an Italian woman satirize this self-satisfaction, while at the same time providing the traveller with further reason to conclude that it is only in the cold North that liberty is properly comprehended:

> National character is a great matter: I did not know there had been such a difference in the ways of thinking, merely from custom and climate, as I see there is; though one has always read of it: it was however entertaining enough to hear a travelled gentleman haranguing away three nights ago at our house in praise of English cleanliness, and telling his auditors how all the men in London, *that were noble,* put on a clean shirt every day, and the women washed the street before his house-door every morning. '*Che schiavitù mai* !' exclaimed a lady of quality, who was listening: '*ma naturalmente sarà per commando del principe.*' – '*What a land of slavery!*' says Donna Luisa, I heard her; '*But it is all done by command of the sovereign, I suppose.*'[74]

---

72 Montagu, *Works*, vol. I, pp. 174–5.

73 Park, *Travels*, p. 132. For a very different analysis of 'reciprocal vision', see Pratt, *Imperial Eyes*, pp. 81–5.

74 Piozzi, *Observations*, vol. I, p. 105; see also vol. I, pp. 355–6 and vol. II, p. 196. The device of quoting foreigners who look back and inadvertently satirize familiar concepts – in this case, the reverence that travellers pay to 'contemptuous ruins' – is employed, too, in Eliza Parsons's Gothic novel *The Mysterious Warning: A German Tale*, vol. III, p. 169.

Absorptive viewing

The traveller, in all these commentaries, registers a desire to enjoy the pleasures and advantages of both the two positions mapped out by pictorial viewing. The transmutation into spectacle is classified as an experience that is gratifying and at the same time dangerous: the perils located within it must, travellers suggest, be kept at bay by ensuring that the position of spectator is always maintained. A second sub-strategy within the option of pictorial viewing explores the possibilities of moving across the boundary between spectator and spectacle in a rather different way. This is the strategy of absorptive viewing – or imaginative evocation of absorptive viewing. Michael Fried, in *Absorption and Theatricality: Painting and Beholder in the Age of Diderot,* has argued that eighteenth-century French art criticism registers an admiration of paintings that absorb the beholder: works, in other words, that seem to remove the beholder from a position of spatial detachment in front of the work of art. By virtue of the eighteenth-century and early nineteenth-century assumption that other domains of objects will also be viewed pictorially, the fascination with the absorptive power of painting is, in both French and English writings, easily transferred to human figures discerned by the traveller-spectator within the topography of the foreign, or conjured up by the imagination. Accounts of absorption in objects and figures encountered or imagined in this way construct a continuity between this mode of viewing and the state of enthralment demanded by the 'wonder'. Absorptive descriptions have the obvious rhetorical advantage that they establish a strong claim to unaffected responsiveness.

Two sorts of painting, Fried argues, were, in turn, defined as possessing a praiseworthy ability to draw in the beholder: first, 'the representation of figures absorbed in quintessentially absorptive states and activities' (such as reverie, or reading) and, secondly, 'the representation of figures absorbed in action or passion (or both)' – in other words, the genre of the history painting.[75] In each case, the figures absorb the spectator by virtue of their own unawareness of themselves as spectacle – their lack of any recognition that they are being looked at.

Travel writing makes frequent use of the first of these concepts of absorption: travellers often note the power to enthral the viewer that is exercised by figures observed or imagined in the 'quintessentially absorptive states and activities' that characterize Fried's first category of paintings. The traveller-narrator, in commentaries of this kind, initially

---

75   Fried, *Absorption and Theatricality*, p. 107.

describes such figures in distanced, pictorial terms, and then experiences a moment of intense emotional identification. Yorick, in Sterne's *Sentimental Journey*, having located Maria within a pictorial vignette, charts in elaborate detail the process by which her unremitting self-absorption draws him into her sorrows: as the tears trickle down her cheeks, he uses his handkerchief to stage a drama of identification that verges on a comic confusion of identities:

> I sat down close by her; and Maria let me wipe them away as they fell with my handkerchief. – I then steep'd it in my own – and then in hers – and then in mine – and then I wip'd hers again...[76]

Feminized responsiveness and effeminate foreigners

Unsurprisingly, given the eighteenth-century rhetorical principle that the topography of the warm South cannot be mapped out as a domain of unreserved pleasure, travellers sometimes voice suspicions about the intense allurements located in those sights that appear as pictures and then induce an enthralled forgetfulness of pictorial distance. John MacCulloch, in his treatise *On Malaria* (1827), argues that Sterne's Maria has become all too seductive a site of enthralment, intensifying the lure of foreign attractions and the power of hidden dangers:

> If the banks of the Loire smile in the imaginations of those whose knowledge is derived from poetry and romance, if Sterne and his Maria have enticed many a wandering Englishman to breathe its zephyrs and listen to its pipe, and – to lay up a long stock of bitter repentance, let future speculators qualify the pages of fancy with those of Monfalcon, ere they trust themselves to its seductions or to those of its ally, the Cher.[77]

Even when describing themselves in the grip of absorptive identification, travellers, on occasion, produce an effect of sudden unease. Piozzi, through her abrupt conclusion to an account of absorptive viewing in Naples, registers a fear that she has been straying into a dangerous imaginative domain. The traveller-narrator begins the description as a detached spectator assessing foreign manners: 'It is... observable, and surely very

---

[76] pp. 113, 114.

[77] p. 410. The reference is, presumably, to Jean Baptiste Monfalcon, author of *Histoire des marais, et des maladies causées par les émanations des eaux stagnantes*. For another reference to Maria as a topographically specific site of enthralment, see Piozzi, *The Piozzi Letters*, vol. I, p. 391.

praiseworthy, that if the Italians are not ashamed of their crimes, neither are they ashamed of their contrition.' A precise piece of spectacle is then cited in support of this point: one that confirms the traveller in her pictorial detachment (and grasp of cultural difference) by positioning her as a northern European traveller struck by a sight that seems unremarkable to the Italians themselves (Like the confessor in Piozzi's account of cicisbeism, the native inhabitants are clearly 'used to it'):

> I saw this morning an odd scene at church, which, though new to *me*, appeared, perhaps from its frequent repetition, to strike no one but myself.
> A lady with a long white dress, and veiled, came in her carriage, which waited for her at the door, with her own arms upon it, and servants better dressed than is common here, followed and put a lighted taper in her hand.[78]

As the story continues, Piozzi attempts to maintain her position of detachment: she introduces figures who, like the confessor in her account of cicisbeism, are 'used to it', in order to emphasise that her own reactions are the product of cultural difference. At the same time, however, the *sangfroid* of the Italians serves to emphasise, by contrast, her own view of the scene as not simply striking but moving as well:

> *En cet état*, as the French say, she moved slowly up the church, looking like Jane Shore in the last act, but not so feeble; and being arrived at the steps of the high altar, threw herself quite upon her face before it, remaining prostrate there at least five minutes, in the face of the whole congregation, who, equally to my amazement, neither stared nor sneered, neither laughed nor lamented, but minded their own private devotions – no mass was saying – till the lady rose, kissed the steps, and bathed them with her tears, mingled with sobs of no affected or hypocritical penitence I am sure.[79]

Piozzi then confesses that her heart is 'quite penetrated' by this display of penitence, and compares the penitent to Milton's Eve. Suddenly, however, she wrenches herself out of her state of enthralment, and swiftly restores herself to the position of a detached, comparative observer of manners, by remarking severely: 'Let not this story, however, mislead any one to think that more general decorum or true devotion can be found in churches of the Romish persuasion than in ours – quite the reverse. This burst of penitential piety was in itself an indecorous thing.'[80]

---

78 Piozzi, *Observations*, vol. II, p. 28.

79 *Ibid.*, vol. II, pp. 28–9; the reference is presumably to Nicholas Rowe's *Jane Shore* (1714).

80 *Ibid.*, vol. II, p. 29.

Piozzi concludes, therefore, by sharply dissociating herself from the effeminate indecorum and excess of the warm South. In doing so, she imprints on her commentary a fear that her identification with a woman so clearly at the mercy of passion might call into question her own authority as a detached observer of manners. Up until this point, however, she positively courts this danger, by proclaiming her feminized responsiveness in a context where it might easily lead her into sympathizing with effeminate unrestraint. In toying with the possibility that femininity and effeminacy might coincide, she provides an interval of suspense, as the reader wonders how far her absorption will take her.

At the same time, the abrupt conclusion emphasizes that the penitent is, like all sights and wonders, a spectacle encountered in the course of an itinerary: the site of pleasures that acquire a particular piquancy from the awareness that the traveller will inevitably move on – and will, therefore, detach herself from the absorptive spectacle of 'penitential piety'. Travel writings of this period often issue such reminders of the need to continue the journey. As Dupaty describes his intense pleasure in the dinner in the Temple of the Sibyl at Tivoli, with the 'jeune Tivolienne' waiting at table, he breaks off by reflecting that such pleasure is too intense to last: 'Les plaisirs sont suivis des peines: il faut quitter Tivoli.'[81] At the end of Shandy's encounter with the 'poor hapless damsel' Maria in Laurence Sterne's *Tristram Shandy* (1759–67), the traveller, having listened to 'such a tale of woe' from the suffering woman 'that I rose up, and with broken and irregular steps walked softly to my chaise', then detaches himself from Maria's sorrows by the cheerful exclamation: ' – What an excellent inn at Moulins!'[82]

Selecting human attractions

The human attractions accorded the most elaborate and complex commentaries in travel writings of this period are those who are not simply features within the topography, but who assume an anomalous role, as travellers who become part of the spectacle, or foreigners who turn out to be travellers and detached spectators as well. By virtue of their status as

---

[81] Dupaty, *Lettres*, vol. I, p. 257; 'But pleasures are attended with pain. – Alas! I must quit Tivoli' (vol. I, p. 199).

[82] pp. 601, 602 (volume IX, chapter 24). Maria is 'unsettled in her mind' (p. 600) as a result of a cruel reversal in love. Maria appears again in Sterne's *Sentimental Journey*; the traveller-narrator's visit to her in this later work is discussed in Chapter 3, 'Spectator and spectacle'.

anomalies, capable of destabilizing the established opposition between subjects and objects of observation, such figures are invested with intense fascination: as Mary Douglas argues, our reaction to disorder – for example, the disordering of carefully separated categories that is entailed in anomaly and ambiguity – is not simply one of condemnation: 'We recognise that it is destructive to existing patterns; also that it has potentiality. It symbolises both danger and power.'[83]

Emma Hamilton and Paolina Borghese fall into the first of these two categories of anomaly. Maria and Corinne both fall into the second category. Maria unexpectedly reveals to Yorick that she has completed her own version of the Grand Tour – a tour unorthodox in the style of travel adopted, but strikingly conventional as far as the crucial elements of the itinerary are concerned:

> She had..., she told me, stray'd as far as Rome, and walk'd round St Peter's once – and return'd back – that she found her way alone across the Apennines – had travell'd over all Lombardy without money – and through the flinty roads of Savoy without shoes.[84]

Maria's role as a traveller, moreover, is accentuated by her strong impulse to wander, which is dramatized all the more strongly by a metaphorical elision with the vagaries of her mind: Yorick defines her penchant for aimless perambulations as one of her primary characteristics when, fantasizing about taking her into his home, he specifies that 'in all thy weaknesses and wanderings I would seek after thee and bring thee back'.[85]

Corinne, too, turns out to be a traveller as well as a sight; from an early point in the novel onwards, the narrator hints that she may have more complex geographical affiliations than might be expected from her initial role as part of the spectacle of Rome. The reader is alerted to these complexities when the prince Castel-Forte, at her first appearance on the Capitol, describes her as uniting 'l'imagination, les tableaux, la vie brillante du Midi' with 'cette connoissance, cette observation du cœur humain qui semble le partage des pays où les objets extérieurs excitent moins l'intérêt'. In the course of the narrative, it is revealed that Corinne herself has experience of travel: she has spent her adolescence in England, as the daughter of an Englishman, and is well able to exert the traveller's characteristic power of

---

83 Douglas, *Purity and Danger*, p. 94.
84 Sterne, *A Sentimental Journey*, p. 115.
85 *Ibid*. Maria is a figure whom Mary Wollstonecraft invokes in the course of her own travels in Scandinavia, implicitly drawing attention to their shared capacity for desolate wandering; see *Letters*, p. 111.

comparison, having decided to live in Italy because the confined domestic life that women are expected to lead in Britain prevents her from making any public display of her talents. Even while judging England severely, she claims to have derived from her early study of English literature qualities that are unmistakeably feminine yet manly: 'la manière profonde de penser et de sentir qui caractérise vos poètes, avoit fortifié mon esprit et mon âme'.[86]

Corinne's Italian admirer emphasizes, moreover, that she is not merely a performer, for others to gaze at: she is, rather, a creative artist, whose talents extend to those of the spectator: '– C'est une chose si rare, dit le prince Castel-Forte, de trouver une personne à la fois susceptible d'enthousiasme et d'analyse, douée comme un artiste, et capable de s'observer elle-même...'[87]

At the same time, Corinne's delight in performance is imbued with an element of excess that aligns her, in an especially compromising manner, with the effeminate immoderation and self-display of the South. She herself expresses a fear that she has, in a fateful moment in earlier years, carried her love of exhibiting her talents too far: she describes an occasion when, back in England in her adolescence, she devised an entertainment for Lord Nelvil's father:

> Je désirai de lui plaire, je le désirai peut-être trop, et je fis, pour y réussir, infiniment plus de frais qu'il n'en falloit: je lui montrai tous mes talents; je chantai, je dansai, j'improvisai pour lui; et mon esprit, long-temps contenu, fut peut-être trop vif en brisant ses chaînes.[88]

As already noted, any traveller who transmutes into spectacle is, during this period, liable to be perceived as effeminate simply by virtue of an

---

86 Staël, *Corinne; ou, l'Italie*, vol. I, p. 48 (book II, chapter 2): 'He pointed out the particular merit of her works as partly derived from her profound study of foreign literature, teaching her to unite the graphic descriptions of the South, with that observant knowledge of the human heart which appears the inheritance of those whose countries offer fewer objects of external beauty' (p. 22). (See also the reference to Corinne's English accent: vol. I, p. 75; book III, chapter 3.) Vol. II, p. 101 (book XIV, chapter 3): 'The depth of thought and feeling which characterises your poets had strengthened my mind without impairing my fancy' (p. 246).

87 *Ibid.*, vol. I, p. 60 (book III, chapter 3): '"It is so rare a thing," said Castel Forte, "to find a person at once susceptible of enthusiasm, and capable of analysis; endowed as an artist, yet gifted with so much self-knowledge, that we ought to implore her revelation of her own secret."' (p. 43).

88 *Ibid.*, vol. II, p. 96 (book XIV, chapter 2): 'When I was presented to Lord Nelvil I desired, perhaps but too ardently, to please him; and did infinitely more than was required for success; displaying all my talents, dancing, singing, and extemporising before him: my long imprisoned soul felt but too blest in breaking from its chain' (p. 242).

imputed inclination for self-display. Travellers identifying with such figures therefore run the rhetorical risk of appearing compromisingly com-
plicit with such effeminacy. The danger of identifying with a feminized
slide into spectacle is, however, a danger that traveller-narrators repeatedly
court: when positioning themselves as enthralled spectators, they almost
always select as their preferred sites of enthralment figures who are in
some way feminized: either women, or men who invite an accentuated
awareness of their feminized role. John Moore, for example, devotes nearly
eight pages of his *View of Society and Manners in Italy* to describing a visit
to Lady Mary Wortley Montagu's son Edward in Venice, during which
Montagu, by his determination to adopt and champion all Turkish customs, both aligns himself with the effeminate luxuriousness of the Middle
East and also seems consciously to reaffirm his own spectacular status: he
sits 'on a cushion on the floor, with his legs crossed in the Turkish fashion',
and perfumes his beard with the steam from 'some aromatic gums', which
are 'burnt in a little silver vessel'.[89]

Travellers who transmute into sights can be rescued from imputations
of effeminacy, however, by an insistence that, through their own evident
self-absorption, they demonstrate a complete lack of interest in their own
role as spectacle. Maria is unequivocally presented as too involved in her
own sorrows to reflect upon how she must appear to others. Another such
sight is the gladiator (implicitly invoking the classical sculpture known as
the *Dying Gaul*), in Canto IV of Byron's *Childe Harold's Pilgrimage* (1818):
the narrator, in the moonlit Coliseum, conjures up in his imagination a
vision of a captive, taken from his home 'by the Danube' in order to supply
the Romans with theatrical entertainment. The role of the gladiator as a
traveller, albeit an unwilling one, is emphasized by the fact that his own
imagination, at the moment of his death, makes a geographical leap back,
reverting to the scenes of domestic happiness that he has left behind. His
dreams of his 'young barbarians all at play' at their 'rude hut by the
Danube' might seem sufficient to rescue him definitively from any imputations of effeminacy that his role within a Roman theatrical spectacle
might prompt, and classify him as feminized (by virtue of his devotion to
sentimental domesticity) yet manly (by virtue of the simplicity of his
domestic life, and his understandable disgust for the excesses of the
Romans in their decadence). The narrator, however, is at pains to refute
such imputations yet more thoroughly, by pointing out that the gladiator
utterly refuses to acknowledge his own place within the spectacle, and

---

[89]   Vol. I, p. 31; the account of Montagu continues until vol. I, p. 38.

completely ignores the presence of his audience: as an 'inhuman shout' hails the victory of 'the wretch who won', Byron notes the dying captive's imaginative removal from the scene: 'He heard it, but he heeded not – his eyes | Were with his heart, and that was far away...'[90]

Another strategy for rescuing human travellers who transmute into spectacle from imputations of effeminacy – and thereby rescuing the speaking subject from the suspicion of complicity with foreign excesses – is to register a fascination with travellers who, however spectacular, align themselves with the detached spectator by virtue of their profession. Foreign artists in Italy, for example, are easily rescued from the charge that they have effeminately allowed themselves to become mere objects of vision, simply by reference to their role as professional spectators. Equivocation between viewing artists as spectacle and as detached observers is especially conspicuous in accounts of female painters, who are often described away from the professional setting of the studio, displaying charms unrelated to their profession. Angelica Kauffman, in Naples and Rome from 1782 until her death in 1807, is regularly designated as one of the attractions of these cities. Piozzi remarks: 'Beside her paintings, of which the world has been the judge, her conversation attracts all people of taste to her house, which none can bear to leave without difficulty and regret.'[91]

The travellers who provide most excitingly dangerous sites of enthralment, however, are those who compromise themselves the most – who depart most dramatically from a position of spectatorial detachment. Two women in particular are cited as figures who seem to accomplish an especially disturbing move to the side of the spectacle, in not only transforming themselves – more or less – into works of art, but actually displaying themselves in a state of nakedness, or semi-nakedness: in other words, the very state that supplies Sterne with a metaphor for vulnerable travel, and that Montagu, Mungo Park and Mrs Belzoni hold out before the reader as a looming threat, and then just manage to avoid. These women, already mentioned as figures who excite an awareness of the comic disjunction between the feminine and the antique, are Emma Hamilton and Paolina Borghese. Oscillations between the elevated classical ideal with which the two women identify themselves, as works of art, on the one hand, and the

---

[90] Stanza 141, lines 5, 4, 1–2; in Byron, *Complete Poetical Works*, vol. II, p. 171.

[91] Piozzi, *Observations*, vol. II, p. 141; see also vol. I, p. 178. Piozzi's explicit claim that it is Kauffman's personality as much as her paintings that 'attracts all people of taste to her house' is echoed by Catherine Wilmot (*An Irish Peer*, p.178) and by Vigée-Lebrun (*Souvenirs*, vol. I, p. 156). See also de Boigne's account of Vigée-Lebrun herself, in Rome (*Mémoires*, vol. I, p. 110).

bathetic reality of their social existence, on the other, only heighten the curiosity which they excite. The seventeen-year-old Englishwoman Harriet Charlotte Beaujolais Campbell, in Florence in 1817, tells the story about Paolina posing naked to Canova, and happily noting that there was a good fire in the room; she describes the Principessa as 'past all excuse'. Having noted another instance of Paolina's fondness for making a spectacle of herself – she has, it seems, forced Lady Jersey to kiss her foot in public – Harriet Campbell declares:

> But nevertheless I should be curious to visit a woman who has been and still is so universally celebrated. Publickly it would not be right as at present it would be against the propriety necessary for an English person, but could I go to her privately I should not waver for a moment. Mr Bury has visited her and will do so again… for a man any thing is allowable. He may visit any woman particularly of such a rank and visit her as a curiosity. He is still himself and returns from her the same and his curiosity is satisfied. Propriety is a sad barrier and I am not the first who has sighed to pass it.[92]

Harriet Campbell's evocation of a model of spectator and spectacle in which 'Mr Bury' views the princess 'as a curiosity' and 'returns from her the same' provides a means of denying, in effect, that the traveller, in crossing the boundary of the Alps, need also cross any symbolic boundaries, of the kind that might lead to an immersion in the dangers of the foreign. The next chapter considers the positive impulse, within travel writing from the final decades of the eighteenth century onwards, to dramatize and endorse the view of the foreign as a domain in which the traveller both crosses boundaries and evinces an awareness that it might prove difficult to remain 'the same'.

---

[92] Campbell, *A Journey to Florence*, pp. 125–6.

4

Destabilized travel

Crossing boundaries

Part of the story of Og of Basan, as told by William Beckford in his *Biographical Memoirs of Extraordinary Painters* (1780), has been recounted in the last chapter. As related there, Og is prompted to fly southwards by 'the shade of her he loved', who appears to him as a ghost in a dream, reproaching him for abandoning her. He finally reaches Sicily, and travels to the foothills of Mount Etna with his devoted young follower Benboaro. In this 'sequestered habitation', Og grows 'restless and melancholy', and utters a long soliloquy in which he recalls the 'beloved nymph': 'The time of expiating my baseness draws near, and methinks at this instant I see the pale form of her I betrayed hovering over me, and beckoning me up to the summit of yonder volcano.' He eventually rushes into the forests. His disciple follows him: 'traversing wildernesses where no one had ever penetrated', he reaches 'the mouth of that tremendous volcano, which the superstition of the times led him to believe the entrance of Hell'. Failing to find Og, Benboaro elicits from some peasants a description of him falling into the abyss in a violent storm, 'wrapped in a blue flame'.[1]

This final episode ekphrastically invokes Salvator Rosa's painting of Empedocles, hurling himself into this same crater in a sublimely ambitious attempt to investigate the mysteries of natural phenomena (late 1660s; Palazzo Pitti, Florence); the allusion to the painting reinforces the association already established between Og and Salvator, by reference to the wild, turbulent subject-matter of Og's paintings. Og, however, differs from Salvator Rosa in one conspicuous way, which aligns him with travellers on the Grand Tour: his origins are not in the warm South, but in northern Europe, and he therefore has to cross the Alps in order to embark on his Italian travels. The Alpine landscape proves highly congenial to him:

---

1 pp. 57, 81, 82, 83, 84–5, 86.

The rude scenery of these mountains suited the melancholy of Og's imagination, which delighted in solitude and gloom. He sequestered himself from his companions, hid himself in the forests of pines, and descended into caverns where no one had ever penetrated.[2]

His fellow-artist Andrew Guelph, identified with Claude Lorrain, travels through the Tyrol with him, and adopts a very different approach to the region:

While Og was delivering himself up to his genius in these wildernesses, Andrew, whose imagination was less fervid, contented himself with the humbler prospect of the valleys. He took pleasure in the conversation of the peasants, and on a moonlight evening would take his guitar, and accompanying it with his voice, enliven the assembled peasants before their simple habitations.[3]

Og, in rejecting such social, domestic pursuits in favour of artistic aspiration, implicitly invokes Longinus's opposition between the domestic and the sublime, in the section of *Peri Hypsous* which asserts that we are impressed not by 'the sight of a small fire that burns clear, and blazes out on our own private hearth', but by 'the boiling furnaces of *Ætna*, which cast up stones, and sometimes whole rocks, from their labouring abyss, and pour out whole rivers of liquid and unmingled flame':

Andrew waited near half the summer for his companion, and had nearly given him up for lost, when one morning, as he was straying by the banks of a rivulet, he saw a strange figure descending a precipice with wonderful alertness. Judge of his surprise, when shortly after he recollected the well known features of Og of Basan, most reverently mantled in a long beard. Andrew desired his friend to quit this savage state, and then begged to know for what purpose he had undertaken so wild an expedition. 'For the love of my art,' replied Og with some warmth; 'I have beheld nature in her sanctuary, I have contemplated the tempest gathering at my feet, and venting its fury on these contemptible habitations. You have idly remained amongst these herdsmen, these unfeeling clowns, whilst I have discovered the source of rivers and the savage animals that inhabit them.'[4]

As a tale that exemplifies Og's inclination to traverse behavioural limits and geographical boundaries simultaneously, this narrative anticipates later stages in the artist's travels, in which crossing boundaries and exceeding

2   *Ibid.*, p. 30.
3   *Ibid.*
4   Longinus, *Dionysius*, pp. 145–7; Beckford, *Biographical Memoirs*, pp. 33–4.

limits prove more dangerous: the artist sets in train the disasters that spring
from the death of the 'beloved nymph' by crossing the Campagna, and
moving from Tivoli to Rome, and it is after traversing the limits that separate 'lively society' from savage regions that he falls to his death in the crater
of Mount Etna. In setting out for Mount Etna, moreover, Og strongly
reaffirms his earlier need to move beyond the limits of domestic life: he
leaves Andrew Guelph behind in Messina, married to 'a beautiful Sicilian
with considerable riches', and pleading 'the cares of a family for his excuse'
in not accompanying his friend into the wilds.[5]

'Og of Basan and Andrew Guelph' is not the only late eighteenth-century narrative in which the danger and destabilization that may result from
traversing boundaries are indicated while the traveller is still engaged in
crossing the geographical barrier of the Alps. Laurence Sterne's
Sentimental Journey (1768) concludes with a section in which Yorick is
trapped in an Alpine inn by the transgressive propensities of sublime
nature. He introduces the landscape as one already heavily mediated by the
established rhetoric of hyperbole:

> Let the way-worn traveller vent his complaints upon the sudden turns and
> dangers of your roads – your rocks – your precipices – the difficulties of
> getting up – the horrors of getting down – mountains impracticable – and
> cataracts, which roll down great stones from their summits, and block the
> road up. [6]

This last feature, however, is suddenly invested with practical as well as
rhetorical force: Yorick reveals that one such stone has in fact blocked up
the road along which he himself is travelling. This event traps him in an
inn, where he soon learns that he must share his bedchamber with two
women, a lady ('a Piedmontese of about thirty, with a glow of health in her
cheeks') and her *fille de chambre* ('as brisk and lively a French girl as ever
moved'). It soon becomes evident that the maid will sleep in a small closet,
leaving Yorick and the lady with two adjoining beds, 'so very close to each
other as only to allow space for a small wicker chair betwixt them'.
Deploying a trope that he has earlier dubbed 'the French sublime' (appealing to the grandeur of nature when speaking of the trivia of everyday life),
Yorick takes up one of the stock features of Alpine scenery favoured by 'the
way-worn traveller', and ironically transfers its hyperbolic force to the situation in the inn, as he and the lady negotiate their sleeping arrangements:

5 Beckford, *Biographical Memoirs*, p. 80.

6 Sterne, *A Sentimental Journey*, pp. 120–1.

'the obstacle of the stone in the road..., great as it appeared whilst the peasants were removing it, was but a pebble to what lay in our ways now'.[7]

At the very beginning of this concluding narrative, 'The Case of
Delicacy', Yorick issues a warning against proceeding too hastily and
incautiously across boundaries: 'When you have gained the top of mount
Taurira', he observes, 'you run presently down to Lyons – adieu then to all
rapid movements! 'tis a journey of caution; and it fares better with sentiments not to be in a hurry with them.' In the light of these premonitory
words, it becomes possible to read the events that follow as an ironic
reminder of the dangers of too hasty an onward rush. He and the lady
agree to maintain a boundary between the beds, by pinning together the
'flimsy' and 'scanty' curtains. Once they are both in bed, however, Yorick
lies awake for some time, 'when Nature and patience both wearing out – O
my God ! said I -'. The Piedmontese woman, 'who had no more slept than
myself', now claims that he has broken a clause of their agreement that
imposes silence: 'The lady would by no means give up her point, tho' she
weakened her barrier by it; for in the warmth of the dispute, I could hear
two or three corking pins fall out of the curtain to the ground.' The barrier
seems unequal to its task of maintaining a separation:

> Upon my word and honour, Madame, said I – stretching my arm out of bed
> by way of asseveration –
>
> – (I was going to have added, that I would not have trespass'd against the
> remotest idea of decorum for the world) –
>
> – But the Fille de Chambre hearing there were words between us, and
> fearing that hostilities would ensue in course, had crept silently out of her
> closet, and it being totally dark, had stolen so close to our beds, that she had
> got herself into the narrow passage which separated them, and had
> advanc'd so far up as to be in a line betwixt her mistress and me –
>
> So that when I stretch'd out my hand, I caught hold of the Fille de
> Chambre's – [8]

The narrative ends here, with the crossing of the Alps and the traversal of
the lesser boundary between the beds both thrown off course by unexpected obstacles. Crossing boundaries, 'The Case of Delicacy' implies, is a

---

7 *Ibid.*, pp. 122, 122–3; Yorick's explanation of the French sublime is prompted by a barber
   commenting on the buckle of his wig: 'You may immerge it... into the ocean, and it will
   stand', at which the traveller himself ironically endorses such hyperbolic flights by declaring: 'I... am generally so struck with the great works of nature, that for my own part, if I
   could help it, I would never make a comparison less than a mountain at least' (pp. 49,
   49–50).

8 *Ibid.*, p. 120, 123, 124, 124–5.

feature of the Grand Tour that is less predictable than readers might expect.[9]

In Book VI of Wordsworth's *Prelude,* too (completed, in its first version, in 1805), the narrator sets out to cross the Alps, but discovers that his plans have been unexpectedly thwarted. He and his travelling companion famously find themselves balked of the anticipated delights of traversing the crucial symbolic boundary by taking the wrong path, and then finding that they have made the crossing inadvertently. Such a complication strongly confirms the suspicion that the desire to cross the Alps might positively invite unsettling consequences – a suspicion raised by the poet's punning insistence on the 'irregular' nature of the desire that leads him to the wild irregularity of nature's 'mighty forms' earlier in the narrative:

> When the third Summer brought its liberty
> A Fellow Student and myself, he, too,
> A Mountaineer, together sallied forth
> And, Staff in hand, on foot pursu'd our way
> Towards the distant Alps. An open slight
> Of College cares and study was the scheme,
> Nor entertain'd without concern for those
> To whom my worldly interests were dear:
> But Nature then was sovereign in my heart,
> And mighty forms seizing a youthful Fancy
> Had given a charter to irregular hopes.[10]

John Whitaker's *Course of Hannibal over the Alps Ascertained* (1794), a book entirely devoted to the question of which route Hannibal may have taken over the mountain range, presents the Carthaginian general as a traveller who, like Wordsworth, finds himself diverted from 'the regular road' in the course of his traversal.[11] As noted in Chapter 1, 'Opposition and intensification', Hannibal is often introduced into travel writings, from the beginning of the Grand Tour onwards, as a figure whose story anticipates the dangers that the contemporary traveller may encounter: having crossed the Alps, according to the established narrative, the Carthaginian

---

[9] For a more extended analysis of this part of Sterne's *Sentimental Journey*, see Chard, 'Crossing Boundaries'.

[10] Lines 549, 338–48. Pleasure in traversing established boundaries is further emphasized by lines 339–59, which describe Europe 'rejoiced' at revolution in France, and by a passage at the end of book VI (660–1), displacing the transgressiveness of travel on to the transgressive digressiveness of translating travel into narrative: travel is, the narrator declares, 'A theme which may seduce me else beyond / All reasonable bounds'.

[11] Vol. I, p. 285.

fails to march on Rome, despite a series of victories, and he and his army
fall victim to the effeminating pleasures of the warm South.[12] A number of
eighteenth-century and early nineteenth-century writings remind the
reader of the narrative of behavioural transgression that is to follow the
traversal of the Alps by assigning a prominent place to the moment when
the general revives the spirits of his troops by pausing on a piece of high
ground to point out to them 'the rich and beautiful plains of Italy' below.[13]
This moment not only draws attention to the fact that a boundary between
two distinct regions is being crossed; it also allegorizes the desire for the
foreign as a place which promises superior pleasure – and, at the same
time, indicates the dangers that such a desire may bring in its wake. Sydney
Morgan's account of this episode, in *Italy*, accentuates the reference forward to the delights of Italy by a progression from Hannibal to a successor
in aspiring geographical transgression, who enjoys on this spot an antici-
patory 'beaker full of the warm South' that serves as a synecdoche for sensory indulgences to come:

> From such a site as this, it is said, Hannibal halted his Carthaginians, and
> pointed to the recompense of all their arduous undertakings. From such a
> site as this, the Lombard Alboin paused amidst his ferocious hosts, to con-
> template the paradise of his future conquest, and quaffed from the skull of
> his enemy his first draught of Italian wine.[14]

In Canto III of *Childe Harold's Pilgrimage* (1817), the narrator, gazing out
upon Italy from the Alps, implies that obstacles may impede his vision:
'The clouds above me to the white Alps tend, / And I must pierce them,
and survey whate'er / May be permitted'. The suggestion here of a transgressiveness inherent in attempting to glimpse the pleasures of the South
is then elaborated into an anticipation of danger by an oblique reminder
that Hannibal, after experiencing a similar moment, did not in fact quite
succeed in winning Italy:

> Italia! too, Italia! looking on thee,
> Full flashes on the soul the light of ages,
> Since the fierce Carthaginian almost won thee...[15]

---

12 For one version of this narrative, see Moore, *View of Society*, vol. II, p. 117.

13 Starke, *Letters*, vol. II, p. 186. See also, for example, Moore's reference to the army gazing
    out upon 'the fertile plains of Italy' (*View of Society*, vol. II, p. 461).

14 Vol. I, pp. 24–5; in using the expression 'beaker full of the warm South', I am, of course,
    quoting Keats's 'Ode to a Nightingale', line 15, in *Complete Poems*, p. 346.

15 Stanza 110, lines 1–3; in Byron, *Complete Poetical Works*, p. 117.

The moment of looking down upon Italy is handled in a premonitory manner, too, in Ann Radcliffe's Gothic novel *The Mysteries of Udolpho* (1794). The heroine, Emily, listens to a dispute between two men, Montoni and Cavigni, about Hannibal's route, and reconstructs a scene from 'this bold and perilous adventure' in her imagination. Radcliffe then describes a moment of gazing out over Italy, in which the dreamer is not Hannibal, but Madame Montoni, Emily's aunt, whose status as an inadequate traveller has just been emphasized by an account of her insensibility towards the sublime. In her own version of 'the French sublime', Radcliffe emphasizes that Hannibal is not alone in giving himself up to ill-fated visions of conquering Italy:

> Madame Montoni, meantime, as she looked upon Italy, was contemplating in imagination the splendour of palaces and the grandeur of castles, such as she believed she was going to be mistress of at Venice and in the Apennine, and she became, in idea, little less than a princess. Being no longer under the alarms which had deterred her from giving entertainments to the beauties of Tholouse, whom Montoni had mentioned with more éclat to his own vanity than credit to their discretion, or regard to truth, she determined to give concerts, though she had neither ear nor taste for music; conversazioni, though she had no talents for conversation; and to outvie, if possible, in the gaieties of her parties and the magnificence of her liveries, all the noblesse of Venice.[16]

Madame Montoni dies in Italy, a prisoner of her Italian husband, exhausted by his ill-treatment. Even Emily, whose 'rapture, when… she caught a first view of Italy' is of a more elevated nature, soon discovers that sublime natural scenery can excite not only 'various emotions of delight', but also a heightened awareness of the dangers that await her, as a woman at the mercy of Montoni's 'arbitrary disposition'; by the time the party reach the Apennines, 'she saw only images of gloomy grandeur, or of dreadful sublimity, around her; other images, equally gloomy and equally terrible, gleamed on her imagination.'[17]

The consequences of transgression: danger and destabilization

The suggestion that traversing and exceeding limits might entail hidden complications and dangerous consequences is made more directly and explored in greater detail in a much later travel narrative. Comparing this

---

[16] pp. 166, 166–7.

[17] *Ibid.*, pp. 325, 165, 166, 224.

text with the two narratives just discussed provides a way of elucidating some of the transformations in the formation of concepts of travel that take place from the late eighteenth century onwards. This piece of writing is Freud's essay 'A Disturbance of Memory on the Acropolis' (1936), which tells the story of a holiday that Freud has spent in the company of his brother. Their travels together are marked by two odd experiences. First, at Trieste, an acquaintance advises the brothers to travel on to Athens rather than their intended destination, Corfu. They spend the hours that elapse before they can buy their tickets in a state of gloom, foreseeing 'nothing but obstacles and difficulties'; once the Lloyd offices open, however, they book their passages 'as though it were a matter of course, without bothering in the least about the supposed difficulties'. Freud describes their initial response as 'no more than an expression of incredulity: "We're going to see Athens? Out of the question! – it will be far too difficult!"'[18]

The second odd experience occurs once they reach Athens: 'When, finally... I stood on the Acropolis and cast my eyes around upon the land-scape, a surprising thought suddenly entered my mind: "So all this really *does* exist, just as we learnt at school!"'. Freud identifies the thought as a displaced expression of 'a momentary feeling: "*What I see here is not real.*"' He classifies this 'derealization' as a defence mechanism, aimed at the dis-avowal of his distressing boyhood doubts as to whether he would in fact ever be able to go to Greece and see the Acropolis – doubts that were 'linked up with the limitations and poverty of our conditions of life in my youth'. These doubts were, he notes, accompanied by a 'longing to travel', which must also have expressed his wish to escape such limitations; 'I had long seen clearly that a great part of the pleasure of travel... is rooted... in dis-satisfaction with home and family.' The desire to travel is, Freud suggests, also closely linked to the universal human desire to go 'further than one's father'. In perceiving such a link, Freud is able to explain the earlier inci-dent at Trieste. Some internal impulse can be assumed to be at work, inter-fering with their enjoyment. 'It must be', Freud concludes, 'that a sense of guilt was attached to the satisfaction in having gone such a long way... It seems... as though to excel one's father was still something forbidden.'[19]

The guilt that Freud ascribes to himself and his brother, however, is not a manifestation of inadequacy, to be judged with reference to the social con-text of a particular practice of travel, but a form of danger, to be assessed with reference to the domain of the personal, and the way in which travel

---

[18] pp. 449, 448, 450.

[19] *Ibid.*, pp. 449, 453, 455, 456.

functions as a variety of personal adventure. While the satisfaction of 'having gone such a long way' turns out to have 'something about it that was wrong', the narrator obviously does not endorse the view that moving beyond Trieste and further than his father is somehow culpable; the sense of something wrong makes itself felt, rather, through the 'obstacles and difficulties' that interfere with the travellers' purposeful pursuit of pleasure.[20]

Danger, at each of the two points at which it intervenes in Freud's holiday, is manifested as a form of destabilization: in analysing the despondency that the travellers evince at Trieste, Freud likens it to the experiences of people 'wrecked by success': people driven by an internal barrier to happiness to 'fall ill or even go entirely to pieces, because an overwhelmingly powerful wish of theirs has been fulfilled'. His description of the 'derealization' on the Acropolis emphasizes the unsettling effect of travel yet more explicitly: he notes a division between the subject of the remark 'So all this really *does* exist...', and the subject who takes cognizance of this remark, and describes both subjects as 'astonished'. The first behaves 'as though he were obliged, under the impact of an unequivocal observation, to believe in something the reality of which had hitherto seemed doubtful', and the second is 'justifiably astonished, because he had been unaware that the real existence of Athens, the Acropolis, and the landscape around it had ever been objects of doubt'. The hyperbole by which Freud describes the first of these two responses of astonishment takes him into the domain that Fielding, in the 'Author's Preface' to his *Journal of a Voyage to Lisbon*, typifies as 'the wonderful':

> If I may make a slight exaggeration, it was as if someone, walking beside Loch Ness, suddenly caught sight of the form of the famous Monster stranded upon the shore and found himself driven to the admission: 'So it really *does* exist – the sea-serpent we've never believed in!'[21]

Fielding, in considering 'the true source of the wonderful', ironically identifies a sublime impulse to exceed limits as the source of travellers' claims that they have in fact seen marvels: 'Why then should not the voyage-writer be inflamed with the glory of having seen what no man ever did or will see but himself?'[22] When Freud investigates the feeling that he has seen a marvel, he does so in order to emphasize the unsettling rather than the self-affirmatory aspect of his encounter with the foreign. At the same time, however, he too

---

20 *Ibid.*, p. 456.

21 *Ibid.*, pp. 450, 449.

22 Fielding, *Jonathan Wild and A Journal of a Voyage to Lisbon*, p. 187.

links travel to sublime aspiration. Having charted the impulse to escape 'our own private hearth' that prompts his 'longing to travel', he then merges this desire to leave behind the limitations of home and family with the experience of crossing 'the Ocean', one of the features noted by Longinus as an instance of the sublime in nature, and further invokes *Peri Hypsous* by linking travel to the sublime aspiration 'ardently to contend in the pursuit of glory':

> When first one catches sight of the sea, crosses the ocean and experiences as realities cities and lands which for so long had been distant, unattainable things of desire – one feels oneself like a hero who has performed deeds of improbable greatness.[23]

Personal need

'A Disturbance of Memory', then, resembles 'The Case of Delicacy' and 'Andrew Guelph and Og of Basan' not only in mapping out a narrative in which the traveller crosses boundaries and undergoes destabilization, but also in drawing the sublime into the narrative of transgression. The three pieces of travel writing, however, differ from one another in their approach to the sublime, and to the motivation that prompts the traveller to cross boundaries and exceed limits. Yorick, in travelling, does not present him-self as a man motivated by impelling personal need; he presents his travels, initially, as the result of mere caprice, and happily allows himself to be dis-tracted by each of the vignettes of social and sentimental life that offers itself to him. Unlike Og and Freud, he feels no great urge to escape scenes of domesticity; just before the final sections of the narrative, he takes pos-itive pleasure in such scenes, in 'The Supper' and 'The Grace'.[24] The sub-lime disregard of limits exemplified by the cataracts in 'The Case of Delicacy', moreover, sets in motion a narrative that (as noted in the Introduction) is more digressive than transgressive: far from identifying with this disregard of limits, Yorick and the Piedmontese woman become thoroughly preoccupied with the trivial details of their embarrassing situation.

In the story of Og, in contrast, the traveller is consistently presented as a man driven onwards by inner needs – needs that are generated not by the conditions of his childhood but simply by the aspiring and disordered per-sonality that Beckford satirically sets up as an attribute of this particular

---

23   Longinus, *Dionysius*, p. 45; Freud, 'A Disturbance of Memory', p. 455.

24   Sterne, *A Sentimental Journey*, pp. 118–20.

version of the artist-hero.[25] As in 'A Disturbance of Memory', the narrator presents the crossing of geographical boundaries as an activity that merges with sublime aspiration precisely because it is prompted by a passionate need for self-realization.

This view of travel as an adventure of the self, in which the traveller is propelled across boundaries by his or her personal needs and desires, is voiced very often in early nineteenth-century narratives of encounters with the foreign: Beckford's biography anticipates the travel writings of some decades later. The first canto of Byron's *Childe Harold's Pilgrimage* (1812) begins by explaining that Childe Harold is driven to set out on his travels by a 'satiety' that is specifically defined as the product of his own personality, as expressed in his proclivity towards a life of 'revel and ungodly glee': 'With pleasure drugg'd he almost long'd for woe, / And e'en for change of scene would seek the shades below.' This weariness of pleasure fills the Childe with a determination to cross boundaries that goes way beyond the extent of the journey actually chronicled by Byron in the cantos that follow:

> ... all that mote to luxury invite,
> Without a sigh he left, to cross the brine,
> And traverse Paynim shores, and pass Earth's central line.[26]

Thomas Love Peacock, satirizing the fourth canto of *Childe Harold* in *Nightmare Abbey* (1818), summarizes this view of travel as motivated by personal need through the Byronic figure of Mr Cypress. When criticized by Scythrop (Shelley) for forsaking his own country, Mr Cypress replies simply: 'Sir, I have quarrelled with my wife; and a man who has quarrelled with his wife is absolved from all duty to his country.'[27] Stendhal, at the beginning of *Rome, Naples et Florence* (1826), happily affirms the view that travel entails a disregard of responsibility. The narrator, learning that he has been granted a period of leave from his employment, exclaims: 'Transports de joie, battements de cœur... Je verrai donc cette belle Italie! Mais je me cache soigneusement du ministre; les eunuques son en colère permanente contre les libertins.'[28] Such a view of travel as a response to

---

[25] For an analysis of the role of Beckford's *Biographical Memoirs* within the history of the life of the artist, see Shaffer, 'Death of the Artist'.

[26] Stanza 4, line 7; stanza 2, line 6; stanza 6, lines 8–9; stanza 11, lines 7–9; in Byron, *Complete Poetical Works*, vol. II, pp. 9, 10, 12.

[27] p. 99.

[28] p. 27: 'What transports of joy do I experience! – How my heart palpitates!. . . I shall then see this enchanting Italy. But I must hide myself carefully from the minister: eunuchs entertain a permanent wrath against libertines' (*Rome, Naples and Florence, in 1817*, p. 1).

individual desires, demands, needs and impulses is in obvious contrast to the concept of travelling as an opportunity for acquiring and ordering knowledge of the world, formed within the eighteenth-century commentary of observation and comparison.

The earlier attitude to travel does not entirely disappear; comparison between the foreign and the familiar, however, no longer incorporates an assumption that the adequate, authoritative subject of commentary will necessarily judge the two domains from a position of detachment. (Some of the commentaries quoted in the last chapter, in which an elision between the antique and the feminine allows the ancient past to erupt within the present, emphasize the ease with which detached viewing can transmute into destabilized reaction, when travellers position themselves not simply as subjects of knowledge but as subjects of desire.) Personal need is regularly cited in early nineteenth-century travel commentaries not only as the primary motive for travel, but also as the primary point of reference to be adopted when judging the foreign: the eighteenth-century assumption that participation in the Grand Tour imposes a commitment to detached observation and comparison is, in many writings, completely displaced. Mary Shelley, in a note on Shelley's *Prometheus Unbound*, assesses Italy almost solely on the basis of its effect on her husband's health, spirits and creative abilities: 'In almost every respect his journey to Italy was advantageous... The first aspect of Italy enchanted Shelley; it seemed a garden of delight placed beneath a clearer and brighter heaven than any he had lived under before... The poetical spirit within him speedily revived with all the power and more than all the beauty of his first attempts.'[29] At the beginning of her *Diary of an Ennuyée* (1826), Jameson speculates on whether travel through France and Italy can soothe her 'torn and upset' mind (upset, it swiftly becomes evident, as a result of an unhappy love affair): 'Who knows but this dark cloud may pass away. Continual motion, continual activity, continual novelty, the absolute necessity for self-command may do something for me.' The traveller then minutely and elaborately assesses her stay in every place that she visits for its therapeutic or destructive effect. In Venice: 'Pleasure and wonder are tinged with a melancholy interest; and while the imagination is excited, the spirits are depressed.' Travelling southwards, she remarks: 'I will say nothing of Bologna; – for the few days I have spent

---

[29] Shelley, *Poetical Works*, p. 270. The arguments formulated within the early nineteenth-century debate about whether or not travel to Italy and the warm South is therapeutic are very clearly dependent upon the concept of travel as an activity prompted by personal need. See, for example, the short story 'Change of Air', in Normanby, *The English in Italy*, and Johnson, *Change of Air*.

here have been to me days of acute suffering.' In Florence, at Santa Croce, she declares: 'All memory, all feeling, all grief, all pain were swallowed up in the sublime tranquillity which was within me and around me.' Once Jameson sets out for Naples, the reader is almost encouraged to feel that she might recover: ' – my senses and my imagination have been so enchanted, my heart so very heavy – where shall I begin?' At Autun, however, on the return journey, an editorial note informs the reader – mendaciously – that the writer has died 'in her 26th year'.[30]

Such appeals to personal need are often deployed, in early nineteenth-century writings, to endorse the approach to travel as an escape from constraint: the same approach that the traveller-narrator adopts in 'A Disturbance of Memory'. The opposition between constraint and freedom is readily smuggled into travel commentaries as though it were simply one more binary opposition between the familiar and the foreign: it nonetheless forces the subject of commentary to abandon any position of impersonal detachment, and entirely obviates the need to register a 'manly understanding' of the advantages of the familiar, so central to the commentary of opposition and comparison. In early nineteenth-century French and English travel writings, Italy is still repeatedly classified as a land of despotism, but is nonetheless greeted as a domain of personal liberty for the traveller. In Mary Shelley's journal of 1823, written after her return to London as a widow, the traveller proclaims her own lack of concern as to whether or not her sense that Italy offers her greater freedom can in some way be assessed and justified:

> Why am I not in Italy – Italian sun & airs & flowers & earth & hopes – they are akin to love enjoyment freedom – exquisite delight – if they are not them they are masked unto them – but here all wears the hue of grimmest reality – a reality to make me shriek upon the ear of midnight.[31]

Another passage from this journal, written during the same unhappy phase of Mary Shelley's life, reveals more clearly the specific need that is invoked in order to endorse such expressions of a desire for superior freedom: the need for self-exploration, self-discovery or self-realization. A complaint about 'the imprisonment attendant on a succession of rainy days' in London is followed by a description of Genoa which suggests not only an imaginative freedom, but also a greater possibility of self-fulfilment – a movement towards a self that transcends mundane existence:

---

[30] pp. 4, 5, 65, 84, 114, 208, 354.
[31] Vol. II, p. 469.

I can hardly tell but it seems to me as if the lovely and sublime objects of nature had been my best inspirers & wanting these I am lost. Although so utterly miserable at Genoa, yet what reveries were mine as I walked on the road and looked on the changing aspect of the ravine – the sunny deep & its boats – the promontories clothed in purple light – the starry heavens – the fireflies – the uprising of spring – then I could think – and my imagination could invent and combine, and self become absorbed in the grandeur of the universe I created – Now my mind is a blank – a gulph filled with formless mist.[32]

The sublime, in this passage, supplies a metaphor for the impulse towards freedom and self-realization: in many early nineteenth-century writings, as in 'A Disturbance of Memory', the experience of sublimity is elided with the expression of a sense of liberation from the oppressive limitations of the familiar. In another journal entry, Mary Shelley goes beyond her equation of rainy London with a 'formless mist' of the mind, and brusquely dismisses her own country as one that offers her only a 'prison'. She then invokes the aesthetic pleasures of sublime infinitude ('the resplendent sky', 'the blue expanse of the tranquil sea', 'the unclouded stars') in order to endorse her need to transcend the bounds of personal grief:

I have now been nearly four months in England and if I am to judge of the future by the past and the present, I have small delight in looking forward. I even regret those days and weeks of intense melancholy that composed my life at genoa [sic] – Yes – solitary and unbeloved as I was there, I enjoyed a more pleasurable state of being than I do here. I was still in Italy, & my heart and imagination were both gratified by that circumstance. I arose with the light and beheld the theatre of Nature from my windows – The trees spread their green beauty before me – the resplendent sky was above me – the mountains were invested with enchanting colours – I had even begun to contemplate painlessly the blue expanse of the tranquil sea speck-led by the snow white sails bounded by rocky promontories, gazed upon by the unclouded stars – there was morning & its balmy air; noon and its exhil-arating heat – evening and its wondrous sunset; Night and it[s] starry pag-eant both on heaven and earth... Then my solitary walks and my reveries – They *were* magnificent, deep, pathetic, wild and exalted – I sounded the depths of my own nature.[33]

---

32 *Ibid.*, vol. II, p. 476.
33 *Ibid.*, vol. II, pp. 470–1; the 'intense melancholy' that Mary Shelley mentions is in response to Shelley's death in 1822.

Freud's appropriation of this same Romantic vision of travel as an escape to a domain of freedom is no chance anachronism. The option of declaring unequivocally that the foreign offers the powerful pleasure of superior freedom, so conspicuously absent from eighteenth-century travel literature, continues to be available to the traveller commenting on the foreign throughout the two succeeding centuries. Many later nineteenth-century writings attempt to reconcile the impulse to seek out greater pleasure and excitement within exotic regions with loyalty towards familiar places and familiar cultural values. During the early decades of the twentieth century, however – the period when 'A Disturbance of Memory' was written – declarations of unreserved pleasure in escaping the constraints of the familiar once again proliferate.[34] In D.H. Lawrence's short story 'Sun' (1928), a woman's increasingly enthuasistic removal of her clothes, in order to take 'sun-baths' in Sicily, serves as a metaphor for her escape (or, as it eventually transpires, her partial escape) from her 'grey', joyless life at home in New York.[35] The sublime, in these early twentieth-century writings, is once again caught up in plots of pleasurable liberation. In a conversation in Norman Douglas's novel *South Wind* (1917), Mr Keith, a long-standing inhabitant of the island of Nepenthe (which greatly resembles Capri), establishes a sharp opposition between freedom abroad and constraint at home, and invokes sublime infinitude – the absence of limits – in order to provide authentication for the pleasures of freedom. An English bishop, Heard, a relative newcomer to Nepenthe, expresses doubts about whether the alleged 'vices' of another foreigner on the island should be condoned. Mr Keith replies by appealing to the natural sublimity around them:

> 'Vices. My dear bishop! Under a sky like this. Have a good look at it; do.'
> Mr Heard, barely conscious of what he was doing, obeyed the counsel. Raising his hand, he pushed the silken awning to one side. Then he peered skyward, into the noonday zenith; into an ocean of blue, immeasurable. There was no end to this azure liquid. Gazing thus, his intelligence became aware of the fact that there are skies of different kinds. This one was not quite like his native firmament. Here was no suggestion of a level space overhead, remote, but still conceivable – a space whereon some god might have sat, enthroned, note-book

---

34 Paul Fussell, in *Abroad: British Literary Traveling between the Wars*, puts forward an analysis of this kind, with, as the title suggests, specific reference to British travel and travel writing: 'Robert Louis Stevenson and Rupert Brooke were pleased to journey away from England and equally pleased to return. But with Lawrence and Douglas and Huxley and Graves. . . and later, Durrell, Isherwood, and Auden, departure is attended by the conviction that England is uninhabitable because it is not like abroad' (p. 15).

35 p. 439.

in hand, jotting down men's virtues and vices, and what not. A sky of this kind
was obviously not built to accommodate deities in a sitting posture.[36]

Sublimity and escape

In its emphasis on 'an ocean of blue, immeasurable', this passage demonstrates
the survival of another element in the early nineteenth-century rhetoric of
crossing boundaries and exceeding limits: the use of the clear blue of sea and
sky in the warm South (opposed, implicitly or explicitly, to the cloudiness of
the North) as a metaphor for an escape from constraining bounds. Mary
Shelley, in her account of her relative imaginative freedom in Genoa, refers to
'the blue expanse of the tranquil sea'.[37] Anna Jameson, describing the Bay of
Naples, also notes the absence of spatial limitations on the prospect as one of
the factors contributing towards its pleasures: in declaring 'I never saw or felt
any thing like the enchantment of the earth, air, and skies', Jameson implicitly
defines the view across the bay as one in which a vast sweep of the natural
world is visible. After referring to 'the atmosphere without a single cloud', she
places 'the blue sea' that results from this unbounded infinitude in implicit
contrast to the 'vapoury atmosphere' of the North:

> To stand upon my balcony, looking out upon the sunshine, and the glorious
> bay; the blue sea, and the pure skies – and to feel that indefinite sensation of
> excitement, that *superflu de vie*, quickening every pulse and thrilling
> through every nerve, is a pleasure peculiar to this climate, where the mere
> consciousness of existence is happiness enough. Then evening comes on,
> lighted by a moon and starry heavens, whose softness, richness, and splen-
> dour, are not to be conceived by those who have lived always in the vapoury
> atmosphere of England.[38]

At this point, the pleasure produced by crossing the boundary between
North and South is elided with the pleasure that Freud, in 'A Disturbance
of Memory', presents as central to the delights of travel: escape from the

---

[36] pp. 173–4. Both self-realization and sublime traversal of boundaries are dominant
themes, too, within a popular genre of the 1920s, founded by E.M. Hull's *The Sheik*
(1919): the 'desert romance' or 'desert passion story'. (Within the narrative pattern that
this novel establishes, a young, virginal Englishwoman or Frenchwoman experiences a
sexual awakening which is accompanied by an increasing attraction towards a wild,
nomadic life, beyond the restraints of convention – and, at the same time, towards the
sublime boundlessness of the desert.)

[37] Shelley, *Journals*, vol. II, p. 471; see also the description of 'the blue and pellucid element'
at Baiæ in Shelley, *The Last Man*, p. 1.

[38] Jameson, *Diary*, pp. 239–40.

constraints of domesticity. Initially, the traveller seems to endorse the domestic 'comforts' of England, in much the same manner as the narrator in a passage of Charlotte Smith's Gothic novel *Montalbert* (1795), cited in Chapter 1, 'Opposition and intensification', as an example of the eighteenth-century strategy of suddenly reminding the reader of the merits of the familiar. Smith's heroine, Rosalie, travelling to Italy with her half-Italian husband, feels 'pleasure, amounting sometimes to rapture, when, as they approached the Alps, the most sublime and magnificent scenes of nature were opened to her astonished view.' The narrator, however, carefully notes that 'she was of an age and disposition to forget, or at least be indifferent to those circumstances which can hardly fail to remind English travellers, that, though other countries may have more bold and attractive scenery, their own is that where life is enjoyed with the greatest comfort'.[39] Jameson, apparently embarking on a similar reminder of the merits of the familiar, after the implied criticism of England's 'vapoury atmosphere', nonethless concludes by vaunting once again the enchantment of the 'deep blue skies', and unworriedly suggests that she prefers Italy to England simply because it does more to satisfy her need for inner regeneration:

> – dear England! I love, like an Englishwoman, its fire-side enjoyments, and home-felt delights: an English drawing-room with all its luxurious comforts – carpets and hearth rugs, curtains let down, sofas wheeled round, and a group of family faces round a blazing fire, is a delightful picture; but for the languid frame, and the sick heart, give me this pure elastic air 'redolent of spring;' this reviving sun shine and all the witchery of these deep blue skies.[40]

In positioning this passage just after a long description of the eruption of Vesuvius, moreover, and emphasizing English 'fire-side enjoyments' and 'hearth rugs', Jameson obliquely invokes Longinus's opposition between volcanoes and 'our own private hearth' – an opposition within which natural grandeur is unequivocally classified as a source of greater and more ennobling delight.[41] The reference to Longinus is all the clearer because at least two of the features of the English 'private hearth' that Jameson cites suggest claustrophobic enclosure and boundedness: the curtains are 'let down' and the sofas are 'wheeled round'. Far from dismissing the sublime, as

---

39 Vol. II, pp. 143, 144.
40 Jameson, *Diary*, p. 240.
41 *Ibid.*; for the account of the eruption of Vesuvius, see pp. 226–39.

the narrator of *Montalbert* does, when loyalty to the familiar is in question, she actually allows the sublime to undermine her declaration of loyalty, by endorsing her reservations about bounded, domestic existence.

This mapping of the Longinian opposition between bounded domestic space and the aspiration to escape boundedness on to the opposition between the familiar and the foreign is repeated not only in Freud's 'Disturbance of Memory', but in many other writings. Charlotte Mansfield, describing the grandeur of Victoria Falls in *Via Rhodesia: A Journey through Southern Africa* (1911), remarks: 'Without the slightest wish to be disloyal or lese-majestic, I must confess that the name of the Falls seems to be its one drawback. The name Victoria suggests solid English comfort and stolid dignity'; the 'native name Mosi-oa-tunya ("Smoke that sounds")', Mansfield observes, possesses a far greater ability to evoke 'Nature in her deepest notes proclaiming her omnipotence'.[42]

Oppositions between escaping constraint and accepting the boundedness of home and family play a central part in Germaine de Staël's *Corinne; ou, l'Italie*. Lord Nelvil, after meeting the heroine in Rome, comes to see her influence as operating in direct opposition to the authority of his dead father. From an early point in the novel, it is emphasized that, for Oswald, 'le souvenir de son père étoit si intimement uni dans sa pensée avec sa patrie, que ces deux sentiments s'accroissoient l'un par l'autre'. It transpires that the father has already singled out Corinne as a woman whom Oswald must *not* marry, and has chosen her younger, English half-sister Lucile to be his son's future wife, on the grounds that Lucile will be better suited to the limited, domestic life which women are expected to lead in England. The sphere of action that Corinne's personality and talents map out for her is placed in yet sharper opposition to English domesticity by her account of her unhappiness in an English household: describing the tedium of sitting round the tea-table after dinner with her stepmother's friends, the heroine declares: 'J'avois été dans les couvens d'Italie, ils me paroissoient pleins de vie à côté de ce cercle.'[43]

---

[42] p. 131.

[43] Vol. I, p. 161 (book VI, chapter 4): 'The memory of his father was so entwined with that of his native land, that each sentiment strengthened the other' (*Corinne; or, Italy*, p. 105; further translations in footnotes are all taken from this edition); vol. II, p. 91 (book XIV, chapter 1): 'The convents I had seen in Italy appeared all life to this' (p. 238); see also Monsieur Edgermond's warning to Oswald (vol. I, p. 194; book VIII, chapter 1). For another variant on the opposition between travel and domesticity, see *Childe Harold's Pilgrimage*, Canto I, stanza 5; in Byron, *Complete Poetical Works*, vol. II, p. 10: while describing Childe Harold's need to travel, Byron explains that the Childe is a man ill–disposed towards 'calm domestic peace' (line 9).

From the very start of Oswald's Grand Tour, the sublime plays a part in this plot of intertwined romantic and topographical adventure, dramatizing the transgressive force of the impulse to move away from home and family quite as strongly as it does in 'A Disturbance of Memory'. Lord Nelvil, in setting out from Edinburgh for Italy, 'se reprochoit d'abandonner des lieux où son père avoit vécu'. His sense of the momentousness of his departure is intensified when he reaches the natural boundary of the English Channel. In the Alps, his antics alert the reader yet more clearly to the perils of crossing boundaries: to the fright of the local peasants, he gallops about 'sur le bord des abîmes', on a horse that he has brought from Scotland. The narrator observes that 'Oswald aimoit assez l'émotion du danger'.[44]

Natural sublimity is once again elided with the dangers of disregarding limits when Oswald and Corinne travel down to Naples together – a journey that two of Corinne's admirers warn her not to undertake. The heroine and her Scottish lover, arriving in Naples, are confronted by the sublime natural feature of Vesuvius, which impresses upon them a sense that their destinies are beyond their control:

> Ce phénomène du Vésuve cause un véritable battement de coeur. On est si familiarisé d'ordinaire avec les objets extérieurs, qu'on aperçoit à peine leur existence, et l'on ne reçoit guère d'émotion nouvelle, en ce genre, au milieu de nos prosaïques contrées; mais tout à coup l'étonnement que doit causer l'univers se renouvelle à l'aspect d'une merveille inconnue de la création: tout notre être est agité par cette puissance de la nature, dont les combinaisons sociales nous avoient distraits long-temps; nous sentons que les plus grands mystères de ce monde ne consistent pas tous dans l'homme, et qu'une force indépendante de lui le menace ou le protège, selon des lois qu'il ne peut pénétrer.[45]

44 Staël, *Corinne; ou, l'Italie*, vol. I, p. 22 (book I, chapter 1): 'Sometimes, too, he reproached himself for abandoning the place where his father had dwelt' (p. 2); vol. I, p. 26 (book I, chapter 2): 'The astonished peasants began by shrieking with fright, as they saw him borne along the precipice's edge'; 'he loved the sense of danger' (pp. 5–6). For the account of the solemnity of crossing the Channel, see vol. I, pp. 22, 23 (book I, chapter 1).

45 *Ibid.*, vol. II, p. 16 (book XI, chapter 2): 'This phenomenon really makes the heart palpitate. We are so familiarised with the works of heaven, that we scarcely notice them with any new sensation in our prosaic realms; but the wonder which the universe ought to inspire is suddenly renewed at the sight of a miracle like this: our whole being is agitated by its Maker's power, – from which our social connections have turned our thoughts so long: we feel that man is not the world's chief mystery; that a strength independent of his own at once threatens and protects him, by a law to him unknown' (p. 186). The comte d'Erfeuil (vol. I, pp. 263–5; book X, chapter 6) warns Corinne of the threat to her reputation that this journey with Lord Nelvil poses; the Prince Castel-Forte tells Corinne, at this juncture, that she will be unhappy if she marries Oswald and is exiled from her native land (vol. I, p. 267; book X, chapter 6).

The final sentence in the chapter again draws attention to the dynamic role of crossing boundaries as a narrative function, opening up exciting and dangerous possibilities: 'Oswald et Corinne se promirent de monter sur le Vésuve, et ce qu'il pouvoit y avoir de périlleux dans cette entreprise, répandoit un charme de plus sur un projet qu'ils devoient exécuter ensemble.' When Corinne improvises at Capo Miseno (Figure 7), several chapters later, she ensures that the reader has grasped the role of volcanoes as metaphors for a dangerous exceeding of limits. She notes the transgressive nature of the landscape itself ('Ici la terre est orageuse comme la mer, et ne rentre pas comme elle paisiblement dans ses bornes') and then observes: 'La campagne de Naples est l'image des passions humaines: sulfureuse et féconde, ses dangers et ses plaisirs semblent naître de ces volcans enflammés qui donnent à l'air tant de charmes, et font gronder la foudre sous nos pas.'[46]

The desire to escape and the sublime impulse towards self-realization are frequently entangled with romantic and sexual adventure in other early nineteenth-century narratives of travel. (This feature of early nineteenth-century imaginative geography is appropriated with particular enthusiasm in early twentieth-century travel narratives[47]). In Sydney Morgan's *Life and Times of Salvator Rosa* (1824), the young painter, born and brought up in Naples, is possessed by an overwhelming desire to travel, as a result of a need to realize his talents that resists all constraint:

> Parental authority now in vain opposed itself to a vocation which made a part of constitutional temperament. Obstacles became stimulants,

---

[46] *Ibid.*, vol. II, p. 16 (book XI, chapter 2): 'Oswald and Corinne promised themselves the pleasure of ascending Vesuvius, and felt an added delight in thinking of the danger they thus should brave together' (p. 186); vol. II, pp. 72, 73 (book XIII, chapter 4); these two pieces of the improvisation are translated by Landon, in Isabel Hill's edition (pp. 224, 225), as:

> For here the earth is stormy as the sea,
> But doth not, like the sea, peaceful return
> Within its bounds.

> Were but a surface ready to unclose
> Naples! How doth thy country likeness bear
> To human passions; fertile, sulphurous:
> Its dangers and its pleasures both seem born
> Of those inflamed volcanoes, which bestow
> Upon the atmosphere so many charms,
> Yet bid the thunder growl beneath our feet.

[47] Juliet, in D.H. Lawrence's 'Sun', for example, feels an attraction towards the Sicilian sun which is described in explicitly sexual terms (p. 425), and displaces this attraction on to a male peasant who catches glimpses of her sunbathing naked (p. 442).

difficulties served but '*to bind up each corporal faculty*' to the cherished purpose; and the young enthusiast... set forth upon *his* giro, animated by that
zeal which leads to the great truths of scenic, as of moral nature, and flushed
with that ardour without which there is no genius, no success![48]

Sublime natural scenery, it seems, is essential to Salvator's path of self-
realization: like Corinne and Lord Nelvil, the artist is attracted to natural
features that share his impatience of bounds and limits. He reaches such
spectacular sights on interludes in his travels when he goes beyond even
the 'last boundaries of social aggregation':

> It appears... that he directed his wanderings to the higher chain of the
> Abruzzi, and that he studied and designed amidst those amphitheatres of
> rocks, which, clothed with dark pines, and dashed with bursting torrents,
> were still freshly stamped with the commotions of that Nature, which in
> such altitudes knows no repose. There, almost within view of the bold and
> solitary student, hills sunk to valleys, valleys swelled to hills, – rivers shifted
> their courses, and latent fires broke forth to scathe the vigorous vegetation
> which their own smothered ardours had produced.[49]

Salvator is then captured by *banditti*, and finds himself in particular danger when he attracts the attention of a woman, 'the mistress, or the wife of
the Chief', a character who is herself no stranger to exceeding limits:
'whose strong passions may have flung her out of the pale of society, but
whose feminine sympathies still remain unchanged'. She pleads 'artfully'
for Rosa's life, attempting to save him 'by contemptuously noting his
insignificance'; once 'her bandit lover' returns, and sees her 'melancholy
severity' softening in response to the artist's 'musical and poetical' tributes,
his 'stern features... now contract into looks of dark distrust'.[50]

Effemination: Hannibal in Siren Land

Salvator Rosa's proclivity for crossing boundaries results in temporary
danger rather than any permanent threat to identity: when he returns to
Naples, his existing proclivity for painting sublime nature is strongly confirmed by his experiences.[51] Some pages before Lady Morgan embarks on
the story of Salvator's capture by the *banditti*, however, she introduces a

---

48 Vol. I, p. 96.

49 *Ibid.*, vol. I, pp. 107, 106, 107–8.

50 *Ibid.*, vol. I, pp. 118, 119, 119–120.

51 *Ibid.*, vol. I, p. 121: 'Fresh from the stupendous altitudes of the Abruzzi, with all their
   mightiness impressed upon his mind, the ardent disciple of Nature must have felt the
   superiority of her great school over all of mere human institution.'

historical figure who, after crossing boundaries and undergoing the consequences, never recovers his purposefulness, and who therefore provides a model for a more thoroughly destabilized approach to the foreign. This figure is Hannibal, in the final phase of his travels, after he has been diverted from any warlike enterprise by the pleasures of Capua. Describing one of the paintings that result from Salvator's wanderings, Morgan remarks that 'a dark and desolate plain, dimly lighted by the livid flushes of a turbulent and stormy sky, retraces what was once the site of seductions which Hannibal found more irresistible than the Roman legions'.[52]

Corinne's improvisation at Capo Miseno, too, introduces Hannibal as a figure relevant to the understanding of the warm South:

> Les Romains dont nous envions la splendeur, n'envioient-ils pas la simplicité mâle de leurs ancêtres? Jadis ils méprisoient cette contrée voluptueuse, et ses délices ne domptèrent que leurs ennemis. Voyez dans le lointain Capoue, elle a vaincu le guerrier dont l'âme inflexible résista plus longtemps à Rome que l'univers.[53]

Corinne, then, places 'cette contrée voluptueuse' – and, by implication, the man who has so notably succumbed to its charms – in direct opposition to the 'simplicité mâle' of the ancient Romans'. The destabilization in Capua, in other words, is identified as a form of effemination: the effeminated failure in bellicosity, in fact, to which Montesquieu refers when he remarks, in Book XIV of *De l'esprit des lois:* 'Mettez un homme dans un lieu chaud et enfermé; il souffrira... une défaillance de cœur très grande'.[54] The possibility that such effeminatory effects might continue to determine the experiences of contemporary travellers is explicitly raised by James Johnson, in *Change of Air; or, the Pursuit of Health* (1831):

---

52 *Ibid.*, vol. II, p. 103.

53 Staël, *Corinne; on l'Italie*, vol. II, p. 73 (book XIII, chapter 4); translated by Landon, in Isabel Hill's edition (p. 225), as:

> We envy Roman grandeur – did they not
> Envy their fathers' brave simplicity?
> Once this voluptuous country they despised;
> Its pleasures but subdued their enemies.
> See, in the distance, Capua! She o'ercame
> The warrior, whose firm soul resisted Rome
> More time than did a world.

54 Vol. I, p. 374 (book XIV, chapter 2): 'Put a man in a close warm place, and he will... feel a great faintness' (*The Spirit of Laws*, vol. I, p. 317). For a useful account of Roman concepts of effeminacy, some of which are implicitly invoked in the travel writings considered here, see Edwards, '*Mollitia*: Reading the Body'.

It is not for me, in this place, to predict the influence of frequent travels or protracted sojourns in a climate so celebrated, in all ages, for its enervating effects on the minds and bodies of the inhabitants – a climate which unmanned not only the conquering Romans but the conquerors of Rome.[55]

The effeminatory stage in Hannibal's campaign is set in contrast to the enterprise of crossing the Alps, which is invariably defined as an act of aspiration and self-affirmation. Narratives of this campaign allegorize the impulse to cross boundaries both by reference to the Carthaginian's quality of sublime aspiration, driving him across the great mountain range of Europe, and by reference to the sublimity of the landscape, which, in its vastness and wildness, tests and confirms this aspiration. Thomas Gray's description of Hannibal's traversal as a topic fit for Salvator Rosa – the painter whose name is regularly used as a metonym for wild sublimity – names as a central feature of the imagined painting the hazards which the untamed inhabitants of untamed regions thrust in the general's way: 'Hannibal passing the Alps; the mountaineers rolling down rocks upon his army; elephants tumbling down the precipices.'[56] Whitaker, over the course of his two volumes on the subject, chronicles Hannibal's journey as a succession of obstacles overcome.[57] The sublime identification with the power of nature entailed in crossing the Alps is emphasized, from 1795 onwards, by parallels – explicit or implicit – between Hannibal and Napoleon. After her evocations of Hannibal and 'the Lombard Alboin' gazing out over Italy, Sydney Morgan leaps forward in time to summon up an imaginative vision of the French army during Napoleon's Italian campaign, sharing in the propensity of sublime natural features to exceed their own bounds:

From such a site as this Napoleon Bonaparte, at the head of an ill-appointed, long suffering, and neglected army, pointed to the plains of Lombardy, and promised victory. His soldiers accepted the pledge, rushed like an Alpine torrent over crags and precipices, and won that Italy, in two brief and splendid campaigns, which had through ages resisted the forces, and witnessed the disasters, of millions of Frenchmen, led on by kings, and organized by experienced generals.[58]

---

55 p. 293.

56 Gray, *The Poems of Mr Gray*, p. 305. Radcliffe's *Mysteries of Udolpho*, silently quoting this passage (p. 166), describes the heroine reconstructing an imaginative picture of the scene, in which sublime aspiration is similarly pitted against sublime nature.

57 This same narrative structure is also adopted, for example, in Thomas Watkins's much briefer account of the general's progress through the Alps, in his *Travels*, vol. I, p. 194.

58 Morgan, *Italy*, vol. I, pp. 22, 25.

Vague and languid enjoyment

The plot of self-affirmatory aspiration on the Alps, followed by destabilizing effemination in the warm South, is repeated in other narratives of travel to Italy. Anna Jameson, in Geneva, describes herself as rising above her sorrows: through the sublime, she implies, intensified emotional responsiveness may be transmuted not only into suffering but also into a form of power:

> Now I feel the value of my own enthusiasm: now am I repaid in part for many pains and sorrows and errours it has cost me. Though the natural expression of that enthusiasm be now repressed and restrained, and my spirits subdued by long illness, what but enthusiasm could elevate my mind to a level with the sublime objects round me, and excite me to pour out my whole heart in admiration as I do now.[59]

At Naples, in contrast, Jameson implicitly allies herself with Hannibal in her experience of effeminating loss of purposefulness:

> I know not whether it be incipient illness, or the enervating effects of this soft climate, but I feel unusually weak, and the least exertion or excitement is not only disagreeable but painful. While the rest were at Capo di Monte, I stood upon my balcony looking out upon the lovely scene before me, with a kind of pensive dreamy rapture, which if not quite pleasure, had at least a power to banish pain...
>
> All my activity of mind, all my faculties of thought and feeling, and suffering, seemed lost and swallowed up in an indolent delicious reverie, a sort of vague and languid enjoyment, the true '*dolce far niente*' of this enchanting climate.[60]

Keats's sonnet 'Happy is England!' (1817) traces out a similar itinerary. Having first suggested that 'I could be content' with England, the speaker then voices a desire for the 'transport and... inward pride' of the Alpine sublime, an experience which, placing him 'as on a throne', confers a sense of authority and mastery:

> Yet do I sometimes feel a languishment
>   For skies Italian, and an inward groan
>   To sit upon an Alp as on a throne,
>   And half forget what world or worldling meant.[61]

---

[59]   Jameson, *Diary*, pp. 32–3.

[60]   *Ibid.*, pp. 261–2.

[61]   Lines 1, 5–8; in Keats, *Complete Poems*, p. 95.

The sestet of the sonnet, however, moves beyond the Alps to an aquatic, southern domain of alluring females, possessed of a power to divert the traveller's purposeful progression into gratifyingly aimless floating:

> Happy is England, sweet her artless daughters;
>   Enough their simple loveliness for me,
>   Enough their whitest arms in silence clinging:
>   Yet do I often warmly burn to see
>   Beauties of deeper glance, and hear their singing,
> And float with them about the summer waters.[62]

The destabilizing powers of the 'beauties of deeper glance' are emphasized especially strongly by the allegorical invocation of the Sirens' song, luring mariners to their doom: as in the myth of the Sirens, seductive women are singing in a watery setting, while the 'deeper glance' of these women suggests some hidden purpose, dangerous precisely because it is not immediately decipherable. This allusion to mythological inhabitants of the Mediterranean, together with the reference to 'beauties of deeper glance' and to the 'summer waters', makes it clear that the speaker has, in his imagination, now moved beyond the Alps to the warm South. The sea, which plays a much larger part in accounts of Naples and its environs than in commentaries on other parts of Italy, supplies a metaphor, in many travel writings, for a pleasure that entails a sense of unmooring.[63] Even Oswald, Lord Nelvil, a traveller notable for the fact that his tastes and opinions remain unchanged by his stay in Italy, is nonetheless described, at the moment when he returns to England and regains his old tastes and opinions, as having experienced a temporary loss of 'fixité', which can be equated with aquatic pleasures: 'il reprenoit pourtant une sorte de fixité dans les idées, que *le vague enivrant* des beaux-arts et de l'Italie avoit fait disparaître'.[64]

The effeminatory character of this unmooring is emphasized by Keats's identifications of female figures as the agents of destabilization. Sirens serve to allegorize the effeminatory effects of a warm climate in

---

62 Lines 9–14; in Keats, *Complete Poems*, p. 96.

63 As Alain Corbin points out in *Le Territoire du vide*, p. 55, the visit to Naples and Campania provides one of the rare occasions on the Grand Tour when the traveller expects to devote specific attention to the Mediterranean sea, and to derive some form of pleasure from it.

64 Staël, *Corinne; ou, l'Italie*, vol. II, p. 167 (book XVI, chapter 4); emphasis added; Hill's translation abandons the metaphor of an 'intoxicating wave': 'He regained *himself*; and though regret prevented his yet feeling any delight, his thoughts began to steady from the Italian intoxication which had unsettled them' (p. 293).

other writings: in Henry Swinburne's *Travels in the Two Sicilies*, the traveller, considering various explanations for the formation of the myth of these destabilizing figures, observes:

> The sweet retreats that abound in the Surrentine peninsula; the enchanting prospects; the plenty of all the necessaries, and even luxuries of life, and the soft temperature of the climate could not fail of attracting strangers: there they must insensibly have acquired a relish for pleasure and indolence that enervated both their bodies and minds, and rendered every other country odious to them.[65]

Jameson, too, defines the lure of the South by direct reference to the seductive powers of the sirens:'Naples wears on her brow the voluptuous beauty of a syren – Rome sits desolate on her seven-hilled throne.' In the 'Song of the Syren Parthenope', inserted in her travel narrative, the siren, addressing 'Ye who have wander'd hither from far climes', observes that these northerners have come to her shores 'To breathe my bland luxurious airs'.[66]

Despite the contrast between this effeminatory experience of being 'lost and swallowed up' and that of self-affirmatory identification with powerful, aspiring nature on the Alps, it is not only the earlier stage in the itinerary of the Grand Tour that is defined with reference to the sublime impulse to transcend limits. In both these two pieces of imaginative geography, the traveller's experience is marked by a movement beyond bounds or, to define it more precisely, by a dissolution of the bounds that separate the self from the world. Keats, in his vision of floating with the 'beauties of deeper glance', sees these siren-like women as luring him not only beyond the constraining bounds imposed by the 'artless daughters' of England ('their whitest arms in silence *clinging*'), but also beyond any sense of personal boundedness. Such a movement follows the same trajectory as Anna Jameson's, when, reaching Naples, she finds that 'All my activity of mind, all my faculties of thought and feeling, and suffering, seemed lost and swallowed up in an indolent delicious reverie.'[67]

A dissolution of this kind has been charted in a number of contexts in the twentieth century, usually with reference to Freud's formulation of a 'Nirvana principle', or tendency towards the suppression of all internal tensions, and corresponding extinction of a sense of individual

[65]   Vol. II, p. 164.
[66]   Jameson, *Diary*, pp. 286, 224.
[67]   *Ibid.*, p. 262.

being.[68] Bice Benvenuto, in *Concerning the Rites of Psychoanalysis; or, The Villa of the Mysteries*, provides an elucidation of the relation between self-confirmatory pleasure and 'this otherwise fatal Nirvana and its consuming "enjoying" activity':

> I wrote 'enjoying', and not pleasurable, as Freud himself says that the pleasure principle does not apply to the life and death drives but to the ego. We can use the word 'enjoyment' to describe precisely this 'beyond pleasure' which Nirvana entails for both Eros and Thanatos. Where is this incomprehensible enjoying flow of life going? Nowhere else, Freud concludes, than towards death.[69]

The expression 'this incomprehensible enjoying flow of life' might seem to paraphrase not only Anna Jameson's account of the 'indolent delicious reverie' induced by the South but also the concept of the beautiful formed in Burke's *Philosophical Enquiry* when he asks: 'Who is a stranger to that manner of expression so common in all times and in all countries, of being softened, relaxed, enervated, dissolved, melted away by pleasure?'[70] This concept is, of course, in Burke's account of it, placed in direct opposition to the sublime. It becomes possible to merge free-floating enjoyment into the sublime, however, within the context of the enervating South, by virtue of the ease with which the sea, which is acclaimed as one of the most striking elements of the landscape around Naples, can be elided with Longinus's 'ocean', one of the main natural features cited in his list of examples of the sublime in nature, and invested with the sublime qualities of infinitude and indeterminacy. Such qualities are emphasized by the new preoccupation with the blue of sea and sky. At the same time, the indeterminacy of the sea readily supplies metaphors for an erasure of boundaries, which is explicitly described, in some commentaries, as encouraging a dissolution of the sense of a fixed and bounded self. Dupaty, in his account of the coast near Naples, already quoted in the chapter 'Hyperbole and observation', attributes his feelings of inner melting and softening to a lack of visual definition and delimitation which can be equated not only with the 'gradual variation' and

68 Freud, 'Beyond the Pleasure Principle', pp. 55–6. ('The dominating tendency of mental life, and perhaps of nervous life in general, is the effort to reduce, to keep constant or to remove internal tension due to stimuli. . . and our recognition of that fact is one of our strongest reasons for believing in the existence of death instincts.') For a definition of the Nirvana Principle, see also Laplanche and Pontalis, *Vocabulaire de la psychanalyse*, pp. 331–2.
69 p. 9.
70 p. 150.

'easy gradation' of the beautiful, but also with sublime indeterminacy: 'je sens mes pensées s'amollir à... cette ombre vague, légère, qui, successivement, éteint... les dernières lueurs du jour'. Even the ruins in the area display a determination to erase limits: the coast is 'couvert de ruines qui pendent et tombent, et disparoissent incessamment dans les ondes'.[71]

Canto IV of *Childe Harold's Pilgrimage* concludes with an address to the sea (Roll on, thou deep and dark blue ocean – roll!'), which also emphasizes its indeterminacy, as manifested in the power of its 'wild waves' to erase the boundary between past and present: 'Time writes no wrinkle on thine azure brow – / Such as creation's dawn beheld, thou rollest now.' Byron energetically attempts to persuade the reader that the enjoyable surrender to forces beyond the traveller's control induced by such erasures of boundaries is in fact compatible with a self-confirmatory identification with the power of nature: the ocean is 'Dark heaving; – boundless, endless, and sublime', and the trustfulness with which the traveller gives himself up to its pleasures is, he argues, made possible by the fact that its 'terror' can be equated with the 'pleasing fear' of Burkean sublimity:

> And I have loved thee, Ocean! and my joy
> Of youthful sports was on thy breast to be
> Borne, like thy bubbles, onward: from a boy
> I wanton'd with thy breakers – they to me
> Were a delight; and if the freshening sea
> Made them a terror – 'twas a pleasing fear,
> For I was as it were a child of thee,
> And trusted to thy billows far and near,
> And laid my hand upon thy mane – as I do here.[72]

Within early nineteenth-century travel writings, moreover, the implication that the relation between the sublime and the beautiful is not necessarily one of opposition is reinforced by the formation of a category of 'wild luxuriance', or simply 'luxuriance'. This category not only allows the more languorous and enervating elements within the beautiful to be absorbed

---

71 Dupaty, *Lettres*, vol. II, pp. 308–9: 'the thoughts are incessantly rendered more flexible by that vague and light shade, spreading a sable veil over the last glimpses of day'; 'covered with hanging and falling ruins, every instant disappearing under the waves' (*Sentimental Letters*, vol. II, p. 211; see Burke, *Philosophical Enquiry*, p. 122 (for an account of 'the easy gradation of the beautiful') and p. 73 (for an account of the relation of indeterminacy to sublime infinitude: 'the eye not being able to perceive the bounds of many things, they seem to be infinite, and they produce the same effects as if they were really so').

72 Stanza 179, line 1; stanza 182, lines 7, 8–9; stanza 183, line 5; stanza 184; in Byron, *Complete Poetical Works*, vol. II, pp. 184, 185, 186.

into the sublime, but also, through the power of etymological and phono-
logical association, compromises the masculine, self-affirmatory character
of sublimity by inviting an elision with another category used to describe
the South: that of 'luxury' (as exemplified by the 'bland luxurious airs' that
the siren Parthenope offers travellers in Jameson's 'Song of the Syren').
The two terms are often used interchangeably to describe natural abundance, as in William Beckford's account of the landscape near Lucca, in
which he first of all describes himself as 'a native of the north, unused to
such luxuriance', and then declares: 'But such luxury did not last, you may
suppose, for ever.'[73] Richard Payne Knight, in his *Analytical Inquiry into
the Principles of Taste* (1805), explicitly argues that sublimity, as exemplified by the southern Italian landscapes of Salvator Rosa, gains in aesthetic
force by incorporating the fertility usually associated with the beautiful:

> Weakness is nearly always allied to meanness in vegetable, as well as animal
> productions; so that scenery of this kind, to be really sublime, should be,
> not only wild and broken, but rich and fertile; such as that of Salvator Rosa,
> whose ruined stems of gigantic trees proclaim at once the vigour of the
> vegetation, that has produced them, and of the tempests, that have shivered
> and broken them. There is also a sort of comfort and satisfaction felt in
> beholding every production around us strong and luxuriant; which, though
> it arise from sympathies of another class, is of no less importance in ren-
> dering the scenery pleasing.[74]

Shelley, in a letter from Naples, voices his delight in the fusion of opposites
displayed by 'scenery at once sublime and tranquil', while Maria Graham,
near Tivoli, observes: 'there is, altogether, a mixture of wild and cultivated
nature, peculiarly agreeable'.[75] Anna Jameson, travelling southwards from
Rome, expresses her enjoyment of 'this savage but luxuriant wilderness'.[76]

The reader is also encouraged to see early nineteenth-century accounts
of the warm South as forming an alternative concept of the sublime by the
added dynamic charge that the final traversal of limits mapped out by the
established narrative of the Grand Tour acquires once travel writing begins
to define the crossing of boundaries as central to the activity of travelling.
The South, within this narrative of the Tour, forms a sequel not only to the
traversal of the Alps but also, more immediately, to the visit to Rome: the

[73] Beckford, *Dreams*, vol. I, p. 152.

[74] p. 368.

[75] Shelley, *Letters*, vol. II, p. 68 (letter of 21 December 1818 to Thomas Jefferson Hogg);
Graham, *Three Months*, p. 114.

[76] Jameson, *Diary*, p. 210.

site of self-confirmatory pleasure and cultural consolidation, the site of an encounter with authority (the authority of the ancients, for example, and the authority represented by the great works of art in the city) and, at the same time, the major geographical goal that the Grand Tour sets up. The traveller to Naples, then, moves beyond the duty to combine pleasure with cultural benefit, and moves on to a domain of carefree irresponsibility, a region visited as an indulgence rather than as an obligatory element within the itinerary of the Tour. In a moment of sublime exceeding of limits, therefore, he or she is able to throw aside not only the constraints of the familiar but also the constraints of the Tour itself. Matilda's reactions to Naples, in the short story 'L'Amoroso', in the Marquis of Normanby's *English in Italy* (1825), are mapped out in a way that emphasizes the status of the part of the conventional itinerary that lies beyond Rome as an anomaly: a domain that throws into question the whole concept of the Tour. These reactions are summed up in a baffling oxymoron - 'pleasing disappointment' - which is produced by the narrator as though it sums up the pleasure of encountering a place of which not too much, in the field of mingled pleasure and benefit, has been expected:

> Upon the English travellers of the present day, so willing to be pleased and prone to be delighted... the residence at Naples, its crowd, its bustle, the prospects of it and from it, form, with the exception perhaps of Rome to the classic visitor, objects of more interest and delight, than the rest of Italy contains. After imperial Rome too, the traveller is in fancy apt to underrate the magnificence of Naples; and he pursues his journey Southward, more to enjoy the climate, the view of Vesuvius, perhaps, and of the Bay, than for the sake of visiting the loveliest and most regal city of modern Italy. To Matilda this pleasing disappointment, that generally strikes the traveller on the sight of Naples, was even stronger, from her having, very justly indeed as an unlearned female, thought Rome a hideous place.[77]

Unsurprisingly, the irresponsibility induced by such a city proves highly destabilizing: Matilda marries a Neapolitan nobleman, and is extremely unhappy.

Restlessness

During the same period - the early decades of the nineteenth century - another, rather different plot of destabilization is introduced into travel

---

[77] Vol. I, pp. 30–1.

writing. Even the more extreme forms of effeminatory unmooring envisaged in the environs of Naples limit the experience of deracination to a
particular place; in all the texts examined in the last few sections of this
chapter, the threat to identity appears as the sequel to crossing a specific
geographical boundary. In some late eighteenth-century and early nineteenth-century texts, however, the argument that travel is potentially
destabilizing is taken one stage further: the power of travel to disrupt the
life of the traveller is brought forward to the point at which the traveller
experiences an impulse to move onwards. Anna Jameson begins her *Diary*
by placing some hope in the benefits of 'continual motion'. The potential
pitfalls of moving onwards, however, are indicated when she remarks, on
setting out for Naples, 'I left Rome this morning exceedingly depressed',
and adds: 'Madame de Staël may well call travelling *un triste plaisir:* my
depression did not arise from the feeling that I left behind me any thing or
any person to regret, but from mixed and melancholy emotions.'[78] The
passage from *Corinne* that she invokes is one in which de Staël, charting
Lord Nelvil's progress through northern Italy, implies that the urge to
move on is something that takes hold of us against our better judgement,
and is beyond our conscious control:

> Voyager est, quoi qu'on en puisse dire, un des plus tristes plaisirs de la vie.
> Lorsque vous vous trouvez bien dans quelque ville étrangère, c'est que
> vous commencez à vous y faire une patrie; mais traverser des pays incon-
> nus, entendre parler un langage que vous comprenez à peine, voir des vis-
> ages humains sans relation avec votre passé ni avec votre avenir, c'est de la
> solitude et de l'isolement sans repos et sans dignité; car cet empressement,
> cette hâte pour arriver là où personne ne vous attend, cette agitation dont la
> curiosité est la seule cause, vous inspirent peu d'estime pour vous-même,
> jusqu'au moment où les objets nouveaux deviennent un peu anciens, et
> créent autour de vous quelques doux liens de sentiment et d'habitude.[79]

'Empressement' and 'hâte' play only a minor and inconspicuous part in
eighteenth-century travel writings: the subject of commentary, in these

---

78 pp. 5, 206.

79 Vol. I, p. 25 (book 1, chapter 2): 'Travelling, say what we will, is one of the saddest pleasures in life. If you ever feel at ease in a strange place, it is because you have begun to make
it your home; but to traverse unknown lands, to hear a language which you hardly comprehend, to look on faces unconnected with either your past or your future, this is solitude
without repose or dignity; for the hurry to arrive where no one awaits you, that agitation
whose sole cause is curiosity, lessens you in your own esteem, while, ere new objects can
become old, they have bound you by some sweet links of sentiment and habit' (pp. 4–5).

writings, is positioned, for the most part, as an immobile spectator, pro-
gressing from one moment of static contemplation to the next, and only
rarely as a traveller caught up in the process of movement. Yorick, in
Sterne's *Sentimental Journey*, claims the authority of a man possessed of
the privilege of mobility, but presents the moments that allow him to
become absorbed in a sequence of sentimental tableaux as the moments at
which he is forced to stop – by 'a shoe coming loose from the fore-foot of
the thill-horse, at the beginning of the ascent of mount Taurira', for example (the mishap that leads him to scenes of rural domesticity in 'The
Supper' and 'The Grace'), and by the stone in the road that leads him into
'The Case of Delicacy'.[80]

The idea that travel might entail the excitement of motion is not
entirely excluded from eighteenth-century writings, however. Smollett, at
the end of his tour of Italy, suggests, in an analysis very similar to Burke's
account of the power of the sublime to disperse melancholy, that the mental
and physical agitation involved in moving from place to place can combat a
deleterious 'relaxation of the fibres'.[81] As a number of the passages quoted
in the Introduction demonstrate, curiosity is often defined as entailing an
active 'giddiness, restlessness and anxiety'.[82] Early nineteenth-century
travel writings, taking these concepts of movement as pleasurable stimula-
tion and of anxious restlessness as their starting-points, repeatedly explore
the possibility that agitation and the giddy pursuit of novelty might gather
sufficient momentum to exclude any moment of satisfaction, of the kind
that is taken for granted in many eighteenth-century accounts of restless
curiosity (for example, in Lord Kames's declaration that curiosity finds its
gratification in 'the emotion… known by the name of *wonder*')[83]. The concept of restlessness, moreover, now, like the concept of travel itself, easily
splits away from 'a perseverance of delight in the continuall and indefatigable generation of Knowledge', as Hobbes puts it, and acquires a new motivation in the inner needs, demands, desires and impulses of the traveller.[84]

---

[80]   p. 118. In Sterne's *Tristram Shandy*, the narrator plunges into ebullient comic absurdity
when he looks forward to the accellerated 'velocity' with which travel by water will enable
him to speed past a series of sights (p. 493). Wallace, at the beginning of *Walking,
Literature, and English Culture*, argues that the Grand Tour, in the seventeenth and eighteenth centuries, was a form of travel in which the crucial emphasis was on destination
rather than on the journey as process (see pp. 37–40).

[81]   Smollett, *Travels*, p. 294. See also Montesquieu's listing of travel, in *De l'esprit des lois*, as
one of the stimulants sought out by the inhabitants of the cold North (vol. I, pp. 3, 6).

[82]   Burke, *Philosophical Enquiry*, p. 31.

[83]   *Elements of Criticism*, vol. I, pp. 319–20.

[84]   Hobbes, *Leviathan*, p. 124.

Michael Cooke has suggested that, in Romantic writing, 'the element of transgression... involves the crossing of the boundaries of one's own competence'.[85] At the beginning of *Childe Harold's Pilgrimage,* Harold's impulse to travel bears the imprint of a transgressiveness of this kind, in that it marks a stage in his life where he has gone beyond any limits which might have ensured some degree of purposeful agency. Danger is first introduced through the words 'Worse than adversity the Childe befell', which identify the menace besetting Harold not within the consequences of crossing boundaries, but within the motive that prompts him to travel:

> He felt the fulness of satiety:
> Then loath'd he in his native land to dwell,
> Which seem'd to him more lone than Eremite's sad cell.[86]

The initial account of the 'satiety' that prompts Harold to leave England establishes a structure of desire in which pleasures, once attained, lose their power to please. When Harold reaches the mountains around Cintra, in Portugal, travel itself is shown to be subject to this same self-defeating mechanism. He does, it is suggested, enjoy moments of rest here, when he contemplates the landscape and reflects. These moments are introduced, however, by lines which indicate any repose is brief: 'Sweet was the scene, yet soon he thought to flee, / More restless than the swallow in the skies.' The next stanza presents him in the grip of a relentless fever to continue:

> Again he rouses from his moping fits,
> But seeks not now the harlot and the bowl.
> Onward he flies, nor fix'd as yet the goal
> Where he shall rest him on his pilgrimage;
> And o'er him many changing scenes must roll
> Ere toil his thirst for travel can assuage,
> Or he shall calm his breast, or learn experience sage.[87]

In visiting the Fountain of the nymph Egeria, outside Rome (Figure 5), in Canto IV, the traveller, reflecting upon 'the dull satiety which all destroys' in the context of Egeria's amorous entanglement with Numa, once again links satiety to addictive movement onwards: as noted in the last chapter, Byron introduces an allegory of Passion as a restless traveller, driven by a

---

85 Cooke, *Acts of Inclusion*, p. 102.
86 Canto I, stanza 4, line 6, lines 7–9; in Byron, *Complete Poetical Works*, vol. II, p. 9; see, too, stanza 8 (vol. II, pp. 10–11), for Byron's account of the 'strange pangs' that assail the Childe from the very outset.
87 Canto I, stanza 27, lines 3–4; stanza 28, lines 3–9; in *ibid.*, vol. II, p. 21.

delusory longing for an unattainable goal. The reflections that follow then use the concept of restless movement as a metaphor for the power of passion to exercise its power even amid disillusionment: 'yet still it binds / The fatal spell, and *still it draws us on*, / Reaping the whirlwind from the oft-sown winds.'[88]

An account of the life of a sailor in Chateaubriand's *Itinéraire de Paris à Jérusalem, et de Jérusalem à Paris* (1811) incorporates the same concept of travel as an addictive search for an unattainable goal, in which we are constantly deprived of the moment of satisfaction and repose that hovers tantalizingly before us:

> Il y a dans la vie du marin quelque chose d'aventureux qui nous plaît et qui nous attache. Ce passage continuel du calme à l'orage, ce changement rapide des terres et des cieux, tiennent éveillée l'imagination du navigateur. Il est lui-même, dans ses destinées, l'image de l'homme ici-bas: toujours se promettant de rester au port, et toujours déployant ses voiles; cherchant des îles enchantées où il n'arrive presque jamais, et dans lesquelles il s'ennuie s'il y touche; ne parlant que de repos, et n'aimant que les tempêtes...[89]

The disorderly nature of restlessness is emphasized especially strongly in commentaries where various forms of thematic, narrative and topographical digression are allowed to override the incipiently purposeful structure of narratives of traversing limits. Peacock, in *Nightmare Abbey*, assigns ironically condensed paraphrases of the reflections on the Fountain of Egeria in *Childe Harold* to the Byronic 'Mr Cypress the poet', who visits the abbey of the title as he is about to set out for Italy. Explaining his need to travel, he rapidly sketches out the plot of desire outlined in the passages just quoted: 'The mind is restless, and must persist in seeking, though to find is to be disappointed.' The utterances that follow are described by another guest as 'false and mischievous ravings'; they repeatedly map out this same plot in sentences that, like Byron's own stanzas, rapidly digress thematically from the topography of Italy (the starting-point of the conversation in

---

88 Canto IV, stanza 119, line 8; stanza 123, lines 5–7 (emphasis added); in *ibid.*, vol. II, pp. 164, 165.

89 Vol. II, p. 210: 'There is in the life of the sailor something adventurous that pleases and attracts us. This continual passage from calm to storm, this rapid change of lands and skies keep the imagination of the navigator alive. He is himself, in his destiny, the image of man here on earth: always promising himself that he will rest at the next port, and always unfurling his sails; seeking enchanted isles at which he scarcely ever arrives, and in which, if he does find them, he at once grows bored; speaking only of rest, and loving only storms.'

which Mr Cypress participates) to the character of human desire and passion. In doing so, moreover, they also resemble Byron's reflections in reaching out to more exotic topographies in search of metaphors for passion's
restless movement onwards; Mr Cypress reworks, in more wildly disordered language, Byron's references to the fruits of Passion as 'trees whose
gums are poison, and to human life as blighted by the 'all-blasting' Upas
Tree of Java, supposedly poisoning the ground for fifteen miles around. In
one of his passages of précis, Peacock's poet declares breathlessly that 'the
eye shall never see the form which phantasy paints, and which passion pur-
sues through paths of delusive beauty, among flowers whose odours are
agonies, and trees whose gums are poison'.[90]

As though to affirm the divagatory force of restlessness, Peacock then
restages Childe Harold's departure, as recounted by Byron, in a satirically
accellerated form, in which drunken digressiveness overrides even the
urge to cross boundaries and exceed limits. Instead of breaking abruptly
away from his life of 'revel and ungodly glee', as the Childe does, Mr
Cypress leaves England almost in the midst of a rambling drinking song,
about mariners 'in charmed bowl', aiming only 'To rake the moon from
out the sea'; the song concludes with the line 'And our ballast is old wine',
and the traveller then envisages his travels not as a series of traversals of
geographical boundaries, in the manner of Childe Harold's resolution to
'cross the brine, / And traverse Paynim shores, and pass Earth's central
line', but as an exploration of the fluid, uncertain lines of various extents
of water and waterways: 'Mr Cypress, having his ballast on board, stepped,
the same evening, into his bowl, or travelling chariot, and departed to rake
seas and rivers, lakes and canals, for the moon of ideal beauty.'[91]

In late twentieth-century works concerned with travel, in contrast,
movement onwards, however hasty, is often associated neither with transgression nor divagation, but with an orderly progression, in which swift-
ness of topographical displacement actually serves as a guarantee of

---

[90] Peacock, *Nightmare Abbey*, pp. 96, 98, 102; *Childe Harold's Pilgrimage*, Canto IV, stanza
     120, lines 6, 126, 4; Peacock, *Nightmare Abbey*, p. 102, paraphrasing parts of *Childe
     Harold's Pilgrimage*, Canto IV, stanzas 120 and 121; *Complete Poetical Works*, (in Byron,
     vol. II, pp. 164, 166).

[91] *Childe Harold's Pilgrimage*, Canto I, stanza 2, line 6 (in Byron, *Complete Poetical Works*,
     vol. II, p. 9); Peacock, *Nightmare Abbey*, p. 105; *Childe Harold's Pilgrimage*, Canto I,
     stanza 11, lines 8–9 (in Byron, *Complete Poetical Works*, vol. II, p. 12); Peacock, *Nightmare
     Abbey*, p. 106; the reference to 'ideal beauty' invokes *Childe Harold's Pilgrimage*, Canto IV,
     stanza 123 (in Byron, *Complete Poetical Works*, vol. II, p. 165) – one of the many points in
     the reflections on the Fountain of Egeria at which the speaker insists that we are in rest-
     less pursuit of unattainable goals.

detachment. The title of the film *If it's Tuesday, this Must be Belgium* (directed by Mel Stuart, 1969) indicates a European tour too brisk to allow dangerous forces within the topography to erupt and transform the coachload of Americans who embark on it. My final chapter considers an alternative approach to travel, which, like the view of travelling as transgressive and destabilizing, first appears around the end of the eighteenth century and the begining of the nineteenth, but which, in contrast to destabilized travel, produces a range of strategies for keeping danger and destabilization at bay.

5

Tourism

Managing pleasure and managing danger

At the beginning of Elaine Dundy's novel *The Dud Avocado* (1958), the heroine, Sally Gorce, a young American woman in Paris, bumps into a compatriot, Larry Keevil, who outlines a series of four types of traveller (or 'Tourist', as he terms all of them): two 'Organized' and two 'Disorganized'. The first type of 'Disorganized' traveller begins by attempting 'to see Europe casually, you know, sort of vaguely, out of the corner of the eye'. After a while, however, 'all restraint is thrown to the wind and anything really *old* enough is greeted with animal cries of anguish at its beauty'. Sally recognizes something of herself in this picture:

> Blushingly I recalled a night not so long before when I had suddenly fallen in love with the Place de Furstenberg in the moonlight. I had actually – Oh Lord – I had *actually* kissed one of the stones at the fountain, I remembered, flung my shoes off, and executed a crazy drunken dance.[1]

Larry, however, identifies Sally not only with this type but also with another variety of 'Disorganized' American in Europe, yet more conspicuously committed to frenzied destabilization and restless motion:

> The last type is the Wild Cat. The I-am-a Fugitive-from-the-Convent-of-the-Sacred-Heart. Not that it's ever really the case. Just seems so from the violence of the reaction. Anyhow it's her first time free and her first time across and, by golly, she goes native in a way the natives never had the stamina to go. Some people think it's those stand-up toilets they have here. . . After the shock of that kind of plumbing something snaps in the American girl and she's off. The desire to bathe somehow gets lost. The hell with all that, she figures. Then weird haircuts, weird hair-colours, weird clothes. Then comes drink and down, down, down. Dancing in the streets all night, braying at the moon, and waking up in a different bed each morning.[2]

---

[1] pp. 11, 12.
[2] *Ibid.*, p. 14.

Like references to Hannibal in earlier travel narratives, the account of 'the Wild Cat' indicates proleptically the dangers that await the traveller later in the narrative: Sally, in keeping with the approach to travel outlined in the last chapter, does her best to live up to Larry's description.

The two 'Organized' types, in their grim determination to maintain control over their travels, emphasize by contrast the abandoned demeanour of the 'Disorganized' travellers:

> First the Eager-Beaver-Culture-Vulture with the list ten yards long, who just manages to get it all crossed off before she collapses of aesthetic indigestion each night and has to be carried back to her hotel; and second, the cool suave Sophisticate who comes gliding over gracefully, calmly and indifferently. But don't be fooled by the indifference. This babe is determined to maintain her incorruptible standards of cleanliness and efficiency if the entire staff of her hotel dies trying. She belongs to the take-your-own-toilet-paper set. Stuffs her suitcases full of nylon, Kleenex, soapflakes, and D.D.T. bombs. . . Finds the hairdresser who speaks English, the restaurant who knows how she likes her steak, and the first foreign word she makes absolutely sure of pronouncing correctly is the one for drugstore.[3]

The heroine's response to these two types is to reflect cheerfully that 'they neither one had the slightest, smallest, remotest connection with me'. In the course of the narrative of giddy deracination that follows, the option that the 'Organized' types follow, in carefully keeping at bay the more dangerous and destabilizing elements within the foreign, is ironically shown to have a certain good sense to recommend it.[4]

The commitment of Larry's 'Organized' travellers to caution and control, like the reckless attitude of his 'Disorganized' types, is anticipated in early nineteenth-century writings. In *Corinne*, the comte d'Erfeuil explains to Lord Nelvil, his travelling companion on the road to Rome, that he expects to find little amusement in Italy, since it is said to lack the diversions of his own country: 'Un de mes amis, qui y a passé six mois, m'a dit qu'il n'y avoit pas de province de France où il n'eût un meilleur théâtre et une société plus agréable qu'à Rome.' A consoling thought nonetheless suggests itself: 'mais dans cette ancienne capitale du monde, je trouverai sûrement quelques Français avec qui causer, et c'est tout ce que je désire'. The exchange concludes with a cheerful dismissal of one of the main forms of engagement with foreign culture endorsed by the Grand Tour:

3 *Ibid.*, p. 11.
4 *Ibid.*

– Vous n'avez été tenté d'apprendre l'italien? interrompit Oswald. – Non, du tout, reprit le comte d'Erfeuil, cela n'entroit pas dans le plan de mes études. – Et il prit, en disant cela, un air si sérieux, qu'on auroit pu croire que c'étoit une résolution fondée sur de graves motifs.[5]

D'Erfeuil is not unreflective; he repeatedly explains to Lord Nelvil the advantages of his own cheerful refusal to embroil himself too deeply in Italian culture. When Oswald refuses to discuss the impression that Rome has made upon him amid the frivolity of a ballroom, the comte replies equably: 'je suis plus gai que vous, j'en conviens; mais qui sait si je ne suis pas plus sage? Il y a beaucoup de philosophie, croyez-moi, dans mon apparente légèreté; la vie doit être prise comme cela.'[6] As in *The Dud Avocado*, the events that follow demonstrate that travellers such as d'Erfeuil, who make a conscious decision not to give themselves up to whatever the foreign has to offer, have a certain amount of common sense on their side.

The comte explicitly emphasizes that he is concerned not only with avoiding trouble, but also with selecting and managing sources of pleasure. In his disparaging remarks on Roman ruins, cited in the Introduction, he explains to Lord Nelvil that he has done his best to find some interest in ancient monuments and fragments, but has concluded that the pleasure to be derived from them is purchased at too dear a cost: 'Un plaisir qu'il faut acheter par tant d'études, ne me paroît pas bien vif en lui-même; car, pour être ravi par les spectacles de Paris, personne n'a besoin de pâlir sur les livres.'[7] Managing pleasure and avoiding trouble are closely linked, too, in a passage in Anna Jameson's *Diary of an Ennuyée* (1826); in Rome, the traveller declares that she is concerned not with the people of Italy but with landscape and art. She describes this approach as conducive both to detachment and to delight:

---

5 Staël, *Corinne; ou, l'Italie*, vol. I, p. 139 (book VI, chapter 1): 'A friend of mine passed six months there, and tells me that there is not a French province without a better theatre, and more agreeable society, than Rome; but in that ancient capital of the world I shall be sure to find some of my countrymen to chat with; and that is all I require' (*Corinne; or, Italy*, p. 8; further translations in footnotes will all be taken from this edition); vol. I, p. 28 (book I, chapter 2): '"Then you have not been tempted to learn Italian?" – "No, that was never included in the plan of my studies," he answered, with so serious an air, that one might have thought him expressing a resolution founded on the gravest motives' (p. 8).

6 *Ibid.*, vol. I, p. 139 (book VI, chapter 1): 'I own I am gayer than you; but who can say that I am not wiser too? Trust me, there is much philosophy in taking the world as it goes' (p. 88). See also vol. I, p. 73 (book III, chapter 2).

7 *Ibid.*, vol. I, p. 139 (book VI, chapter 1): 'A rapture which one must purchase by study cannot be very vivid in itself. One needs not spoil one's complexion over musty books, to appreciate the sights of Paris' (p. 88; the final words might more helpfully be translated as 'the theatre and opera of Paris').

Let the modern Italians be what they may, – what I hear them styled six times a day at least, – a dirty, demoralized, degraded, unprincipled race, – centuries beyond our thrice blessed, prosperous, and comfort-loving nation in civilization and morals: if I were come among them as a resident, this picture might alarm me; situated as I am, a nameless sort of person, a mere bird of passage, it concerns me not. . . I have not many opportunities of studying the national character; I have no dealings with the lower classes, little intercourse with the higher. No tradesmen cheat me, no hired menials irritate me, no innkeepers fleece me, no postmasters abuse me. I love these rich delicious skies; I love this genial sunshine. . . this pure elastic atmosphere. . . and all the treasures of art and nature, which are poured forth around me; and over which my own mind, teeming with images, recollections, and associations, can fling a beauty even beyond their own.[8]

Jameson's aim is, she emphasizes, to maintain 'that state of *calm benevolence* towards all around me, which leaves me *undisturbed* to enjoy, admire, observe, reflect, remember, with pleasure, if not with profit'.[9] The positive pleasure to be derived from avoiding potentially jarring encounters with other human beings is affirmed yet more resolutely in a twentieth-century travel book: Roland Barthes, commenting on Japan in *L'Empire des signes* (1970), argues that 'la masse bruissante d'une langue inconnue constitue un protection délicieuse', and exclaims: 'Aussi, à l'étranger, quel repos! J'y suis protégé contre la bêtise, la vulgarité, la vanité, la mondanité, la nationalité, la normalité.'[10]

The very different programmes outlined by the comte d'Erfeuil, Jameson and Barthes, and attributed to 'Organized' travellers by Larry Keevil, have one obvious feature in common: they all entail a commitment to limiting and containing the experience of the foreign. (Even the 'Eager-Beaver-Culture-Vulture', who so conspicuously takes on more than she can manage, follows the same principle of exclusion as Anna Jameson, in devoting herself to art and nature rather than to human society.) In their assumption that the foreign is best enjoyed by keeping at bay the more troubling elements within it, or editing these elements out of the traveller's experience altogether, these programmes can all be seen as part of a single approach to the encounter with alterity, formed in opposition to the view of travel as transgressive and destabilizing. This approach can usefully be

---

8   pp. 293–4.

9   *Ibid.*, p. 294; emphasis added.

10 p. 18: 'The murmuring mass of an unknown language constitutes a delicious protection'; 'Hence, in foreign countries, what a respite! Here I am protected against stupidity, vulgarity, vanity, worldliness, nationality, normality' (*Empire of Signs*, p. 3).

termed *tourism*. While the Romantic view of travel positions the traveller as the subject of urgent desires, impulses and inner needs, the touristic view affirms the position of the traveller as the subject of more modest demands, seeking out carefully regulated pleasures.

This view is often endorsed within the same commentaries that proclaim a fascination with crossing boundaries and encountering danger; in describing the foreign and relating the narratives that it generates, travellers move constantly between destabilized and detached positions. The touristic attitude to the foreign remains in continued tension with destabilizing travel today; together, the two approaches still determine the range and limits of what can be said and written about encounters with foreign places.

The formation of a concept of tourism as carefully controlled and delimited travel is, then, dependent upon the concept explored in the last chapter: a notion of travelling as an activity that may well get out of control, and dramatically destabilize the traveller who allows himself or herself to be governed by the overpowering force of desire. Destabilization and danger, however, assume a double role within tourism: on the one hand, they are seen as threats to be contained; on the other, when kept at a proper distance, they may provide acceptable touristic gratification, by allowing the traveller to combine a frisson of excitement and a reminder of risk with a self-congratulatory awareness of having survived. The many references to *banditti* on the roads in early nineteenth-century accounts of travel in Italy assure the reader that the topography of the Grand Tour, however frequently traversed over the centuries, may well contain lurking dangers.[11] Allusions to cannibalism introduce a similar frisson into twentieth-century guide books to Fiji.[12] An analysis of tourism in Evelyn Waugh's *Labels* (1930), already quoted in the Introduction, offers an astute assessment of the gratification to be derived from flirting with danger from a position of safety. The traveller analyses the powerful effect of 'the advertisements of steamship companies and travel bureaux' upon 'the middle-aged widow of comfortable means'. In considering the 'assembly of phrases – half poetic, just perceptibly aphrodisiac – which can produce at will in the unsophisticated a state of mild unreality and glamour', he

11 See, for example, Morgan, *Italy*, vol. II, p. 167. A whole travel book of this period is devoted to *banditti*: Graham, *Three Months*.
12 See, for example, Jones and Pinheiro, *Fiji*, p. 208 (for a 'boxed text' account of the Reverend Thomas Baker, famed as the only missionary eaten by Fijian cannibals) and p. 181 (for an account of the Fiji Museum, in Suva; the Museum's collection includes 'the Reverend Baker's old boot, which was reportedly cooked along with his body parts').

invokes the plot of abduction by a sheik established by the desert passion novel of the 1920s:

> There is no directly defined sexual appeal. That rosy sequence of associa-
> tion, desert moon, pyramids, palms, sphinx, camels, oasis, priest in high
> minaret chanting the evening prayer, Allah, Hichens, Mrs Sheridan, all
> delicately point the way to sheik, rape, and harem. . . [13]

Waugh then emphasizes that such fantasies must, nonetheless, remain fantasies – that the crucial trick to the touristic management of pleasure is to
respect the boundaries that more reckless travellers might cross:

> – but the happily dilatory mind does not follow them to this forbidding
> conclusion; it sees the direction and admires the view from afar. The actual
> idea of abduction is wholly repugnant – what would the bridge club and the
> needlework guild say when she returned? – but the inclination of other
> ideas towards it gives them a sweet and wholly legitimate attraction.[14]

While incipiently dangerous fantasies may be rendered 'sweet and wholly
legitimate' by careful management, the touristic approach also incorporates
a suspicion that the activities that seem to keep the foreign most safely controlled and distanced may themselves prove dangerous and unpredictable.
The literature of tourism is full of accounts of danger suddenly erupting
amid the most sedate varieties of encounter with alterity. A particularly
striking example of a narrative of this kind is E.M. Forster's 'Story of a
Panic' (written in 1902), in which a party of English picnickers in the countryside near Florence are visited by the god Pan, who appears to take possession of a young boy in the group, dramatically transforming his character.

Threats to stability are perceived even within the activity that Jameson
blithely imagines to offer the most 'undisturbed' experience of pleasure:
sightseeing. Larry Keevil summons up the figure of the 'Eager-Beaver-
Culture-Vulture' who all but 'collapses of aesthetic indigestion each night
and has to be carried back to her hotel'. Waugh is yet more darkly premonitory in his account of 'those pitiable droves of Middle West school teach-
ers whom one encounters suddenly at street corners and in public
buildings, baffled, breathless'; he describes their 'haggard and uncompre-
hending eyes, mildly resentful, like those of animals in pain, eloquent of
that world-weariness we all feel at the dead weight of European culture'.[15]

---

[13] pp. 41, 42.

[14] *Ibid.*, p. 42.

[15] *Ibid.*, p. 36.

Stendhal, in his *Promenades dans Rome* (1830), also looks into the eyes of tourists for signs of exhaustion: 'Plus une sensation est inaccoutumée, plus vite on s'en fatigue. C'est ce qu'on lit dans les yeux ennuyés de la plupart des étrangers qui courent les rues de Rome un mois après leur arrivée.' On leaving St Peter's, he warns, the traveller must move on to 'un objet absolument différent', such as the Borghese gardens or the Villa Lante: 'Faute de cette méthode, vous vous fatiguerez étonnamment et arriverez plus vite au *dégoût de l'admiration*.'[16]

Trivial gratification

The aspects of the touristic approach emphasized so far are implicitly acknowledged in travel writings before the period that social historians usually associate with the end of the Grand Tour and the beginnings of tourism. Recent studies have usually set out to define tourism as, primarily, a social phenomenon: in such analyses, any changes in approach that are acknowledged as part of tourism are referred back to such transformations as improvements in transport systems, more widespread access to foreign travel, and the development of organized tours. The beginnings of tourism are therefore located around the 1820s at the very earliest.[17] If tourism is defined as a system for managing pleasure and keeping danger and destabilization at bay, on the other hand, the main precondition for the formulation of a touristic approach to the foreign is the appearance of the Romantic, destabilized approach; in propounding the view of travel as an incipiently dangerous adventure of the self, this approach provides tourism with its crucial starting-point. The main features of tourism, defined in this more abstract, symbolic sense, can be traced in writings of

[16] Vol. I, p. 120: 'The more unaccustomed a sensation is, the more quickly it induces fatigue. This is what one reads in the bored expression of most foreigners who frequent the streets of Rome a month after their arrival'; vol. I, p. 41: 'a completely different object'; 'Unless you try this method, you will become astonishingly tired, and will more swiftly become disgusted with admiration'; see also vol. I, pp. 13, 40, 42, 121. For an account of the destabilized reactions of French artists to the experience of viewing the sights of Rome, see Wrigley, 'Infectious Enthusiasms', pp. 81–7.

[17] James Buzard, for example, in *The Beaten Track*, remarks: 'If the years 1820–1850 saw the expansion and consolidation of the new means of transport, they also saw the establishment of numerous institutions either indirectly enabling tourism or designed expressly to facilitate it' (p. 47). He then embarks on an account of the tours organized by Thomas Cook, and the guidebooks published by John Murray and Karl Baedeker (pp. 47–79). John Pemble, in *The Mediterranean Passion*, observes that 'in the second half of the nineteenth century rising incomes and facilitated travel combined to bring more and more members of the middle classes to the South' (p. 2).

the very beginning of the nineteenth century, and, in some instances, can be discerned in late eighteenth-century writings.

Tourism, then, is viewed here as a set of rhetorical and theoretical options which appear within the discourse that concerns itself with the topography of the Grand Tour. My concern, in analysing these options, is not to chart the points at which they displace or weaken the assumptions that determine the concept of the Tour; during the period with which the present study is concerned, this displacement is only partial. I am concerned, rather, with identifying a range of new strategies and concepts which, for a while, coexist with more long-established notions. New concepts of pleasure are formed, for example, and these concepts are deployed alongside the assumption that the traveller should be committed to establishing a seamless continuity between pleasure and benefit, despite their evident ability to disrupt this continuity.

One such concept is that of a trivial, pointless and innocent gratification, which can be pursued without incurring danger. Stendhal, in *Rome, Naples et Florence* (1826), registers a commitment to trivial diversion, even at the cost of cultural benefit, that is worthy of the comte d'Erfeuil:

> Quelle n'a pas été ma joie, en rentrant à Florence ce matin, de rencontrer au café un de mes amis de Milan!. . . Il me propose une place dans sa calèche; cette idée renverse tous mes projets raisonnables, et j'accepte; car enfin, je voyage non pour connaître l'Italie, mais pour me faire plaisir.[18]

William Hazlitt, in his essay 'On Going a Journey' (1822), also endorses the idea that the pleasure of travel might be situated in relative irresponsibility: in this case, in the lifting of the responsibility of socially imposed identity:

> The *incognito* of an inn is one of its striking privileges – 'lord of one's self, uncumbered with a name.' Oh! It is great to shake off the trammels of the world and of public opinion – to lose our importunate, tormenting, everlasting personal identity in the elements of nature, and become the creature of the moment, clear of all ties – to hold to the universe only by a dish of

---

18   p. 298: 'I can hardly express my joy at meeting one of my friends from Milan at the café, on returning to Florence this morning. . . He offered me a place in his calèche; this idea overturned all my sensible plans, and I accepted his offer; for, in the end, I'm travelling not to get to know Italy, but for my own pleasure.' (The English translation of 1818, obviously enough, translates the French edition of 1817, rather than the text of 1826 used here; in the case of this quotation and of subsequent extracts not included in the earlier version of the text, I have supplied my own translations.) For a discussion of Stendhal's ironic triviality, in his travel writings, see McGann, 'Rome and its Romantic Significance', pp. 328–9.

sweetbreads, and to owe nothing but the score of the evening – and no longer seeking for applause and meeting with contempt, to be known by no other title than *the Gentleman in the parlour*![19]

The idea that travel might actually provide a temporary escape from identity, rather than a consolidation of it, is emphasized yet more strongly in a discussion of the pleasures of travelling in a prose section of Samuel Rogers's poem *Italy* (1822). Rogers comments on those of our 'nation of travellers' who venture abroad: 'whatever they may say, whatever they may believe, they go for the most part on the same errand; nor will those who reflect, think that errand an idle one.' The explanation that follows is in direct contrast to Lassels's definition of the Grand Tour as a *rite de passage* initiating the traveller into adulthood: 'traveling preserves my yong nobleman from surfeiting of his parents, and weanes him from the dangerous fondness of his mother.'[20] Rogers observes: 'Almost all men are over-anxious. No sooner do they enter the world, than they lose that taste for natural and simple pleasures, so remarkable in early life.' A temporary escape from the relentless 'pursuit of wealth and honour' is nonetheless available to them: an escape that leads them away from wearisome adult existence and back towards 'the golden time of their childhood':

> Now travel, and foreign travel more particularly, restores to us in a great degree what we have lost. When the anchor is heaved, we double down the leaf; and for a while at least all effort is over. The old cares are left clustering round the old objects, and at every step, as we proceed, the slightest circumstance amuses and interests. All is new and strange. We surrender ourselves, and feel once again as children. Like them, we enjoy eagerly; like them, when we fret, we fret only for the moment.[21]

Childhood, then, supplies Rogers with a metaphor for an escape, of a safely delimited kind, from care and responsibility. While the traveller stops short of abandoning any commitment to a continuity between pleasure and benefit, he defines this continuity not as one that facilitates a consolidation of cultural and personal identity but, rather, as an echo of a childlike joy in learning, undimmed by adult anxieties.[22] The redemptive force

---

[19] p. 34.

[20] Rogers, *Italy*, pp. 170–1; Lassels, *Voyage*, part I, unpaginated preface.

[21] Rogers, *Italy*, p. 171.

[22] Rogers defines his concept of mingled pleasure and benefit by the observation: 'Our sight is on the alert when we travel; and its exercise is then so delightful, that we forget the profit in the pleasure' (*ibid.*, p. 173).

of such childhood joy, in guaranteeing the safety of the traveller's gratification, authenticates, for Rogers, even the pursuit of novelty, so often
treated with suspicion in literature of the Grand Tour: 'all is new and
strange', he blithely pronounces. Childhood continues to be employed as a
metaphor for the pleasures of travel throughout the nineteenth and twentieth centuries: Freud is quoted by Ernest Jones as writing to his wife that
he takes a 'childish delight in being somewhere else'.[23]

Effeminate and feminized leisure

Childhood is not the only metaphor that plays a part in the formation of
this concept of a pleasurable, temporary escape. Travel books begin to
adopt a new option in classifying the indolence of the Italians: southern
languor and 'mollesse' are viewed as promoting a capacity for pleasure that
is worthy of investigation and even perhaps of imitation. References to the
dolce far niente proliferate in early nineteenth-century commentaries on
Italy, especially in accounts of the warm South; many such references register an interest in the complex, specialized character of the pleasure cultivated by southerners. Anna Jameson, in her account of the effects of a
southern climate, already quoted in Chapter 4, 'Destabilized travel', designates southern indolence as a source of gratification accessible to the traveller as well as to the Italians themselves: 'All my activity of mind, all my
faculties of thought and feeling, and suffering, seemed lost and swallowed
up in an indolent delicious reverie, a sort of vague and languid enjoyment,
the true "*dolce far niente*" of this enchanting climate.'[24] Stendhal, in *Rome,
Naples et Florence*, accentuates the attractive qualities of such 'indolent
delicious reverie' by linking it to an impatience of affectation:

> Accoutumé qu'il est dès l'enfance à observer si les gens qu'il adore ou qu'il
> exècre lui parlent avec sincerité, la plus légère affectation glace l'Italien, et
> lui donne une fatigue et une contention d'esprit tout à fait contraires au

---

23 Jones, *Sigmund Freud*, vol. I, p. 198; letter dated 16 December 1883. This declaration is
    quoted by Harvie Ferguson, in 'Sigmund Freud', p. 55. Ferguson, considering the con-
    cept of leisure, argues that it can be understood, with reference to Freud's oblique pro-
    nouncements on the topic, as an attempt to recapture, through the 'excitement' of
    activities such as travel, a childhood experience of purposeless, unpredictable 'fun',
    unmediated by any structure of desire. This view of leisure is anticipated in some of the
    commentaries quoted here.
24 Jameson, *Diary*, p. 262. For other early nineteenth-century references to the *dolce far
    niente*, see, for example, Morgan, *Italy*, vol. II, p. 393; Normanby, *The English in Italy*,
    vol. I, pp. 178–9, vol. III, p. 178, Stendhal, *Promenades*, vol. I, p. 179, Simond, *Voyage*,
    vol. II, p. 355.

dolce far niente. Par ces mots célèbres, *dolce far niente*, entendez toujours le plaisir de rêver voluptueusement aux impressions qui remplissent son cœur. Otez le *loisir* à l'Italie, donnez-lui le travail anglais, et vous lui ravissez la moitié de son bonheur.[25]

Such references to pleasurable indolence strongly affirm that Italy holds out prospects of a reposefulness which, even when courted by the traveller, may in fact play a perfectly appropriate part in an activity in which, as Rogers puts it, 'for a while all effort is over'. The degree of respectability with which Italian languor is invested by the early twentieth century, as a model of gratification to be imitated by the tourist, is demonstrated in Forster's 'Story of a Panic' when the narrator (a testy Englishman, given to remarks such as 'those miserable Italians have no stamina') equably observes that, after lunch in the open air, 'we reclined, and took a *dolce far niente*'.[26] As noted in the last chapter, enervation in the warm South is, from antiquity onwards, readily defined as a form of effemination; pursuit of the *dolce far niente* is a form of effemination that is nonetheless easily classified as innocent, provided that the traveller defines it as part of a carefully limited experience of the foreign.

Most of the travellers whose views have been quoted in this chapter, however, express more attraction towards excitement and trivial diversion than towards languor and voluptuousness. Larry Keevil's comments that 'all tourists are she', and that 'the only male tourists are the ones loping around after their wives' prompt the reader to wonder whether the feminine might provide a metaphor for varieties of trivial, touristic gratification that demand too much exertion to be assigned to the category of the effeminate *dolce far niente*.[27] Where travel is equated with a trivializing version of the feminine in the early nineteenth century – as it often is, when defined as a form of portable family life, dominated by women – travel writings define it as pointlessly arduous rather than voluptuously languorous, and, at the same time, are hesitant to affirm its innocence. 'L'Amoroso', in common with various other sketches in Lord Normanby's

---

25   p. 188: 'An Italian, accustomed as he is from childhood onwards to observe whether those whom he loves or hates speak to him sincerely, is chilled by the slightest affectation; it fills him with a sense of fatigue and mental strife that are completely opposed to the *dolce far niente*. By these celebrated words, *dolce far niente*, you must understand the pleasure of dreaming voluptuously, in response to the impressions that fill your heart. Take *leisure* away from Italy, give it the English preoccupation with work, and you will take away half of its happiness.'

26   pp. 33, 12.

27   Dundy, *The Dud Avocado*, p. 16.

English in Italy, follows a family on its travels; in this particular short story, Lady Euston, her daughter Matilda and her husband Sir Thomas all grow tired of Paris, and move onwards in pursuit of the attraction that travel writing so frequently brands as superficial: mere novelty: 'it soon become agreed. . . that with the first swallow, their migrating steps should be directed to Italy, in order to explore that hitherto untasted mine of novelty and excitement.'[28] A short story of 1839 in *Blackwood's Magazine*, entitled 'A Family Continental Tour, and its Results', begins with Mr H. declaring, as he and his family are about to set out on their tour: 'I wish it were all over, and we safe back here again.' His wife agrees, but reminds him of the duty to appropriate the foreign that competitive participation in the vanities of a consumer culture imposes: 'Only think with what delight all our neighbours speak of the different places they have seen, while we can only sit and listen, and have nothing to say.'[29]

The feminine, in both these narratives, operates as a metaphor for whims and caprices that prove highly destructive, however different in character from the passionate inner needs that drive transgressive and destabilized travellers. In 'L'Amoroso', Matilda's disastrous marriage to an Italian follows some musings in which she 'did not take the trouble of either examining or understanding what she uttered': 'Sweet land of the south, I love thee: not for thy cloudless skies. . . but for the soul of flame that animates thy sons, the native enthusiasm that renders them alone the only fit worshippers of beauty, in women or in art.'[30] In 'A Family Continental Tour', Mr H. loses large amounts of money at gambling, his daughter marries a foreign fortune-hunter, and his wife dies of chagrin.

Elisions between travel and feminized triviality only serve to guarantee touristic safety, it would seem, once family travel is unequivocally assigned to the domain of stolid domesticity. Evelyn Waugh, in his account of the middle-aged widows on cruise ships, suggests, cruelly, that the impulse of these widows to collect trashy souvenirs might be seen as an attempt to transfer domestic skills to the foreign and the exotic: 'I suppose it is the housekeeping habit run riot after twenty years of buying electric-light bulbs and tinned apricots and children's winter underwear'.[31]

28 Vol. I, p. 23.

29 Vol. 46, no. 285 (July 1839), pp. 56–65; p. 56.

30 Normanby, *The English in Italy*, vol. I, pp. 94–5. The narrator comments (vol. I, p. 95): 'Certainly it was not the kind of sentimental soliloquy, that, sentimental as she had ever been, she would have uttered in England. *There* a mere worshipper of external beauty "in women or in art," she would have shunned with a blush, or contemned.'

31 Waugh, *Labels*, p. 42.

As Waugh suggests in this analysis of compulsive collecting, any symbolic influx of the domestic insulates the traveller against the destabilizing
effects of the foreign; domesticity, it is assumed, is accompanied by a tinge
of bathos which is fatal to any impulse to cross boundaries. In E.M.
Forster's *Room with a View* (1908), the heroine, Lucy, demonstrates an
ironic awareness of the insulating powers of the family when Cecil, to
whom she has become engaged in Rome, remarks to her: 'Such romance as
I have is that of the Inglese Italianato':

> 'Inglese Italianato?'
> 'È un diavolo incarnato! You know the proverb?'
>   She did not. Nor did it seem applicable to a young man who has spent a
> quiet winter in Rome with his mother.[32]

'A momentary hallucination'

While the feminine, in the early nineteenth century, is not yet equated with
bathetic, insulating domesticity, a number of new strategies of distancing do
in fact allow the traveller to register a resistance to danger, while at the same
time expressing an attraction towards pleasures which, in eighteenth-century commentaries, might compromise any claim to a manly understanding
of the superiority of liberty to superficial gratification. One such strategy
has already been mentioned, in discussing Rogers's account of the pleasures
of travel as childlike: the assumption (or explicit assertion) that travel is a
temporary interruption of everyday life, and that its provisional character
allows the traveller to feel free from everyday responsibilities while it lasts.
As Hazlitt explains: 'It is because I want a little breathing-space to muse on
indifferent matters. . . that I absent myself from the town for a while.'[33]
    Earlier writings, of course, also define travelling as a temporary (if protracted) activity. In seventeenth-century and eighteenth-century writings,
however, the anticipation of a return home, far from marking a freedom
from all responsibilities, imposes on the traveller a set of expectations of an
especially demanding kind (expectations which, it is understood, he or she
may or may not manage to satisfy). A daunting list of such expectations is
supplied by Jean Gailhard in his *Compleat Gentleman* (1678):

> Now for men to learn sobriety, civility, frugality, and an universal compli
> ance with all manner of tempers, to be acquainted with persons and places,

---

[32] p. 116.

[33] Hazlitt, 'On Going a Journey', p. 29.

the most considerable in Europe, to be instructed in the way of Governments of several Nations, and with their forces, riches, and nature, to gather all the good there is in them, and at last to know and rule himself, are matters of no small concernment to be gotten by travelling: to say nothing of the advantage of Languages. . .[34]

Hazlitt, in his essay 'On Going a Journey', offers a very different account of travel. He emphasizes that travelling abroad may well be 'in one sense, instructive', but nonetheless throws into doubt its usefulness as a means of acquiring any ability to speculate on such matters as the relative merits of different governments (let alone of gaining the personal merits so blithely enumerated by Gailhard); foreign travel, in his analysis, is too disconnected from everyday life to allow the traveller either to consolidate his own virtues and social skills or to gain permanent intellectual authority. As in Rogers's account of the pleasures of travel, the encounter with the foreign does not pose any permanent threat to the traveller's identity, but it does suspend that identity:

> There is undoubtedly a sensation in travelling into foreign parts that is to be had nowhere else: but it is more pleasing at the time than lasting. It is too remote from our habitual associations to be a common topic of discourse or reference, and, like a dream or another state of existence, does not piece into our daily modes of life. It is an animated but a momentary hallucination. It demands an effort to exchange our actual for our ideal identity; and to feel the pulse of our old transports revive very keenly, we must 'jump' all our present comforts and connections. Our romantic and itinerant character is not to be domesticated. Dr. Johnson remarked how little foreign travel added to the facilities in conversation in those who had been abroad. In fact, the time we have spent there is both delightful, and, in one sense, instructive; but it appears to be cut out of our substantial, downright existence, and never to join kindly on to it. We are not the same, but another, and perhaps more enviable individual, all the time we are out of our own country. We are lost to ourselves, as well as to our friends.[35]

Sights and wonders

The touristic approach is also mapped out through a range of new strategies of distancing, many of which make use of the long-established concepts of the sight and the wonder. One such strategy is the option outlined

---

[34] Part II, pp. 6–7.

[35] pp. 39–40. For Dr Johnson's remark, referring to the conversation of Lord Charlemont, see Boswell, *Life of Johnson* (1791), p. 995.

by Anna Jameson, when she observes with satisfaction that 'no tradesmen cheat me, no hired menials irritate me, no innkeepers fleece me, no post-masters abuse me': avoiding encounters with foreigners, and turning instead to art, architecture and landscape.[36] A device that supplements this strategy of selection and limitation, in ensuring that the traveller will not be drawn into any unsettling encounters with the topography, is that of viewing travel as a progression round a selected itinerary of sights. As noted in the Introduction, the imaginative topography of the Grand Tour is already, by the beginning of the seventeenth century, mapped out as a formalized sequence of places to visit. This topography, therefore, not only accords with the demands of the touristic approach, but actually supplies a model for the structuring of other imaginative topographies as regions for touristic travel.[37]

Within the established itinerary of the Grand Tour, it has already been suggested, some sights are distinguished from others by reference to their uniqueness, and accorded the status of wonders. It is worth quoting a much later travel book, concerned with a quite different topography of the foreign, in order to emphasize the power of such uniqueness to detach the wonder from the surrounding topography, as a point to be recognized and acclaimed in its own right: in *A First Year in Canterbury Settlement* (1863), Samuel Butler describes Mount Cook, in New Zealand:

> It is. . . well worth any amount of climbing to see. No one can mistake it. If a person says he thinks he has seen Mount Cook, you may be quite sure that he has not seen it. The moment it comes into sight the exclamation is, 'That is Mount Cook!' – not 'That must be Mount Cook!' There is no possibility of mistake.[38]

By setting particular sights apart from the topography that surrounds them, the singularity of the wonder operates as a framing device. Dean MacCannell, in *The Tourist: A New Theory of the Leisure Class*, puts forward a concept of framing as part of the process that he terms 'sight sacralization'.

[36] Jameson, *Diary*, p. 294. The advantages of this approach to travel are noted by Tzvetan Todorov in his brief analysis of tourism in *Nous et les autres*, p. 378.

[37] In the late twentieth century, in regions where sights have not been established as such by long tradition and literary mediation, itineraries and 'trails' are nonetheless constructed by tourist authorities and by guide books: see, for example, the mapping out of the Canyon de Chelly through two separate itineraries ('South Rim Drive' and 'North Rim Drive'), each of which is composed of a succession of vantage points ('Spider Rock Overlook', 'Junction Overlook', and so on), in Pritchard, *Fodor's 95 Arizona*, pp. 105–6.

[38] pp. 62–3.

Wonders are sometimes framed in the literal sense of MacCannell's explanation of the concept ('On a practical level, two types of framing occur: pro-
tecting and enhancing. . . When spotlights are placed on a building or a
painting, it is enhanced'); more often, they are separated from the topography in the symbolic sense described by Butler, and are recognizable as self-
contained sites of enthralment, set apart from their surroundings.[39]

It might be expected that, once it becomes possible to define travel as
destabilizing, the wonder, in its heightened intensity, might pose an especially strong threat to the traveller's stability. Wonders do in fact often play
a part in a narrative of destabilization: when Og throws himself into the
crater of Etna, for example, or when, in *Corinne,* the propensity of the
heroine and Lord Nelvil to plunge into danger is emphasized by the observation that the two of them, planning to climb Vesuvius together, feel that
the perils of this enterprise cast an added charm over it.[40] The early nineteenth-century traveller, however, is able to maintain a more detached attitude to wonders by following an alternative option: a plot in which a sight
or wonder invites a responsiveness so extreme as to raise the possibility of
destabilization, but in fact allows the traveller to maintain his or her com-
posure. In *Rome in the Nineteenth Century* (1820), Charlotte Eaton presents
herself as so enraptured by the *Apollo Belvedere* that she teeters on the
brink of derangement; as though anticipating incredulity, she cites another
traveller more unquestionably unhinged than herself:

> You will think me mad – and it were vain to deny it – but I am not the first
> person who has gone mad about the Apollo. Another, and a far more unfor-
> tunate damsel, a native of France, it is related, at the sight of this matchless
> statue, lost at once her heart and her reason. Day after day, and hour after
> hour, the fair enthusiast gazed and wept, and sighed her soul away, till she
> became, like the marble, pale, but not like the marble, cold. Nor, like the lost
> Eloisa, nor the idol of her love, could she 'forget herself to stone,' till death
> at last closed the ill-fated passion, and the life, of the maid of France.[41]

Having raised the possibility of extreme derangement, however, Eaton
cheerfully reimposes touristic distance; the fatal raptures of the 'fair

---

39 p. 44. For references to the effects of 'framing' that are practical as well as symbolic, see
    the allusions to the curtain over Guido Reni's *St Peter Weeping*, in Bologna, in Miller,
    Letters, vol. II, p. 15, and Piozzi, *Observations*, vol. I, p. 252.

40 Beckford, *Biographical Memoirs*, p. 86; Staël, *Corinne; ou, l'Italie*, vol. II, p. 16 (book XI,
    chapter 2).

41 Vol. I, pp. 169–70. (In the text, the inverted commas begin just before the words 'nor the
    idol of her love'.)

enthusiast', like the fantasies of the widows in Waugh's account of the
appeal of cruising ships, simply provides a gratifying frisson of excitement: 'But I have not the least intention of dying; I only congratulate
myself that I have lived to see that glorious work, whose perfection will
never be paralleled upon earth.'[42]

The strategy of qualified identification with a destabilized traveller,
combined with cheerful or even jocular expressions of detachment, is
employed, in various permutations, in other travel books. Anna Jameson,
wandering in the Coliseum, uses a traveller more happily destabilized than
Eaton's 'unfortunate damsel' to hold out the possibility of a mildly
unhinged responsiveness, which can then be shown to end in smiles:

> Looking down through a gaping aperture. . . I saw in the collossal [sic] corridor
> far below me, a young artist, who, as if transported out of his senses by delight
> and admiration, was making the most extraordinary antics and gestures:
> sometimes he clasped his hands, then extended his arms, then stood with
> them folded as in deep thought; now he snatched up his portfolio as if to draw
> what so much enchanted him, then threw it down and kicked it from him as if
> in despair. . . At length, however, he happened to cast up his eyes, as if appeal-
> ing to heaven, and they encountered mine peeping down upon him from
> above. He stood fixed and motionless for two seconds staring at me, and then
> snatching up his portfolio and his hat, ran off and disappeared. I met the same
> man afterwards walking along the Via Felice, and could not help smiling as he
> passed: he smiled too, but pulled his hat over his face and turned away.[43]

The self-affirmatory sublime is easily adapted to the plot in which a danger
is glimpsed and then avoided. The wonder, when invested with sublimity,
supplies a space within which the traveller-narrator can court destabilization just sufficiently to produce a dramatic flourish at the point where the
spectator ceases to feel overwhelmed by the sublime, and begins to experience a 'swelling and triumph'. Byron's description of St Peter's, in Canto
IV of *Childe Harold's Pilgrimage*, uses one of the long-established wonders
of the Grand Tour as the site of a sequence of this kind. Having exclaimed:
'But lo! the dome – the vast and wondrous dome', and proceeded through
two stanzas of hyperboles, the narrator declares: 'Enter: its grandeur over-
whelms thee not'. While unable to assimilate such grandeur all at once, he
explains, we are able to comprehend it a little at a time, until the mind,
'expanded by the genius of the spot', is able to grasp the immensity of the

---

42 *Ibid.*, vol. I, p. 170.
43 Jameson, *Diary*, pp. 185–6.

building in its entirety: 'Thou seest not all; but piecemeal thou must break, / To separate contemplation, the great whole.'[44]

Distraction: the advantages of solitude, moonlight and weeds

Framed isolation is a quality that early nineteenth-century travellers demand not only of wonders, but of all sights: writings of this period repeatedly note the traveller's own imaginative and practical efforts to view sights as though a line were drawn around them, separating them from their surroundings.[45] (One precondition for this strategy is, fairly obviously, the eighteenth-century concept of pictorial detachment, which continues to play a major part in travel writing: the spectator needs to adopt a pictorial sense of distance in order to see the sight as a unified, framed whole.) Travellers insistently scrutinize the topography for features that separate a sight from the continuum of everyday life: above all, for solitude, which guarantees that the traveller's viewing will be undisturbed by the eruption of bathetic elements of the contemporary world. Stendhal explains that, since 'les trois quarts de Rome sont solitaires et silencieux', the city provides a setting in which almost all the sights sought out by travellers are enshrouded by 'ce vaste silence'.[46] Where sights are situated in the inhabited part of the city, however, travellers often register unease at the level of distraction that results from the presence of human beings. Charlotte Eaton, observing that 'the beautiful solitude which surrounds the Coliseum, adds a secret charm to the pleasure we feel in surveying it', notes the lamentable deficiencies of a sight unprovided with such a framing device:

> Not so the Pantheon. Its situation, on the contrary, tends as much as possible to dissolve the spell that hangs over it. It is sunk in the dirtiest part of Modern Rome; and the unfortunate spectator, who comes with a mind filled with enthusiasm to gaze upon this monument of the taste and magnificence of antiquity, finds himself surrounded by all that is most revolting to the senses, distracted by incessant uproar, pestered with a crowd of clamorous beggars, and stuck fast in the congregated filth of every description that covers the slippery pavement.[47]

---

44 Stanza 153, line 1; stanza 155, lines 1, 3; stanza 157, lines 1–2; in *Complete Poetical Works*, vol. II, pp. 175–7.

45 An effect of this kind, in mid-twentieth-century guide books, is described by Roland Barthes in his essay 'The *Blue Guide*', in *Mythologies*, p. 76.

46 Stendhal, *Promenades*, vol. I, p. 120; 'three quarters of Rome are solitary and silent'; 'this vast silence'. See also, among many such accounts of Rome, Jameson, *Diary*, pp. 193–4.

47 Eaton, *Rome*, vol. I, pp. 328–9.

Traveller-narrators voice their demand that architectural monuments should present themselves as neatly bounded by complaints about the distraction and clutter that impinge on the visual scene.[48] Distraction is generated not only by the 'incessant uproar' and 'congregated filth' of foreign life, as described by Eaton (and noted in many other travel books of the period), but also by the unwelcome presence of other travellers.[49] Anna Jameson complains of such figures:

> Last night we took advantage of a brilliant full moon to visit the Coliseum by moon-light; and if I came away disappointed of the pleasure I had expected, the fault was not in me nor in the scene around me. In its sublime and heart-stirring beauty, it more than equalled, it surpassed all I had anticipated – but – (there must always be a *but* ! always in the realities of this world something to disgust;) it happened that one or two gentlemen joined our party – young men too, and classical scholars, who perhaps thought it fine to affect a well-bred *nonchalance*, a fashionable disdain for all romance and enthusiasm, and amused themselves with *quizzing* our guide, insulting the gloom, the grandeur, and the silence around them, with loud impertinent laughter at their own poor jokes; and I was obliged to listen, sad and disgusted, to their empty and misplaced flippancy.[50]

Stendhal, also in the Coliseum, argues that this sense of distraction is inevitable:

> Dès que d'autres curieux arrivent au Colysée, le plaisir du voyageur s'éclipse presque en entier. Au lieu de se perdre dans des rêveries sublimes et attachantes, malgré lui il observe les ridicules des nouveaux venus, et il lui semble toujours qu'ils en ont beaucoup. [51]

---

48 Archaeologists, during this period, often define their task as, in part, one of clearing away accretions of clutter from ruins, and establishing a space around them. Ronald Ridley has chronicled in detail the programmes of *déblayage*, in and around the ancient monuments of Rome, planned and carried out by the French between 1808 and 1814; see, for example, Ridley's account of the clearing of the Coliseum and its surroundings (*The Eagle and the Spade*, pp. 109–23).

49 For another of the many complaints about filth in writings of this period, see Morgan, *Italy*, vol. II, pp. 215–17, describing 'filth and ostentation' (p. 215) in the *palazzi* of Rome. Susan Stewart, in *On Longing*, points out another role that filth assumes in travel writing: that of affirming that the subject of commentary, aiming to make 'what is visible, what is surface, reveal a profound interiority through narrative', gains this interiority 'at the expense of risking *contamination*' (pp. 146, 147).

50 Jameson, *Diary*, p. 137.

51 Stendhal, *Promenades*, vol. I, p. 29: 'As soon as other sightseers arrive at the Coliseum, the pleasure of the traveller is almost entirely eclipsed. Instead of losing himself in sublime and affecting reverie, he will, despite himself, observe the absurdities of the newcomers, and it always seems that they have plenty to observe.'

This theme of the struggle with distraction is a useful one within the rhetoric of tourism, since it partially displaces a fascination with danger. When travellers complain about other travellers, or about distracting foreigners, they impress upon the reader that it is difficult enough to concentrate on the topography of the foreign at all, let alone be seduced by it into crossing symbolic boundaries and limits.

In pursuing their struggle to concentrate, travellers emphasize the practical measures that they take to visit monuments at times when they will appear more visually unified and free from clutter. A moonlit setting, which proves insufficient to guarantee Anna Jameson's enjoyment of the Coliseum, is, nonetheless, often described as imposing a visual unity upon a scene into which other distracting elements might otherwise intrude. Louis Simond, noting the fashion for visiting the monument by moonlight in his *Voyage en Italie et en Sicile* (1828), elaborates on this visual effect:

> Il est certain que nous nous sommes fort bien trouvés d'avoir vu le Colysée par un beau clair de lune. La lumière douce et vague qu'il répandait sur les masses caverneuses entassées autour de l'arène, ne laissait voir aucun des tristes détails de la décadence, ni rien qui rappelât la règle et le compas. Une sorte de grandeur idéale, sans couleur et presque sans forme, se montrait seule, et, au lieu d'un ouvrage artificiel composé de murs et de voûtes, on aurait cru être au fond du cratère d'un volcan éteint dont le cône escarpé s'élevait à l'entour.[52]

'The Forum', in the Marquis of Normanby's *English in Italy*, describes this erasure of 'triste détails' as absolutely necessary in order to elevate a less isolated part of ancient Rome to the status of a framed sight: 'The Roman Forum. . . unless visited in the solitude of moon-light, is sure to

---

52 Vol. I, p. 218: 'We certainly found it well worth while to go and see the Coliseum by night during a full-moon. The light played with more than usual vagueness, softness and harmony among the cavernous masses which rose in fantastic greatness on all sides of us; and such was the general appearance of the whole, that we might have fancied ourselves in the crater of an extinguished volcano rather than in any thing reared by the hand of man, – mere brick and mortar!' (*A Tour*, p. 177).

Among the many other accounts of the Coliseum by moonlight, see Byron, *Childe Harold's Pilgrimage*, Canto IV, stanzas 128–9, in *Complete Poetical Works*, vol. II, pp. 166–7. The 'Au clair de lune' passage of Chateaubriand's *Voyage en Italie* emphasizes the power of moonlight to compose features of the topography into pictures, and so elevate them to the status of framed sights: observing (p. 99) that 'une jeune femme me demande l'aumône', the traveller remarks excitedly: 'la *poverina* ressemble à une Madone: elle a bien choisi le temps et le lieu. Si j'étois Raphaël, je ferois un tableau'.

present some object, so enormously incongrous with its past renown, as to scare away every feeling of divine awe that memory would inspire.'[53]

The effect produced by viewing of the famous classical sculptures in the Belvedere courtyard at the Vatican's Museo Clementino at night is described by travellers from the second half of the eighteenth century onwards.[54] Piozzi comments on the *Apollo Belvedere:* 'It is the fashion for every body to go see Apollo by torch light: he looks like *Phœbus* then, the Sun's bright deity.'[55] Mary Berry, in a journal entry of April 1784, describing visits both to the Vatican and to the sculptures on the Capitoline, explains more fully the advantages of torchlight as an intensificatory device:

> *Tuesday, 27th.* – Museum Clementinum. In the evening to see the statues by torchlight. Nobody that has not seen it can have an idea of the excellent effect of this light, thrown upon them at pleasure; every statue appeared much more beautiful than I had ever seen it by daylight.
> *Wednesday, 28th.* – Capitol, to see the statues by torchlight; the effect is equally good; it is the only method of having a true idea of the beauty of these admirable statues, for both here and in the museum they are mostly ill-placed as to light.[56]

Another way of marking out sights as framed and elevated is to note the vegetation that rampages over them: plants – often referred to in English writings as *weeds* – are constantly mentioned in early nineteenth-century accounts of Italy. Hugh William Williams includes in his *Travels in Italy, Greece, and the Ionian Islands* (1820) an appendix that lists 261 varieties of plants growing in the Coliseum alone, beginning with *Acanthus mollis* and ending with *Xantium spinosum.*[57] Weeds sometimes provide a framing

---

53 Vol. II, pp. 136–7; the narrator explains that it is the use of the Forum as 'the Roman Smithfield' which guarantees such distracting incongruity.

54 Pearlee Freiberg, in 'Roman Nocturne', notes that travellers record torchlit visits to classical sculptures as early as the 1760s.

55 Piozzi, *Observations*, vol. I, p. 429. For a detailed account of this fashion, see Jon Whiteley, 'Light and Shade'.

56 Berry, *Extracts*, vol. I, p. 114. Henry Matthews's *Diary of an Invalid*, p. 135, also includes a detailed analysis of the effects of torchlight.
    Other sights and wonders of the Grand Tour as also seen as demanding a visit at night; one obvious example is the eruption of Vesuvius, which is much less dramatic by daylight. See, for example, Alphonse de Lamartine, *Le Dernier Chant du Pèlerinage d'Harold* (1826), section XII, lines 18–19: 'Sa flamme, dans le jour un moment assoupie, / Lance, au retour des nuits, des gerbes de clartés.' Nocturnal viewing is still used as a framing device in contemporary tourism: in *son-et-lumière* spectacles, for example, and early evening drives round African safari parks in which animals are picked out by floodlights.

57 Vol. I, pp. 389–99.

device in a literal sense: Byron's account of the Fountain of Egeria assigns a 'green, wild margin' to the spot.[58] More often, they supply guarantees of solitude – or, at least, of a relative neglect, which marks out sights as places apart from the activity and bustle of everyday contemporary life: travel writings constantly emphasize that plants – sometimes in connection with birds and animals – have displaced people. John Chetwode Eustace comments on the hall of the imperial palace on the Palatine:

> This hall is now cleared of its encumbrances, and presents to the eye a vast length of naked wall, and an area covered with weeds. As we stood contemplating its extent and proportions, a fox started from an aperture, once a window, at one end, and crossing the open space, scrambled up the ruins at the other, and then disappeared in the rubbish. This scene of desolation reminded me of Ossian's beautiful description. 'The thistle shook there its lonely head; the moss whistled to the gale; the fox looked out from the windows, the rank grass waved round his head,' and almost seemed the accomplishment of that awful prediction: 'There the wild beasts of the desert shall lodge, and howling monsters shall fill the houses; and wolves shall howl to one another in their palaces, and dragons in their voluptuous pavilions.'[59]

The traveller can also isolate sites from their surroundings simply by a declaration of recognition. In Butler's account of Mount Cook, quoted above, the mountain, as a wonder, is defined as recognizable by virtue of its innate singularity. Both wonders and other sights are often defined as recognizable by reference to 'markers'. Dean MacCannell, in the context of tourism of the later twentieth century, defines markers as pieces of information about a sight that allow the tourist to recognize it, and so to perceive it as an attraction. (He adds 'Note that markers may take many different forms: guidebooks, informational tablets, slide shows, travelogues, souvenir matchbooks, etc.')[60] Allusions to such pieces of information (to writings,

---

58 *Childe Harold's Pilgrimage*, Canto IV, stanza 116, line 5, in *Complete Poetical Works*, vol. II, p. 163.

59 Eustace, *A Tour*, vol. I, p. 222; the quotation at the end of the passage is cited as 'Louthe's Isaiah, XIII. v. 21, 22'; the earlier reference is to 'Carthon: a Poem', in Macpherson, *Works of Ossian*, vol. I, p. 186. In Eaton's account of the theatre at Hadrian's Villa at Tivoli, as in Og's encounter with the Tomb of Cecilia Metella, in Beckford's *Biographical Memoirs*, it is crows (this time of a 'black hooded' variety) that merge with vegetation as affirmations of solitude: the 'hoarse complaining clamour' of the birds 'now alone resounds here, instead of the dialogues of Plautus or Terence' (Eaton, *Rome*, vol. III, p. 331; for other accounts of rampant plant life, see, for example, vol. III, pp. 104, 332–3, 421–2).

60 MacCannell, *The Tourist*, p. 41.

engravings, casts and copies of sculptures, for example) play a part in travel
writing long before the formulation of the touristic approach, but prove
especially useful to the rhetoric of tourism, in classifying sights as already
familiar to the traveller – and so affirming that he or she will is well prepared to encounter the intensity that the foreign has to offer. Edward
Wright, describing the Vatican in *Some Observations Made in Travelling
through France, Italy &c* (1730), observes: 'The Statues in the Court of the
Belvedere, are, as to their Attitudes, so well known, not only by the Prints,
but Casts from them, or Models after them, which are in *England,* that I
need only name them.'[61]

In some commentaries, however, references to markers indicate that a
place or sight has already gained a place in the traveller's imaginative life, and
that powerful emotions may be aroused by the on-the-spot encounter with
it; an unspoken assumption of this kind is inscribed in Stendhal's assertion,
just before his famous account of his state of rapture and exhaustion at Santa
Croce (a condition in which 'je marchais avec la crainte de tomber'), that 'j'é-
tais déjà dans une sorte d'extase, par l'idée d'être à Florence', and in Freud's
account of his derealization when he finally visits the Acropolis, after his
boyhood fears that he would never travel to such a place.[62]

Invoking markers, moreover, also provides a means of setting the
diluted intensity of the copy or description in contrast to the undiluted
power of the original. Charlotte Eaton prefaces her declaration that 'I am
not the first person who has gone mad about the Apollo' with an elaborate
hyperbole of unrepresentability, denying that any marker could possibly
convey 'the subtle essence of beauty':

> Description would be the excess of absurdity; even the best copies are vain.
> No cast, drawing, or design, that I ever beheld, had conveyed to my mind
> the faintest image of its perfection. From every attempt to imprison it in
> other models, the subtle essence of beauty escapes. The Divinity disdains
> to inhabit a meaner form.[63]

As already noted, Eaton nonetheless draws back from any suggestion that
she might herself be permanently destabilized by her experience of the

---

61 Vol. I, p. 267. For an earlier reference to markers, see, for example, Evelyn's account of
    the *Dying Gladiator* in the Villa Ludovisi, in *Diary,* vol. II, p. 235; diary entry for 10
    November 1644. For a later reference to markers, see Jameson, *Diary,* p. 257.

62 Stendhal, *Rome, Naples et Florence,* p. 272: 'I was afraid of falling over as I walked along';
    'I was already in a sort of extasy, at the idea that I was in Florence'; Freud, 'Disturbance
    of Memory', p. 455.

63 Eaton, *Rome,* vol. I, p. 169.

Apollo. The intensity that sights acquire by reference to markers can always be distanced, as it is in Eaton's commentary, by implicit reference to the power of the frame to cut off experience of sights from other, more troubling forms of experience.

Reference to different sources of mediation, moreover, allows the traveller to adopt the position of a cheerfully playful consumer of existing visions and fantasies, drawing at will on a range of such visions. In one sense, this position resembles the seventeenth-century positioning of the subject as a scholar, consulting the classics and other texts and viewing them as a store-house full of intensified forms of language. Within the literature of tourism, however, this ability to draw on an established store of signs serves a new rhetorical purpose, in proclaiming the traveller's ability to flit happily from one source of imaginative gratification to the next, without finding any of the available fantasies too alluring or overwhelming. Anna Jameson, at Terracina, emphasizes her own power to play with a variety of mediatory literary texts:

> The Promontory (once poetically the *island*) of Circe is still the Monte Circello: here was the region of the Lestrygons, and the scene of part of the Eneid and Odyssey: and Corinne has superadded romantic and charming associations quite as delightful, and quite as *true*.[64]

Deflecting to the past

Yet another long-established strategy that the rhetoric of tourism deploys is that of using a sight as a starting point for a deflection to the past. As noted in 'Spectator and Spectacle', the traveller, in writings from around the middle of the eighteenth century onwards, often greets a visual feature of the topography as an object that in some way facilitates the task of converting historical time into personal time. He or she assumes, in other words, that through contemplating a particular visual feature, and forcing this feature, in Susan Stewart's words, to 'reveal a profound interiority through narrative', it becomes possible to forge an emotional link with the sight in question.[65] Lady Morgan, proclaiming the uniqueness of Venice, emphasizes that, in observing its *palazzi*, she is also 'reading' the historical narrative that they yield up:

---

64   Jameson, *Diary*, p. 209.

65   Stewart, *On Longing*, p. 146.

In gliding along its great canals, its patrician palaces rise on either side from their watery base, in such majesty of ruin, in such affecting combinations of former splendour and actual decay, that their material beauty is heightened by deep moral touches; and in gazing on fabrics, beyond all others, singular and imposing from their peculiar architecture, we feel that we are reading a history! – a history unparalleled in the annals of humanity![66]

Many of the late eighteenth-century and early nineteenth-century commentaries cited in my chapter on 'Spectator and Spectacle' describe places where the past threatens to resurge, in a way that may prove unsettling to travellers. Tourism, in contrast, designates the sights sought out by the traveller as places where the past, however full of energy, turbulence, danger and excitement, nonetheless maintains its distance. In the conversation between Sydney and Mr Milton in Elizabeth Bowen's *The Hotel* (1927), quoted in 'Spectator and Spectacle', Sydney's remark 'Wouldn't it be nice... if the Saracens were to appear on the skyline, land, and ravage the Hotel?', is followed by the reflection that the 'dust, panic and ecstasy' of the past is all too easy to keep at bay:

'But I wonder,' she added, while a cloud of depression crept over her, 'how many of us they would really care to take away?'

He did not know how she wished him to answer and risked: 'It would be an embarrassing choice.'

She sighed flatly. The dust, panic and ecstasy with which she had filled for a moment the corridors of the Hotel subsided. Once more she saw her fellow-visitors as they were to remain – undesired, secure and null. 'Not many,' she said, and turning away from him seemed to be gazing down some distant, barred-away perspective of feminine loveliness. 'Women must have deteriorated.'[67]

Many early nineteenth-century writings on Italy endorse this view of the past as full of a vitality which might conceivably resurge, with dramatically destabilizing effects, but which is far more likely to remain in a state of indefinite quiescence. Such writings often, in fact, establish the separation between narratives of 'dust, panic and ecstasy' and the flatness of contemporary life rather more firmly than Sydney does. A change in the way in which Italian history is divided up serves to accentuate the gap between past and present. Until the early decades of the nineteenth century, Renaissance and Baroque Italy, and sometimes even medieval Italy, are assumed to be more or less culturally continuous with the contemporary topography

---

[66] Morgan, *Italy*, vol. II, p. 452.

[67] p. 35.

encountered by the traveller – or, at least, are not overtly distinguished from this contemporary topography. Early nineteenth-century writings, in contrast, suggest that the past that has vanished is not only that of antiquity but also a more modern one. During the chapters in *Corinne* in which the heroine is conducting Lord Nelvil round the sights of Rome, the two include in their tours 'les palais des grands seigneurs'. The narrator provides a description of these *palazzi* in which the Italians, colluding with the demand for framing, edit themselves out of the sights in which they live, and leave the Renaissance paintings within them to the scrutiny of foreigners:

> Ces vastes demeures des princes romains sont désertes et silencieuses; les paresseux habitans de ces palais se retirent chez eux dans quelques petites chambres inaperçues, et laissent les étrangers parcourir leurs magnifiques galeries, où les plus beaux tableaux du siècle de Léon X sont réunis.[68]

The description concludes by emphasizing the sharp separation between contemporary Rome and the Rome of recent centuries: 'Ces grands seigneurs romains sont aussi étrangers maintenant au luxe pompeux de leurs ancêtres, que ces ancêtres l'étoient eux-mêmes aux vertus austères des Romains de la république.'[69] In Chateaubriand's *Voyage en Italie* (1827), the traveller, equating medieval Rome with Christianity in general, and with its monuments, declares: 'Non-seulement l'ancienne Italie n'est plus, mais l'Italie du moyen âge a disparu.'[70]

As the opposition between luxury and the ancient and austere virtues in *Corinne* suggests, the two pasts to which early nineteenth-century travellers deflect are not simply characterized as ancient and modern. On the one hand, Italy is presented as bearing the traces of a past of classical grace, sunshine, tranquillity and (in some instances) liberty, shared with Greece and other lands on the shores of the Mediterranean. On the other hand, the traveller can also deflect back to a violent, turbulent, 'Gothic' past, full of blood, horror, luxury and excess. These two alternative histories are already established in late eighteenth-century writings; the change that

---

68   Staël, *Corinne, ou, l'Italie*, vol. I, p. 129 (book V, chapter 3): 'The palaces of the Roman lords are vast in the extreme. . . They have none of those elegant apartments invented elsewhere for the perfect enjoyment of social life. Superb galleries, hung with the chefs-d'œuvre of the tenth Leo's age, are abandoned to the gaze of strangers, by their lazy proprietors' (p. 83; Leo X was elected pope in 1513, and succeeded by Hadrian VI in 1522).

69   *Ibid.*, vol. I, p. 129 (book V, chapter 3): '. . . their lazy proprietors, who retire to their own obscure little chambers, dead to the pomp of their ancestors, as were *they* to the austere virtues of the Roman republic' (p. 83).

70   p. 100: 'Not only is ancient Italy no more, but medieval Italy has disappeared as well.'

takes place early in the nineteenth century is simply that more recent centuries are now frequently allotted to 'Gothic' history.[71] The traveller very frequently deflects to the two Italies in commentaries on works on art: the tranquil past is rediscovered in classical sculpture, and the turbulent past in Renaissance and Baroque painting, which travel writings continue to view as most strikingly represented by scenes of blood and horror.[72] One of the sights mentioned by a great many travellers in the early nineteenth century is a painting not directly representing a scene of horror but, as Shelley notes in his preface to *The Cenci* (1820), connected to a narrative of 'fearful and monstrous' events: Guido Reni's portrait of Beatrice Cenci.[73]

No chronological dividing line is ever definitively established between the two Italian pasts: turbulence can be seen as replacing tranquillity at any point, although the replacement of ancient Roman virtues by the decadence of the emperors and the invasion of Italy by northern barbarians provide two favourite dates at which to situate the beginnings of horror. Lady Morgan's *Italy* follows the second of these two options, arguing that it was 'on the fall of the Roman Empire' that Europe loses 'every trace of the Asiatic characteristics, which distinguished her southern regions': at this point in history, 'the brilliant mythology she had adopted and naturalized, which had so long peopled her temperate climes with the bright imagery of more fervid zones, faded away like the fantasms of a gay dream'.[74] Shelley, in a letter to Thomas Love Peacock, describing a visit to Pompeii, offers a different chronological schema; he selects the Greek colonies of the South as the primary repositories of Italian tranquillity, and sees not only Christianity but, before it, 'that series of wretched wars which terminated in the Roman conquest of the world', as displacing 'the harmony the unity the perfection the uniform excellence' of Greek art.[75]

71 For a late eighteenth-century formulation of the opposition between the two Italies, see Piozzi, *Observations*, vol. I, p. 126.

72 In commentary on the Italian paintings that are seen as representative of the turbulent past, the degree and variety of horror admissible in art is debated as frequently as ever. Forsyth, for example, in *Remarks*, commenting on the depiction of an 'inexplicably horrible' story in Poussin's famous and 'admirable' *Massacre of the Innocents*, describes the painting as a work 'where the horror is not, as usual, dissipated in a multitude of details', and notes: 'Expression is just on the extreme. Agony carried one point further would fall into the ludicrous' (p. 211).

73 In Shelley, *Poetical Works*, p. 276; among the accounts of the portrait in travel books, see Jameson, *Diary*, pp. 146–7 (and also pp. 299–300, describing Sestini's improvisation on 'La Morte di Beatrice Cenci'), and Dickens, *Pictures from Italy*, pp. 211–12.

74 Vol. I, p. 3.

75 Shelley, *Letters*, vol. II, p. 74 (letter dated 23–4 January 1819).

Wherever the division is placed between them, both pasts, tranquil and violent, are invested with vitality and animation. This vitality is, unsurprisingly, more strongly evident in deflections to turbulent epochs: in commentary on the Italian paintings that are seen as representative of the violent and excessive past, the dramatic depiction of cruelty and suffering is invested with a passionate intentionality through the new option of eliding an artist's formal traits of style and characteristic choice of subject-matter not simply with his (or occasionally her) character, but also with details of his or her biography. Morgan's account of Jusepe Ribera, or 'Lo Spagnoletto', in her *Life and Times of Salvator Rosa* (1824), describes the artist as giving 'full play to those dark passions, which, while they pointed his poniard, directed his pencil to the representation of human suffering, the deformities of Nature, torture methodized into system, and agonies detailed with frightful fidelity.'[76]

As both Morgan and Shelley emphasize, however, in their accounts of the contrast between the two histories, the serenity of the tranquil past does not preclude a 'brilliant mythology' and a flourishing artistic life. Commentaries on antique sculptures invest these works not only with grace but also with vitality: Shelley's enraptured description of a version of the *Crouching Venus*, in Florence, presents the sculpture as full of animation and 'vital energy'.[77]

Italy emptied of vitality

Vitality and energy are, on the other hand, described in many writings of the period as conspicuously absent from contemporary Italy. From Napoleon's Italian campaign of 1795 onwards, the presence of foreign armies of occupation in Italy supplies travellers with evidence to support the contention that Italy is sunk in slavish torpor. This claim is often made without direct reference to the political state of Italy, as though Italian servitude can simply be taken for granted. Both the description of the silent and deserted palaces of Rome in *Corinne* and Chateaubriand's assertion that Christian as well as Pagan Rome is sinking into the dust designate the present as a time of lifelessness, dramatized as such by the spatial emptiness of the parts of the city described. Empty space is also invoked as evidence of a loss of vitality in Lamartine's *Dernier Chant du pèlerinage d'Harold* (1826):

---

[76] Vol. I, p. 142.

[77] Shelley, *Notes on Sculptures*, pp. 27–8. See also, for example, the heroine's account of the combined force and graceful charm of antique sculpture in Staël, *Corinne; ou, l'Italie*, vol. I, p. 206 (book VIII, chapter 2).

Le Scythe et le Breton, de leurs climats sauvages
Par le bruit de ton nom guidés vers tes rivages,
Jetant sur tes cités un regard de mépris,
Ne t'aperçoivent plus dans tes propres débris.[78]

Some writings of this period following the more extreme option of denying that the Italians display one of the forms of vitality traditionally
imputed to them: a proclivity for immoderate indulgence of the passions.
The narrator of 'L'Amoroso', in the Marquis of Normanby's *English in
Italy*, embarks on what seems to be a routine affirmation of Italian excess,
but swiftly transmutes this incipient excess into lifeless insipidity:

> The marriage tie in these countries is not the sacred, indissoluble bond;
> that kind of despotic law, which it is sweet to transgress. Intrigue there has
> not even the charm of being esteemed a sin, – it is an every day and a vulgar
> occupation.[79]

This analysis of Italian sexual mores implicitly invokes an existing option
for explaining cicisbeism (or *serventismo* as it is often termed in the nineteenth century, with reference to the new term *cavaliere servente,* replacing
that of *cicisbeo*). As already noted, this custom is, in some eighteenth-century writings, presented as an effect of Italian male slavishness, and of the
absence of political liberty in Italy. In early nineteenth-century writings,
this explanation is almost invariably the one adopted; in addition, cicisbeism is often cited not only as a result of Italian political enslavement, but
as a cause of it. Hugh William Williams's *Travels in Italy, Greece, and the
Ionian Islands* (1820) observes that a married woman, in Rome, 'is never
without her cavaliere servente. . . attending to all her capricious whims',
and comments: 'Is it not disgraceful, that men of rank should be thus
employed, instead of attending to the general good of their country?'[80]

The heroine of *Corinne* has a cicisbeo – or, at least, a devoted and unde-
manding male friend, the Prince Castel-Forte.[81] This urbane, unassertive
figure provides a useful example for the Marquis of Normanby, in affirming

---

78 Section XIII, lines 11–14: 'The Scythian and the Breton, guided towards your shores
    from their savage climes by your reputation, and throwing a scornful glance over your
    cities, can no longer discern you amid your own rubble.' The early nineteenth-century
    view of Rome as a city emptied of people is emphasized by McGann in 'Rome and its
    Romantic Significance', pp. 313–5; McGann also (pp. 329–31) considers equivocations in
    Stendhal's view of energy and vitality in Rome.

79 Vol. I, p. 148.

80 Vol. I, pp. 362–3. See also, for example, Morgan, *Italy*, vol. I, p. 252.

81 For an account of the point to which Castel-Forte is prepared to take his devotion, see
    Staël, *Corinne; ou, l'Italie,* vol. I, p. 75 (book III, chapter 3).

his view of Italy as a country drained of vitality. The narrator of 'L'Amoroso' reveals that Matilda, unhappily married to the Count Avellino, has given way to the influence of the 'epicurean clime', and has herself acquired a cicisbeo. In explaining how it is that 'a grave and serious character, such was Antonio's, accustomed too, to interest itself in political and patriotic considerations, could give up his time and his independence to a kind of slavery', the narrator casts serious doubt on the view of the Italians as a people of 'boiling blood':

> The universal *dolce* of an Italian's *far niente* is female society; and that admits of many very different modes of connection. Youth, and after manhood looks for passion – but, in spite of the boiling blood and fervid passions of the clime, this is not the prevailing link. In general it is of purer, chaster kind; and Italian life, so corrupt in the mass and in principle, is not by any means so much so in practice as is supposed. The Prince of Castelforte's attachment to Corinna, sketched by De Stael, and limited to the simple wish of daily beholding her, and passing a few languid hours in her company, may be taken as a very fair type of the greater part of these *liaisons*.[82]

Luxuriance, gastronomy and trivial gratification

The vanished vitality of Italy is displaced not only onto the past but also onto nature; as already noted, the sublime and the beautiful are regularly merged into a new category of luxuriance. The luxuriant landscape, bristling with vigorous and flourishing vegetation, provides a means of accentuating, by contrast, the torpor and general degradation of the country's inhabitants. Anna Jameson, having discerned in the region around Terracina 'a picture of the most wonderful and luxuriant beauty', plunges into an account of human 'depravity and dirt' in the 'two wretched towns' of Itri and Fondi.[83] Accounts of ruins returning to nature, as weeds rampage over them, set natural luxuriance in yet more dramatic contrast to the decline of vitality in

---

82 In Normanby, *The English in Italy*, vol. I, pp. 178, 179. For a similar analysis of cicisbeism, see Simond, *Voyage en Italie*, vol. II, p. 355. Byron, describing his own role as cicisbeo to Teresa Guiccioli in a letter of 1819, also identifies 'this Cicisbean existence' with an abnegation of wider responsibilities (*Letters and Journals,* vol. VI, p. 214). This particular part of the Byron legend – the power of the warm south to draw even the foreigner into a passively 'Cicisbean existence' – is dramatized at some length by Lamartine in his *Dernier Chant du pèlerinage d'Harold* (see, for example, section IV, lines 1–4; section VIII, lines 27–32).

83 Jameson, *Diary*, p. 268.

human culture. As Corinne and Lord Nelvil visit the Palatine, the narrator
asserts that the Domus Aurea covered the whole of that hill, but observes
that 'des pierres, recouvertes par des plantes fécondes, sont tout ce qu'il en
reste aujourd'hui: la nature y a repris son empire sur les travaux des
hommes, et la beauté des fleurs console de la ruine des palais'.[84]

By affirming the separation between Italian nature and Italian culture
and society, this new emphasis on natural luxuriance allows travel writing
to accord much more attention to a pleasure which is largely ignored in the
eighteenth century, but which begins to play a major part in the rhetoric of
tourism, in affirming that the foreign may be enjoyed safely: the pleasure
to be derived from food and wine.

Eighteenth-century travel writings, it has been noted, accord relatively
little attention to food and wine as the products of nature, and adopt a tone
of positive complaint when describing food as the product of Italian culture. While seventeenth-century travel writings, with gentle, self-protective irony, positively acclaim gastronomic products as worthy objects of
attention, the Earl of Cork and Orrery's *Letters from Italy* (1773) brusquely
dismisses an interest in wine as a mark of the inadequate traveller:

> The English are a happy people, if they were truly conscious, or could in
> any degree convince themselves, of their own felicity. . . Let them travel
> abroad, not to see fashions, but states, not to taste different wines, but dif-
> ferent governments.[85]

In the early nineteenth century, however, references to food and wine once
again proliferate, and are once again employed, as they are in seventeenth-
century writings, to affirm the fertility of the country. Descriptions of luxuriance often allude to the edible products of the terrain: Henry Sass, for
example, declares, in Naples:

> The deliciousness of the climate, the fertility of the earth, producing excel-
> lent corn in abundance, and quantities of the finest fruits and vegetables,
> the grandeur of the bay, and the magnificence of the scenery, caused that
> degree of inspiration which renders us above ourselves.[86]

---

84 Staël, *Corinne; ou, l'Italie*, vol. I, p. 108 (book IV, chapter 5): 'a heap of stones, overgrown
    with shrubs, is all that now remains. Nature reclaimed her empire over the works of man;
    and her fair flowers atone for the fall of a palace' (p. 68). See also, for example, Shelley's
    well-known account of the Baths of Caracalla, in a letter to Thomas Love Peacock (*Letters*,
    vol. II, p. 85; dated 23 March 1819).

85 p. 246.

86 Sass, *A Journey*, pp. 176–7.

Joseph Forsyth, in his *Remarks on Antiquities, Arts, and Letters* (1813), elides 'some red wine' with a southern Italian landscape by using the term *crater* (or 'drinking-bowl') to describe the natural formation before him:

> On the cliffs above is a cottage which commands a view of the two promontories of Misenum and Minerva, the whole crater of sea, all the islands before, and the volcanoes behind. Here I drank some red wine of volcanic growth, still more delicious than the *lacrime* of Vesuvius.[87]

From early in the nineteenth century onwards, the traveller, in a great many writings, displays an interest in the gastronomic products to be encountered as he or she moves from one region to the next. Forsyth, at Bibbiena, considers the argument that 'the dryness of the air' might contribute towards the 'superior flavour' of the hams, which 'are esteemed the best in Italy, and require no cooking'. At Cortona, he remarks: 'This is a favourite seat of "Bacco in Toscana;" for good table-wine costs here but a penny the large flask.'[88] Louis Simond, in his *Voyage en Italie et en Sicile* (1828), offers detailed accounts both of meals consumed by himself and his companions and of the foods eaten by the inhabitants of different localities.[89]

Such commentaries do not always endorse the quality of the products consumed: Eustace embarks on a long discussion of 'why Italy does not now produce wines so excellent, and in such variety as anciently', while Forsyth, having 'stopped at Sta AGATA in hopes of drinking some real Falernian', on his way to Naples, is disappointed in such an ambition: 'we found this degenerate wine far inferior to the Formian which we had drunk at Mola.'[90] Most travel writings of this period nonetheless take it for granted that consuming food and wine will play a part in the process of managing the pleasures of Italy. Anna Jameson's unhappiness in love does not prevent her from perceiving the need for some refreshment after climbing Vesuvius to watch its eruption at close quarters:

> After a slow and difficult descent, we reached the Hermitage. I was so exhausted that I was glad to rest for a few minutes. My good friend

---

[87] pp. 304–5.

[88] *Ibid.*, pp. 101, 105.

[89] See, for example, Simond's account of a supper at Girgenti (now known as Agrigento; vol. II, p. 206), and his summary of the gastronomic pleasures of the Neapolitans (vol. II, pp. 143–4).

[90] Eustace, *A Tour*, vol. I, p. 481 (the discussion continues for two more pages, to p. 483); Forsyth, *Remarks*, p. 290. Travel writings of the early nineteenth century are full of allusions to the observations of Latin poets on Roman wine: Best, *Italy as it is*, p. 47, laments the English neglect of 'the wines of Italy, which contented the masters of the world'.

Salvador, brought me a glass of *Lachryma Christi* and the leg of a chicken; and with recruited spirits we mounted our animals and again started.[91]

Samuel Rogers describes in some detail his own success in extracting pleasure from the most unpromising of meals. He begins glumly:

> It was in a splenetic humour that I sate me down to my scanty fare at TER-RACINA; and how long I should have contemplated the lean thrushes in array before me, I cannot say, if a cloud of smoke, that drew the tears into my eyes, had not burst from the green and leafy boughs on the hearth-stone. 'Why,' I exclaimed, starting up from the table, 'why did I leave my own chimney-corner?'[92]

Soon, however, Rogers indicates an imminent reversal:

> 'But am I not on the road to BRUNDISIUM? And are not these the very calamities that befel HORACE and VIRGIL, and MÆCENAS, and PLOTIUS, and VARIUS? HORACE laughed at them – Then why should not I? HORACE resolved to turn them to account; and VIRGIL – cannot we hear him observing, that to remember them will, by and by, be a pleasure?'[93]

The traveller's initial discontent, it seems, has been voiced in order to underline his achievement in overcoming all obstacles to gratification:

> My soliloquy reconciles me at once to my fate; and when, for the twentieth time, I had looked through the window on a sea sparkling with innumerable brilliants, a sea on which the heroes of the Odyssey and the Eneid had sailed, I sat down as to a splendid banquet. My thrushes had the flavour of ortolans; and I ate with an appetite I had not known before. 'Who,' I cried, as I poured out my last glass of Falernian (for Falernian it was said to be, and in my eyes it ran bright and clear as a topaz-stone) 'Who would remain at home, could he do otherwise?'[94]

Jameson includes in her *Diary of an Ennuyée* two passages of reflection on how a picnic in Italy should be organized, in order to produce the greatest delight; describing a dinner in the gardens of the Villa Pamphili, in Rome, she emphasizes the joys of 'admirably managed' commensality:

---

91 Jameson, *Diary*, p. 237.
92 Rogers, *Italy*, p. 169.
93 *Ibid.*
94 *Ibid.*, pp. 169–70.

Our luxurious dinner, washed down by a competent proportion of Malvoisie and Champagne, was spread upon the grass, which was literally the *flowery turf,* being covered with violets, iris, and anemones of every dye. Instead of changing our plates, we washed them in a beautiful fountain which murmured near us, having first by a libation propitiated the presiding nymph for this pollution of her limpid waters. For my own peculiar taste there were too many servants (who on these occasions are always *de trop*) too many luxuries, too much fuss; but considering the style and number of our party it was all consistently and admirably managed: the grouping of the company, picturesque because unpremeditated, the scenery round, the arcades and bowers and columns and fountains, had an air altogether quite poetical and romantic; and put me in mind of some of Watteau's beautiful garden pieces, and Stothard's fêtes-champêtres.[95]

The new proliferation of gastronomic references is dependent upon a change in aesthetic theory (and in the internalized assumptions that it generates) that makes it possible to classify food and wine as sources of trivial yet innocent gratification: the variety of pleasure that proves so useful within the rhetoric of tourism. At times, eighteenth-century writings introduce food as a point of bathos, in relation to art, as in Spence's observation, in Florence, that 'though the statues here in the Great Duke's gallery are something better than what we meet with at Hyde Park Corner, the Florentine beef is not half so good as our English'.[96] Eighteenth-century theoretical speculations about taste, however, do not take it for granted that taste in food and drink must obviously be completely distinct from taste in aesthetic matters. In the 'Introduction on Taste' that begins the second edition (1759) of his *Enquiry,* Burke notes the persistence of 'the original natural causes of pleasure' that lead 'all men' to enjoy butter or honey, even when addicted to drugs such as opium, tobacco, fermented spirits, tea and coffee. He then suggests that his conclusions about taste in food can very readily be extended to taste in its metaphorical sense: 'Thus the pleasure of all the senses, of the sight, and even of the Taste, that most ambiguous of the senses, is the same in all, high and low, learned and unlearned.'[97]

Early nineteenth-century reflections on art and literature, in contrast, often establish an explicit opposition between taste in each of these two domains, assigning a frivolity to gastronomic taste that distinguishes it

---

95 p. 280.

96 Spence, *Letters*, p. 125; 11 October 1732.

97 Burke, *Philosophical Enquiry*, p. 16.

from the complex sensibility required by the arts. Wordsworth, in the Preface to the second edition of *Lyrical Ballads,* published in 1800, refers scornfully to 'men who speak of what they do not understand; who talk of Poetry as of a matter of amusement and idle pleasure; who will converse with us as gravely about a *taste* for Poetry, as they express it, as if it were a thing as indifferent as a taste for rope-dancing, or Frontiniac or Sherry'.[98] Coleridge, in a fragment known as 'The Definition of Taste', from his lectures of 1808, asks:

> But first, what is taste, in its metaphorical sense. Its primary sense is only an accident. The Greeks, who have left us the finest models of taste, and who are justly believed to have possessed the faculty of taste in the highest degree, did not adopt this metaphor.[99]

In his essay 'On the Principles of Genial Criticism concerning the Fine Arts', Coleridge establishes this distinction with specific reference to the sights of the Grand Tour. Reflecting on 'the essential difference between the beautiful and the agreeable', he poses a question about the delight occasioned by 'the noblest productions of human genius' which ends up differentiating between taste in literature and taste in food, and begins by listing among the productions of genius a series of major sights to be seen in Rome or Florence:

> Whether the noblest productions of human genius (such as the Iliad, the works of Shakspeare and Milton, the Pantheon, Raphael's Gallery, the Michael Angelo's Sistine Chapel, the Venus de Medici and the Apollo Belvedere, involving, of course, the human forms that approximate to them in actual life) delight us merely by chance, from accidents of local associations – in short, please us because they please us (in which case it would be impossible either to praise or to condemn any man's taste, however opposite to our own, and we could be no more justified in assigning a corruption or absence of just taste to a man, who should prefer Blackmore to Homer or Milton, or the Castle Spectre to Othello, than to the same man for preferring a black-pudding to a sirloin of beef). . .[100]

The reader, then, is invited, in a roundabout way, to consider the absurdity of responding to sights such as the *Stanze di Raffaele* in the Vatican by

---

98 Wordsworth. *Poetical Works,* p. 737.

99 p. 158; Coleridge adds (p. 162): 'If in drinking choice wine from a goblet cast and adorned by Myron, a man should say, "A beautiful flavor from a beautiful bowl"; and a friend should observe that it would be better to say, "A delightful flavor from a beautiful vase," there are few even among the uneducated who would not feel the superior propriety.'

100 pp. 226–7.

exercising the same powers of differentiation required in order to discern the superiority of beef to black-pudding. Sydney Morgan is rather more straightforward in defining any confusion between gastronomic delights and the pleasures of the great works of art in Italy as highly comic. She describes the Cavaliere Puccini, a former director of the 'Gallery' in Florence:

> Of this arduous director of the museum, and zealous guardian of the Venus de Medicis, the Hesperian dragon '*was but a type:*' one object only had ever divided his passion for the fine arts, and that was his taste for the *gastronomic* ones. Torn by contending inclinations toward the cabinet and the kitchen, he is said to have habitually confounded the phraseology of both – to have talked of the Venus, as a '*cosa da mangiare,*' and of '*mouton à la braise,*' as being of the true French school.'[101]

Elaborating on this confusion of two discourses in a footnote, Morgan sums it up by deploying the term *culinary criticism* as an ironic oxymoron:

> Pointing out the best pictures of the gallery one day to a Roman gentleman, in his usual strain of culinary criticism, he observed of *one,* 'Come questo quadro è butiroso' (how buttery this picture is!) of another, 'Come *è midol-loso!*' (how full of marrow is this!) 'If you say another word,' interrupted the Virtuoso, licking his lips, 'I shall eat them,' – '*State zitto; se non, lo mangio.*'[102]

Both in Coleridge's commentary and in Morgan's, the definition of gastronomic pleasure as innocently trivial depends, in part, on the relation between this pleasure and curiosity. Hobbes, when he defines curiosity as 'a Lust of the mind, that. . . exceedeth the short vehemence of any carnall Pleasure', cites as one of the pleasures to be set in opposition to this 'Lust of the mind' the 'appetite of food' which, with 'other pleasures of Sense', characterizes not only humans (the sole beings who evince the '*Desire,* to know why, and how'), but other animals.[103] Coleridge, when he implies that the relative ability to please that can be ascribed to black-pudding and a sirloin of beef neither invites nor requires any great effort of investigation, takes it for granted that gastronomic appetite is quite distinct from the speculative fervour aroused by the problem of distinguishing between 'the noblest productions of human genius' and inferior works of literature. Lady Morgan, describing the 'Roman gentleman' ironically 'licking his

---

[101]   Morgan, *Italy*, vol. I, p. 71.

[102]   *Ibid.*

[103]   Hobbes, *Leviathan*, p. 124.

lips', assumes that this physical reaction, unlike the blushes and shudders that are intermittently mentioned by travellers as evidence of their intensified responses to works of art, introduces a concept of pleasure too simple, straightforward and down-to-earth to have any relevance to the complex business of assessing paintings.

References to food and drink, then, both in accounts of paintings and sculptures and in descriptions of landscape, can readily be used to indicate that the traveller is ingeniously managing the incipient intensity of aesthetic pleasure by merging this pleasure with innocently gastronomic gratification. In a long account of a picnic at Pompeii, Jameson implies that a meal in such a place, if properly organized, could increase the delight afforded by 'the loveliness and solemnity of the scenes around' and 'our deep impressions of the past'. Her account of how such a picnic should be conducted begins by specifying the exact spot ('the platform of the old Greek Temple which commands a view of the mountains and the bay'), but then details, just as exactly, the fare to be consumed: 'There we would make our cheerful and elegant repast, on bread and fruits, and perhaps a bottle of Malvoisie or Champagne'.[104]

Travellers often betray an uncertainty as to whether the rhetorical risk involved in demonstrating a capacity for the down-to-earth gratification of food and wine is in fact outweighed by the advantages of forging continuities between frivolous diversions and incipiently destabilizing pleasures. Anna Jameson, at the Villa Pamphili, is careful to establish that aesthetic considerations are dominant for her: 'What I most admired was the delicious view', she states firmly, and adds: 'What I most felt and enjoyed was the luxurious temperature of the atmosphere, the purity and brilliance of the skies. . .' Both here and at Pompeii, moreover, she emphasizes her repudiation of any element of gastronomic excess or luxury as strongly as possible: the simplicity of her own programme, at the latter spot, is placed in sharp contrast to the items actually consumed. ('Besides more substantial cates, we had oysters from Lake Lucrine (or Acheron), and classically excellent they were; London bottled porter, and half a dozen different kinds of wine.')[105]

References to gastronomic pleasure, however, whether literal or metaphorical, nonetheless offer the traveller an enormous rhetorical advantage: that of strongly rebutting any suspicion of affectation or pretentiousness. In Hazlitt's *Notes of a Journey through France and Italy*

---

[104] Jameson, *Diary*, pp. 247–8.

[105] *Ibid.*, pp. 281, 245–6.

(1826), a food metaphor makes it clear that the traveller has no intention of launching into affected raptures at one of the great works of art in Florence: Raphael's *Fornarina:*

> Assuredly no charge can be brought against it of *nimini-piminee* affectation or shrinking delicacy. It is robust, full to bursting, coarse, luxurious, hardened, but wrought up to an infinite degree of exactness and beauty in the details. It is the perfection of vulgarity and refinement together. The Fornarina is a bouncing, buxom, sullen, saucy baker's daughter – but painted, idolized, immortalized by Raphael! Nothing can be more homely and repulsive than the original; *you see her bosom swelling like the dough rising in the oven;* the tightness of her skin puts you in mind of Trim's story of the sausage-maker's wife – nothing can be more enchanting than the picture – than the care and delight with which the artist has seized the lurking glances of the eye, curbed the corners of the mouth, smoothed the forehead, dimpled the chin, rounded the neck, till by innumerable delicate touches and the 'labour of love,' he has concerted a coarse, rude mass into a miracle of art.[106]

In his description of the cascade at Terni, Hazlitt maintains robustly that he is well able to assume a cheerful irreverence in the face of a natural wonder:

> To say the truth, if Lord Byron had put it into *Don Juan* instead of *Childe Harold,* he might have compared the part which her ladyship has chosen to perform on this occasion to an experienced waiter pouring a bottle of ale into a tumbler at a tavern. It has something of the same continued, plump, right-lined descent.[107]

Destabilized drinking

These two descriptions both use gastronomic metaphors to affirm that there is no question of giving way to restlessness or destabilization: Hazlitt introduces dough and ale as reassuringly mundane points of reference, which affirm that, far from feeling overwhelmed by the topography of alterity, he perceives it as a topography that is, after all, understandable in familiar terms. Like other elements in the rhetoric of tourism, however, food and drink can easily assume a quite different rhetorical role: gastronomic products function not only as metaphors for innocent gratification but also for the foreign as an object of potentially destabilizing longing: in

---

106 pp. 262–3; emphasis added.
107 *Ibid.*, p. 329.

the cry 'O for a beaker full of the warm South' in Keats's 'Ode to a Nightingale', there is no moment of bathos or jocularity to distance the speaker from the dangers of desire.[108] In a much later travel book, Samuel Butler's *First Year in Canterbury Settlement* (1863), wine and fruit are poignantly made to accentuate Butler's desperate desire to escape New Zealand and taste once again the delights of Switzerland and Italy: 'How one does long to see some signs of human care in the midst of the loneliness! How one would like, too, to come occasionally across some little auberge, with its vin ordinaire and refreshing fruit!'[109]

Drunkenness, moreover, as indicated by the account of Mr Cypress's departure for Italy in Peacock's *Nightmare Abbey* (1818), supplies a metaphor for the restlessness and destabilization which, from the late eighteenth century onwards, are so often presented as elements in the experience of travelling.[110] Sterne's inclusion of the drunken Noah in an epic simile designed to indicate the uncertainties of the traveller's fate metaphorically elides intoxication with the dangers of travel.[111] In this same tradition, the 1995 Baedeker guide to Australia, advising its readers on handling 'Food and Drink', supplies a bland, generalized admonition that nonetheless evokes one of the central fears of the tourist: the fear of unspecified perils, lurking ineluctably amid even the most simple and straightforward of pleasures:

> In view of the great heat it is better to abstain from alcohol during the day.[112]

Beckford, travelling down the River Brenta from Venice, hovers between visions of restless and reassuring drinking. The countryside prompts him to an imaginative digression to a more exotic topography: 'Our navigation, the tranquil streams and cultivated banks. . . had a sort of Chinese cast which led me into Quang-Si and Quang-Tong.' Feverishly, he conjures up an exotic object of the kind that Byron's reflections on Egeria characterize as 'some celestial fruit forbidden to our wants': 'when I beheld the yellow nenupha expanding its broad leaves to the current, I thought of the Tao-Sé, and venerated one of the chief ingredients in their beverage of immortality.' Failing to find 'the kernels' of these waterlilies (the source of the

---

[108] Stanza 2, line 5, in *Complete Poems*, p. 346.

[109] p. 59. Butler's gloom prompts an unnecessarily pessimistic attitude towards the future of wine in this region: 'As for *vin ordinaire*, I do not suppose that, except at Akaroa, the climate will ever admit of grapes ripening in this settlement.'

[110] pp. 105–6; see the summary of this episode in chapter 4.

[111] Sterne, *A Sentimental Journey*, pp. 11–12.

[112] *Baedeker Australia*, p. 558.

beverage's 'wonderful effects'), he nonetheless comes across some bowers of vines, and is reminded of the more attainable pleasures of drinking wine – which, reassuringly, retain an air of cosy familiarity even when the traveller invokes the drunken Noah: 'Under these garlands I passed, and gathered the ripe clusters which dangled around, convinced that Noah had discovered a far superior beverage to that of the Tao-Sé.'[113]

---

[113] Beckford, *Dreams*, vol. I, pp. 110, 111. (For my refererence to Byron, see *Childe Harold's Pilgrimage*, Canto IV, stanza 120, line 9, in *Complete Poetical Works*, vol. II, p. 164.) Shaffer, in "'To remind us of China'", p. 228, discusses this passage in relation to other deflections to China in the same work.

Bibliography

Travel writings and other primary texts, 1600–1830

[Addison, Joseph,] *Remarks on Several Parts of Italy, &c. In the Years 1701, 1702, 1703*, London, 1705.

Addison, Joseph, *The Works of the Right Honourable Joseph Addison*, edited by Richard Hurd, 4 vols, London, 1854.

Addison, J[oseph], and Richard Steele, *Selections from the Tatler and the Spectator*, edited by Angus Ross, Penguin, London, 1988.

[D'Alembert, Jean le Rond, and Diderot, Denis (editors),] *Encyclopédie; ou, Dictionnaire Raisonné des sciences, des arts et des métiers, par une société de gens de lettres*, 17 vols, Paris, 1751–65.

Alison, Archibald, *Essays on the Nature and Principles of Taste*, sixth edition, 2 vols, Edinburgh, [1790] 1825.

Austen, Jane, *Northanger Abbey and Persuasion*, edited by John Davie (Oxford: Oxford University Press, [1818/1818] 1975).

Baillie, [John,] *An Essay on the Sublime*, London, 1747.

Baretti, Joseph [Giuseppe], *An Account of the Manners and Customs of Italy: with Observations on the Mistakes of some Travellers, with Regard to that Country*, 2 vols, London, 1768.

Barry, James, *An Inquiry into the Real and Imaginary Obstructions to the Acquisition of the Arts in England*, London, 1775.

Beckford, William, *Biographical Memoirs of Extraordinary Painters*, London, [1780] 1824.

Beckford, William, *Dreams, Waking Thoughts and Incidents* [1783], in *The Travel Diaries of William Beckford of Fonthill*, edited by Guy Chapman, 2 vols, London, Constable and Houghton and Mifflin, 1928; vol. I, pp. 1–310.

Behn, Aphra, *The Feigned Courtesans* [1679], in *Female Playwrights of the Restoration: Five Comedies*, edited by Paddy Lyons and Fidelis Morgan, London, Everyman, 1991.

Belzoni, G[iovanni Battista], *Narrative of the Operations and Recent Discoveries within the Pyramids, Temples, Tombs, and Excavations, in Egypt and Nubia; and of a Journey to the Coast of the Red Sea, in Search of the Ancient Berenice; and another to the Oasis of Jupiter Ammon*, London, 1820.

Bénard, Nicolas, *Le Voyage de Hierusalem et autres lieux de la Terre-Sainte, faict par le Sr Bénard Parisien Chevalier de l'ordre du Saint Sepulchre de Notre Seigneur Jesus Christ. Ensemble son retour par l'Italie, Suisse, Allemagne, Holande et Flandre, en la tres fleurissante et peuplée ville de Paris*, Paris, 1621.

Bergeret [de Grancourt, Pierre-Jacques-Onésyme], and Jean Fragonard, *Journal inédit d'un voyage en Italie 1773–74*, edited by M.A. Tomézy, Paris, 1895.

Berry, [Mary,] *Extracts of the Journals and Correspondence of Miss Berry from the Year 1783 to 1852*, edited by Lady Theresa Lewis, 3 vols, London, 1865.

[Best, Henry,] *Italy as it is; or, Narrative of an English Family's Residence for Three Years in that Country. By the Author of 'Four Years in France'*, London, 1828.

Blair, Hugh, *Lectures on Rhetoric and Belles Lettres*, 2 vols, London, 1783.

Boccage, [Marie Anne Fiquet du,] *Recueil des œuvres de Madame du Bocccage*, 3 vols, Lyons, 1762.

Bocage, Madam du [Marie Anne Fiquet du Boccage], *Letters concerning England, Holland and Italy... Written during her Travels in those Countries. Translated from the French*, 2 vols, London, 1770.

Boigne, [Charlotte-Louise-Éléonore-Adélaïde de,] *Mémoires de la Comtesse de Boigne*, edited by Charles Nicoullaud, 4 vols, Paris, Plon-Nourrit, 1907.

Boswell, James, *Boswell on the Grand Tour: Italy, Corsica, and France 1765–1766*, edited by Frank Brady and Frederick A. Pottle, Heinemann, London, 1955.

Boswell, James, *Life of Johnson*, edited by R.W. Chapman, introduced by Pat Rogers, Oxford, Oxford University Press, [1791] 1985.

Bouchard, Jean-Jacques, *Journal*, edited by Emanuele Kanceff, 2 vols, continuous pagination, Turin, Giappichelli, 1976. The journal is concerned with the years 1630 to 1632.

Broderick, Thomas, *The Travels of Thomas Broderick, Esq; in a late Tour through Several Parts of Europe, &c*, 2 vols, London, 1754.

Bromley, William, *Remarks in the Grande Tour of France and Italy. Lately Performed by a Person of Quality*, London, 1692.

Brooke, N., *Observations on the Manners and Customs of Italy, with Remarks on the Vast Importance of British Commerce on that Continent*, London, 1798.

Brydone, Patrick, *A Tour through Sicily and Malta*, 2 vols, London, [1773] 1796.

Burke, Edmund, *A Philosophical Enquiry into the Origin of our Ideas of the Sublime and Beautiful*, edited by James Boulton, Oxford, Blackwell, [1757] 1987.

Burnet, Gilbert, *Some Letters. Containing an Account of what Seemed most Remarkable in Switzerland, Italy, &c.*, Amsterdam, 1686 [in fact 1687]; first published in Rotterdam, 1686.

Burney, Charles, *The Present State of Music in France and Italy; or, The Journal of a Tour through those Countries, Undertaken to Collect Materials for a General History of Music*, London, 1771.

Burney, Frances, *Camilla; or, A Picture of Youth*, edited by Edward A. Bloom and Lilian D. Bloom, London: Oxford University Press, [1796] 1983.

Byron, [George Gordon Noel Byron, Baron,] *Letters and Journals*, edited by Leslie A. Marchand, 13 vols, London, John Murray, 1973–94.

Byron, [George Gordon Noel Byron, Baron,] *The Complete Poetical Works*, edited by Jerome J. McGann, 7 vols, Oxford, Oxford University Press, 1980–92.

Cailliaud, Frédéric, *Voyage à Méroé, au Fleure Blanc, au-delà de Fâzoql dans le midi du royaume de Sennâr, à Syouah et dans cing autres oasis; fait dans les années 1819, 1820, 1821 et 1822*, edited by the author and E.F. Jomard, 4 vols, [Paris,] 1826–27.

Campbell, Harriet Charlotte Beaujolais, *A Journey to Florence in 1817*, edited by G.R. de Beer, London, Bles, 1951.

Castelvetro, Giacomo, *Brieve racconto di tutte le radici di tutte l'erbe di tutti i frutti che crudi o cotti in Italia si mangiano*, edited by Emilio Faccioli, Mantua, Gianluigi Arcari, 1988.

Chateaubriand, [François René de,] *Itinéraire de Paris à Jérusalem*, edited by Émile Malakis, 2 vols, Baltimore and London, Johns Hopkins University Press, [1811] 1941.

Chateaubriand, [François René de,] *Voyage en Italie*, Textes littéraires français no.153, Geneva, Droz, [1827] 1968.

[Clenche, John,] *A Tour in France and Italy, Made by an English Gentleman, 1675*, London, 1676.

Cochin, Charles Nicolas [the Younger], *Voyage d'Italie, ou recueil de notes sur les ouvrages de peinture et de sculpture, qu'on voit dans les principales villes d'Italie*, 3 vols, Paris, 1758.

Coleridge, S[amuel] T[aylor], 'On the Principles of Genial Criticism concerning the Fine Arts, More Especially those of Statuary and Painting, Deduced from the Laws and Motions which Guide the True Artist in the Production of his Works', in *Biographia Literaria, with his Aesthetical Essays*, edited by J. Shawcross, 2 vols, Oxford, Clarendon Press, 1907, II, 219–46.

Coleridge, Samuel Taylor, 'The Definition of Taste', in *Shakespearean Criticism*, edited by Thomas Middleton Raysor, second edition, 2 vols, London and New York, Dent and Dutton, 1960, I, 158–65. A fragment from lectures of 1808.

Corke and Orrery, John [Boyle], Earl of, *Letters from Italy, in the Years 1754 and 1755*, edited by John Duncombe, London, 1773.

Coryate, Thomas, *Coryats Crudities. Hastily gobled up in five moneths travells in France, Savoy, Italy, Rhetia comonly called the Grisons Country, Helvetia alias Switzerland, some parts of High Germany, and the Netherlands. Newly digested in the hungry aire of ODCOMBE in the County of Somerset, and now dispersed to the norishment of the travelling members of this kingdome*, London, 1611.

Coyer, L'Abbé, *Voyages d'Italie et de Hollande*, 2 vols, Paris, 1775.

Dallington, Sir Robert, *Survey of the Great Dukes State of Tuscany*, Facsimile edition, Amsterdam/Norwood, NJ, Johnson/Theatrum Orbis Terrarum, [1605] 1974.

Dennis, John, *Miscellanies in Verse and Prose*, London, 1693.

Dryden, John, *Virgil's Æneis*, edited by William Frost, Volume V in *Works*, 20 vols, University of California Press, Berkeley, 1956–89.

[Dupaty, Charles Marguerite Jean Baptiste Mercier,] *Lettres sur l'Italie, en 1785*, 2 vols, Rome, 1788.

Dupaty, [Charles Marguerite Jean Baptiste Mercier,] *Sentimental Letters on Italy*, translated by J. Povoleri, 2 vols, London, 1789.

Eaton, Charlotte, *Rome in the Nineteenth Century*, 3 vols, London, 1820.

Eustace, John Chetwode, *A Tour through Italy*, 2 vols, London, 1813.

Evelyn, John, *Diary*, edited by E.S. de Beer, 6 vols, London, 1955.

[Evers, Samuel,] *A Journal Kept on a Journey from Bassora to Bagdad; over the Little Desert to Aleppo, Cyprus, Rhodes, Zante, Corfu; and Otranto, in Italy; in the Year 1779. By a Gentleman, Late an Officer in the Service of the Honourable East India Company: Containing an Account of the Progress of Caravans over the Desert of Arabia; Mode and Expences of Quarantine; Description of the Soil, Manners and Customs of the Various Countries on this Extensive Route, &c., &c.*, Horsham, 1784.

Fielding, Henry, *Jonathan Wild and The Journal of a Voyage to Lisbon*, edited by Douglas Brooks, London, Dent, [1743/1755] 1973.

Fleckno, Richard, *A Relation of Ten Years Travells in Europe, Asia, Affrique, and America*, London, [1654].

Forsyth, Joseph, *Remarks on Antiquities, Arts, and Letters during an Excursion in Italy in the Years 1802 and 1803*, London, 1813.

Gailhard, Jean, *The Present State of the Princes and Republicks of Italy*, London, [1650] 1668.

Gailhard, Jean, *The Compleat Gentleman: or, Directions for the Education of Youth as to their Breeding at Home and Travelling Abroad. In Two Treatises*, 2 parts, London, 1678.

Galiffe, James Aug., *Italy and its Inhabitants: An Account of a Tour in that Country in 1816 and 1817*, 2 vols, London, 1820.

Gerard, Alexander, *An Essay on Taste*, London, 1759.

Gibbon, [Edward,] *Gibbon's Journey from Geneva to Rome: his Journal from 20 April to 2 October 1764*, edited by Georges A. Bonnard, London, Nelson, 1961.

Gibbon, Edward, *Autobiography of Edward Gibbon, as Originally Edited by Lord Sheffield* [entitled *Memoirs of My Life and Writings* by Gibbon himself], introduced by J.B. Bury, London, Oxford University Press, [1796] 1935.

Graham, Maria, *Three Months Passed in the Mountains East of Rome during the Year 1819*, London, 1820.

Gray, Robert, *Letters during the Course of a Tour through Germany, Switzerland and Italy, in the Years 1791 and 1792, with Reflectons on the Manners, Literature, and Religion of those Countries*, London, 1794.

Gray, [Thomas,]*The Poems of Mr Gray, to which are Prefixed Memoirs of his Life and Writings*, edited by William Mason, York, 1775. The letters from Italy in this work were written during 1739 and 1740.

Gray, Thomas, *The Poems of Thomas Gray, with a Selection of Letters and Essays*, London, Dent, 1912, introduced by John Drinkwater. The letters from Italy in this work were written during 1739 and 1740.

Gray, Thomas, *Works*, edited by the Revd John Milford, 5 vols, London, 1836.

Gray, [Thomas,] and [William] Collins, *Poetical Works*, edited by Austin Lane Poole, London, Oxford University Press, 1974.

Hakewill, James, *A Picturesque Tour of Italy, from Drawings Made in 1816–17*, London, 1820.

Hamilton, Sir W[illiam], *Observations on Mount Vesuvius, Mount Etna, and Other Volcanos: in a series of letters, addressed to the Royal Society*, London, 1772.

Hazlitt, William, 'On Going a Journey' [1822], in *The Essays of William Hazlitt: A Selection*, introduced by Catherine Macdonald Maclean, London, Macdonald, 1949, pp.29–40. The essay was first published in the *New Monthly Magazine*.

Hazlitt, William, *Notes of a Journey through France and Italy*, London, 1826.

Hazlitt, William, *Criticisms on Art: and Sketches of the Picture Galleries of England*, edited by William Hazlitt Junior, 2 vols, London, 1843–4.

[Hitchcock, Robert,] *The Macaroni. A Comedy. As it is Performed at the Theatre-Royal in York*, York, 1773.

Hoare, Sir Richard Colt, *A Classical Tour through Italy and Sicily; Tending to Illustrate some Districts, which Have Not Been Described by Mr. Eustace, in his Classical Tour*, London, 1819.

Hobbes, Thomas, *Leviathan*, edited by C.B. Macpherson, Harmondsworth, Penguin, [1651] 1976

Hobhouse, John Cam, *Historical Illustrations of the Fourth Canto of Childe Harold: Containing Dissertations on the Ruins of Rome; and an Essay on Italian Literature*, London, 1818.

Houel, Jean, *Voyage pittoresque des isles de Sicile, de Malthe et de Lipari. Ou l'on traite des antiquités qui s'y trouvent encore; des principaux phénomènes que la nature y offre; du costume des habitans, et de quelques usages*, Paris,1782.

Howell, James, *Instructions and Directions for Forren Travell. Shewing by what Cours, and in what Compas of Time, one may Take an Exact Survey of the Kingdomes, and States of Christendome, and Arrive to the Practicall Knowledg of the Languages, to Good Purpose*, London, [1642] 1650.

H[owell], J[ames], *Epistolæ Ho-Elianæ. Familiar Letters Domestic and Forren; Divided into Six Sections, Partly Historicall, Politicall, Philosophicall, upon Emergent Occasions*, 6 parts, London, 1645.

[Huguetan, Jean,] *Voyage d'Italie Curieux et Nouveau*, Lyon, 1681.

[Jameson, Anna,] *Diary of an Ennuyée*, second edition, London, [1826] 1826.

Johnson, Samuel, 'A Journey to the Western Islands of Scotland', in *Johnson and Boswell in Scotland: A Journey to the Hebrides*, edited by Pat Rogers, New Haven and London, Yale University Press, 1993. Parallel texts of the two narratives.

Kames, [Henry Home,] Lord, *Elements of Criticism*, 3 vols, Edinburgh, 1762.

Keats, John, *The Complete Poems*, edited by John Barnard, Harmondsworth, Penguin, 1977.

Knight, Richard Payne, *An Analytical Inquiry into the Principles of Taste*, London, 1805.

Lalande, Joseph Jérôme le Français de, *Voyage d'un françois en Italie*, 8 vols, Venice, 1769.

Lamartine, Alphonse de, *Le Dernier Chant du pèlerinage d'Harold* [1826], in *Nouvelles méditations poétiques avec commentaires*, Paris, 1892, 208–326.

Lassels, Richard, *The Voyage of Italy*, 2 parts, Paris, 1670.

Lodge, William, *The Painters Voyage of Italy. In which all the famous paintings of the most eminent masters are particularised, as they are preserved in the several cities of ITALY*, London, 1679. A translation of Giacomo Barri, *Viaggio Pittoresco in cui si notano distintamente tutte le pitture famose de' più celebri pittori, che se conservano in qualsivoglia città dell'Italia*, Venice, 1671.

Longinus, *Dionysius Longinus on the Sublime*, translated and edited by William Smith, fourth edition, London, [1739] 1770.

MacCulloch, John, *On Malaria: an Essay on the Production and Propagation of this Poison, and on the Nature and Localities of the Places by which it is Produced; with an Examination of the Diseases Caused by it, and of the Means of Preventing or Diminishing them, both at Home and in the Naval and Military Service*, London, 1827.

[Macpherson, James,] *The Works of Ossian, the Son of Fingal*, 2 vols, London, 1775.

Martyn, Thomas, *The Gentleman's Guide in his Tour through Italy. With a Correct Map, and Directions for Travelling in that Country*, London, 1787.

Matthews, Henry, *The Diary of an Invalid; being the Journal of a Tour in Pursuit of Health; in Portugal, Italy, Switzerland, and France, in the Years 1817, 1818, and 1819*, London, 1820.

Middleton, Conyers, *A Letter from Rome, Shewing an Exact Conformity between Popery and Paganism: or, the Religion of the Present Romans to be Derived Entirely from that of their Heathen Ancestors*, second edition, London, [1729]1729.

[Miller, Anne, Lady], *Letters from Italy, Describing the Manners, Customs, Antiquities, Paintings, &c of that Country, in the Years 1780 and 1781, to a Friend Residing in France, by an English Woman*, 3 vols, London, 1776.

Minto, Sir Gilbert Elliott, First Earl of, *Life and Letters of Sir Gilbert Elliot, First Earl of Minto, from 1751 to 1806*, edited by the Countess of Minto, 3 vols, London, 1874.

Misson, François Maximilien, *Nouveau voyage d'Italie, fait en l'année 1688. Avec un mémoire contenant des avis utiles à ceux qui voudront faire le mesme voyage*, 2 vols, The Hague, 1691.

Misson, François Maximilien, *A New Voyage to Italy: with a Description of the Chief Towns, Churches, Tombs, Libraries, Palaces, Statues and Antiquities of that Country. Together with Useful INSTRUCTIONS for those who shall Travel thither ... Done into English, and adorn'd with figures*, 2 vols, London, 1695.

Monfalcon, Jean Baptiste, *Histoire des marais, et des maladies causées par les émanations des eaux stagnantes*, Paris [printed in Lyons], 1824.

Montagu, Lady Mary Wortley, *The Works of the Right Honourable Lady Mary Wortley Montagu*, sixth edition, 2 vols, London, 1811; Montagu's *Letters from Turkey* were first published in 1763.

Montagu, Lady Mary Wortley, *The Complete Letters of Lady Mary Wortley Montagu*, edited by Robert Halsband, 2 vols, Oxford, Oxford University Press, 1966.

Montesquieu, [Charles Louis de Secondat, Baron de,] *Voyages de Montesquieu*, edited by Baron Albert de Montesquieu, 2 vols, Bordeaux, 1894–6.

Montesquieu, [Charles Louis de Secondat, Baron de,] *De l'esprit des lois*, edited by Victor Goldschmidt, 2 vols, Paris, Garnier Flammarion, [1748] 1979.

Montesquieu, [Charles Louis] de Secondat, Baron de, *The Spirit of Laws. Translated from the French ... With Corrections and Additions Communicated by the Author*, [translated by Thomas Nugent] 2 vols, London, 1750.

The Monthly Review; or, Literary Journal. By several hands, 81 vols, London, 1749–89.

Moore, John, *A View of Society and Manners in Italy*, second edition, 2 vols, London, [1781] 1781.

Morgan, Lady [Sydney], *Italy*, 2 vols, London, 1821.

Morgan, Lady [Sydney], *The Life and Times of Salvator Rosa*, 2 vols, London, 1824.

Moryson, Fynes, *An Itinerary, Containing his Ten Yeeres Travell through the Twelve Dominions of Germany, Bohmerland, Sweitzerland, Netherland, Denmarke, Poland, Italy, Turky, France, England, Scotland, and Ireland*, 3 parts, London, 1617.

Normanby, [Constantine Henry Phipps,] Marquis of, *The English in Italy*, 3 vols, London, 1825.

Nugent, Thomas, *The Grand Tour; or, A Journey through the Netherlands, Germany, Italy and France*, third edition, 4 vols, London, [1749] 1778.

Park, Mungo, *Travels in the Interior Districts of Africa*, London, 1799.

Parsons, Eliza, *The Mysterious Warning: A German Tale*, 4 vols, London, 1796.

Peacock, Thomas Love, *Nightmare Abbey, Crotchet Castle*, edited by Raymond Wright, Harmondsworth, Penguin, [1818/1831] 1969.

Piozzi, Hester Lynch, *Observations and Reflections Made in the Course of a Journey through France, Italy, and Germany*, 2 vols, London, 1789.

Piozzi, Hester Lynch, *The Piozzi Letters: Correspondence of Hester Lynch Piozzi, 1784–1821 (formerly Mrs. Thrale)*, edited by Edward A. Bloom and Lillian D. Bloom, 3 vols, Newark, University of Delaware Press, 1989–93.

Pope, Alexander, 'Peri Bathous: or, Of the Art of Sinking in Poetry', in *Works*, 6 vols, Edinburgh, 1764, IV, 109–93.

Pope, Alexander, *Poems*, edited by John Butt, 11 vols, London and New Haven, Yale University Press, 1961–9.

Price, Uvedale, *An Essay on the Picturesque, as Compared with the Sublime and Beautiful; and, on the Use of Studying Pictures, for the Purpose of Improving Real Landscape*, 2 vols, [1794–8] 1796–8.

Radcliffe, Ann, *A Sicilian Romance*, edited by Alison Milbank, Oxford, Oxford University Press, [1790] 1993.

Radcliffe, Ann, *The Mysteries of Udolpho: A Romance, Interspersed with some Pieces of Poetry*, edited by Bonamy Dobrée, Oxford, Oxford University Press, [1794] 1980.

Radcliffe, Ann, *The Italian; or, the Confessional of the Black Penitents. A Romance*, edited by Frederick Garber, London, Oxford University Press, [1797] 1968.

Raymond, Jo[hn], *An Itinerary Contayning a Voyage Made through Italy, in the Yeare 1646, and 1647*, London, 1648.

Reynolds, Frances, *An Enquiry concerning the Principles of Taste, and the Origin of our Ideas of Beauty*, London, 1785.

Richardson, Jonathan [Senior and Junior], *An Account of some of the Statues, Bas-Reliefs, Drawings and Pictures in Italy, &c with Remarks*, London, 1722.

Rogers, Samuel, *Italy, A Poem*, London, [1822] 1830.

Rogissart, de, *Les Délices de l'Italie; ou, Description exacte de ce pays, de ses principales villes, et de toutes les raretez, qu'il contient*, 3 vols, continuous pagination, Leiden, 1706.

Rousseau, Jean-Jacques, *Émile; ou, de l'éducation*, introduced by Michel Launay, Paris, Garnier-Flammarion, 1966.

[Sade, Donatien Alphonse François de,] *La Nouvelle Justine, ou Les Malheurs de la Vertu, suivie de l'histoire de Juliette, sa sœur*, 10 vols, 'en Hollande' [Paris?], 1797.

Sade, Donatien Alphonse François de, *Voyage d'Italie, précédé des premières œuvres, suivi de 'Opuscules sur le théâtre'*, edited by G. Lély and G. Daumas, Paris, Tchou, 1967.

Sandys, George, *A Relation of a Journey begun An: Dom: 1610. Foure bookes containing a description of the Turkish Empire, of Ægypt, of the Holy Land, of the remote parts of Italy, and Ilands adjoyning*, London, 1615.

Sass, Henry, *A Journey to Rome and Naples, Performed in 1817; Giving an Account of the Present State of Society in Italy; and Containing Observations on the Fine Arts*, London, 1818.

Savary, [Charles,] *Lettres sur l'Égypte*, 3 vols, Paris, 1786.

Seignelay, Marquis de [Jean-Baptiste Colbert], *L'Italie en 1671*, Paris, 1867.

Sharp, Samuel, *Letters from Italy, Describing the Customs and Manners of that Country, in the Years 1765, and 1766*, second edition, London, [1766] 1767.

Shelley, Mary, *Journals 1814–1844*, edited by Paula R. Feldman and Diana Scott-Kilvert, 2 vols, continuous pagination, Oxford, Oxford University Press, 1987.

Shelley, Mary, *The Last Man*, introduced by Brian Aldiss, London, Hogarth Press, [1826] 1985.

Shelley, Percy Bysshe, *Essays, Letters from Abroad, Translations and Fragments*, edited by Mrs Shelley, 2 vols, London, 1840.

Shelley, Percy Bysshe, *Notes on Sculptures in Rome and Florence*, London, 1879.

Shelley, Percy Bysshe, *Letters*, edited by F.L. Jones, 2 vols, Oxford, 1964.

Shelley, [Percy Bysshe,] *Poetical Works*, edited by Thomas Hutchinson, corrected by G.M. Matthews, Oxford, Oxford University Press, 1988.

Sherlock, Martin, *Nouvelles Lettres d'un voyageur anglois*, London, 1780.

Sherlock, Martin, *New Letters from an English Traveller. Written originally in French ... and now translated into English by the author*, London, 1781.

Simond, Louis, *Voyage en Italie et en Sicile*, 2 vols, Paris, 1828.

Simond, L[ouis], *A Tour in Italy and Sicily*, London, 1828.

Smith, Adam, *The Theory of Moral Sentiments*, London and Edinburgh, 1759.

Smith, Charlotte, *Montalbert: A Novel*, 3 vols, London, 1795.

Smith, Sir James Edward, *A Sketch of a Tour on the Continent in the Years 1786 and 1787*, 3 vols, London, 1793.

Smollett, Tobias, *Travels through France and Italy*, edited by Frank Felsenstein, Oxford, Oxford University Press, [1766] 1981.

Spence, Joseph, *Letters from the Grand Tour*, edited by Slava Klima, Montreal and London, McGill-Queen's University Press, 1975.

Spon, Jacob, *Voyage d'Italie, de Dalmatie, et de Grèce, et du Levant fait aux années 1675 et 1676*, 4 vols, Lyon, 1678.

Staël, [Germaine] de [Anne Louise Germaine de Staël-Holstein], *Corinne; ou, l'Italie* (1807), edited by Claudine Herrmann, 2 vols, Paris, des Femmes, 1979.

Staël, [Germaine] de [Anne Louise Germaine de Staël-Holstein], *Corinne; or, Italy*, translated by Isabel Hill, London, [1831] 1833.

Starke, Mariana, *Letters from Italy, between the Years 1792 and 1798, Containing a View of the Revolutions in that Country, from the Capture of Nice by the French Republic to the Expulsion of Pius VI from the Ecclesiastical State: likewise Pointing out the Matchless Works of Art which still Embellish Pisa, Florence,*

Siena, Rome, Naples, Bologna, Venice &c. With Instructions for the Use of Invalids and Families who May not choose to Incur the Expence attendant upon Travelling with a Courier, 2 vols, London, 1800.

Stendhal, [Henri Beyle,] *Rome, Naples et Florence*, edited by Pierre Brunel, Paris, Gallimard, [1817; revised edition first published in 1826] 1987.

Stendhal, [Henri Beyle,] *Rome, Naples and Florence, in 1817. Sketches of the Present State of Society, Manners, Arts, Literature, &c in those Celebrated Cities, by the Count de Stendhal*, London, 1818.

Stendhal, [Henri Beyle,] *Promenades dans Rome*, edited by Armand Caraccio, 3 vols, Paris, Champion, [1830] 1938.

Sterne, Laurence, *The Life and Opinions of Tristram Shandy, Gentleman*, edited by Graham Petrie, Harmondsworth, Penguin, [1759–66] 1976.

Sterne, Laurence, *A Sentimental Journey through France and Italy [1768]*, in *'A Sentimental Journey' with 'The Journal to Eliza' and 'A Political Romance'*, edited by Ian Jack, Oxford, Oxford University Press, 1984.

Stevens, Sacheverell, *Miscellaneous Remarks Made on the Spot, in a Late Seven Years Tour through France, Italy, Germany and Holland*, London, 1756.

Swinburne, Henry, *Travels in the Two Sicilies in the Years 1777, 1778, 1779, and 1780*, 2 vols, London, 1783–5.

Temple, Lancelot [John Armstrong], *A Short Ramble through some Parts of France and Italy*, London, 1771.

Veryard, E[llis], *An Account of Divers Choice Remarks, as well Geographical as Historical, Political, Mathematical, Physical and Moral; Taken in a Journey through the Low-Countries, France, Italy, and Part of Spain; with the Isles of Sicily and Malta. As also a Voyage to the Levant*, London, 1701.

Vigée-Lebrun, Elisabeth, *Souvenirs de Madame Vigée Le Brun*, 2 vols, Paris, [1835–7] 1891. The book includes accounts of Italy in 1789 and 1790.

Walker, Adam, *Ideas, Suggested on the Spot, in a Late Excursion through Flanders, Germany, France, and Italy*, London, 1790.

Walpole, Horace, *The Yale Edition of Horace Walpole's Correspondence*, edited by W.S. Lewis, 40 vols, London, Yale University Press, 1937–83.

Warcupp, Edmund, *Italy, in its Original Glory, Ruine and Revival, Being an Exact Survey of the whole Geography and History of that Famous Country*, London, 1660. Translated from *Itinerario, overo nova descrittione de' viaggi principali d'Italia*, an Italian version of Franciscus Schottus, *Itinerarii Italiae rerumque Romanarum libri tres*.

Watkins, Thomas, *Travels through Switzerland, Italy, Sicily, the Greek Islands to Constantinople; through Part of Greece, Ragusa, and the Dalmatian Isles*, second edition, 2 vols, London, [1792] 1794.

Weston, Stephen, *Viaggiana*, London, [1776?].

Whitaker, John, *The Course of Hannibal over the Alps Ascertained*, 2 vols, London, 1794.

Williams, Helen Maria, *A Tour in Switzerland*, 2 vols, London, 1798.

Williams, H[ugh] W[illiam], *Travels in Italy, Greece, and the Ionian Islands, in a Series of Letters, Descriptive of Manners, Scenery, and the Fine Arts*, 2 vols, Edinburgh, 1820.

Wilmot, Catherine, *An Irish Peer on the Continent (1801–1803): Being a Narrative of the Tour of Stephen, Second Earl Mount Cashell, through France, Italy, etc., as Related by Catherine Wilmot*, edited by Thomas U. Sadleir, second edition, London, Williams and Norgate, 1924.

Winkelmann, Jerome Joachim, *Histoire de l'art chez les anciens... traduite de l'allemand; avec des notes historiques et critiques de différens auteurs*, 2 vols, Paris, 1790–1803. Translation of Jerome Joachim Winckelmann, *Geschichte der Kunst des Alterthums*, Dresden, 1764.

Wollstonecraft, Mary, *A Vindication of the Rights of Woman*, edited by Miriam Brody, London, Penguin, [1792] 1985.

Wollstonecraft, Mary, *Letters Written during a Short Residence in Sweden, Norway, and Denmark* [1796], in Mary Wollstonecraft and William Godwin, *'A Short Residence in Sweden, Norway and Denmark' and 'Memoirs of the Author of "The Rights of Woman"'*, edited by Richard Holmes, London, Penguin, 1987.

Wordsworth, [William,] *The Prelude; or, the Growth of a Poet's Mind (Text of 1805)*, edited by Ernest de Selincourt, corrected by Stephen Gill, Oxford, Oxford University Press, 1970.

Wordsworth, [William,] *Poetical Works*, edited by Thomas Hutchinson, revised by Ernest de Selincourt, Oxford, Oxford University Press, 1981.

Wright, Edward, *Some Observations Made in Travelling through France, Italy &c in the Years 1720, 1721, and 1722*, 2 vols, continuous pagination, London, 1730.

Young, Arthur, *Travels, during the Years 1787, 1788, and 1789. Undertaken More Particularly with a View of Ascertaining the Cultivation, Wealth, Resources, and National Prosperity of the Kingdom of France*, 2 vols, Bury St Edmunds, 1792.

Travel writings and other primary texts from 1830 onwards

Anon., 'A Family Continental Tour, and its Results', *Blackwood's Magazine*, 46:285 (July 1839), 56–65.

Anon., *The South Pacific with Air New Zealand*, London, Air New Zealand, 1995.

Auden, W.H. and Louis MacNeice, *Letters from Iceland*, London, Faber and Faber, [1937] 1985.

Baedeker Australia, translated from the German, London, Jarrold and Sons Ltd, 1995.

Barthes, Roland, *L'Empire des signes*, Geneva, Skira, 1970.

Barthes, Roland, *Empire of Signs*, translated by Richard Howard, London, Cape, 1983.

Benvenuto, Sergio, *Capire l'America: Un europeo negli States di oggi*, Genoa, Costa & Nolan, 1995.

Butler, Samuel, *A First Year in Canterbury Settlement*, Auckland and Hamilton, Blackwood and Janet Paul, [1863] 1964.

Bowen, Elizabeth, *The Hotel*, London, Penguin, [1927] 1987.

Dickens, Charles, *Pictures from Italy*, second edition, London, [1846] 1846.

Douglas, Norman, *South Wind*, London, Penguin, [1917] 1953.

Dundy, Elaine, *The Dud Avocado*, London, Virago, 1993.

Forster, E.M., 'The Story of a Panic', in *Collected Short Stories*, London, Penguin, 1954, 9–33. Written in 1902.

Forster, E.M., *A Room with a View*, edited by Oliver Stallybrass, Harmondsworth, Penguin, [1908] 1980.

Freud, Sigmund, 'Delusions and Dreams in Jensen's "Gradiva"' [1907; first English translation 1917], in *The Pelican Freud Library*, translated under the general editorship of James Strachey, Harmondsworth, Penguin, 1973–, vol. 14, edited by Albert Dickson, 27–118.

Freud, Sigmund, 'A Disturbance of Memory on the Acropolis' [1936; first English translation 1941], in *The Pelican Freud Library*, Harmondsworth, Penguin, 1973–, translated under the general editorship of James Strachey, vol. 11, edited by Angela Richards, 443–56.

Hull, E.M., [Edith Maud Winstanley,] *The Sheik: A Novel*, London, [1919] 1920.

Huxley, Aldous, *Along the Road: Notes and Essays of a Tourist*, London, Chatto and Windus, 1925.

Johnson, James, *Change of Air; or, the Pursuit of Health; an Autumnal Excursion through France, Switzerland and Italy, in the Year 1829, with Observations and Reflections on the Moral, Physical, and Medical Influence of Travelling-Exericise, Change of Scene, Foreign Skies, and Voluntary Expatriation*, fourth edition, London, [1831] 1831.

Jones, Robyn, and Leonardo Pinheiro, *Fiji: A Lonely Planet Travel Survival Kit*, fourth edition, Hawthorn, Victoria, Australia, Lonely Planet Publications, [1986] 1997.

Lawrence, D.H., 'Sun' [1928], in *Selected Short Stories*, edited by Brian Finney, Harmondsworth, Penguin, 1982, 424–43.

Lévi-Strauss, Claude, *Tristes Tropiques*, Paris, Plon, 1955.

Mansfield, Charlotte, *Via Rhodesia: A Journey through Southern Africa*, London, 1911.

Pritchard, Marcy (editor), *Fodor's 95 Arizona*, New York, Fodor's Travel Publications, Inc., 1994.

Waugh, Evelyn, *Labels: A Mediterranean Journal*, Harmondsworth, Penguin [1930] 1985.

Wharton, Edith, *Old New York: False Dawn (The 'Forties)*, London and New York, [1923] Appleton, 1924.

Secondary material

Ashfield, Andrew, and Peter de Bolla (editors), *The Sublime: A Reader in British Eighteenth-Century Aesthetic Theory*, Cambridge, Cambridge University Press, 1996.

Bann, Stephen, *Under the Sign: John Bargrave as Collector, Traveler, and Witness*, Ann Arbor, University of Michigan Press, 1994.

Barrell, John, *The Political Theory of Painting from Reynolds to Hazlitt: 'The Body of the Public'*, London and New Haven, Yale University Press, 1986.

Barrell, John, *The Birth of Pandora and the Division of Knowledge*, London, Macmillan, 1992.

Barthes, Roland, *Mythologies*, selected and translated by Annette Lavers, London, Cape, 1972. A translation of *Mythologies*, Paris, Seuil, 1957.

Benedict, Barbara, 'The "Curious Attitude" in Eighteenth-Century Britain: Observing and Owning', *Eighteenth-Century Life*, 14:3 (1990), 59–98.

Benvenuto, Bice, *Concerning the Rites of Psychoanalysis; or, The Villa of the Mysteries*, Cambridge, Polity Press, 1994.

Black, Jeremy, *The British Abroad: The Grand Tour in the Eighteenth Century*, New York, St Martin's Press, 1992.

Buzard, James, *The Beaten Track: European Tourism, Literature, and the Ways to 'Culture', 1800–1918*, Oxford, Oxford University Press, 1993.

Campbell, Mary C., *The Witness and the Other World: Exotic European Travel Writing, 400–1600*, Ithaca and London, Cornell University Press, 1988.

Cascardi, Anthony J., *The Subject of Modernity*, Cambridge, Cambridge University Press, 1992.

Chaney, Edward, *The Evolution of the Grand Tour: Anglo-Italian Cultural Relations since the Renaissance*, London, Frank Cass, 1998.

Chard, Chloe, 'Horror on the Grand Tour', *Oxford Art Journal*, 6:2 (1983), 3–16.

Chard, Chloe, 'Rising and Sinking on the Alps and Mount Etna: the Topography of the Sublime in the Eighteenth Century', *Journal of Philosophy and the Visual Arts*, 1:1 (1989), 60–9.

Chard, Chloe, 'Effeminacy, Pleasure and the Classical Body', in *Femininity and Masculinity in Eighteenth-Century Art and Culture*, edited by Gill Perry and Michael Rossington, Manchester, Manchester University Press, 1994, 142–61.

Chard, Chloe, 'Nakedness and Tourism: Classical Sculpture and the Imaginative Geography of the Grand Tour', *Oxford Art Journal*, 18:1 (1995), 14–28.

Chard, Chloe, 'Crossing Boundaries and Exceeding Limits: Destabilization, Tourism, and the Sublime', in *Transports: Travel, Pleasure, and Imaginative Geography, 1600–1830*, edited by Chloe Chard and Helen Langdon, New Haven and London, Yale University Press, 1996, 117–49.

Chard, Chloe, 'The Road to Ruin: Ghosts, Women, Moonlight and Weeds', in *Receptions of Rome in European Culture 1789–1945*, edited by Catharine Edwards, Cambridge, Cambridge University Press, forthcoming.

Chard, Chloe, 'Comedy, Antiquity, the Feminine and the Foreign: Emma Hamilton and Corinne', in *Aspects of the Grand Tour: Some Writers, Architects and Artists in Italy 1600–1845*, edited by Clare Hornsby, The British School at Rome, forthcoming.

Chard, Chloe and Helen Langdon (editors), *Transports: Travel, Pleasure, and Imaginative Geography, 1600–1830*, New Haven and London, Yale University Press, 1996.

Clifford, James, *Routes: Travel and Translation in the Late Twentieth Century*, Cambridge, MA, Harvard University Press, 1997.

Cohen, Michèle, *Fashioning Masculinity: National Identity and Language in the Eighteenth Century*, London and New York, Routledge, 1996.

Cooke, Michael, *Acts of Inclusion: Studies Bearing on an Elementary Theory of Romanticism*, New Haven and London, Yale University Press, 1979.

Corbin, Alain, *Le Territoire du vide: L'Occident et le désir du rivage 1750–1840*, Paris, Flammarion, 1988.

de Man, Paul, *Allegories of Reading: Figural Language in Rousseau, Nietzsche, Rilke, and Proust*, New Haven and London, Yale University Press, 1979.

de Man, Paul, 'The Rhetoric of Temporality', in *Blindness and Insight: Essays in the Rhetoric of Contemporary Criticism*, London, Methuen, 1986, pp. 187–228.

Derrida, Jacques, *Memoires for Paul de Man*, translated by Cecile Lindsay, Jonathan Culler, and Eduardo Cadava, New York, Columbia University Press, 1986.

Derrida, Jacques, *Mal d'archive: une impression freudienne*, Paris, Galilée, 1995.

Douglas, Mary, *Purity and Danger: An Analysis of the Concepts of Pollution and Taboo*, London, Routledge,1966.

Edwards, Catharine, '*Mollitia*: Reading the Body', in *The Politics of Immorality in Ancient Rome*, Cambridge, Cambridge University Press, 1993, 63–97.

Ellison, Julie, *Delicate Subjects: Romanticism, Gender, and the Ethics of Understanding*, Ithaca and London, Cornell University Press, 1990.

Ferguson, Frances, *Solitude and the Sublime: Romanticism and the Aesthetics of Individuation*, New York and London, Routledge, 1992.

Ferguson, Harvey, 'Sigmund Freud and the Pursuit of Pleasure', in Chris Rojek, *Leisure for Leisure: Critical Essays*, London, Macmillan, 1989, pp. 53–74.

Fontanier, Pierre *Les Tropes*, with a commentary by César Chesneau Dumarsais, 2 vols, Geneva, Slatkine, [1818] 1967.

Foucault, Michel, 'Réponse à une question', *Esprit*, 5 (1968), 850–74.

Foucault, Michel, *L'Archéologie du savoir*, Paris, Gallimard, 1969.

Freiberg, Pearlee, 'Roman Nocturne: Classical Sculpture Illuminated', paper presented at the Annual Meeting of the North-Eastern American Society for Eighteenth-Century Studies, Boston, 1997.

Freud, Sigmund, 'Beyond the Pleasure Principle', in *The Standard Edition of the Complete Psychological Works of Sigmund Freud*, edited by James Strachey in collaboration with Anna Freud, vol. 18, London, Hogarth Press and Institute of Psycho-Analysis, 1955, 7–64.

Fried, Michael, *Absorption and Theatricality: Painting and Beholder in the Age of Diderot*, Berkeley, University of California Press, 1980.

Fussell, Paul, *Abroad: British Literary Traveling between the Wars*, Oxford and New York, Oxford University Press, 1980.

Greenblatt, Stephen, *Learning to Curse: Essays in Early Modern Culture*, London: Routledge, 1990.

Grosrichard, Alain, *Structure du sérail: la fiction du despotisme asiatique dans l'Occident classique*, Paris, Seuil, 1979, 'Connexions du champ freudien'.

Gross, Kenneth, *The Dream of the Moving Statue*, Ithaca and London, Cornell University Press, 1992.

Hamblyn, Richard, 'Private Cabinets and Popular Geology: The British Audiences for Volcanoes in the Eighteenth Century', in Chloe Chard and Helen Langdon (editors), *Transports: Travel, Pleasure, and Imaginative Geography, 1600–1830*, New Haven and London, Yale University Press, 1996, 179–205.

Hertz, Neil, *The End of the Line: Essays on Psychoanalysis and the Sublime*, New York, Columbia University Press, 1985.

Jacob, Christian, *L'Empire des cartes: Approche théorique de la cartographie à travers l'histoire*, Paris, Albin Michel, 1992.

Jacobus, Mary, *Reading Woman: Essays in Feminist Criticism*, London, Methuen, 1986.

Jones, Ernest, *Sigmund Freud: Life and Work*, 3 vols, London, The Hogarth Press, 1953–7.

Kerr, Joan (editor), *Heritage: The National Women's Art Book*, Sydney, G+B Arts International Limited, 1995.

Lamb, Jonathan, *The Rhetoric of Suffering: Reading the Book of Job in the Eighteenth Century*, Oxford, Oxford University Press, 1995.

Laplanche, Jean, and J.-B. Pontalis, *Vocabulaire de la psychanalyse*, Paris, Presses Universitaires de France, 1967.

Lowe, Lisa, *Critical Terrains: French and British Orientalisms*, Ithaca and London, Cornell University Press, 1991.

MacCannell, Dean, *The Tourist: A New Theory of the Leisure Class*, New York, Schocken Books, 1976.

Marchese, Angelo, *Dizionario di retorica e di stilistica: arte e artificio nell'uso delle parole*, Milan, Mondatori, 1979.

Marshall, David, *The Figure of Theater: Shaftesbury, Defoe, Adam Smith and George Eliot*, New York and Guildford, Columbia University Press, 1986.

McGann, Jerome J., 'Rome and its Romantic Significance', in *The Beauty of Inflections: Literary Investigations in Historical Method and Theory*, Oxford, Oxford University Press, 1985, 313–33.

Melville, Stephen, *Philosophy Beside Itself: On Deconstruction and Modernism*, Manchester, Manchester University Press, 1986.

Mullan, John, *Sentiment and Sociability: The Language of Feeling in the Eighteenth Century*, Oxford, Oxford University Press, 1988.

Pemble, John, *The Mediterranean Passion: Victorians and Edwardians in the South*, Oxford, Oxford University Press, 1987.

Perry, Gill, "'The British Sappho": Borrowed Identities and the Representation of Women Artists in late Eighteenth-Century British Art', *Oxford Art Journal*, 18:1 (1995), 44–57.

Pointon, Marcia, 'Portraiture, Excess, and Mythology: Mary Hale, Emma Hamilton, and Others... "in Bacchante"', in *Strategies for Showing: Women, Possession, and Representation in English Visual Culture 1665–1800*, Oxford, Oxford University Press, 1997, 173–227.

Pomian, Krzysztof, *Collectionneurs, amateurs et curieux: Paris, Venise: XVIe–XVIIIe siècle*, Paris, Gallimard, 1987.

Porter, Dennis, *Haunted Journeys: Desire and Transgression in European Travel Writing*, Princeton, Princeton University Press, 1991.

Pratt, Mary Louise, *Imperial Eyes: Travel Writing and Transculturation*, London and New York, Routledge, 1992.

Redford, Bruce, *Venice and the Grand Tour*, New Haven and London, Yale University Press, 1996.

Ridley, Ronald T., *The Eagle and the Spade: Archaeology in Rome during the Napoleonic Era*, Cambridge, Cambridge University Press, 1992.

Said, Edward, *Orientalism*, London, Routledge, 1978.

Sedgwick, Eve Kosofsky, *Between Men: English Literature and Male Homosocial Desire*, New York, Columbia University Press, 1985.

Shaffer, E.S., 'The Death of the Artist and the Birth of Art History: Appearance, Concept and Cultural Myth', in *Reflecting Senses: Perception and Appearance in Literature, Culture and the Arts*, edited by Walter Pape and Frederick Burwick, Berlin and New York, De Gruyter, 1995, 189–222.

Shaffer, E.S., '"To remind us of China" – William Beckford, Mental Traveller on the Grand Tour: The Construction of Significance in Landscape', in *Transports: Travel, Pleasure, and Imaginative Geography, 1600–1830*, edited by Chloe Chard and Helen Langdon, (New Haven and London: Yale University Press, 1996), 207–42.

Sheriff, Mary D., *The Exceptional Woman: Elisabeth Vigée-Lebrun and the Cultural Politics of Art*, Chicago and London, University of Chicago Press, 1996.

Smith, Bernard, *European Vision and the South Pacific*, second edition, New Haven and London, Yale University Press, 1985.

Stafford, Barbara Maria, *Voyage into Substance: Art, Science, Nature, and the Illustrated Travel Account, 1760–1840*, Cambridge MA and London, MIT Press, 1984.

Stewart, Susan, *On Longing: Narratives of the Miniature, the Gigantic, the Souvenir, the Collection*, Durham and London: Duke University Press, 1993.

Thomas, Nicholas, 'Licensed Curiosity: Cook's Pacific Voyages', in *The Cultures of Collecting*, edited by John Elsner and Roger Cardinal, London, Reaktion Books, 1994, 116–36.

Thomas, Nicholas, *In Oceania: Visions, Artifacts, Histories*, Durham and London, Duke University Press, 1997.

Todorov, Tzvetan, *Les Genres du discours*, Paris, Seuil, 1978.

Todorov, Tzvetan, *Nous et les autres: la réflexion française sur la diversité humaine*, Paris, Seuil, 1979.

Urry, John, *The Tourist Gaze: Leisure and Travel in Contemporary Societies*, London, Thousand Oaks, CA, and New Delhi, Sage Publications, 1994.

Vincent-Buffault, Anne, *The History of Tears: Sensibility and Sentimentality in France*, London, Macmillan, 1991. A translation of *Histoire des larmes XVIIIe–XIXe siècles*, Paris, Rivages, 1986.

Wallace, Anne D. (1993), *Walking, Literature, and English Culture: The Origins and Uses of Peripatetic in the Nineteenth Century*, Oxford, Oxford University Press, 1993.

Weiskel, Thomas (1986), *The Romantic Sublime: Studies in the Structure and Psychology of Transcendence*, Baltimore and London, Johns Hopkins University Press, 1986.

Whiteley, Jon, 'Light and Shade in French Neoclassicism', *Burlington Magazine*, 117 (1975), 768–73.

Wrigley, Richard (1996), 'Infectious Enthusiasms: Influence, Contagion, and the Experience of Rome', in *Transports: Travel, Pleasure, and Imaginative Geography, 1600–1830*, edited by Chloe Chard and Helen Langdon, New Haven and London, Yale University Press, 75–116.

Index

Note: page numbers in *italics* refer to illustrations; 'n.' after a page reference indicates a note number on that page.

Virgil, *Aeneid*, 73–4, 83, 87, 138, 232, 241
vitality
    absent from contemporary Italy, 236–8
    and the Italian past, 236
volcanoes, and exceeding limits, 112, 125, 192

Waldie, Jane, Byron's annoyance with, 35 n.90
Walpole, Horace, letters of, 4, 88 n.16, 89, 96 n.36
Warcupp, Edmund, *Italy*, 62, 63 n.77, 71, 82
waste of plenty, theme of, 109–10
Watkins, Thomas, *Travels*, 42, 87 n.12, 92, 93 n.29, 117, 195 n.57
Waugh, Evelyn, *Labels*, 1–2, 3, 31, 213–14, 220, 225
Weston, Stephen, *Viaggiana*, 103 n.56
Wharton, Edith, 'False Dawn', 115
Whitaker, John, *The Course of Hannibal over the Alps Ascertained*, 177–8, 195
Williams, Hugh William, *Travels*, 229, 237
Wilmot, Catherine, journal of, 116, 122, 125, 171 n.91
Winckelmann, Jerome Joachim, 16
    Geschichte der Kunst des Altertums, 16, 43
wine
    complaints about, 108–10
    and 'esteem', 79, 82
    and excess, 58, 59, 61
    and gratification, trivial, 242–6
    and hyperbole, 62, 69–71
    and intensification, the commentary of, 53
    and travel, metaphorical links between, 159, 247–8
    selection of, as object of commentary, 50–1, 108–10, 239, 242–5
    and tourism, 239–48
    unworthy of attention, 23, 239
    see also drinking

Wollstonecraft, Mary
    Letters, 38, 162
    A Vindication of the Rights of Woman, 107, 161
women
    as objects of commentary, 126–30
    see also feminine, the; travellers, female
wonder, 31, 85, 90, 181, 204.
    see also marvellous, the
wonders, 4, 18–20, 55, 62, 113, 167, 223
    female performers as, 136
    and tourism, 222–32
Wordsworth, William
    Lyrical Ballads, preface to, 243
    The Prelude, 177
Wright, Edward, *Some Observations*, 88–9, 91–2, 231
Wright, Joseph, *Maria, from Sterne*, 154, *154*
writing, role in appropriating the foreign, 24–6

Young, Arthur, *Travels*, 101, 109 n.74